Makers of Worlds, Readers of Signs

Makers of Worlds, Readers of Signs

Israeli and Palestinian Literature
of the Global Contemporary

Kfir Cohen Lustig

VERSO
London • New York

First published by Verso 2019
© Kfir Cohen Lustig 2019
Foreword © Fredric Jameson 2019

1 3 5 7 9 10 8 6 4 2

Verso
UK: 6 Meard Street, London W1F 0EG
US: 20 Jay Street, Suite 1010, Brooklyn, NY 11201
versobooks.com

Verso is the imprint of New Left Books

ISBN-13: 978-1-78873-757-9
ISBN-13: 978-1-78873-556-8 (HB)
ISBN-13: 978-1-78873-557-5 (UK EBK)
ISBN-13: 978-1-78873-558-2 (US EBK)

British Library Cataloguing in Publication Data
A catalogue record for this book is available from the British Library

Library of Congress Cataloging-in-Publication Data
A catalog record for this book is available from the Library of Congress

Typeset in Minion Pro by MJ & N Gavan, Truro, Cornwall
Printed in the UK by CPI Group (UK) Ltd, Croydon, CR0 4YY

For Erica

Contents

Foreword

Fredric Jameson

Important compositional or formal problems confront a truly theoretical work of literary criticism such as this one is (they are rare). First, that of the theory and the example, something always calculated to raise misconceptions and encourage misreadings. A book on Israeli and Palestinian literature will at once be taken to be a statement about the Israeli-Palestinian conflict, which this one emphatically is not. Not because of its neutrality or some secret prejudice in favor of this faction or that: this work has in fact some of the icy coolness of all the great dialectical standpoints on such struggles: that is to say, it is profoundly historical, and history is unfortunately necessity. But in fact it is not really "about" any of those partisan issues at all (except insofar as the very concept of "partisan" necessarily enters the literary judgments of its various exhibits).

In fact, this is a book about (for one thing) historical periodization; and that is its stunning originality. To be sure, any truly dialectical study —and I believe that that is what this book is and what makes for its originality among a host of lesser "theoretical" studies—will, by uncovering the tangle of relationships, be "about" several problems all at once as we shall see. And these include so-called world literature; a kind of Wallersteinian question about centers (European forms) and peripheries which can have several different modes of development—a genuinely "third-world" subaltern or "war-of-independence" colonization, and a satellite, settler-colony capitalist enclave. The various peripheries will produce works which are, appearances to the contrary, necessarily radically different in their form-problems from those of the center (even if in some ways the forms of the center secretly derive from the peripheries, and sometimes the underclasses, as is the case with so-called Western modernisms). Class is also a problem here, insofar as the class situations of the peripheries will always be skewed with relations to some classical mode of the center and its class struggles. Finally, as is evident here, the cultural area which takes as its framework a constituted nation (or better still the struggle to constitute a nation where none existed) will be very different in its experiences and its form-problems from the literature of a struggling or oppressed minority which itself would seem to derive from a very different linguistic, "national," political, tradition (so that, for example, Palestinian literature will be confused with the Arabic or even Islamic literary-historical tradition). Incidentally, this last misconception will raise the question of tradition itself and of imports: we probably don't believe in idealist notions of tradition any more—although at that point religion also rears its head—but the question of the export and import of forms from other places is a central, and poorly enough explored, question on the agenda of current "world-literature" studies, if indeed it has an agenda.

There thus overlap two kinds of issues: the First World/Third World opposition, which is asymmetrical to the degree that there are a set of First-World forms which have been developed and stand, like the automobile, ready for export (the Western one is called the naturalist novel); while the so-called Third World shows a variety of very different impulses and form-temptations, ranging from the traditional storytelling of the griot to modern resistance literature, agitprop, socialist realism, etc. Now then, can a single instance of Third World—or better still, peripheral—literary development and invention be at all representative or exemplary of the larger First/Third World distinction? And indeed, everyone knows how unique the Palestinian conflict is and has decided that it is no longer politically "exemplary" (in the way it was in the 1970s when the Palestinian struggle was really at the center and beating heart of all the then struggles of national independence, and indeed of internal politics as a politics of liberation as well). So this book has yet a supplementary dilemma: how to overcome the general cultural fatigue with what is certainly still a burning dilemma, and how to avoid some inevitable "avoidance behavior" on the part of readers and scholars alike.

So in a more general way, the book faces the primary problem or potential misconception: Is it about a theory, which will always bear within it an urge towards universality (should it not somehow apply to all third-world literature, or to all literary comparison, or to all of the intersections of global literatures and cultures, etc.); or is it about a specific literature and literary history—the Israeli one or the Palestinian one—and somehow stands as one more contribution to those specialized fields, in which case the theory is more or less independent? So: class or political problems with classification of the area in question (colonies, Wallersteinian peripheries, etc.); the more traditional "Marxist-literary-critical" problems about social content and expression, form, political tendency, didacticism, etc.; the current debate about "world literature" which has its own dynamic today; the questions about the novel as a form (realism/modernism/postmodernism); and of course the problem of the Western reader, for whom all these books and references in impenetrable foreign languages, and all these unknown works, even in translation, easily become an excuse for a lack of interest altogether (where a responsible Americanist, for example, might feel obligated to look at something as unfamiliar as Chicano literature, even if it lies outside of his or her specialization in American transcendentalism, for example).

There are theoretical issues hidden away even in this last seemingly more individual matter of "interest" (I'm not interested in foreign literatures like Vietnamese; I'm not interested in acquiring all the historical background and reference I would need to read a Kyrgyz novel or play, etc.). They are twofold: the domination of English today, as lingua franca and world language (this seems to be at the center of what is called the world-literature debate today); but second, the reluctance to read about works you have never read, even if the story is briefly outlined.

I won't go into the first, but the second is interesting, for it is possible to take a heightened interest in what Franco Moretti would call the distant reading of a text that is only available to you in some reader's plot rehash: I take the example of music analysis. For a non-specialist, or indeed a non-musical reader who cannot read music or even play, it is possible—when of course many specialist works remain closed, with their plates and musical illustrations—to derive the greatest profit from an abstract work like Adorno's *Philosophy of Modern Music*. In the absence of available concrete detail, the movement of form it describes—development, regression, dilemmas and contradictions—can be an object in its own right which one can then transfer to other fields and objects such as the novel (or even social or political situations). Phenomena like repetition become clearer, and issues like familiarity, shock, autonomy, exteriority, suddenly emerge from the tangle of musical detail and become visible and theoretically usable in their own right. This is what happens in the present work, I think, with some of the more luminous critical analyses of unfamiliar novels in an utterly unfamiliar language. They become an abstract play of solutions and problems, a theoretical object, which is then a kind of exemplary model in its own right. (I think one should avoid the detestable word method which has nothing to offer in this context). This, then, is at least one of the strengths of this work, whose discussion of that import which is the Israeli modern novel sheds an extraordinary light on the insufficiencies of the readings of modern European literature in the West and proposes altogether new concepts and solutions for its rewriting.

But I have not mentioned one final and determinate innovation of the present study, and that is, cutting across all the local, formal and regional contradictions of these literatures, the fact of History itself. What we are witnessing here is real (literary) History, the use of literature to make genuine History appear behind it as though the former were a symptom and an expression of a reality itself unrepresentable. Suddenly History, in the form of periodization, appears in the fateful cut-off point of 1980 (relatively speaking), and we confront that "great transformation" which has been variously termed postmodernity, neoliberalism, globalization, total subsumption to capital, the world market, the third stage of capitalism, and even "the end of history," terms on which no one is agreed but a reality that by now no one doubts. It is this great transformation which is at issue uniquely in this book, and followed across several contiguous literatures, which turn out to be somehow about each other in a mirror situation in which they are locked in mortal conflict—apartheid on the one hand, reduction to a powerless minority status on the other—and which have very different formal achievements to their credit, but which are suddenly, as in some universal world eclipse, caught in the blinding light of a single universal event, like a meteor hitting the earth or an epidemic that knows no boundaries.

Universal commodification suddenly seizes on the entire world population—rich or poor, industrialized or nomad, advanced or primitive, alike—and something emerges from this moment of universal transformation which few enough critics have studied and indeed which could not become so blindingly visible except through the lens of a comparison of this kind. This is a unique historical and theoretical, indeed dialectical, vision which is only rarely available in other literary or cultural studies and which is essential, not only to our literary readings, but to social reality and above all to politics itself. For the question of the novel and the question of political movement and revolution are in some deeper way the same: What is it in the development of capitalism today, in the development of many different kinds of daily life and culture, that makes both the novel and political praxis problematic? This is the moment of the emergence of History as such, which can only show itself through contradiction and dilemma: this is what we suddenly glimpse, in a seemingly irrelevant discussion of books we have never heard of, in languages we cannot decipher, and from far away, from "people of whom we know nothing," as Chamberlain so memorably put it. This work gives us not only a unique chance to experience History but sets the example (or I would rather say, the model) of how we should be dealing with cultural phenomena in a historical moment which itself presents utterly new dynamics for which the "methods" of the past are no longer useful. This is what work in world literature ought to look like today, and seldom does.

Note on Translations and Transliterations

Unless otherwise mentioned, all translations from Hebrew and Arabic are mine. Transliteration of titles in Arabic and Hebrew follow IJMES and Encyclopedia Judaica.

Introduction

On Social and Aesthetic Abstraction

Part I

1.

What had started in the late 1970s as neoliberal economic restructuring and, after the fall of the Berlin Wall, became associated with the political promise of "globalization" remains today the name for our historical moment and a central fact in inquiries into the contemporary.[1] This rather recent reality, about whose origin and scope there is still some debate, serves in this book as the departure point for rethinking what

---

1 Globalization is a relatively new approach to social and cultural life and as such its concepts, scope, and claims are still being tested and contested. Scholarly literature on globalization is quite large by now so I mention only a few notable contributions: for social and anthropological theory see, for example, Arjun Appadurai, *Modernity at Large: Cultural Dimensions of Globalization* (Minneapolis: University of Minnesota Press, 1996); Anthony Giddens, *The Consequences of Modernity* (Cambridge: Polity Press, 1991); Roland Robertson, Mike Featherstone, Scott Lash (eds.) *Global Modernities* (London: Sage, 1995); Saskia Sassen, *A Sociology of Globalization* (New York: Norton, 2007). For early attempts to conceptualize global relations see Andre Gunder Frank, "The Development of Underdevelopment," *Monthly Review* 18.4 (September 1966): 17–31; Immanuel Wallerstein, "The Rise and Future Demise of the World Capitalist System: Concepts for Comparative Analysis," *Comparative Studies in Society and History* 16.4 (September 1974): 387–415. For cultural theory, including postmodernity, see David Harvey, *The Condition of Postmodernity: An Enquiry into the Origins of Cultural Change* (Cambridge, Mass: Blackwell, 1991); Fredric Jameson, *Postmodernism, or The Cultural Logic of Late Capitalism* (Durham: Duke University Press, 1991). For theories of world literature and circulation, see Pascale Casanova, *The World Republic of Letters*, translated by M.B. DeBevoise (Cambridge: Harvard University Press, 2004); David Damrosch, *What is World Literature?* (Princeton: Princeton University Press, 2003); Franco Moretti, *Distant Reading* (London/New York: Verso, 2013); Roberto Schwarz, *Misplaced Ideas: Essays on Brazilian Culture* (London/New York: Verso, 1996).

Immanuael Wallerstein calls the periphery, its morphing relation to the center, and the modes of life, culture and knowledge that can no longer be said to be simply its own. While the world surely remains culturally heterogeneous and uneven in ways that make claims of standardization inaccurate, the global, as it is conceived here, will not be understood as the borderless movement of peoples and things, as if the world is the sum-total of groups and practices whose mixture and hybridization the scholar registers, but rather as a set of abstract conditions that mediate and limit such encounters and subjects, and their modes of knowledge and action. If the current study can make one contribution, it is to explain and interpret the manner in which social or real abstraction, as Alfred Sohn-Rethel would say, comes to matter for the political valence of symbolic forms.

Thus, while the immediate object of this inquiry concerns the political and aesthetic transformation of Israeli and Palestinian literature (specifically the novel), the reader will not find here the familiar conversation about Israelis and Palestinians, Arabs and Jews, but rather a conversation about globality as an Other with which the novel, in form and political import, must ultimately contend. For, as of the late 1980s, despite the persistence of the Israeli-Palestinian conflict, the story of Israel and Palestine—their cultural production and political and economic structures, not to mention the day-to-day experiences of Israelis and Palestinians—has changed significantly. These changes, which are often shaped and determined outside Israel and Palestine's sovereign areas, in the circuits of capital and politics in the US and Europe, the IMF and the World Bank, thus necessitate an account that goes beyond national categories, hitherto the preferred framework in studies by Zionists and non-Zionists alike.

Tracing the impact of these changes, the road ahead follows a historical and conceptual itinerary. While taking into account the transformations affected by globalization, I propose here, without falling into a static mapping of characteristics à la Hegel's *Zeitgeist*, a socio-poetic periodization of Israeli and Palestinian literature before and after the global moment, a narrative that will help us tell a different history about these literatures not yet acknowledged in current studies. Making a point to answer the idiographic humanist reproach of reductionism (the concern that a social nomothetic etiology of literary form forfeits the question of autonomy), I have placed the question of autonomy at the very center of this study, but instead of an a priori attribution of "autonomy" to works of art—an uncritical and ahistorical gesture—I have historicized the way the Israeli and Palestinian literary artwork think this concept in each period and compared these to the concept's emergence in Europe, especially in Kant, a comparison that will eventually allow us to form the basis for rethinking the concept of world literature. Correlating, as subtly and fully as possible, between poetic and social form, interpretation and explanation, would then be the burden of this study. It will require patient shifts between literary, socio-historical and theoretical levels of analysis, resulting in what I hope will be one possible model for comparative interdisciplinary work in the global humanities.

Before delving into what is meant here by globalization, it is important to quickly distinguish the current attempt from existing ones. In the humanities today, the term globalization, or one of its variants, is often studied via the twin concepts "circulation" and "hybridization." Cultural forms, we are told, do not simply arise organically but are always implicated in other circulating cultural forms, a hybridity whose presence is often denied by the ideologies of nationalism or other identitarian investments. While useful in many regards, both politically and analytically, hybridity and circulation reduce globalization to the phenomena of trade and immigration and are thus open to several challenges. First, that immigration and trade across borders have probably existed for thousands of years and thus globalization is nothing new. Second, that the intensity of immigration and trade were even higher at the end of the nineteenth century than they are today. And third, that hybridity is the norm of human interaction rather than a new phenomenon coming about with globalization. If we concede these points—which I believe we must—we realize that the qualitative transformation is not after all in the world, but in our way of thinking about the world. That is to say, we realize that it was the ideologies of the Cold War, nationalism, Area Studies and the like that prevented us from seeing the interconnected world for what it was all along. This admission shifts attention to the subject's modes of analysis, an inward move which uses globalization as an institutional critique of disciplinary protocols and, by doing that, forfeits the object. Moreover, as the concept of cultural circulation is used at times to criticize the alleged purity and homogeneity of national culture, it gives new license to a dominant variant of literary studies whose political priorities are still beholden to a liberal and humanist stance, and whose critical object continues to be the state. Posited vis-à-vis the state and its rigid borders (symbolic and real), "circulation" takes up the opposite number of excess, of overflowing connections whose underlying concepts—plurality and difference—ultimately reaffirm the problematic notion of the transcendent power of culture.

Seeking to avoid these limitations, this inquiry advances a different argument. It takes globalization to mean something quite different than a borderless world, a reality more recent than the spread of trade and immigration, and a critical object whose aim is as much the new forms of capital as the state. For this concept of cultural circulation as a critique of the state does not register how global capital itself weakens states and their symbolic logic, and this perspective usually overlooks the fact that it is not only cultural objects and people in circulation, but capitalist social relations themselves. This perspective is not altogether new: in 1984, Fredric Jameson's inquiry into postmodernity alerted us to the new reality in which late capitalism has exceeded the limits of nation-states, crippling our epistemological and political engagement. This stage of capitalist development, as we are told, too, by Giovanni Arrighi, sees the locus of power shifting, around the 1970s, from the Westphalia system of European nation-states to a network of global corporations. Put in Michael Hardt and Antonio Negri's terms, globalization signals the global moment of what Marx calls "real subsumption," in which the extensive reach of capital turns intensive.[2] In this moment, that is, capitalist relations do not only exploit the "periphery" by techniques of surplus value extraction, but fundamentally transform the very structure of labor and social relations in the periphery, leaving in fact "no outside."[3] Understood thusly, globalization is then more recent than what "trade" and "immigration" can allow, and it brings with it new political, social and aesthetic conditions that hybridity and circulation do not adequately address.[4] For example, while on the regional and global stage, Palestine, specifically

2   Giovanni Arrighi, *The Long Twentieth Century: Money, Power and the Origins of Our Times* (London/New York: Verso, 1994); Michael Hardt and Antonio Negri, *Empire* (Boston, Mass: Harvard University Press, 2000).

3   For bibliographic details of Wallerstein, see footnote 1

4.   For example, that globalization proper is outside the purview of Pascale Casanova's study and appears there as an afterthought is clearly evident in the fact that of her incredibly rich study—whose central concept of autonomy will be pivotal to this inquiry—only a handful of remarks are devoted to the new development of global literature and global publishing, a new period with which her model, and Pierre Bourdieu's, does not contend but considers an aberration. Franco Moretti's otherwise useful theory also betrays its own historical limit when we notice that its signature contribution— the imbalance between the imported Western form and local content/narrator in the periphery—no longer characterizes the structure of fiction coming out of Israel and Palestine (and surely other regions). Not only do such formal imbalances no longer exist, but the literary form in the periphery begins to resemble the core. Casanova, *The World Republic of Letters*, 164–72. On the new commercialization of art and the threat to autonomy, see also Pierre Bourdieu, *The Rules of Art: Genesis and Structure of the Literary Field*, translated by Susan Emanuel (Stanford: Stanford University Press, 1996), 344–5. For Moretti's study see footnote 1.

the West Bank, is dominated politically, economically, and aesthetically in terms of value, it nonetheless shares in a new global condition in the periphery—i.e., the emergence of a private, liberal subject—that makes its literary production equivalent, rather than identical, to other literatures. Thus, although a world of difference separates life in the West Bank from life in Tel Aviv, and these two differ from life in England, and although novels depicting such experiences take up various ideological solutions, these heterogeneous lives and diverse ideologies are nonetheless imagined from a common global *condition*—i.e., a form of private life for whom politics has become a problem, and social life has turned into a text to be read rather than an object to be made. This structural similarity provides the shared basis—the shared historical and aesthetic categories—for a global comparative study.

Three key characteristics of globalization will be developed throughout this inquiry and distinguish it from current literary studies: first, globalization is here understood as a new stage of capitalism whose social relations, underlined by the principle of value production, now subsume the entire world. The novelty of this stage, as we said, is not simply in the reach of the world market, but rather in the fact that these social relations now remake more and more areas of the world. This transformation has several political, social and aesthetic consequences I examine closely below, but it can be summed up as the moment when the concept of political finality or end (telos) is replaced by endless accumulation for which human life, let alone political organization, is but a means. Calling it "real subsumption," Marx argues that "it is a form of production not bound to a level of needs laid in *advance* and hence it does not predetermine the course of production itself."[5]

In and of itself such a transformation from quality to quantity is inherent to capitalism and therefore not new. In Europe and the US, the more recent substantive and historical shift pertains to those entities —e.g., the Keynesian state and civil society—which in the period between the 1940s and the 1970s were able, to a certain degree, to subordinate capitalist production to political ends. In the periphery, the shift concerns, among other things, a transition from state-building, where resources are directed to communal ends, to more market-oriented policies, usually dictated by global lenders. For this reason, globalization in Israel and Palestine (and in other parts of the world) has a dual and

---

5   Karl Marx, *Capital* I, translated by Ben Fowkes (London: Penguin Books, 1976), 1037.

contradictory meaning—on the one hand, since it comes after a long period of state-building, it represents freedom (especially of the body) from such collective duty, and, on the other, it confronts its new subjects as a radical release from any kind of social obligation against which nationalism, ethics, and other forms of spirituality are called in to fill the void, to confront it with an end (in the dual sense of purpose and limit). Globalization is then first and foremost a crisis of political ends which is sometimes characterized as the "end of the state" and demonstrated in the subordination of the needs of political communities to global corporations and networks of finance that we associate with neoliberalism.[6] This political crisis underlies Israeli and Palestinian literary production despite the enormous significance of the conflict and its attendant nationalisms. In fact, in Israel, it would be fair to say that nationalism is today posited—as in Britain and the US and other European states—as a cure for the effects of global capital.

Second, one of the consequences of the supersession of the nation-state as the "container" of social life concerns the abstraction of the local. Jameson saw this kind of separation between the local and the global already arising in a limited fashion in late nineteenth-century imperialism, where life in the metropole was more and more conditioned by distant colonies, a disjunction that was extended and exacerbated by globalization where, for example, private life in Israel is now dependent on abstract networks of global capital. What characterizes the current global moment, according to Jameson, is then a "growing contradiction between [local] lived experience and [global] structure, or between phenomenological description of the life of an individual and a more properly structural model of the conditions of existence of that experience."[7] Separated from its conditions of possibility, now dispersed into global markets, local lived experience comes to acquire a seeming autonomy, especially in the periphery, precisely by dint of being detached from that which determines it.[8]

---

6   By the 1990s, as David Harvey suggests, neoliberal political and economic aspects are "subsumed" under the more encompassing term "globalization." David Harvey, *A Brief History of Neoliberalism* (Oxford/New York: Oxford University Press, 2007). See also, Gérard Duménil, Dominique Lévy, *Capital Resurgent: Roots of the Neoliberal Revolution*, translated by Derek Jeffers (Cambridge, Mass: Harvard University Press, 2004); Michel Foucault, *The Birth of Biopolitics: Lectures at the College de France 1978–79*, translated by Graham Burchell (New York: Palgrave Macmillian, 2008).

7   Jameson, *Postmodernism*, 410.

8   Paraphrasing Alfred Sohn-Rethel, I understand this process as "real abstraction." Placed at the very heart of globalization, abstraction, too, is not entirely new. Marx identifies its emergence with the shift from feudalism to capitalism in Western Europe, first

Arjun Appadurai sees what is designated here as global abstraction as the creation of the illusory autonomy of the local, arguing that "the locality (both in the sense of the local factory or site of production and in the extended sense of the nation-state) becomes a fetish that disguises the globally dispersed forces that actually drive the production process."[9] Now, it is worth noting that while Appadurai and other anthropologists and sociologists working with the same conception of globalization-as-disjuncture[10] are quite averse to Hegelianism, the effects of globalization, separating cause and effect, follow quite faithfully Hegel's definition of "appearance":

> When we speak of an appearance, we associate with it the representation of an indeterminate multiplicity of concretely existing things whose being is simply mediation alone and which accordingly do not rest on themselves . . . The appearance posited in this way does not stand on its own feet and does not have its being in itself but in another [i.e. essence].[11]

To be sure, one does not need to adopt Hegel's teleological closure of historical processes to make use of this conception. Hegel's understanding helps us rather to see the communality between social appearance on the one hand, and aesthetic appearance (*Schein*), especially in Kant and Adorno, on the other, and with this communality to designate the third characteristic of globalization that will bring us closer to aesthetic production.

Recall that for Kant what distinguishes reflective from determining judgment, and fine art from other made objects, is that in the former the determining concept is absent, a condition that allows for both the freedom of the faculties in the moment of aesthetic experience, and the autonomy of the beautiful object that takes after the category of nature

---

when labor is no longer embedded in particular social relations and becomes abstract labor power as such; and second, with the separation of the state from civil society—a process of disembedment of political relations that are now lifted from civil society and placed in the state proper. It is precisely this kind of abstraction that "travels" to the periphery, and transforms its social relations, without, however, making it identical to Europe. Alfred Sohn-Retel, *Intellectual and Manual Labour: A Critique of Epistemology*, translated by Martin Sohn-Retel (Atlantic Highlands: Humanities Press, 1977).

9   Appadurai, *Modernity at Large*, 41–42.
10   See for example Giddens, *The Consequences of Modernity*, 65.
11   G. W. F. Hegel, *Encyclopedia of the Philosophical Sciences in Basic Outline: Part I: Science of Logic*, translated by Klaus Brinkmann and Daniel O. Dahlstrom (Cambridge, Mass: Cambridge University Press, 2010), 198.

as the unmade. Recall, too, that for Adorno, the autonomy of the artwork hinges on its ability to conceal the fact that it was made from the outside, that it was a product of work.[12] It is this concealment that provides the "appearance" of naturalness and autonomy. Globalization, I argue, exhibits the same structure of Kantian aesthetics—for locality (as is its subject) depends precisely on the absence of its global determining cause, turning it into an autonomous and natural object.

With this communality we can also see the twofold meaning of the absence: what is missing is not simply far away as if the problem were a matter of space alone; what is missing and procures the appearance of autonomy is precisely the determining concept of finality or end discussed above. For in Kant, it is not simply the absence of any concept or law that allows for the autonomy of the fine arts and reflective judgment, but specifically the absence of the concept of end, which precisely characterizes capital both in its historic emergence and in its global expansion. In other words, globalization can be cast as a process of social aestheticization (a concept that has a strong affinity with Derrida's concept of textuality, as we shall see). In an environment where reality has been aestheticized and stripped of cause, artworks respond by inventing modes of narration—primary among them is the "search"—that map out laws and rules that condition the life of the subject. In artworks that celebrate private life as newfound freedom from nationalism or any other constraint, the search depicts globalization as a displaced and mystified problem of origin, self-identity and ethics, while conscious political artworks attempt to uncover the global conditions in whichever sphere they consider Real (politics, economics, etc.). For this reason, current political artworks that engage with globalization and take up various techniques of mapping begin to resemble nomothetic social inquiries whose philosophical concept has more to do with Kant's First critique than his Third. Globalization is then the spread of disjuncture and absence—and not simply the circulation of people, commodities and cultural forms—to the rest of the world and especially to the periphery.

---

12 Theodor Adorno, *In Search of Wagner*, translated by Rodney Livingstone (London/New York: Verso, 2005), 71–2.

2.

Moving from this global condition (about which we will say much more in the following pages) to Israeli and Palestinian literature, let us first set the period under discussion and distinguish this periodization from existing ones. To understand the global transformation, we are to look at Israeli and Palestinian literature from the 1940s to the present, when the moment of change, acknowledging the arbitrariness of dates, occurs in Israel in 1985 and in Palestine in 1993. I should alert the reader that dividing the period between the 1940s and the present into only two periods is not the common practice. In existing historical accounts of modern Hebrew literature, shared by both Zionist and non-Zionists critics, we find a pendulum movement between two styles and two political tendencies, usually lasting a decade or so and whose basic unit is the "generation." The first is the realist style which is seen as explicitly endorsing national ideology (Jewish or more specifically Zionist) and whose themes revolve around collective concerns, while the second is the modernist style whose worlds revolve around the individual psyche of the characters whose thoughts and actions challenge (but do not necessarily reject) Zionist ideology. This pendulum movement also underlies the history of Israeli literature (or at least until the 1990s).[13]

The problem with this periodization concerns its underlying assumptions. In historical accounts of Israeli literature, the Israeli nation is conceived as a constant ideal Subject while the different periods of national unity or differentiation function as the Subject's predicates. According to the standard literary history, what prompts the change in

---

13   This periodization is assumed by almost all critics of Hebrew literature as well as by writers and editors. Gershon Shaked's history of modern Hebrew literature in five volumes is credited with establishing the norm of "stylistic generations" and although critics challenge the inclusion or exclusion of writers from each "generation" they accept his periodization in general terms. For a few major historical studies of Hebrew literature that use this periodization or presuppose it, see: Gershon Shaked, *Ha-siporet ha-'ivrit 1880–1980*, 5 volumes (Yerushalayim: Keter, 1977–1998); Nurit Gerts, *Ḥirbet Ḥiz'ah yeha-boker shela-moḥorat* (Tel Aviv: Ha-kibuẓ ha-me'uḥad, 1983); Dan Miron, *'Im lo tihiyeh yerushalayim: Ha-sifrut ha-'ivrit be-heksher tarbuti u-politi* (Tel Aviv: Ha-kibuẓ ha-me'uḥad, 1987), 9–92; Dan Miron, "Hirhurim b-'idan shel proza." In Zisi Stav (ed.) *Sheloshim shana, sheloshim sipurim: mivḥar ha-sipur ha-'ivri ha-kaẓar mi-shenot ha-shishim 'ad shenot ha-tish'im* (Tel Aviv: Yedi'ot aḥaronot, 1993), 397–427; Avraham Balaban, *Gal aḥer ba-sifrut ha-'ivrit : siporet 'ivrit posmodernistit* (Yerushalayim, Keter, 1995); Hannah Herzog, *Ha-kol ha-'omer 'ani: megamot ba-siporet ha-yisra'elit shel shenot ha-shemonim* (Tel Aviv: Ha-'universitah ha-petuḥah, 1998); Hannan Hever, *Sifrut she-nikhtevet mi-kan: kiẓur ha-sifrut ha-yisra'elit* (Tel Aviv: Yedi'ot aḥaronot, 1999); Yigal Shwartz, *Mah she-ro'im mi-kan: sugiyot be-historyografyah shel ha-sifrut ha-'ivrit ha-ḥadashah* (Or Yehudah: Kineret, Zemorah-bitan, Dvir, 2005).

the national mood is a great event—usually wars or elections—whose outcome and consequences influence a critical or endorsing attitude.[14] Critics working with this model presuppose a concept of eventmental history that ignores long-term social structures that change more slowly. Similarly, if the relation between the nation and its mood is one of Subject and predicate so also the relation between the category of Literature and the different styles of each period. The category of literature is assumed to be constant while only its styles change. In such a history all styles are equivalent to one another. The history of Palestinian literature from 1948 onwards follows a similar pattern; historical accounts tend to correlate between the effects of political movements and literary style, where political commitment is expressed in realism and political failure in modernism.[15]

I propose here a different principle of historicization by shifting the underlying Subject from nation to social form, and instead of assuming the continuity of the categories of nation and literature, I identify not only two historical Subjects but also two categories of Literature. The shift from what is called statism in Israel and "political society" in Palestine in the first period to neoliberal globalization in the second indicates a transition between two qualitatively different societies and two different categories of aesthetic production. Enlarging the historical periods beyond the decade and the event on the one hand, and expanding aesthetic categories on the other, will allow us to see the communalities between styles in each period that in existing accounts are considered distinct. To be sure, stylistic distinctions and their accompanying political significance are real literary phenomenon, but they belong to literary practitioners and exist within the history of what Bourdieu calls the literary field. In this

---

14   According to such accounts, the years leading to the 1948 war saw a robust identification of the literary field with the project of state making while the period that followed is considered to be a period of disillusionment and criticism. The wars of 1967, 1973 and 1982 as well as the defeat of the labor party (MAPAI) in the 1977 elections are all considered catalysts for stylistic changes in literature.

15   See, for example, Bashir Abu-Manneh's new history of the Palestinian novel, *The Palestinian Novel: From 1948 to the Present* (Cambridge: Cambridge University Press, 2016); Bashir Abu-Manneh "Palestinian Trajectories: Novel and Politics Since 1948," *Modern Language Quarterly* 75:4 (December 2014): 511–539; Faysal Darraj, "Disparities of the Palestinian Novel," *Banipal* 15–16 (2002–3): 47–52; Kamal Abu-Deeb, "Cultural Creation in a Fragmented Society." In Hisham Sharabi (ed.) *The Next Arab Decade: Alternative Futures* (Boulder: Westview Press, 1988), 160–81. Specifically in the case of Kanafani, Muhammad Siddiq also argues that his experimentation with modernism comes about in a time of political uncertainty. See Muhammad Siddiq, *Man Is a Cause: Political Consciousness and the Fiction of Ghassan Kanafani* (Seattle: University of Washington Press, 1984).

level, writers respond to the immediate political context of the day as well as to one another.[16] This level is also the level of canon formation around whose sanctioned writers, styles, and political tendencies many of the battles in the literary field are waged. Accepting this level of engagement as necessary but insufficient, this inquiry shifts to a broader historical level of analysis—much shorter than Braudel's *longue durée*, but longer and more consistent than the punctual political event or the decade— and identifies this new level as the historical condition of possibility of literary and political form. Since Kant is alluded to here, we could rewrite the difference between the immediate and historical levels of analysis as the difference Kant draws between criticism and Critique. To paraphrase Kant and replace his transcendental assumption with a historical one, we can say that differently from criticism, which prefers one style to another according to its political preferences, literary Critique assumes that all literary styles, in a given period, are conditioned by a shared historical "ground" that underlies imaginary worlds without necessarily appearing in them as such.[17] I argue then that literary positions are to be understood not only laterally, i.e., in relation to one another, but also vertically, in relation to common social structures—the "other" of all positions—that condition their existence and especially their political responses. Hegel's concept of "limit" can help us make the point:

> Something is what it is only *within* its limit and *due to* its limit. Hence one must not regard the limit a something that is merely external to exis-tence; rather it permeates existence as a whole. The construal of the limit as a merely external determination of existence is due to the conflation of the quantitative with the qualitative limit.[18]

Social-form-as-limit is that which "permeates" and conditions literary production "as a whole": it is not something literature confronts as an

---

16   Here I follow Jameson who proposes reading literary texts according to three levels of analysis: the (immediate) *political* context, the *social* (whose literary object are class ideologemes) and the *historical* (whose object is the sign system). See Jameson, *The Political Unconscious: Narrative as a Socially Symbolic Act* (Ithaca: Cornell University Press, 1981), 74–102.

17   As Kant puts it, the critical method "does not consider the question objectively at all [i.e., whether a statement is true or not], but instead asks about the foundations of the cognition [i.e., the presuppositions] on which it is grounded." Immanuel Kant, *Critique of Pure Reason*, translated by Paul Guyer and Allen Wood (Cambridge: Cambridge University Press, 1998), 507.

18   Hegel, *Encyclopedia of the Philosophical Sciences in Basic Outline: Part I*, 147, emphasis in original.

external limit, which it can exceed or transgress as if it were a spatial border. Rather, its forms arise from this limit as a response, and for this reason the limit inheres in its form. The limit conditions the philosophical, aesthetic and experiential dimensions of a particular social organization in a given period. Such dimensions, in their ideological diversity, neither passively reflect the constitutive limit, nor are all of them homologous with the period, but rise as diverse and sometimes opposing responses. To be sure, such limits are socially made and social agents seeks to either establish or depose such limits. Hegel's insight is that there is no "thing" that exists without a limit and yet there isn't a simple identity between the two. Hegel's "limit" can be understood as a form of Freud's Unconscious and Lacan's Real *avant la lettre*.

The fundamental fallacy of certain kinds of literary criticism, especially those that pose literary production as "resistance" to nationalism or to exchange value, is that such accounts posit literature and its "other" as an encounter between two adversaries, two opposite forms (e.g., binarism vs. hybridity; the absolute vs. the iterable). Such accounts objectify or fetishize the limit in one of its formal responses, a move that then allows us to conceive of the alternative form as outside the limit. Since there is no form that does not arise from a limit, such accounts are fallacious, or, to be more precise, they are invested in an ideological project whose limits they disavow. When positing hybridity and iterability as "resistance" we never ask, for example: What is their unconscious? What is it that such forms cannot say? Asking such questions will push us to acknowledge the subject position from which this or that resistance is posited and interrogate its presuppositions. There is no such thing as "resistance" in general. The present task of critique is to articulate this limit in its two historical social forms, explain how it conditions literary worlds, and finally interpret these last and analyze their political significance.

The styles we see emerging in Israel and Palestine after 1985 and 1993 respectively are then qualitatively different than those that came before them; they spring to life from a new historical conjuncture where both the political problem facing writers and their preliminary poetic raw materials are now different and impose new conditions on literary form. Current studies do not register this structural change because their static emphasis on nationalism either generates an ahistorical outlook, or it locates the origin of stylistic change in the writers themselves, offering no explanatory field outside individual innovation. If a historical "outside" is offered it is attributed, as I said, to an historical event rather than to a structural condition.[19] Consider, for example, the Israeli case: even without endorsing the periodization offered here, most if not all literary critics would agree that since the mid-1980s social conditions underlying literary production,[20] as well as literary forms, have utterly changed, while Israeli nationalism remains *unchanged*. Zionism, understood as a separatist ideology and a Jewish redemptive narrative, remains today as virulent as it was a hundred years ago, if not more so, yet the novels published since the second half of the 1980s are the least nationalist Israel has ever known. The adequacy of nationalism as an explanatory category of literary analysis is attenuated further when we shift from literary to social change and note the radical transformations that have affected Israeli society in the last thirty years, cutting across all spheres of life, while national identity and even the Israeli occupation itself remain intact. More damaging is the additional fact that this other reality, tightly tied to the processes of neoliberal globalization, begins to challenge the viability of the separatist ideology within Israel, especially in the labor market, and accordingly modifies the representation of Jews and Arabs, and the political significance allotted them in novelistic writings.[21]

The incongruence between, on the one hand, the constancy of Zionist nationalism and its ubiquitous presence in daily life, and, on the other, the deep structural changes in the forms and modes of this life, points to another, more complex reality that escapes literary studies that pose nationalism as the most important social condition underlying literary production. What is needed is a historical concept that will be at once broader than nationalism, grasping different kinds of social phenomena, and subtler, suggesting a more refined relation between social reality and literary forms. Presupposing Marx's category of "mode of production," the concept of social form, which will be central to this inquiry, will allow us both explanatory breadth and interpretive agility.

---

19 Bashir Abu-Manneh's *The Palestinian Novel* is an example here, offering a political category ("defeat") that conditions Palestinian literary production since the 1970s. Manneh, however, does not attribute a qualitative change to the Oslo Accords, but rather sees in them a continuation of the 1970s failure of liberation strategies. Similarly, Avarham Balaban's study, *Gal aher ba-sifrut ha-'ivrit*, like many others, attributes the emergence of Israeli postmodernism in the late 1980s to the 1977 electoral defeat of the labor party (MAPAI) and to the 1982 Lebanon war that eroded public confidence in the government.

20 I mean here the establishment of privately owned publishing houses and the aggressive commercialization of the field of cultural production that came about with the new communications law of 1992.

21 I attend to these changes in Chapter 2.

With this concept in mind, we can say that what has transpired in Israel and Palestine in the last thirty years is a transformation in the structure of the social form, or in the nature of the "limit," similar to the transformations in Western Europe in the nineteenth century that saw the establishment of liberal creed and capitalism as the dominant social order. To be sure, history does not simply repeat itself. Not only does the tertiary emergence of capitalist social relations, liberalism, and civil society out of the statist/political structure in Israel and Palestine coincide with the neoliberal moment that also undermines the autonomy of civil society—leading to complex political responses that need to be carefully observed—but the particularities of lived experience in Israel and Palestine differ from Europe and the United States. And yet, as of the mid-1980s and the early 1990s, Israel and Palestine share in structural historical conditions that affect the rest of the world.

The transition in the social form, enabled by globalization, can be described as a process of autonomization through which both Israel and Palestine (specifically the West Bank) see the rearticulation of the private and public sphere, or what is equivalent, the autonomization of private life that now comes to be separated from direct political powers, resulting in the real liberal fiction of self-legislation. To articulate this change in the language of globalization previously discussed, the social process of autonomization separates immediate experience (private life) from the conditions of possibility (public life) that are now abstracted and governed by global networks. The shift from what I call heteronomy to autonomy on the social ground is the condition of possibility of a comparable shift from heteronomous to autonomous aesthetic. The categorical homology between these two levels is predicated on the relation between universality and particularity that characterizes both social and aesthetic relations. Put in Kantian terms, if in the first heteronomous period (1940–1985/1993) the political sphere acts as the direct universality (the political end) that both subsumes private life and provides the determinate concept, or universal, for the literary work, in the second autonomous period (1985/1993–) the social separation of the "political" from the "private" allows for the indeterminate relation between the particular and the universal, akin to reflective (aesthetic) judgments in Kant's sense. Such a transformation is of profound historical significance for the lives of both Israelis and Palestinians who now, "for the first time," begin to live private lives separated from communal bonds.

To open up a comparative historical, theoretical and aesthetic perspective let us first go through this transition in Western Europe.

3.

The shift from the pre-modern to the modern period in Europe is often told as a shift from heteronomy to autonomy. Whether the argument revolves around a transition from Absolutism to liberal democracy, religious authority to Enlightenment's scientific inquiry, or sovereign to disciplinary power, what is common to all such transformations is the designation of the pre-modern as determined from the outside, having its cause in an external power, while the modern subject is conceived as self-legislating, being the cause of itself. In the pre-modern, the law-giver is conceived as an agent or entity separated from and usually situated above the world or society, while in the modern period the law-giver is characterized by immanence, whether within the subject or society at large. And last, if the pre-modern is conceived through the category of constitutive inequality and incommensurability (between the earthly and the divine; the different Estates; men and women, etc.) then the modern is characterized by a new equivalence and a common measure.[22]

Marxist accounts ascribe this change to a broader historical shift in modes of production, moving from feudalism to capitalism.[23] In Moshe

---

22   For an intellectual history of the shift from heteronomy to autonomy in Europe, see James Kloppenberg, *Towards Democracy: The Struggle for Self-Rule in European and American Thought* (Oxford/New York: Oxford University Press, 2016). Kloppenberg conceives of the shift to democracy in the US and Western Europe through the categories of popular sovereignty, autonomy and equality. For two useful philosophical surveys of autonomy see, C. B. Macpherson, *The Political Theory of Possessive Individualism: Hobbes to Locke* (Oxford: Clarendon Press, 1962); J. B. Schneewind, *The Invention of Autonomy: A History of Modern Moral Philosophy* (Cambridge: Cambridge University Press, 1998). For Immanuel Kant's conception of enlightenment as autonomous self-legislation see his "An Answer to the Question: What is Enlightenment." Translated by James Schmidt. In James Schmidt (ed.) *What Is Enlightenment? Eighteenth-Century Answers and Twentieth-Century Questions* (Berkeley: University of California Press, 1996), 53–57. For a short social history of the conquest of autonomy and the establishment of the liberal creed, see Immanuel Wallerstein, *The Modern World-System IV: Centrist Liberalism Triumphant 1789–1914* (Berkeley: University of California Press, 2011). For Michel Foucault's discussion on the shift from sovereign to disciplinary power which is based on the same spatial shift from vertical/external power to lateral and immanent power see his *Discipline and Punish: The Birth of the Prison*, translated by Alan Sheridan (New York: Vintage, 1995), and *Security, Territory, Population: Lectures at the Collège de France, 1977–78*, translated by Graham Burchell (Basingstoke/New York: Palgrave Macmillan, 2007). We can find the same distinction between direct and immanent power in Louis Althusser's distinction between coercive State Apparatus (SA) and Ideological State Apparatus (ISA) dispensed through the institutions of civil society. See Louis Althusser, "Ideology and Ideological State Apparatuses (Notes towards an Investigation)." In *Lenin and Philosophy*, translated by Ben Brewster (New York: Monthly Review Press, 1971), 127–86.

23   For a history of the transition from antiquity to feudalism to Absolutism and

Postone's terminology, "overt social relations," prevalent in the pre-capitalist period, are replaced by the self-mediation of abstract labor that displaces direct (i.e., extra-economic) social domination into the impersonal structure of the system of capitalist production.[24] In Louis Althusser's account, this latter structure is conceived in an epistemological idiom as structural totality ("structural causality") with an "absent cause," ever-present but allowing for the relative autonomy of the branches of society.[25] Hence the shift from external to immanent determination, where the causes of social life are no longer directly accessible to experience, and entail new modes of epistemological, social and psychological inquiry.[26]

To explain the social, epistemological and aesthetic significance of this shift I follow Postone's re-interpretation of Marx's theory more closely. As Marx does, Postone argues that one of the conditions of possibility of capitalism is abstract labor, in the moment when labor is lifted up from its subordination to and embeddedness in this or that area of life, to become labor power in general, a commodity like any other.[27] In this moment we see a shift from pre-capitalist social forms, based on what he calls "overt social relations," to capitalism whose social relations are "objective" or "impersonal." In the former, labor receives its meaning and value from the social groupings in which it is embedded, while in

the roots of capitalism in private property, see Perry Anderson, *Passages from Antiquity to Feudalism* (London: New Left Books, 1974); *Lineages of the Absolutist State* (London: New Left Books, 1974).

24   Moshe Postone, *Time, Labor and Social Domination: A Reinterpretation of Marx's Critical Theory* (Cambridge: Cambridge University Press, 1993).

25   Louis Althusser et al., *Reading Capital*, translated by Ben Brewster (London/New York: Verso, 1997), see especially "Marx Immense Theoretical Revolution," 182–193; Louis Althusser, *For Marx*, translated by Ben Brewster (London/New York: Verso, 2005), see especially "Contradiction and Overdetermination," 87–128.

26   It is not accidental that Kant's concept of transcendental philosophy is grounded on the assumption that the conditions of possibility of knowledge (the modalities of time and space, the categories, schematism and apperception) are not accessible to direct experience and need to be detected through the method of critique. Marx's critical theory, too, is grounded on the assumption that capitalist social relations are not present on the surface of commodities and need to be revealed; and in the same way, if to extend the mapping, Freud's concept of the Unconscious and Lacan's concept of the Real presuppose the inaccessibility of the primary cause or limit of mental life which exists only in its effects or symptoms.

27   "The historical conditions of . . . [capital] are by no means given with the mere circulation of money and commodities. It arises only when the owner of the means of production and subsistence finds the free worker available, on the market, as the seller of his own labour-power. And this one historical pre-condition comprises a world's history. Capital, therefore, announces from the outset a new epoch in the process of social production." Marx, *Capital* I, 274.

the later, labor is released from this embeddedness and becomes the abstract form that mediates itself and its specific social relations. Postone calls this character of abstract labor "reflexive" and "self-grounding" in the sense that no other overt determinant exists outside it. This leads to a peculiar shift in the structure of the social world:

> The system constituted by abstract labor embodies a new form of social domination. It exerts a form of social compulsion whose impersonal, abstract and objective character is historically new . . . This compulsion exerted is not a function of direct social domination, as is the case for example, with slave or serf labor; it is, rather, a function of "abstract" and "objective" social structure, and represents a form of abstract, impersonal domination. Ultimately, this form of domination is not grounded in any person, class or institution.[28]

He adds:

> The structure of abstract domination constituted by labor acting as a socially mediating activity does not appear to be socially constituted; rather, it appears in naturalized form. Its social and historical specificity is veiled by several factors. The form of social necessity exerted . . . exists in the absence of any direct, personal, social domination . . . This structure is such that one's own needs, rather than the threat of force or other social sanctions, appear to be the source of such necessity.[29]

As noted, this is the moment where we observe the emergence of social abstraction and absence of direct causes which, by the nineteenth century, makes Western Europe qualitatively different from other social forms around the world that are still characterized by external determination of various types. As we shall see momentarily, this condition leads to a crisis of political finality, which Hegel's theory of the state will try to solve, a solution that reappears in the current moment as well.

Shifting from the historical horizon of capitalist transformation to the more localized field of artistic production we can see the relation between the transition from external to immanent determination and the emergence of aesthetic autonomy in Western Europe. Several varying accounts exist here, and all share the claim that, during the eighteenth

---

28 Postone, *Time, Labor and Social Domination*, 159.
29 Ibid., 161.

century, as art is slowly detached from its cultic or institutional sites (from external determination) it sheds its social function and is assumed to be following its own immanent laws. Historicizing this process, Raymond Williams, for example, argues that with the industrial revolution and the creation of a market for literary goods in late eighteenth-century England, artists were no longer determined externally by political, economic or religious powers (a king, a patron, a church, etc.,), a development that informed the Romantic movement's new conception of the autonomy of art. In Pierre Bourdieu's account, such a transition takes place in France in the second half of the nineteenth century. Borrowing Kant's critical terminology, Bourdieu conceives of autonomization as a shift from an external, heteronomous determination into an immanent one where art now is to be understood only in relation to the positions available in the artistic field. Walter Benjamin, too, offers two such accounts of artistic transformation grounded in a process of autonomization.[30] I develop the aesthetic consequences of this shift later in this chapter.

The second development made possible by this unique structure concerns the separation of the individual and society—a variant of the private/public split—into two distinct poles now confronting one another:

In commodity-determined society, the modern individual is historically constituted—a person independent of personal relations of domination, obligations, and dependence who no longer is embedded overtly in a quasi-natural fixed social position and so, in a sense, is self-determining. Yes, this "free" individual is confronted by a social universe of abstract objective constraints that function in a lawlike fashion. In Marx's terms, from a precapitalist context marked by relations of personal dependence a new one emerged characterized by individual personal freedom within a social framework of "objective dependence." The modern opposition

---

30   Raymond Williams, *Culture and Society 1780–1950* (New York: Columbia University Press, 1958), See especially xiii–xx, 30–41; Bourdieu, *The Rules of Art*; Walter Benjamin, "The Storyteller: Reflections on the Works of Nikolai Leskov" and "The Work of Art in the Age of Mechanical Reproduction." In *Illuminations: Essays and Reflections*, translated by Harry Zohn (New York: Schocken, 1968), 83–109; 217–52. For a short historical account of shifts in modes of aesthetic production see Peter Bürger, *Theory of the Avant-Garde*, translated by Michael Shaw (Minneapolis: University of Minnesota Press, 1989), see especially 35–54. For an intellectual history of the consolidation of the concept Art as a non-utilitarian form of human activity, see Paul Oskar Kristeller "The Modern System of the Arts: A Study in the History of Aesthetics I," *Journal of the History of Ideas* 12.4 (October 1951): 496–527; "The Modern System of the Arts: A Study in the History of Aesthetics II," *Journal of the History of Ideas* 13.1 (January 1952): 17–46.

between the free, self-determining individual and an extrinsic sphere of objective necessity is, according to Marx's analysis, a real "opposition" that is historically constituted . . . and is related to the more general constituted opposition between a world of subjects and a world of objects.[31]

For the sake of the discussion of Israel and Palestine that follows, I emphasize the temporal structure of these two poles: both the individual and "society" are conceived as *ready-made*; the autonomy of the individual is no longer dependent on the community, but rather now limited by it, and society is grasped as an "objective" reality lacking a direct or overt cause.[32] This kind of liberal "self-determining" and "free" individual feeds into Kant's moral and aesthetic theory, for in Kant's understanding, the freedom of the individual has no other ground but the a priori will itself which is free of any external, heteronomous determination in the form of authority (the will of another) or object (a social purpose, for example). Rejecting prior conceptions of freedom in which the subject ought to accomplish an act for the sake or will of another, Kant's categorical imperative severs the subject from any such external determination and places the autonomous will as the source of the act. Correspondingly, the community, or any kind of social mores or conventions, turn into a limit for the freedom of the subject. In this kind of Kantian and liberal conception, the individual is not only "free," it is also utterly abstracted from any kind of preceding social ground.[33]

The removal of external determination and the separation of the world into autonomous subjects and social constraints, private and public spheres, transforms the knowledge of social conditions of possibility into a political and epistemological problem. Hegel's theory of the state, for example, arises out of this problem and attempts to solve it. For Hegel, civil society, as the site of unfettered individual private wills, excess, and infinity, produces the illusion that the particular is free of other people, or what he calls the universal. In this the consciousness of the private individual is erroneous, he argues, because it is enmeshed in appearances and cannot conceive consciously of the conditions that underlie its particular life:

---

31   Postone, *Time, Labor and Social Domination*, 163–4.

32   For individual autonomy and self-legislation see Macpherson and Schneewind's accounts above.

33   For a critique of Western European moral philosophy, see Alasdair MacIntyre, *After Virtue: A Study in Moral Theory* (Notre Dame: University of Notre Dame Press, 2007).

[A] situation arises in which the particular is to be my primary determining principle . . . But I am in fact mistaken about this, since, while
I suppose that I am adhering to the particular, the universal and the
necessity of the connection between particulars remains the primary and
essential thing. I am thus altogether on the level of semblance [Schein].[34]

Thus, in a society that separates the private and the public and advances
the notion of individual self-legislation, *Schein*, or semblance/appear-
ance, as previously discussed, becomes the philosophical property of
private life, a life that is disconnected from its condition of possibility,
making it what it is. Now, Hegel's concept of the state as the explicit
embodiment of universality, a binding social power over and above particular wills, is devised as a fetishized correction in order to overcome
the unfettered will of particularity, and the epistemological and political
problem that accompanies it. In other words, in Hegel, the state-as-
universality is devised so as to solve the disintegration of political finality
that comes with the sanctioned self-interest of individuals in civil society
in modern times. Arguing against a liberal and libertarian conception of
the state, Hegel says:

If the state is confused with civil society, and if its specific end is laid
down as the security and protection of property and personal freedom,
then *the interest of individuals as such* becomes the ultimate end of their
association, and it follows that membership in the state is something
optional. But the state's relation to the individual is quite different from
this. Since the state is objective spirit, it is only as one of its members that
the individual himself has objectivity, truth and ethical life.

Moving closer to literary and cultural theory, Jameson's theory of the
development of the European novel—from realism through modernism to postmodernism—seems to be modeled, in part, on the axis that
traces the growing abstraction between the individual and its social
conditions. In eighteenth- and nineteenth-century realism, we indeed
see the emergence of laws of probability and causality that not only
secularize and banish mythic power (foreshadowed in Cervantes's *Don
Quixote*), but also shift determination from an explicit external cause

---

34   G. W. F. Hegel, *Outlines of the Philosophy of Right*, translated by T. M. Knox.
Edited by Stephen Houlgate (Oxford: Oxford University Press, 2008), 180, brackets in
original.

to the immanent and logical rules of society. "It is a truth universally acknowledged," Jane Austen's narrator tells us, "that a single man in possession of a good fortune, must be in want of a wife."[35] The articulation of these rules, whether explicitly or implicitly through the course of events, is then the primary task of the main character who, precisely by seeking to fulfill their private desires and wishes, must cross paths with "society" conceived now as a limit to its desires.[36] Further, with the separation of self and society, the private individual begins to appear as a sign and riddle whose underlying meaning and cause become the object of novelistic investigation. As Balzac argues in the Introduction to his Human Comedy:

> By adhering to the strict lines of a reproduction a writer might be a more or less faithful, and more or less successful, painter of types of humanity, a narrator of the dramas of private life, an archaeologist of social furniture, a cataloguer of professions, a registrar of good and evil; but to deserve the praise of which every artist must be ambitious, must I not also investigate the reasons or the cause of these social effects, detect the hidden sense of this vast assembly of figures, passions, and incidents?[37]

The coincidence of autonomous characters with the social laws they confront as a natural object, usually in the city, begins to dissolve, according to Jameson, with imperialism and the rise of Western European modernism in the late nineteenth century. At this moment we notice

---

35   The opening line of Jane Austen's 1813 *Pride and Prejudice*.

36   As Nancy Armstrong argues, "the history of the [British] novel and the history of the modern subject are, quite literally, one and the same . . . Novels thus gave tangible form to a desire that set the body on a collision course with limits that the old society had placed on the individual's options for self-fulfillment, transforming the body from an indicator of rank to the container of a unique subjectivity." Nancy Armstrong, *How Novels Think: The Limits of British Individualism from 1719–1900* (New York: Columbia University Press, 2005), 3–4. On the rise of individuality and the new canon of realist description as the central characteristic of the novel see also Ian Watt's classic study *The Rise of the Novel: Studies in Defoe, Richardson and Fielding* (Berkeley/Los Angeles: University of California Press, 1957). Georg Lukács' account of the historical novel and the narrative techniques of "making private" are still very useful in this context. See Georg Lukács, *The Historical Novel*, translated by Hannah and Stanley Mitchell (London: Merlin Press, 1962).

37   Honoré de Balzac, *At the Sign of the Cat and Racket, and & Other Stories*, translated by Clara Bell (London: J. M. Dent, 1910), 6. For a short discussion of the becoming of private life into a sign and the novel into an investigation see also M. M. Bakhtin, *The Dialogic Imagination*, translated by Caryl Emerson and Michael Holquist (Austin: University of Texas Press, 1981), 123–6.

a growing contradiction between lived experience and structure, or between phenomenological description of the life of an individual and a more properly structural model of the conditions of existence of that experience. Too rapidly we can say that, while in older societies and perhaps even in the early stages of market capital, the immediate and limited experience of individuals is still able to encompass and coincide with the true economic and social form that governs that experience, in the next moment these two levels [i.e., experience and economic social form] drift ever further apart and really begin to constitute themselves into that opposition the classical dialectic describes as *Wesen* and *Erscheinung*, essence and appearance, structure and lived experience.

At this point the phenomenological experience of the individual subject . . . becomes limited to a tiny corner of the social world . . . But the truth of that experience no longer coincides with the place in which it takes place. The truth of that limited daily experience of London lies, rather, in India or Jamaica or Hong Kong; it is bound up with the whole colonial system of the British Empire that determines the very quality of the individual's subjective life. Yet those structural coordinates are no longer accessible to immediate lived experience.[38]

As I have noted, this kind of epistemological problem is no longer limited to Western states but, with globalization, comes to characterize the periphery as well. Let us now see how a similar shift from external to immanent determination took place, and continues to occur, in Israel and Palestine.

4.

With the previous discussion in mind, we can see that in the first period (1940–1985/1993) nothing can be more foreign to Israeli and Palestinian societies than the twin characteristics of capitalism that we have already discussed: First, in these societies, and indeed in most of the world, we still have direct external determination by either a strong state in Israel, or colonialism and pre-capitalist modes of life in Palestine. Second, the separation of the individual from society, the private from the public sphere, has yet to occur. These two characteristics separate Israel and Palestine from Western Europe in the first period and distinguish their social form as well as their aesthetic production.

---

38   Jameson, *Postmodernism*, 410–11.

As many social scientists argue, in order to found an autonomous Jewish polity, labor-Zionist leaders of the second wave of colonization ('*Aliya Sheniya*, 1904–1914)[39] established what is sometimes referred to as a statist structure in which the state directly controls almost all aspects of social life and especially the purchase of land, the fabric of the labor market and the circulation of capital.[40] Differently than European "core" states in which capital, the bourgeoisie and its liberal ideology are the hegemonic powers, in Israel, until the mid-1980s, the dominant powers were the state itself and the labor movement. In this period, capital and private life are tethered to the state and cannot develop autonomously, a condition enabling the fusion of the private and the public spheres. I designate this period as heteronomous as both social life and literary production are directly political, that is to say they are directly conditioned by social and political powers. Another way of putting this will be to say that in this period, labor, land and capital are not abstracted yet; they have what Postone would call "overt" political content (Jewish/statist). For this reason, although Zionists imagined themselves as Western Europeans, the real social structure they established did not resemble Western European social forms, a historical fact that is obscured in current literary studies. The contradiction between the Zionist European imaginary and the reality of its social structure goes unattended in post-Zionist and postcolonial studies, which concentrate instead on the East/West imaginary divide.

The first period in Palestine, stretching between the end of the 1948 war and the 1993 Oslo Accords that inaugurated the establishment of the Palestinian Authority, is a period that sees the disintegration and slow re-integration of Palestinian society.[41] In this period, Palestinians

---

39   The first colonization wave took place between 1882 and 1904. The clean language of Zionist scholarship and popular history divides the pre-state colonization period from 1882 to 1948 into several "immigration waves" ('*Aliyot* literally means "ascents").

40   For studies on the establishment of the Zionist statist structure see Yonatan Shapira, *Ha-demokratyah be-yisra'el* (Ramat Gan: Masadah, 1977); Michael Shalev, *Labour and the Political Economy in Israel* (Oxford: Oxford University Press, 1992); Gershon Shafir, *Land, Labor, and the Origins of the Israeli-Palestinian Conflict 1882–1914* (Berkeley: University of California Press, 1996); Gershon Shafir and Yoav Peled (eds.) *The New Israel: Peacemaking and Liberalization* (Boulder: Westview Press, 2000); Uri Ram, *The Globalization of Israel: McWorld in Tel Aviv, Jihad in Jerusalem* (New York: Routledge, 2010).

41   See Ilan Pappe, *A History of Modern Palestine: One Land, Two Peoples* (Cambridge: Cambridge University Press, 2004), 142–61; Rashid Khalidi, *Palestinian Identity: The Construction of Modern National Consciousness* (New York: Columbia University Press, 2010), 177–186; Samih Farsoun and Naseer Aruri, *Palestine and the Palestinians: A Social and Political History* (Boulder: Westview Press, 2006), 105–22.

live either as citizens in Israel[42] and other states around the world, or as refugees.[43] Although different than Israel, the period between 1948 and 1993—in which a mixture of agrarian economy, wage labor, patriarchal political relations and a revolutionary national movement (PLO) existed simultaneously—can be characterized by a similar overlap of the private and political spheres. Middle Eastern and European social scientists call this kind of structure a "political society."[44] As in Israel, I designate this period as heteronomous; it is a period in which social life is directly influenced by political association, national or otherwise. Correspondingly, aesthetic production is heteronomous as well, and is at odds with conceptions of art as an autonomous activity.

The significance of this structure for our inquiry is in its theoretical meaning, its form of causality, and its temporality. Unlike in Western capitalist societies, where "society" has reified into discrete and autonomous social spheres whose underlying conditions of possibility are obscured, in Israel and Palestine society itself (and not simply the "nation") as well as the state are a constant object of making which pervades every sphere such that the home, the schools, the streets, the workplace, the law, personal and professional relationships—all are imbued with political significance. Here, the causes of social life are themselves open to transformation, forcing upon the subject the reality of its heteronomy. The latter is exemplified in the political proposition that the freedom of the individual depends on the freedom of the collective, or, in other words, that the individual cannot be free until the collective is free. The collective project "spiritualizes" society, as it were; it ennobles social life, even the pettiest of moments, and elevates it to the degree of universality that is responsible in part for the high value of the category of literature in this period.

Thus, external determination or heteronomy designates the historical limit of the period itself. It is a limit because it is imposed upon both those who support the project of making and those who find themselves marginalized by it or directly opposing it. In this understanding, heteronomy does not confer homogeneity on all its instances; it is rather the

---

42   Palestinians who remained in Israel after 1948 were under military rule until 1966.

43   Of the 1.4 million Palestinians living in what was mandatory Palestine in 1948, 160,000 remained in Israel while over 750,000–800,000 were displaced and have been living as refugees in TransJordan, the Gaza Strip, Syria and Lebanon. See Farsoun and Aruri, *Palestine and the Palestinians*: 105–43.

44   See Benoît Challand, *Palestinian Civil Society: Foreign Donors and the Power to Promote and to Exclude* (London: Routledge, 2009).

preliminary condition of possibility which different and even opposing positions and ideologies cannot but presuppose. Eventually, since in
Israel the statist state had the power to impose its law and its political
project as the universal, no other project was allowed to establish its
own law and thus alternative political projects either adopted the social
logic and poetic form of the state or disavowed it to achieve freedom in
form alone. In Palestine, especially after 1967, daily existence is by default
conditioned by the Israeli occupation, such that it is quite literally impossible to establish Palestinian autonomy without a process of making and
struggle. In sum, in this period, literature was not simply the site where
ideology was reproduced; rather, it was the site *par excellence* where
autonomy, collective or individual, was thought under pre-existing conditions. What I call statist novels in Israel and anti-colonial novels in
Palestine emerged out of a political struggle, a social form in the making,
while alternatives, mostly liberal and humanist ones, were devoid of such
grounding in the real, a social lack that carried over into their form and
resulted in forms of abstract freedom that are not made but given.

Due to economic crises, the dominance of the Israeli state began
to weaken as of the late 1960s, and a series of privatizations ensued.
However, the second period, which Uri Ram designates as the globalization of Israel, begins to be felt more acutely after 1985, the year in which
the state implemented the US-backed Emergency Plan for Economic
Stabilization, an aggressive liberalization reform that put in place the
institutional structure to separate the state from civil society and allowed
for the autonomization of the latter.[45] The historical importance of this
period is in the foundation of the category of the "private sphere." It is
important to stress the point that private life always existed in Zionism
from its very inception but in a subordinated, negative manner. The
novelty, therefore, is not in the appearance of private life as such, but
in its universalization, autonomization and legitimization. If in the first
period the individual was political by default, now it is by default private.
Separated from its causes in the public sphere, a process exacerbated
by the globalization of Israel, private life now seems self-legislating, the
origin of itself. In this moment, aesthetic production becomes autonomous, and the lofty, sacred meaning given to literature by the state is
replaced by the "vulgarity" of the market. It is in this moment and due

---

45   On this transition, see Shalev, Ram, and Shafir and Peled in footnote 40, but see
also Yoav Peled and Gershon Shafir "The Israeli-Palestinian Conflict and Civil Society
in Israel." In Yoav Peled and Adi Ophir (eds.), *Yisra'el, me-ḥevrah meguyeset le-ḥevrah
ezraḥit?* (Yerushalayim: Makhon van lir/Ha-kibutz ha-me'uḥad, 2001), 183–205.

to these series of privatizations that Israel begins to resemble Western Europe and the US and a global space of equivalence (although not equality) begins to open up between these places.

Similarly, after the 1993 Oslo Accords, Palestine enters into global networks of foreign capital investment. As social scientists explain, this period sees the creation of proto-state institutions such as the Palestinian Authority, but more importantly the establishment of professional, foreign-funded NGOs, which initiate what could be called a symbolic separation between the political and civil spheres.[46] While NGOs existed in the first period, and were subordinated to local political parties,[47] after 1993, especially in secular, left-leaning NGOs, the source of funding has shifted to the international, or global community (including the World Bank, the US and Europe). This global community promotes short term relief and development, curbing the role of political parties, creating an abstract "human."[48] Concomitant with these transformations we see the slow establishment of a Palestinian middle class, mostly in the West Bank, whose life and political activities move away from direct colonial struggle with Israel. Finally, a shift in aesthetic categories takes place—a shift from heteronomous to autonomous aesthetics which alters the imaginary worlds we encounter in Palestinian literature and, correspondingly, the location of Palestinian literature in the global distribution of aesthetic production.

What we see in this period, in both Israel and Palestine, is the condition that Postone described, in which individual autonomy and society are separated from each other and become ready-made, while the process of making either disappears, or it is the localized domain of certain "political" individuals who continue to be subordinated to an external heteronomous law. The process of making the state therefore does not end, it is simply rearticulated. In Israel it is banished to the borders, to the seams of Israel and Palestine where the statist project is still going on, and imbues private life with political meaning, while in Palestine

---

46   In Palestine, see Rema Hammami, "NGOs: The Professionalization of Politics," *Race and Class* 37.2 (1995): 51–63; "Palestinian NGOs Since Oslo: From NGO Politics to Social Movements?" *Middle East Report* 214 (Spring 2000): 16–48; Sari Hanafi and Linda Tabar, *The Emergence of a Palestinian Globalized Elite: Donors, International Organizations and Local NGOs* (Jerusalem: Institute of Jerusalem Studies, 2005); Challand, *Palestinian Civil Society*; Adam Hanieh, *Lineages of Revolt: Issues of Contemporary Capitalism in the Middle East* (Chicago: Haymarket Books, 2013).

47   Ibid., 62.

48   Rema Hammami has described this process as the "depoliticization and professionalization" of NGOs. See footnote 45 for bibliographical details.

"making" is mostly relegated to militants that embody a fusion of the private and public. The separation of private and public life is analogous to the separation of the political spirit from the body, a process leading to the materialization and secularization of private life, which some take to be a vulgarization. It is a source of liberation of the individual body from the abstract, the edicts of political commitment, leading to new pleasures and desires, but it also confronts the subject as a loss of way, for no explicit universal is now available. (This is in part the meaning of postmodernism in Israel, a meaning that is far less present in Palestine.)

Finally, now immanent determination or autonomy becomes the historical limit—it is a condition of possibility that political action, social thought, and aesthetic form must presuppose. Postmodernity in Israel and Palestine is not then a literary or philosophical style; such an understanding reduces the historical real into one of its ideological instances, i.e., postmodernism. The latter's philosophical marker—the absence of explicit unifying universals or "grand narratives" à la Lyotard—is the kind of thought that uncritically takes the historical transformation in the form of the limit from external to immanent determination as real ontological absence, ending up in equivalent iterativity, or the infinite series.[49]

5.

The previous discussion can now serve as the basis for a series of elaborations that will allow us to see how the social form conditions aesthetic and political possibilities in each period.

As I have noted, the Western European concept of aesthetic autonomy develops in the course of the eighteenth century alongside the broader shift from external to immanent determination. This historical change underlies the transition from political to civil societies, as well as the gradual autonomization of literary production, seeing its release from overt authority and entry into the abstract market of literary commodities. Kant's conception of the aesthetic object (modeled on his understanding of nature) as "purposiveness without a purpose," and

---

49   See, for example, Jameson's review and critique of Lyotard's stance in his foreword to *The Postmodern Condition*. Jean-François Lyotard, *The Postmodern Condition: A Report on Knowledge*, translated by Geoff Bennington and Brian Massumi (Manchester: Manchester University Press, 1984), vii–xi. See also Michael Hardt and Antonio Negri's critique of postmodern thinking, especially in its "hybrid" variant, *Empire*, 137–59.

his conception of reflective judgment as an activity lacking a concept or universal, are to be understood then in the larger context of the autonomization of private life and the disembeddedness of both the artwork and the individual from what Postone calls "overt social relations." As we have seen, with the shift to immanent determination, autonomy and freedom do not result from a real release from determination, but rather from the latter's abstraction and concealment, ending in the individual and the artwork appearing as "natural"[50] or unmade.

I will attend in detail to Kant's formulation tying between nature and artworks, but for now let us note how this understanding inheres in one of Adorno's formulations of art:

> Works of art owe their existence to division of labor in society, the separation of physical and mental labor. At the same time they have their own roots in existence. Their medium is not pure mind, but the mind that enters into reality, and by virtue of such movement, is able to maintain the unity of what is divided. It is this contradiction that forces works of art to make us forget that they have been made. The claim implicit in their existence, and hence, too, the claim, that existence has a meaning is the more convincing, the less they contain [sic] to remind us that they have been made, and that they owe their own existence to something external to themselves, namely to a mental process. Art that is no longer able to perpetrate this deception with good conscience, has implicitly destroyed the only element in which it can thrive ... A contradiction of all works of Art is the concealment of the labor that went into it, but in high capitalism, with the complete hegemony of exchange value, and the contradictions arising out of that hegemony, autonomous art becomes both problematic and programmatic at the same time.[51]

Echoing Kant, as we shall see momentarily, Adorno centers autonomy on the concepts of making and concealment. For Adorno, the division of physical and mental labor allows for the autonomy of art. However,

---

50   "The political revolution thereby abolished the political character of civil society [present in feudalism] ... A person's particular activity and situation in life sank to the level of a purely individual significance ... Political emancipation was at the same time the emancipation of civil society from politics ... Egoistic man [of civil society] is the passive and merely given result of the society which has been dissolved, and object of immediate certainty ... a *natural* object." Karl Marx, "On the Jewish Question." In *Early Writings*, translated by Rodney Livingstone and Gregor Benton (London: Penguin, 1992), 232–4, emphasis in italics in original.

51   Adorno, *In Search of Wagner*, 71–2.

since the artwork always has its "roots" in existence, since it is, as he says in his *Aesthetic Theory*, "a thing in which the world of things is embedded a priori"[52] it ends up in a form of appearance (semblance; *Schein*) that conceals the fact it has been made by "something external." Concealment, or what Adorno sometimes calls the hermetic or monadic nature of the artwork, makes possible the illusory nature of the work as a whole onto itself. "The illusory quality of artworks is condensed in their claim to wholeness."[53] Illusoriness, wholeness or *Schein* are, to be sure, not simply a matter of formal choice that the artist can simply discard; they are not simply a matter of style but rather the default condition of the artwork. "The dialectic of modern art is largely that it wants to shake off its illusoriness like an animal trying to shake off its antlers. The aporias in the historical development of art cast off their shadows over its possibility as a whole."[54] For this reason, as Peter Bürger argues, avant-garde art in twentieth-century Europe tried to re-embed art within social life, and make it purposeful again, or in other words, tie it to its external determination.[55]

Whether Adorno situates this concept of art and concealment in modernity or whether it is a trans-historical attribute of art is not clear.[56] Either way, this conception is incompatible with literary production in Israel and Palestine in the first period. In this period, the two characteristics of Western European society—separation of individual and society and autonomization of literary production—as well as the two aesthetic characteristics—lack of purpose and the appearance of being unmade—do not obtain. As I have argued, individuality or particularity is not yet autonomous, and this is so in a historically specific way; since the freedom and autonomy of the community itself is in the making, the individual is bound to it in a dual sense: one passive, the other active.

---

52   Theodor Adorno, *Aesthetic Theory*, translated by Robert Hullot-Kentor (Minneapolis: University of Minnesota Press, 1997), 102.

53   Ibid., 101.

54   Ibid.

55   "Only after art, in nineteenth century Aestheticism, has altogether detached itself from the praxis of life can the aesthetic develop 'purely.' But the other side of autonomy, art's lack of social impact, also becomes recognizable. The avant-gardist protest, whose aim it is to reintegrate art into praxis of life, reveals the nexus between autonomy and the absence of any consequences." Peter Bürger, *Theory of the Avant-Garde*. Translation by Michael Shaw (Minneapolis: University of Minnesota Press, 1989), 22.

56   The fact that Adorno traces this conception all the way back to the division of physical and mental labor in the Sirens scene in the *Odyssey*, and that he sees it operating in the Greek epic more generally, makes one think he is talking about transhistorical aesthetic autonomy.

In the passive sense, the individual is directly and explicitly tied to the conditions of possibility that make up social life; in such a situation the fiction of autonomous self-legislation cannot emerge because the individual is always aware of its heteronomy, its dependence on conditions other than itself. In the active sense, by needing to act on these conditions through various forms of antagonism, and making possible a degree of separation from direct conditions of possibility, the individual is bound to this making which makes it in return. In the latter sense, social life is guided by an explicit telos, by a concept of finality and purpose whose object is precisely the autonomy of the community itself. In other words, the community is not an inert starting point; it is the very object of a self-reflexive making. In this kind of reality, literary production is not autonomous but rather embedded within social and political finality. And, most importantly, the artwork is an activity directed explicitly by political purpose and hence the fact that it is made by something "external" to itself is its default state. *Schein*, the illusory sense of wholeness, or an existence autonomous and separate from social reality, is not accorded to the artwork, and consequently readers see in it an extension of their reality; it is judged by the criteria of objective truth, which refuses to accept the boundary between reality and art, a boundary that relegates art to mere art. This is especially the case in novels that describe historical events, for example, since the reader may reject the work's claim to aesthetic autonomy, to its freedom to depict reality according to its own formal law. Lastly, the artwork here is not only imitating reality; it is also an object of imitation that provides exemplary characters for readers to emulate. As I show in Chapter 3, Benjamin's concept of the storyteller as a heteronomous art of narration is a fitting aesthetic mode for literature written in this period.

With this historical reality in mind, acting as a limit on literary production, let us see what kind of political responses and aesthetic forms were taken up in this period.

Poiesis, or the poetics of making, was an aesthetic and political position of the first period that was practiced by what I call statist (rather than simply Zionist) writers in Israel and anti-colonial writers in Palestine. At the heart of *poiesis* stands a constitutive antagonism between unequal subjects whose meaning, as does the meaning of the world itself, depends on this antagonism.[57] These imaginary worlds earn the attribute

57   As Gershon Shaked argues, the "act" (*ma'aseh*) is the fundamental narrative and temporal category in such novels. See Shaked, *Gal Ḥadash ba-siporet ha-'ivrit* (Merḥavyah: Sifriyat po'alim, 1971), 27.

of "making" because in them characters, and sometimes the social world and nature itself, are made through the antagonism. Such worlds, and *only* such worlds, are homologous with the historical limit, for in both the social and literary world the freedom and autonomy of the individual is impossible without an act of collective making. What characters "make" in these worlds is not so much themselves but their autonomy and freedom, which is bound up with the autonomy and freedom of the community/nation. The antagonism subordinates (almost) all other materials and allegorizes them such that each concrete moment stands in for a larger (collective) spiritual meaning. Likewise, it generates the Time of the world and it accordingly localizes, particularizes or otherwise completely blocks any other times and histories.[58] In narratological terms, this is accomplished by emplotment in which (most) narrative materials turn into plot functions. In conceptual terms, universal, abstract meaning—freedom—does not only bind the particular and its body to a spiritual project, it also subordinates it in the form of an instance. For this reason, characters seem doubly "unfree": on the level of the world, they are bound to their duty, while on the level of the plot, they are bound to their function. This aspect lays bare the political finality of the work; or to put it differently, such novels make redundant Shklovsky's "lying bare the device" because their motivations are already transparent. The relation between the poetics of making and the various political positions making use of it can be compared not only with Benjamin's conception of practical tales but also to the older form of parables we find in the Bible and the Quran, and thus show the continuity of the modern novel with older forms of narration. In the Jewish context, for example, the relation between the Halakha—the abstract Jewish law—and Haggada—the illustrative tale—is one of exemplarity. The Haggada is supposed to exemplify the law and for this reason it is a heteronomous from of writing. While all novels presuppose a political position, the novel of making makes this position explicit. The explicit politics of novels of making should not be confused with mere propaganda. Here lies another crucial difference between contemporary literary criticism on Israel and Palestine and the current inquiry. While Israeli nationalist novels of making naturalize the colonial project and deny the equally valid claim to freedom of Palestinians—they are "monologic" novels as Bakhtin would say—they still

---

58 To anticipate a future discussion, the fact that in the second, liberal, period, we see a proliferation of local histories associated usually with multiculturalism is not simply a matter of a new conception of nationalism but an outcome of the privatization of the state and its time.

represent Zionist life for what it was: a collective struggle of making. The fact that even such nationalist novels contain what Adorno would call "truth content," the existence in them of the conditions of possibility of Zionist collectivity—shows not so much that art transcends ideology, but rather that political ideology is broader and more complex than its narrow cast within contemporary studies.[59] Similarly, the fact that Palestinian anti-colonial novels underplay class and gender questions that complicate national unity does not detract from the "truth-content" of such novels. Finally, as I said, since all other political projects are blocked or repressed, any resistance—and there is often resistance even in the most nationalist novels—can exist only *alongside* the main antagonism, in a parallel, usually personal time and form.

While Jameson's concept of "national allegory" based on the overlap of the private and public sphere does justice to Israeli and Palestinian literature written in this first period, it still needs further elucidation to allow us a better grasp of the historical specificity of the form of "making."[60] While novels written in this period are surely national allegories, what is most operative in them is the *heteronomy* of the characters, for not only that they, as Jameson indeed argues, must know the causes of their own self and world—as Hegel's slave—they are also bound to these causes as an outside law (such as war, settlement, family, and other forms of duty). This is also the reason why, although Israel is not exactly a third-world state, Ashkenazi Zionist culture does not belong to the order of European "Masters" whose reality is made by others. The explicit presence of these causes, and the fact that here autonomy and freedom is the

---

59   Discussing Balzac, Pierre Macherey argues that political ideology can and indeed does register the "real" in spite of itself. Thus, Balzac's royalist position does not blind him to the real struggle between the nobles, and the bourgeoisie and the place of the peasants in this conjuncture. See Pierre Macherey, *A Theory of Literary Production,* translated by Geoffrey Wall (New York: Routledge, 2006). Jameson elaborates on this point in his reading of Balzac. See Jameson, *The Political Unconscious,* 151–84. On the same matter, see Georg Lukács, *Studies in European Realism,* translated by Edith Bone (New York: Grosset & Dunlap, 1964).

60   Jameson, "Third World Literature in the Era of Multinational Capitalism," *Social Text* 15 (1986): 65–88. Jameson's argument was contested by Aijaz Ahmed in the case of India, but I find its general proposal suitable to the literatures studied here. More generally, I do not accept Ahmad's claim that we cannot draw comparisons between different national situations based on shared historical conditions. See Aijaz Ahmad, "Jameson's Rhetoric of Otherness and the 'National Allegory.'" In *In Theory: Class, Nations, Literatures* (New York: Verso, 1992), 95–122. For response and counter critique see Fredric Jameson, "A Brief Response." *Social Text* 17 (Autumn, 1987): 26–7; Madhava Prasad, "On the Question of a Theory of (Third World) Literature," *Social Text* 31/32 (1992): 57–83; Imre Szeman, "Who's Afraid of National Allegory? Jameson, Literary Criticism, Globalization," *The South Atlantic Quarterly* 100.3 (Summer 2001): 803–27.

very problem of the world, differentiates these imaginary worlds as well as the novels themselves from "Western" novels and relegates them to the pole of "heteronomy" in what Pascale Casanova calls the world republic of letters. This political and aesthetic condition explains why Israeli literature in this period, no matter how "Eurocentric," failed to "pass" as autonomous and hence as "European." This fact points to a fundamental lacuna in studies that do not differentiate adequately between "Eurocentrism" and European social form.

In Israel (and even earlier in the pre-state Palestine), imaginary worlds of making were dominant in the 1940s and 1950s and could be found in Moshe Shamir, Yonat and Alexander Sened, Hanokh Bartov, and many more,[61] but they also existed throughout the first period (until 1985), in a less-dominant form. Given that Palestine is occupied rather than a sovereign state, it is not only "making" that underlies narrative time but also liberation by antagonism. The dominant position here is that of national resistance of varying types, exemplified in certain novels by Ghassan Kanafani and Sahar Khalifeh as well as by Rashad Abu Shawar, Ahmad Harb, Yahya Yakhlif and others.[62] These diverse writers share the fact that they think of freedom as a goal to be achieved (at least partly) through antagonism, while their ideological positions cast this antagonism in different ways.

Two political and aesthetic responses emerged in reaction to heteronomy: humanism and liberalism, both marked by an historical impossibility which fractured their imaginary worlds. When considered on the level of the literary field (literary criticism), these responses

---

61 See for example Yigal Mosinzon, *Aforim ka-sak* [*Grey as Cloth*] (Merḥavyah: Sifriyat po'alim, 1946); Moshe Shamir, *Hu halakh ba-sadot* [*He Walked in the Fields*] (Tel Aviv: Yedi'ot aḥaronot and 'Am 'oved: 2006 [1947]); Emma Talmi, *Le-'et ohalim: pirke kibuẓ* [*Time of Tents: Kibbutz Chronicles*](Merḥavyah: Sifriyat po'alim, 1949); Yonat and Alexander Sened, *Adama lelo ẓel* [*Land without Shadow*] (Tel Aviv: Ha-kibuẓ hame'uḥad, 1953); Hanokh Bartov, *Shesh kenafayim le-'eḥad* [*Six Wings Each*] (Merḥavyah: Sifriyat po'alim, 1954); Yehudit Hendel, *Reḥov ha-madregot* [*Street of Steps*] (Tel Aviv, 'Am 'oved, 1955). Novels of making had appeared by the 1930s but were not the dominant style. See for example Aharon Ever ha-Deni, *Ẓerif ha-'eẓ: sipur me-ḥaye ha-sadeh ba-'areẓ* [*Wood Cabin: A Story of Rural Life*] (Yerushalayim: Miẓpeh, 1930); Yosef 'Arikha, *Leḥem ve-ḥazon* [*Bread and Vision*] (Tel Aviv: Shtibel, 1932); Yehuda Ya'ari, *Ka-or yahel* [*Shining as Light*] (Tel Aviv: Masadah, 1944 [1937]); Avigdor Hameiri, *Tenuvah* [*Yield*] (Yerushalayim: Miẓpeh, 1933).

62 See for example, Ghassan Kanafani, *Rijāl fī al-shams* [*Men in the Sun*] (Bayrūt: Dār al-Ṭalī'ah, 1963); Sahar Khalifeh, *al-Ṣubār* [*Wild Thorns*] (Bayrūt: Manshūrāt Dār al-Ādāb, 1999); Rashad Abu Shawar, *al-'Ushaq* [*Lovers*], 1977; Ahmad Harb *Ismā'īl* [*Ishmael*](Bīr Zayt: Jāmi'at Bīr Zayt, 1994); Yahya Yakhlif, *Buḥayrah wara'a al-rīḥ* [*A Lake beyond the Wind*](Bayrūt: Dār al-Ādāb, 1991).

are a reaction to the poetics of making and its constitutive antagonism among unequals, but when considered from the point of view of history (literary critique) they emerge in response to the historical limit, the binding of the particular to the universal, limiting individual freedom. In Israel, while these aesthetic responses succeed in displacing the poetics of making in the literary field, no political project, if there even was one, managed to displace statism. In Palestine, the novel of resistance was the dominant form in this period although its exponents are rarely translated or taught in the US or the "West."[63] The humanist and liberal aesthetics of this period is meaningful then only in light of the practical impossibility of its political goal; its form is conditioned by this historical limit.

In Israeli literature, the humanist position was expressed most clearly in works by S. Yizhar in the late 1940s and through the 1950s. Yizhar's works affirm the statist project and the poetics of constitutive antagonism while trying to find in nature and its infinite time alternative, non-antagonistic forms of freedom and human equivalence (not equality). To accomplish this without giving up *poiesis*, the imaginary world is split in two, one part unfolds according to the temporality of the constitutive antagonism where nature, mind, body and language are subordinated to the utility and purpose of war, while a second part, existing *alongside* the antagonism (rather than against it), unfolds in a static, eternal natural and psychic time, where nature, body, mind, and poetic language can regain a non-utilitarian existence, that is, an existence unburdened with purpose.[64] The fact that the non-purposeful world is imagined only alongside a world of purpose points to the impossibility of the alternative political project to reformulate its "other" in real history, and for this reason it is written as passivity. The passivity, taking the poetic form of additive relation, existing in a metaphysical time outside historical time, reflects the failure of an Israeli humanist alternative and continues to characterize projects on the left today that advance a similar project. In Palestinian literature, we see humanist aspects in all

---

63   It is a rarely acknowledged fact that it is mainly the liberal and humanist Palestinian novels that "cross over" into academic syllabi and publishing houses in the "West."

64   See for example S. Yizhar, *Ha-Shavui* [*The Captive*] and *Sipur Ḥirbet-Ḥiz'ah* [*The Story of Hirbet Hizah*] (Merḥavyah: Sifriyat po'alim, 1949); *Shayarah shel ḥazot* [*Midnight Convoy*] (Tel Aviv: Ha-kibuẓ ha-me'uḥad, 1950). Aharon Megged's fantastic tale, *Mikre ha-kasil* [*As It Happens to a Fool*] (Tel Aviv: Ha-kibuẓ ha-me'uḥad, 1959), tries to reconcile constitutive antagonism through a last moment appeal to an absolute divine power and in this way resembles Yizhar's position.

the writers previously mentioned,[65] but especially in Emile Habibi's 1974 *The Secret Life of Saeed, the Ill-Fated Pessoptimist* and to a certain degree in Ghassan Kanafani's 1970 *Returning to Haifa*.[66] In the latter novella, Kanafani accomplishes the split by, on the one hand, pushing antagonism to the past (the 1948 war) and advancing an ideology of equivalent humanity in the present in the form of a conversation and rhetorical persuasion, and on the other, by stressing the difference between the parents' generation (Said and Safiyya, who live in the past) and their son's (Khalid, who desires to join the resistance).[67] A similar split takes place in Habibi, where the antagonism between Arabs and Jews is undermined by the humanist naiveté of the narrator.

The second response, coming to the fore in the 1960s and 1970s, was practiced by diverse writers such as Yeshayahu Koren, Aharon Megged, A. B. Yehoshua, Amos Oz and others in Israel, and Kanafani and Jabra Ibrahim Jabra in Palestine.[68] Their modernist novels were an attempt to think individual freedom and autonomy and at the same time to achieve "visibility" in the world republic of letters by producing, on the level of language, aesthetic autonomy not determined from the outside.[69]

---

65   See footnote 62 for examples.

66   Emile Habibi, *The Secret Life of Saeed, the Ill-Fated Pessoptimist*, translated by Salma Khadra Jayyusi and Trevor Le Gassick (New York: Vantage Press, 1982). In Arabic: *al-Waqā'i' al-gharībah fī ikhtifā' Sa'īd Abī al-Naḥs al-Mutashā'il* (al-Qāhirah: Dār al-Hilāl, 1998); Ghassan Kanafani, "Returning to Haifa." In *Palestine's Children and Other Stories*, translated by Barbara and Karen E. Riley (London/Boulder: Lynne Rienner, 2000), 149–96. In Arabic, *'Ā'id ilá Ḥayfā* (Beirut: Dār al-'Awdah, 1970).

67   Said names this split directly when he says that for Khalid, his son, "Palestine is something worthy of a man bearing arms for, dying for. For us, for you and me, it's only a search for something buried beneath the dust of memories." Kanafani, "Returning to Haifa," 187. See also Kanafani, *'Ā'id ilá Ḥayfā*, 89.

68   See for example in Israel, A. B. Yehoshua, *Mot ha-zaken* [*The Death of the Old Man*] (Tel Aviv: Ha-kibuẓ ha-me'uḥad, 1962); Aharon Megged, *Ha-ḥay 'al ha-met* [*The Living on the Dead*] (Tel Aviv: 'Am 'oved, 1965); Yeshayahu Koren's *Levaya ba-ẓohorayim* [*Funeral at Noon*] (Tel Aviv: Ha-sifriya ha-ḥadasha/Ha-kibuẓ ha-me'uḥad, 2008 [1974]; Amos Oz, *Mikha'el Sheli* [*My Michael*] (Tel Aviv: 'Am 'oved, 1968); Amalia Kahana-Carmon, Ve-*yareaḥ be-'emek ayalon* [*And Moon in the Valley of Ayalon*] (Tel Aviv: Ha-kibuẓ ha-me'uḥad, 1971). In Palestine, see Ghassan Kanafani, *All that's Left to You: A Novella and Other Stories*, translated by May Jayyusi and Jeremy Reed (Austin: Center for Middle Eastern Studies, the University of Texas at Austin, 1990), 1–50. In Arabic: *Mā tabaqqá lakum* (Bayrūt, Mu'assasat al-Abḥāth al-'Arabīyah, 2001); Jabra Ibrahim Jabra, *The Ship* (Washington, DC: Three Continents Press, 1985). In Arabic: *Al-Safinah* (Bayrūt, Dār al-Nahār, 1970).

69   In poetry, it was Nathan Zach who rejected the pathetic poetics of collective making (attributed to the writers of the 1940–50s, but especially to the national poet Nathan Alterman) for a more individualist negative poetics that cut off the concrete body from the abstract spirit of the state, ending up in a quotidian, sometimes aimless, subject. Zach explicitly says that this kind of new poetics aspires to be "translated . . . [and] recognized abroad . . . in the "big world."" His manifestos are rooted in the

Since this kind of individual freedom has become possible only in the form of liberal freedom springing to life in the US and Western Europe, the borrowing of US/Western European modernism was in actuality a borrowing of political time and freedom not yet possible in Israel and Palestine. These texts bear the mark of this impossibility, which received different theoretical formulations in Jameson, Franco Moretti and Roberto Schwartz.[70] This style will require slower elucidation as it will be crucial for understanding the difference between "peripheral" and "core" modernisms and the developments in the second period.

I recall that, in terms of politics, the overlap of the private and the public made the causes of the social world directly visible to individual experience such that no liberal freedom based on self-legislating individuality could emerge. Likewise, in literature, allegorical characters betrayed the fact that they were made, and thus gave the sense of being merely the instantiation of a political program. Writers, who did not resist so much Zionism or Palestinian nationalism themselves, but rather their total binding power, tried to wrestle the particular from the universal, and imagine a liberal and indeterminate relationship between the personal and the political. However, given the power of the state in Israel, and the occupation in Palestine, all such projects could not materialize in the real social world and could be accomplished only in the imagination as *abstract negation*. To stress the point, unlike novels of *poiesis* which were rooted in the historical social form (the overlap of the private and public spheres), modernist works had no autonomous (liberal) social ground from which to draw their materials, and thus they could imagine this social relation only as a negation of existing reality

---

ideology of liberal freedom for which the allegorical and national poetry of Alterman serves as the aesthetic foil. For the quoted statement above and his poetic manifesto, see "Le-'akliman ha-signoni shel shnot ha-ḥamishim be-shiratenu." In *Ha-shira she-me'ever la-milim: te'orya u-vikoret 1954–1973* (Tel Aviv: Ha-kibuẓ ha-me'uḥad, 2011), 165–71. Zach also notes, quite admiringly, the difference between the realist prose writing of the writers of the 1940s and 1950s that managed to "create a world," and the new writers of the 1960s whose symbolic and "literary" worlds are unconvincing and empty. He says of one poet, "things no longer refer to what's around them: it is obvious that such [symbolic] poetry would be 'literature' [*literatura*] . . . [but] since it no longer relates to any reality [*mamashut*] outside it, it falls back on a secondary aesthetic world." In other words, the aesthetic itself becomes the material of the poem rather than an outside world. See Zach, "*Sifrut beli 'olam.*" In *Ha-shira she-me'ever la-milim*, 132.

70 Fredric Jameson, "In the Mirror of Alternate Modernities." In *The Modernist Papers* (London/New York: Verso, 2007), 281–93; Franco Moretti, "Conjectures on World Literature," *New Left Review* 1 (January–February 2000):54–68; Roberto Schwarz, "A Brazilian Breakthrough," *New Left Review* 36 (November–December, 2005): 91–107. It is notable that Casanova's account does not register these kinds of stylistic/political breaks.

rather than as a positive political project. Their strategy—taking many variants—sought to break or block the relation between the personal and the political, body and spirit, signifier and signified so to create an indeterminate relationship between the particular and the universal.

To bring this description closer to known examples of peripheral modernism, I use the example of Kafka. Adorno and Benjamin characterized Kafka's style as one where the signifier is released from the signified, the concrete from the abstract. Adorno writes: "Nowhere in Kafka does there glimmer the aura of the infinite idea; nowhere does the horizon open. Each sentence is literal and each signifies. The two moments are not merged ... Walter Benjamin rightly defined it as parable. It expresses itself not through expression but by its repudiation, by breaking off."[71] Placing Kafka's parables in the tradition of Haggada mentioned earlier, Benjamin also argues that Kafka refuses the subsumption of the abstract law—the Halakha. "[Kafka's parables] don't simply lie down at the feet of doctrine, the way Haggadah lies down at the feet of Halakha. Having crouched down, they unexpectedly cuff doctrine with a weighty paw."[72] While Kafka's worlds are more abstract than any Israeli and Palestinian literature in the 1960s and the 1970s, the underlying gesture of "breaking off" can serve as the concept tying together different peripheries.

Now, the splitting of the abstract from the concrete, the particular from the universal, is, I argue, a figure of Kantian aesthetics. In other words, in the period of heteronomy where the liberal program was blocked, modernist novels thought politics in terms of Kantian aesthetics. Let us look at Kant's distinction between determining and reflective (aesthetic) judgment in the *Critique of the Power of Judgment* to see how this is done:

> The power of judgment in general is the faculty for thinking of the particular as contained under the universal. If the universal (the rule, the principle, the law) is given then the power of judgment, which subsumes the particular under it ... is determining. If, however, only the particular is given, for which the universal is to be found, then the power of judgment is merely reflecting.[73]

---

71   Theodor Adorno, *Prisms*, translated by Samuel and Shierry Weber (Cambridge, Mass: MIT Press, 1981), 246. See also Adorno, *Aesthetic Theory*, 178.

72   Walter Benjamin, "Letter to Gershom Scholem on Franz Kafka" in *Selected Writings*, vol. 3, (Cambridge: Harvard University Press, 1996), 326.

73   Immanuel Kant, *Critique of the Power of Judgment*, translated by Paul Guyer and Eric Matthews (Cambridge: Cambridge University Press, 2000), 66–7, emphasis in original removed.

I will comment in the following pages on the fact that these two judgments are not as exclusive as they are thought to be; but for now I note that the unique characteristic of reflective aesthetic judgment has to do with the absence of conceptuality, where particularity is not determined by the universal, and the subject's activity is engaged in "finding" or searching for the concept. The affinity between mystery novels, techniques of mapping typical of modernism and postmodernism, as well as the absence of overt determining causes we saw in Postone is already here in embryo. But more urgent now is the fact that Kant (and subsequent similar theories of the aesthetic) associates the act of finding the universal—where our faculties are engaged in combining and comparing elements in the imagination without a determining concept—with "play" and "freedom." The sense of play and freedom is made possible not simply by the absence of conceptuality in general, but with the absence of the concept of purpose or end (telos) in particular. Different than determining judgment in which we assign a purpose and a guiding principle, reflective and teleological judgments whose objects are art and nature respectively are those types of judgments where we cannot assign a purpose. This brings Kant to compare works of art with nature, and to distinguish between two kinds of art objects. Here is Kant's discussion of fine art:

> In a product of art one must be aware that it is art, and not nature; yet the purposiveness in its form must still seem to be free from all constraint by arbitrary rules as if it were a mere product of nature. On this feeling of freedom in the play of our cognitive powers, which must yet at the same time be purposive, rests that pleasure which is alone universally communicable though without being grounded on concepts . . .
>
> Now art always has a determinate intention of producing something . . . If the intention were aimed at the production of a determinate object, then if it were achieved through art, the object would please only through concepts . . . . It would not please as beautiful but as mechanical art. . . beautiful art must be regarded as nature . . . A product of art appears as nature, however, if we find it to agree punctiliously but not painstakingly with rules in accordance with which alone the product can become what it ought to be, without the academic form showing through i.e., without showing any sign that the rule has hovered before the eyes of the artist and fettered his mental powers.[74]

---

74   Kant, *Critique of the Power of Judgment*, 2000, 185–6; emphasis in bold removed.

Kant makes use of determinant and indeterminate judgment to differ-entiate between mechanical and beautiful art respectively. Mechanical art is un-free because it is a direct product of determining concepts. I call this kind of art "heteronomous aesthetics" because it is, as Kant says, "fettered" by a guiding concept. Such "fetters" expose the fact that the work was made, and moreover that it presupposes a telos: finality or purpose. Now, we would think that the beautiful object, or what can be called "autonomous aesthetics" will be diametrically opposed to the mechanical object, but here comes the unexpected complication that brings to mind Adorno's concept of art: beautiful art is free and pro-duces a sense of freedom not because it is actually free from the guidance of concepts—"art always has a determinate intention"—but because it *conceals* the guiding concept, the rule that indeed "hovered before the eyes of the artist" but was made to disappear in the artwork. It is this "concealment" of the concept, of the determinant cause, that acts as the condition of possibility for the appearance of freedom and for its universality—the fact that it can now be taken as a manifestation of humanity at large rather than this or that situated and particular audi-ence, this or that particular finality. We can see here, in embryo, how concealment is intimately tied to abstraction, for by removing the cause/concept we separate the object from what makes it what it is and in this way we make it universal or abstract.

Now, to see how Kant's conception of the aesthetic and fine art underlies Israeli and Palestinian modernist novels we need to make one substitution: while in Kant the concept or telos "fetters" the freedom of the artist and the work, the liberal position was fettered by the telos of state-making in Israel and the occupation in Palestine, which limited both the liberal political program and its aesthetic autonomy. To gain liberal freedom, such novels concealed the determinant concept, the determining ground of the characters and sometimes of the world itself. More specifically, to achieve freedom, the characters and the imaginary world had to be cut off from their underlying causes. On the level of the literary field, this aesthetic technique was directed against the poetics of "making" and was intended to gain autonomy in the field (and vis-ibility in the world). On the level of historical analysis, it was the way that writers thought about liberal freedom in a period that made such freedom impossible.

As a consequence, as Kant would argue, the main character and parts of the world itself turned "natural," that is, unmade. In terms of character, psychic states seemed to emanate from the depths of the self itself rather than from any political project, while the social world was rendered ready-made by the fact that historical antagonism was now evacuated from the surface of the work. In such worlds, both the world and the main character are instantiations of Kant's aesthetic and for this reason they are often aestheticized or self-reflexive, turning the entire world, as in Kafka's novels, into a mysterious text to be read or deciphered, and in which we need to "find" the universal, as Kant says. The act of searching and deciphering not only becomes the main activity of the reader; it is projected inward and becomes the chief activity of the main character. But what the character is in fact looking for is the political telos that was evacuated.

Such novels are not only riddle-like; they are written as and turn the world into what Derrida calls a "text." To see the relation between Kant's aesthetics and Derridean textuality let us go back to the distinction between reflective and determinant judgment.

As we said, in reflecting (aesthetic) judgment the determining universal is absent. However, reflecting judgment is not a process of logical induction where the mind simply generates general laws from particulars. This last is indeed a basic and fundamental activity of the understanding, what Kant scholar Béatrice Longuenesse calls the activity of comparison/reflection/abstraction that is the preliminary condition of empirical concept generation in Kant. In her path-breaking study, Longuenesse insists that reflective and determinative judgments are not two separate categories of judgments. Rather, in the latter, reflection is a *preliminary* activity of determination, while in the former determination never arrives. This is why, she points out, Kant argues that the case where the universal is missing and has to be found is *merely* reflecting:

> [Reflective judgments] differ in this regard from other judgments relating to the sensible given, which are not *merely* reflective, but determinative *as well*. What makes judgments merely reflective is that in them, the effort of the activity of judgments to form concepts *fails*. And it fails because it *cannot* succeed. This is the case in "merely reflective" *aesthetic* judgment, where the agreement of imagination and understanding is of such a nature that it cannot be reflected under any concept. And it is the case also in "merely reflective" *teleological* judgment, where no cognitive concept of a final cause can legitimately be employed to account for the objective purposiveness of organisms . . . Thus, the peculiar feature of aesthetic and teleological judgments is not that they are reflective

judgments . . . ; it is rather that they are . . . judgments in which reflection can never arrive at a conceptual *determination*.[75]

In determinant judgment, reflection is then the act of the mind that is busy comparing in order to find a concept which then, with the final moment of abstraction, stops the movement and creates a concept. Reflective judgment cuts off this final determination, ending in a potentially infinite movement. Now compare this understanding to Derrida's concept of text:

> A text is not a text unless it hides from the first comer, from the first glance, the *law* of its composition and the rules of its game. A text remains, moreover, forever imperceptible. Its law and its rules are not, however, harbored in the inaccessibility of a secret; it is simply that they can never be booked, in the present, into anything that could rigorously be called a perception. And hence, perpetually and essentially, they run the risk of being definitively lost.[76]

And this perpetual deferring where the rules are lost is the hallmark of Derridean "free play," a form of freedom from constraints. Thus, projecting inward Kant's reflective judgment is akin to textualization, where the imaginary world turns into a sign whose rules have been concealed and the character is attempting to find them (Kafka's Josef K. being the most paradigmatic example). But with Kant we see that this is not the nature of all art objects or all texts in general ("a text is not a text unless . . ."), but rather precisely those whose causes or telos have been concealed so to allow for this form of freedom. This form of freedom then has what Hegel would call a determinant content: unlike novels of *poiesis* that conceive of freedom as a result of antagonism with determining causes, where the freedom achieved takes the particular stamp of the struggle itself, literary textuality is that freedom that is the outcome of an act of disavowal—concealment—of heteronomy, which precisely procures its universality, that is to say, abstract character. To be precise, abstraction and universalization are not simply the obfuscation of local detail, but rather of historical conditions of possibility. Novels

75   Béatrice Longuenesse, *Kant and the Capacity to Judge: Sensibility and Discursivity in the Transcendental Analytic of the Critique of Pure Reason*, translated by Charles T. Wolfe (Princeton and Oxford: Princeton University Press, 1998), 164.

76   Jacques Derrida, *Dissemination*, translated by Barbara Johnson (Chicago: University of Chicago Press, 1981), 63.

can be steeped in local detail and still be abstract and universal and vice versa.

Finally, if *poiesis* was characterized by antagonism among unequals, these modernist novels end up creating a world governed by formal *equivalence*. If in the humanist novels equivalence is imagined within the world in the form of nature or sometimes art itself[77] (a sphere in which unequals can find a shared measure) in modernist novels, equivalence appears as form. The latter results, as I said, from the deferral or evacuation of antagonism, which often empties the plot and its causal connections, turning everything into a form of thought. In Longuenesse's terms, equivalence comes out of the fact that the determinant moment, in which certain features of the object become more salient than others in distinguishing the object, is deferred, thus giving all features an equivalent weight. Abstract equivalence is then the (impossible) utopian alternative to antagonistic inequality.

Now, since eventually the aesthetics of unmade textuality is at odds with the historical period, it is a form of impossible freedom, it does not cover the entire world, and antagonism or *poiesis* enters as an "other," which splits the imaginary world. This split takes many forms, but in general, antagonism returns in the form of inequality and finitude, breaking the infinity of equivalence, usually through a violent abrupt end. Such imaginary worlds are split then between two forms and two temporalities: one unfolding through antagonism, the other eternal, or static, and undergirded by a technique of textuality. As we shall see in Part II of this introduction, the fact that Israeli and Palestinian modernism in the 1960s and 1970s is rooted in negation and split worlds distinguishes it from Western European modernism where, with the separation of the private and the public already accomplished, modernism arises from the social form itself rather than from an abstract aesthetic negation. I should mention one qualification here: such split imaginary worlds in the periphery will emerge only if the novel is rooted in some local historical reality. If the text completely rejects this reality it will be free of such formal breaks as well as from any relation to local or national experience.

Before moving to the fourth position, it is important to mention here the position of female writers in Israel. While the scholarship on women's writing is split between universality (politics of resemblance)

---

77   In the sense that art knows no national boundaries and thus can serve as a utopian equivalent measure that trumps national animosity.

and particularity (politics of difference), or in other words whether female writers have a unique experience/form, this inquiry argues that any novel by a woman will be subjected to the same historical limit, and that any differences in form will stem from the ideological positions hitherto mentioned: statist, humanist or liberal. Thus, female writers who identify with the state—as did Yonat Sened or Emma Levin Talmi, for example—will adopt the poetics of making, while those taking up humanist and liberal positions, such as Amalia Kahana Carmon and Shulamit Hareven, will attempt to invest female protagonists with liberal autonomy that will ultimately prove impossible.[78] In other words, protagonists will be unable to attain self-legislation and especially creative license in their personal or professional world, or when they engage with the state; rather, they will be relegated to a subordinate position within its structure. Some studies see this failure of autonomy by Carmon and Hareven (pre-1985) as a consequence of male domination,[79] and, conversely, consider other writers (significantly post-1985), such as Ruth Almog, as able to create autonomy for their protagonists.[80] Two crucial points are missing in such accounts: first, critics usually underplay the fact that often the desired autonomy is modeled on liberal artistic self-expression and is thus limited to the individual private subject. What was impossible to imagine pre-1985 then was not simply women's autonomy but the autonomy of the private sphere more generally. This claim is affirmed when we notice the second point, namely that post-1985 we can see not only felicitous narratives of women's liberal self-expression (artistic or otherwise), but also an inordinate increase in female writers and the very invention of the category "women's writing" (*sifrut nashim*). This development is conditioned, I argue, precisely by capital-related processes, especially in terms of work and the privatization of the literary field. As Sylvia Fogiel Bijaoui explains, women's autonomy in Israel began to gain momentum after 1967 when the labor market needed more working hands and thus women (mostly of the Ashkenazi middle

---

78 Both cases do not preclude expressing a critique of the misogyny embedded in statist forms of association.

79 See for example the pioneering study by Esther Fuchs, *Israeli Mythogynies: Women in Contemporary Hebrew Fiction* (Albany: State University of New York Press, 1987).

80 Yael Feldman, *No Room of Their Own: Gender and Nation in Israeli Women's Fiction* (New York: Columbia University Press, 1999), but see also her previous study, Yael Feldman, "From Feminist Romance to an Anatomy of Freedom: Israeli Women Novelists." In Alan Mintz (ed.), *The Boom in Contemporary Israeli Fiction* (Hanover, NH: Brandeis University Press, 1997), 71–113.

class) could gain relative autonomy from "traditional" roles at home. As a consequence, the role of the "housewife" was changed, the structure of the family slowly transformed into the site of inter-personal relationship only, and birth rates declined.[81] Similarly, the rapid and wide-spread commercialization of cultural production in the early 1990s, especially in film, television and literature, corresponded with the boom in female writers. It is at this moment that the literary market begins to be segmented according to market categories, one category being "romance," now sanctioned by the cultural industry and whose object is women, both as readers and writers. In other words, it is the shift from statism to neoliberalism that enables the felicitous transition to women's liberal autonomy, both as writers and as fictional characters.

The fourth position that I identify in Israel (and there are others that are less visible) is the one taken by Mizrahi writers. As a dominated ethnic class within Israel suffering from systemic racism and exploitation, Mizrahim could not, and still cannot, enjoy the emancipatory promises of Zionism (or liberalism for that matter), for their labor, their un-freedom, is very much the condition of possibility of Ashkenazi freedom, Zionist or not. Excluded in this way, but still considering themselves a part of the Israeli polity, Mizrahi writers take up a split position that both criticizes Zionist inequality and tries to find a domain of equivalence in which the Mizrahi could be included as an equal member. Thus, while Mizrahi imaginary worlds structurally resemble Ashkenazi liberal and humanist worlds in that they are internally split, their political priority is to find "a way in" to the polity, expanding its political boundaries rather than breaking away from it. Here we find the second meaning of "liberalism" as the expansion of the principle of civic equivalence.

All other communities, in so far as they write literature, will be rooted in heteronomous social relations and a heteronomous aesthetic.

6.

In the second period, with the shift of autonomy from the project of state-making to private life—a process concomitant with the shift of literary production from the field of the state to the field of civil society—a new concept became possible: the Kantian concept of aesthetic activity

---

81   Sylvia Fogiel Bijaoui, "Mishpaḥot be-yisra'el: Ben mishpaḥtiyut le-post-moderniyut." In Dafna Izraeli et al., *Min, Migdar, Politica* (Tel Aviv: Ha-kibuẓ ha-me'uḥad, 1999), 107–66.

without a purpose. As Adorno argued, artworks in this period appear unmade, as an object of nature. But unlike in the modernist moment discussed previously, this appearance is not a matter of technique, of a style of concealment that cuts off the characters and sometimes the world itself from its conditions of possibility in the real; rather, such concealment has already befallen the artwork's preliminary social and symbolic materials themselves so that *Schein* now becomes the default category of literature.

Another way to put this is to say that the negativity of the modernist style has now become a property of the social itself where the structure of immanent determination takes on the attributes of Kantian aesthetics and Derridean textuality. The removal of the state as the determinant cause brings about a social structure, which, like Kant's conception of fine art, conceals its law and appears, to private life, as natural, unmade and free. Similarly, with the inability to locate in any one institution the positive governing law of a capitalist structure unhinged from its subordination to a political project, the social appears, to private life, as a Derridean text premised on the infinite deferral of determination and a series of equivalences (e.g., identities). Finally, the most important shift that takes place is the crisis of political finality. For unlike any other previous social forms, capitalism, based on abstract labor, is that form which eschews finality itself whence emerges its unbound and infinite nature. Thus, the literary artwork is now faced with a social world based on private and autonomous individuals whose conditions of possibility are absent and whose political purpose is put into doubt. In response to this historical situation, aesthetic negativity changes its priorities: if in the modernism of the 1960s it responded to the poetics of making and the determination of the state by projecting inward the concept of Kantian aesthetic and concealing the law, now aesthetic negation, in the instances that it occurs, projects into itself Kant's concept of critique which resists the structure of capital by searching for the governing law. In other words, in the previous moment, negativity meant a movement of interiority and redoubling (the work of art represented its own principle within itself), while in the neoliberal moment, negativity means abandoning the concept of art and becoming its other (as art wants to become a form of discursive knowledge). Thus, as much as we see the emergence of postmodern styles of measure-less worlds we also see the development of a type of search whose quintessential instance is the detective novel. The "search" is a broad literary type that can include several genres and literary styles in which a missing object, broadly defined, serves as the absent center around which the imaginary world is weaved. This latter development goes unattended because critics seek historical development in what Bourdieu calls the field of limited-production (so-called high literature), while the most important transformations have taken place in the field of large-scale production (or commercial literature), especially since the nineties.

In Israel, two kinds of searches can be discerned according to their object: in novels where Israel is conceived as a nation, i.e., as a spiritual concept, the search is for a principle of national unity or national origin whose definition will differ according to ideology. In novels where Israel is conceived as a society, i.e., as a form of material forces, the search is for the governing social conditions of daily life, the character and definition of which will again differ by ideology. In Palestine, since national unity is still defined by the priority of national liberation, the search is for conditions of possibility of Palestinian life that have become foreign and unfamiliar to the private Palestinian. If in Israel the detective novel is the quintessential new form of the second period, in Palestine, although far less ubiquitous, it is the novel of return, in which a private Palestinian returns to Palestine and finds its (heteronomous) daily life an odd text he or she can only observe from the outside. The cause of the foreignness is usually attributed to the Israeli occupation and its ruinous effects, but such reading covers over the fact that the observer has changed, for, turning autonomous, the observer finds the realities of the occupation almost unfathomable.

In general, in the worlds of the second period the constitutive antagonism (rooted in inequality) is either reduced to local political events within the world or vacated completely, especially in modernist-style texts. This new development creates a world peopled with equivalent characters who inhabit the infinite time of routine and mundane existence that is usually wrapped in random causality. This kind of daily experience confronts the characters as a problem, and a narrative figure, usually an abrupt violent event, is invented to provide closure and finitude. The entry of such figures of finitude suggests the existence of inequality and heteronomy which, demoted from their previous status as constitutive condition, become a localized event that enters the world as a narrative "other" and disrupts the time of the private subject.

With this initial description let us examine a few new political positions. In Israel, the first position affirms the new liberal society in which social life is strictly private. Here we can discern three variants: the first is what commentators call "postmodern"—a world cast from the vantage point of private life for which all universal measures are put into doubt or ridiculed.[82] These novels are the mirror image of statist novels of "making" of the first period, not only because they undermine the existence of any universal that the latter position took for granted, but also because they are *homologous* with the historical condition, taking as absolute what is in fact a historical development, and thus do not go beyond the surface of social life. The second variant affirms the formation of new social and cultural identities (woman, Mizrahi, Israeli-Palestinian, LGBTQ, Russian, Ethiopian, etc.) for whom, however, political commitment is a problem and (at times) a new principle of national unity (multiculturalism) is thought out as a solution.[83] The third variant is the mainstream commercial literature in which the main characters are the new private (mostly Ashkenazi) Israeli.[84] The distinction between the second and third variants hinges on the fact that the latter is identified with a universal imagined Israeliness whose identity-markers are considered normative.

The second political response is conservative nostalgia for the lost paternal world of Zionism, now shed of its colonial violence and reduced to "values" of sacrifice, authenticity, making do, and so-called refined European culture that no longer have a place in a fallen materialist Israel.[85] The third and more recent position is the critique of Israeli capitalism as such in both its local and global appearances. These are worlds that see

---

82   See for example Avraham Hefner, *Kolel ha-kol* [*Everything Included*] (Yerushalayim: Keter, 1987); Orly Castel-Bloom, *Hekhan ani nimẓet* [*Where Am I*] (Tel Aviv: Zemorah bitan, 1990); Etgar Keret, *Ga'agu'ay le-kisinjer* [*Missing Kissinger*] (Tel Aviv: Zemorah bitan, 1994); Gafi Amir, *'Ad gil 21 tagi'a la-yareaḥ* [*By 21 You'll Reach the Moon*] (Yerushalayim: Keter, 1997).

83   See for example, Ruth Almog, *Shorshe Avir* [*Roots of Air*] (Yerushalayim: Keter/Ha-kibuẓ ha-me'uḥad, 1987); Amalia Kahana-Carmon, *Liviti otah ba-derekh le-vetah* [*I Walked Her Home*] (Tel Aviv: Ha-kibuẓ ha-me'uḥad, 1991); Ronit Matalon, *Zeh 'im ha-panim 'elenu* [*The One Facing Us*] (Tel Aviv: 'Am 'oved, 1995); Yossi Avni-Levy, *Gan ha-'eẓim ha-metim* [*The Park of Dead Trees*] (Tel Aviv: Zemorah bitan, 1995); Yehudit Katzir, *Le-matis yesh et ha-shemesh ba-beten* [*Matisse Has the Sun in His Belly*] (Tel Aviv: Ha-kibuẓ ha-me'uḥad, 1995); Ẓeruya Shalev, *Ḥaye ahavah* [*Love Life*] (Yerushalayim: Keter, 1997); Dorit Rabinyan, *Ha-ḥatunot shelanu* [*Our Weddings*] (Tel Aviv: 'Am 'oved, 1999); Dudu Busi, *Ha-yareaḥ yarok ba-vadi* [*Green Moon over the Creek*] (Yerushalayim: Keter, 2000); Dana Peleg, *Te'enim ahuvati* [*Figs, My Dear*] (Tel Aviv: Shufra le-sifrut yafah, 2000); Ilan Sheinfeld, *Rak atah* [*Only You*] (Tel Aviv: Shufra le-sifrut yafah, 2000); Shimon Ballas, *Yalde-ḥuẓ* [*Outsiders*]. In *Tel Aviv Mizraḥ: Trilogya* [*Tel Aviv East: Trilogy*] (Tel Aviv: Ha-kibuẓ ha-me'uḥad, 2003); Sayed Kashua, *Va-yehi boker* [*Let It Be Morning*](Yerushalayim: Keter, 2004).

84   This category includes the majority of mainstream literary production.

85   See for example Batya Gur, *Reẓaḥ be-shabat ba-boker* [*A Saturday Morning Murder*](Yerushalayim: Keter, 1988).

the capitalist logic of equivalence and infinite exchange as a threat to the autonomy of private life and the operation of politics.[86]

The modernist position of negation and concealment surely continues but now, bereft of the historical and political situation that it had in the first period, it is no longer split between two temporalities and weaves the homogenous world of a thought closed onto itself. The novel of "making" is now a historical impossibility, and it may live on only beyond the borders of Israel, in literature written by settlers for whom the Israeli frontier is a constant object of making.

In Palestine, mostly in the West Bank, novels written from the position of private life begin to take center stage as the dominant new social relation. Here, too, the literary type of the search begins to characterize new Palestinian imaginary worlds, and politics becomes a narrative problem.[87] In such novels, the Israeli occupation is either relegated to the background or enters into the lives of the main characters as an external shock. Novels in this category are written by Palestinians all over the world in multiple languages.[88] Novels of national resistance, where the collective fate of Palestinians is the main object of narration, continue to be written but no longer take center stage.[89]

Part II

1.

I argued in Part I that the twin concepts of autonomy and heteronomy could exceed the scope of Israel and Palestine and serve as categories

---

86   See for example Assaf Gavron, *Tanin Pigu'a* [*Croc Attack*] (Or Yehuda: Zemora bitan, 2006); Nir Baram, *Ẓel 'Olam* [*World Shadow*] (Tel Aviv: 'Am 'oved, 2013).

87   Sahar Khalifeh, *The Inheritance* (Cairo/New York: The American University in Cairo, 2005). In Arabic, *al-Mīrāth* (Bayrūt: Dār al-Ādāb, 1997); Adania Shibli, *Touch*, translated by Paula Haydar (Northampton: Clockroot Books, 2010); In Arabic, *Masās* (Bayrūt: Dār al-Ādāb / Mu'assasat 'Abd al-Muḥsin al-Qaṭṭān, 2003); *We Are All Equally Far from Love* (Northampton, Mass.: Clockroot Books, 2012). In Arabic, *Kullunā ba'īd bi-dhāt al-miqdār 'an al-ḥubb* [*We Are All Equally Far from Love*](Mu'assasat 'Abd al-Muḥsin al-Qaṭṭān; Bayrūt: Dār al-Ādāb, 2004); Rabai al-Madhoun, *The Lady from Tel Aviv* (London: Telegram, 2013). In Arabic, *al-Sayyidah min Tall Abīb* (Bayrūt: al-Mu'asasah al-'Arabiyah lil-Dirasāt wa-al-Nashr, 2009); Selma Dabbagh, *Out of It* (London: Bloomsbury Publishing, 2011); Ahmed Masoud, *Vanished: The Mysterious Disappearance of Mustafa Ouda* (Cyprus: Rimal Publications, 2015).

88   In May 2015, the literary journal *Words without Borders* published selections from "New Palestinian Literature" written in English, Spanish, Danish and Arabic.

89   See for example, Ahmad Harb, *Baqāyā* [*Remainder*](Bayrūt: al-Mu'assasah al-'Arabīyah lil-Dirāsāt wa-al-Nashr, 1997); Yahya Yakhlif, *Mā' al-samā'* [*Sky Water*] ('Ammān: Dār al-Shurūq lil-Nashr wa-al-Tawzī, 2008).

for a broader inquiry into world literature, and I turn in this direction now.

Since the publication in 2000 of Franco Moretti's "Conjectures on World Literature," and David Damrosch's *What Is World Literature* in 2003, as well as the translation into English in 2004 of Pascale Casanova's *The World Republic of Letters*, world literature as a concept and as a field of literary knowledge has become a major object of inquiry. Although the idea of world literature goes back two hundred years to Goethe and Marx, it operates as a new concept today that, as Theo D'haen explains, opens up new research avenues on the graduate level in Europe, and has made inroads into undergraduate syllabi (and perhaps one day into disciplinary structures) in the United States.[90] Whether affirmative or critical of the field itself, what many of the studies on world literature have in common is a central opposition between the nation-state and the world: between a concrete, bounded locality and a more diffuse network that in Moretti is conceived as circulation of forms underlined by the capitalist world system, and in Casanova as a world distribution system of aesthetic value situated against and parallel to nation-states. Such accounts seek to contest the boundedness of national literature and make us see that literary form, especially in the periphery, cannot be explained solely by reference to the nation-state and its local culture, but rather by its "debt" and relation to other, "worldly" forms (Moretti) or by its position within a world system of aesthetic value (Casanova). And yet, however useful in getting us out of national boundaries, Moretti and Casanova's accounts might not be fully adequate for the moment of neoliberal globalization, nor is their object of study fully satisfying if we want to understand the relation between literary form and the Real, rather than between one form and another. First, these two accounts seem to arrive on the scene very much like Minerva's owl. For the literary reality that they describe can enter thought as concept and indeed system only at the moment when this system passes from the world and thus appears to our minds as such. What is different today is the conception of the "world:" as discussed above, the older concept relied on a world composed of distinct states, while today we work with a different concept: that of a globe in which capital, by weakening states, imposes an abstract equivalent space. To be sure, the world is still underlined by inequality but the relation between center and periphery begins to

---

90   Theo D'haen, *The Routledge Concise History of World Literature* (New York: Routledge, 2012).

change its characteristics. Second, by emphasizing systemic relations, in which accounting for formal variations is the main concern, both Moretti and Casanova focus on the lateral relation, as it were, between forms and underplay the vertical relation between the literary work and its social conditions in which lies its political import.

What I set out to do here, then, is to propose a critique of Moretti and Casanova whose conclusions will serve as the beginning for a different approach to world literature, one that will take the significance of neo-liberal globalization into consideration.

2.

Moretti's inquiry into world literature begins by borrowing a theoretical preposition from Jameson's introduction to Kojin Karatani's study on modern Japanese literature. Like Roberto Schwarz in the Latin American context, Jameson proposes that "the raw material of Japanese social experience and the abstract formal patterns of Western novel construction cannot always be welded together seamlessly."[91] Slightly rewriting this formulation, Moretti argues:

> In cultures that belong to the periphery of the literary system . . . the modern novel first arises not as an autonomous development but as a compromise between western influence (usually French and English) and local materials.[92]

To thicken his abstract proposition, Moretti offers elsewhere a useful example of this difference in a short discussion of Antonio Candido's comparative study of Emile Zola's *L'Assomoir* (France), Giovanni Verga's *Malavoglia* (Italy), and Aluísio de Azevedo's *O Cortiço* (Brazil). Candido notices a "disjunction" between the imported plot and the local styles that took on, in Verga, Sicilian-Tuscan collective speech, and, in Azevedo, "racial-political allegory" and ethical commentary. Moretti adds that Verga and Azevedo transformed "the analytico-impersonal style which had been the great invention of nineteenth-century France

---

91 Fredric Jameson, "Foreword: In the Mirror of Alternate Modernities," in Kojin Karatani, *Origins of Modern Japanese Literature* (Durham: Duke University Press, 1993), xiii. See also Schwarz, "A Brazilian Breakthrough."

92 Moretti, "Conjectures," 58.

with judgmental, loud, sarcastic, emotional voices."[93] Based on this insight, I argue that the "compromise" (breaks or discontinuities) in the form arises out of the qualitative difference between the social form of immanent determination in England and France and external determination (in their wide varieties) in the periphery, where capitalism might very well have penetrated in terms of trade, fashion, architecture and the like; but the social form itself has yet to transform into a structure where individuals and social laws become separate and autonomous from one another.[94] In Candido, we see this distinction between the scientific, objective narrator of Zola who levels off novelistic materials (equivalence) and the situated narrator (inequality) in Verga and Azevedo that colors the imaginary world with collective, popular, and political voices.

The same argument is found in Schwarz's account of Brazilian realism. Examining the relationship between Brazil's history and the novel, Schwarz offers an explanation of what he calls the "mismatch" between Brazilian social form and Balzacian realism.[95] Reading José de Alencar's 1872 Senhora, Schwarz notices a break in the novel between the main and secondary plot. The main love intrigue replicates the abstract and tragic contradictions in nineteenth-century French society between, on the one hand, extreme individualism, self-interest and the pursuit of money, and, on the other, love and fidelity, while in the comic and more relaxed world of the secondary characters such abstract contradictions have no purchase. Although he does not use these terms, Schwarz's description of the secondary plot and the pre-modern social form as clientelist and paternalist fits precisely Postone's term of "overt social relations" where abstract individuality, which does characterize the main protagonists,

---

93 Moretti, "World-Systems Analysis, Evolutionary Theory, 'Weltliteratur.'" *Review* (Fernand Braudel Center) 28.3 (2005): 225. Pierre Bourdieu attributes the invention of the "analytico-impersonal style" to Flaubert's *Madame Bovary*. See his discussion in *The Rules of Art*, 105–12.

94 These two steps in the contact with capital are designated by Marx as formal and real subsumption. In the first, as capitalist accumulation is extended, world regions as well as domestic branches of the economy are subsumed by capital as they are: the labor process is not changed but inherited from previous modes of production. In the second moment, capitalist relations transform the labor process itself and make it an organic part of capital. Following Marx, Hardt and Negri use these two terms to discuss the shift from a world structured by a capitalist center and a non-capitalist periphery (under formal subsumption) to a global society where capital now subsumes its outside and transforms the fabric of society itself. Appealing to and modifying Foucault's theory they name this transition a shift from disciplinary to control society where society as a whole is immersed in capitalist social relations. See, Marx, *Capital* I, 1019–38; Hardt and Negri, *Empire*, 254–5.

95 Schwarz, "Brazilian Breakthrough," 92

has yet to become possible for the secondary characters, who must still "obey the many ties that bind" them together. The fact that the two parts are not connected in a meaningful way (as they would be in a Balzacian novel) but rather exist side by side prompts Schwarz to offer this historical explanation:

> What is the content of this dissonance? The answer can only be historical. Brazilian independence was a conservative process that did not bring about a restructuring of society. The colonial heritage of landownership, slavery, traffic in human beings, extended family and generalized clientelism went almost untouched. Brazil's insertion in the modern world proceeded by way of a social confirmation of the colonial Ancien Régime, not its supersession. This made for a disconcerting kind of progress, in which pre-modern inequalities were simply replicated in newer and newer contexts, rather than being eradicated. This pattern may be a key to the peculiarities of Brazilian culture, with its penchant for both radical modernism and unending compromise. What is one to think of the strange lack of tension between the ultra-modern and the indefensibly pre-modern?[96]

For Schwarz, Alencar's importation of Balzacian realism is a superficial and failed attempt, motivated mostly by the desire to mimic Europe. It is so because its narrative structure reverses the historical reality of Brazil, pushing to the background, as local color, paternalistic social relations that in actuality characterize Brazilian society as a whole. However, we can also see how the importation of individualism in its Balzacian form can be interpreted as an unconscious wish for liberal autonomy from those paternalistic forms. By endowing her with an unexpected inheritance and great beauty, allowing her freedom to choose a husband as well as to show the corrupt effects of money, Aurelia's character, precisely because improbable in Brazil at that time, embodies a wish for freedom not yet possible, and for this reason it takes the form of perversion. The importation of Balzacian realism is then a stylistic choice meant to put Brazil on the world map of literature and to imagine a way out of paternalism. As I show in Chapters One and Three, similar narrative breaks, a reversal of historical forms, and an impossible wish for liberal autonomy appear in Israeli and Palestinian modernism, in Yeshayahu Koren's 1967 *Funeral at Noon*, and in Ghassan Kanafani's 1966 *All That's Left to You*.

---

96   Schwarz, "Brazilian Breakthrough," 98–99, emphasis in original removed.

So far Moretti's theory seems to explain the local articulation of travel-ing forms,[97] but this theory finds its limit when, in the neoliberal period, forms of capitalist socialization arise domestically in Israel, Palestine and other states, and create an equivalent (if uneven) space between core and periphery states that smoothes over the breaks we notice in the earlier moment. This new transformation draws our attention to the historical and methodological limits of Moretti's theory. First, Moretti's perception is underlined by a "figure-ground" schema in which the new worldly "figure" (literary form, e.g., realism) arises organically as it were out of local social conditions in Europe, then travels to new "grounds" (states on the periphery) where it is domesticated or rearticulated. The fact that Moretti concedes that figures can also travel in the other direction, from the periphery to the center, does not alter the main presupposition that the ground is static and it is only the figure that moves around. But since the beginning of neoliberal globalization in the 1970s, the ground itself has been traveling, a transformation that allows for worldly literary forms to arise from local experience instead of being imported from elsewhere. The world is still uneven, but its social fabric, especially in the periphery, is changing. Moretti's metaphors of "trees" (states) and "waves" (markets) can be recalibrated to account for this change. In his theory, the state-as-tree is figured as a barrier that bifurcates or "cracks" the traveling form, a process resulting in diverse cultural branches, while the market-as-wave erases local difference and produces homogeneity.[98] To put the new historical situation in Moretti's terms, the global "waves" (not of cultural production but of economic and political forms) are washing over not simply domestic culture but the "trees"—the states—themselves.

Second, once we realize that unevenness can still produce equivalence we begin to notice another limit in Moretti's theory, the conceptualiza-tion of which would contribute to a resolution of some of the criticisms that it has received. Although Moretti is attentive to history and offers us a literary account rooted in Wallerstein's theory of the capitalist world system, his "object" of analysis is shaped by a strong scientific assump-tion, drawn from the natural sciences (evolution), whose fundamental premise, the exclusion of meaning, is at odds with that which drives studies of society. The much-attacked method of "distant reading," based on general principles, does not simply wipe out "close reading" and the

---

97   But see what follows for critical responses.

98   "Trees and branches are what nation-states cling to; waves are what markets do." Moretti, "Conjectures," 67.

category of the example, as critics argue. This is, I would say, the usual tendency of humanists to defend idiographic against nomothetic knowledge, a binary that must disavow the fact that any reading of an example presupposes abstract (nomothetic) assumptions, operative already in the very choice of an example. Moretti's method involves rather a far more radical amputation, for what it really does is to replace interpretation with explanation, and thus must remain mostly silent when asked what morphological change actually *means*.[99] On the explanatory level, the morphological change provides evidence of the heterogeneity of the world system, or vice versa, the heterogeneity of the system serves as the cause of literary mutation; beyond that, the text and its inner workings remain mute. In the same manner that Darwin, and science in general, eradicates god from nature and replaces spiritual meaning with material causality, Moretti sucks the meaning out of literary phenomena, giving us its empty shell alone. The charge of "formalism" is not unfair here. But unlike nature that is indeed devoid of any spiritual (i.e., teleological) meaning, literature is nothing but what German idealists call "spirit," that is, society and its ends.[100] For this reason, however limited by the premises of a sociological approach, Casanova's theory is closer, in my mind, to understanding literary difference, for in her study form is simply the writer's way to think autonomy, that is, politics, under certain historical conditions.

Third, once the quality of literary form is minimized, Moretti is left with a field governed by quantities: weak and strong states underlie the capacity of "strong" forms to influence "weaker" ones. Here the theory is open to a charge of imprecision that threatens to destabilize the assumption of the autonomous development of the "core": although England and France are supposed to influence the periphery, critics argue, how does Moretti explain the influence of Cervantes on Fielding, or in other words the periphery on the core?[101] Moretti concedes the point,

---

99   For the absence of the category of interpretation in Moretti see also Christopher Prendergast, "Evolution and Literary Theory: A Response to Franco Moretti," *New Left Review* 34 (July–August 2005): 40–62, as well as Moretti's response "The End of the Beginning: A Reply to Christopher Prendergast," *New Left Review* 41 (September–October 2006): 71–86.

100   As Moretti himself says, Schwarz, a sympathetic reader of his studies, expressed concern with the absence of social critique in his evolutionary theory. See Moretti, "The End of the Beginning," 83–4.

101   For these objections and others see Jale Parla, "The Object of Comparison," *Comparative Literary Studies* 41.1 (2004): 116–25; Jonathan Arac, "Anglo-Globalism?" *New Left Review* 16 (July–August 2002): 35–45; Efraín Krystal, "Considering Coldly . . ." *New Left Review* 15 (May–June 2002): 61–74; Francesca Orsini, "Maps of Indian Writing:

and argues that indeed all literatures are a matter of "compromises" and subject to pressures from without. But, since we are in the field of quantities, the original claim holds when the levers are shifted from the absolute to the relative. Moretti's point is that there are different kinds of pressures (again note Moretti's appeal to hydraulic imagery typical of Newtonian mechanics), and the pressure England and France exerted on all the rest at that point in time is far more significant to the evolution of the novel than the pressure that was exerted on these two states.[102] This acknowledgment could however be interpreted differently if we readmit quality into the theory and consider the argument that it is not only a matter of which form is stronger or more influential symbolically, but the political function that the imported form plays in each text, and the way it relates to other materials. Itamar Even Zohar, upon whose insights Moretti draws consistently, argues in the same vein. Under the heading "Interference occurs when a system is in need of items unavailable within itself," he argues that when dominating forms do not fit the needs of new generations, forms can be imported from an adjacent system.[103] Moretti's theory erases the concept of "need" and replaces it simply by the sheer forces of circulation. It is quite plausible to argue that European literature "needed" an aspect of peripheral literature not possible in England and France in order to think certain political thoughts.[104] Finally, Moretti does mention his overall political concern to study literature "against the background of the unprecedented possibility that the entire world may be subject to a single centre of power—and a centre which has long exerted an equally unprecedented symbolic hegemony."[105] While I share this concern, two modifications are necessary with the advent of neo-liberal globalization. First, we can no longer talk of a "center" in any simple way, but rather of a network of capitalist relations (especially in the highly abstract moment of financialization) that subordinates states

---

India in the Mirror of World Fiction," *New Left Review* 13 (January–February 2002): 75–88. Emily Apter, "Global *Translatio*: The 'Invention' of Comparative Literature, Istanbul 1933," *Critical Inquiry* 29 (Winter 2003): 253–281.

102   Moretti, "More Conjectures," *New Left Review* 20 (March–April 2003): 78–80.

103   Itamar Even Zohar, "Laws of Literary Interference," *Poetics Today* 1.11 (1990): 69.

104   Eileen Julien makes this point about the way French modernism uses African art. "In the French sphere [noting, among others, the pre-Surrealists, Apollinaire, Cendrars, Tzara] . . . African languages, oral traditions, and mythopeia were seen as means of rejuvenation for an anemic French language and a civilization racked by war and in decline. "Eileen Julien, Arguments and Further Conjectures on World Literature." In Gunilla Linberg-Wada (ed.), *Studying Transcultural Literary History* (Berlin/New York: Walter de Gruyter, 2006), 126.

105   Moretti, "More Conjectures," 81.

themselves to its dictates. Second, once parts of the periphery become socially equivalent with the "core," one cannot simply speak of symbolic hegemony per se, because now cultural forms of the "core" arise "organically" in the periphery. This does not mean that the cultural products of "strong" states do not dominate the market of cultural goods; the unevenness remains.

3.

Moving now to Casanova. Although they differ in scope, Casanova's *The World Republic of Letters* and Bourdieu's *The Rules of Art* will be treated here as complimentary texts that should be taken together when approaching the question of world literature. First, both texts arrange their objects and their histories so to debunk two contradictory positions, to affect a "double rupture," to use Bourdieu's conception of Flaubert's project, from both idealism and Marxism: from the position that takes the author as the pure originator of the work, and the work itself as a singular text, as well as from the counterposition that reduces the work and the author to social origins and historical circumstance. In broad terms, Kant is the object of the first rupture; Marx is the object of the second. Their sociological project rejects literary idealism by re-inserting the work and the author into a historical "field" of cultural production in which the meaning of both work and author are made possible, or "thinkable" only in relation to other positions and other works. Likewise, they reject Marxism (for Bourdieu the targets are Sartre, Goldmann and Williams) by insisting on the (historical) autonomy of the literary field that, in Bourdieu's terms, "refracts" such external conditions, or in Casanova's, "translates" these conditions into its own aesthetic mechanisms. Second, both studies argue that literary autonomy, and the "refracted" styles it makes possible, are enabled by the social autonomization of the field of literary production, a process that reached its culmination in the second half of the nineteenth century, first in France and then in other states throughout the twentieth century, and both studies spend a considerable amount of time providing a history of the social genesis of this autonomization. Bourdieu limits his study to France, while Casanova expands it to the rest of Europe, the US, and Latin America, but in essence provides a model for what she calls the world republic of letters. To further understand the implications of Casanova and Bourdieu's studies on world literature, we need to look more closely at Bourdieu's claims about the French field and see how they are treated in Casanova's global model.

Bourdieu's first concern lies in historicizing literary autonomy, in showing that the claim that artists should submit to no law but their own, is preconditioned by sociological developments ("morphological changes") in literary production. Similar to Raymond Williams in the English case,[106] Bourdieu argues that one such precondition has to do with the enlargement of the reading and writing public (producers and consumers of cultural goods). The expansion of the press offers new ways to make a living to an influx of young people from the lower and middle classes who, impressed by the symbolic capital and the romantic allure of writers and painters, aspire to become artists. Seeking to avoid unimaginative professions, these new cultural producers "live by their art" and eventually invent "the art of living," a socio-symbolic process creating a bohemian "society within society."[107] This kind of society is directly opposed to the "bourgeois," and especially to the "new money" of wealthy industrialists and businessmen whose practical habitus is inimical to cultural and intellectual matters. Setting up the historical moment in this way, Bourdieu makes his first claim (whose form will sound familiar I hope in light of our previous discussions), arguing that what characterizes this moment is a shift from "direct dependence" (on a patron) to "structural subordination."[108] Not accidently, this shift happens alongside the broad shift from feudalism to capitalism, external to immanent determination, that Postone has described. Thus, the precondition of the pre-condition is the shift in the social form, making possible specialized autonomization of the literary field. To be sure, discussing the new position of the writer on the market of cultural goods, Bourdieu does draw our attention to the affinity between the writer for hire and the "free" laborer. He says:

> To understand this transformation, one might think of it by analogy with the oft-analysed shift from the servant, attached by personal ties to a family, to the free worker . . . who, freed from the ties of dependence which limited or prevented the free sale of his labour, is available to put himself on the market and to undergo its anonymous constraints and sanctions.[109]

106 Williams, *Culture and Society 1780–1950*.
107 Bourdieu, *The Rules of Art*, 47–55.
108 Ibid., 49.
109 Ibid., 55.

But Bourdieu mentions this affinity only to caution his reader not to think of this process only negatively, i.e., as a process of alienation, for the writer can now make a ("miserable") living from new positions linked to the commercial market. However useful, the remark displaces the real effect of this historical shift onto the construction of imaginary worlds, and as we shall see, blinds Bourdieu and Casanova to the way this new form of "freedom" informs the new autonomous styles.[110]

I will return to the affinity between the structural subordination in the "field" of literary production and the immanent determination of capitalism, but in the meantime, I move to Bourdieu's second claim. Now that we have shifted from external to immanent determination, the writer, according to Bourdieu, is dependent on two poles: the market (appearing directly through the demands of profit-making, and indirectly through the professional demands of commercial publications) and social ties, mediated by the salons, that enable writers to benefit from the support of the state.[111] In short, the state and the market, politics and economics, through their variant constraints, constitute the two *heteronomous* poles, determining literary production from the "outside," as it were.[112] In the same time that the social autonomization of the literary field is underway, the field is separated into two literary positions: first, what is called "bourgeois" or "idealist" art (split between the "high" value of the theatre, and the "low" value of commercial literature), and second what is called "social art" and sometimes "realism." The former is subservient to the tastes and morals of the bourgeois public and the market, while the latter puts art in the service of a popular political cause. At this moment, "bohemian society" seeks to break with both the twin heteronomous poles and the two dominant literary positions by imposing its own law of autonomy upon the field of cultural production, a position that comes to be defined as "art for art's sake" in which art liberates itself from the constraints of political and economic demands, from the "law of others" (*heter-nomos*) by giving itself its own law, the law of form. The sociological condition of possibility of this aesthetic development according to Bourdieu is the oft-neglected fact that "bohemia,"

---

110   Bourdieu completes this displacement by mentioning this process in relation to Weber's work rather than Marx.

111   Bourdieu, *The Rules of Art*, passim.

112   I stress that to consider such constraints as the outside of literature presupposes the position of autonomy, and thus we should be careful not to collapse the category of literature with one of its dominant articulations. To be sure, the field of literary production is indeed dominated by such a definition but we should not reproduce it in our critical studies as Casanova does in hers.

the "society" of producers, is also its own market (a self-reflexive market as in it producers are also consumers). Around the 1880s, this niche market develops into the "subfield of restricted production" in which cultural producers are also the clients, a position set against the "subfield of large-scale production," producing for the general public.[113] Finally, Bourdieu argues that since the 1880s in France, autonomy, understood as independence from external demands, becomes the dominant law of the field, discrediting and excluding any art that depends on external powers or serves a cause.

Let us see now how Casanova modifies and expands Bourdieu's model into the global literary field. Casanova sets up a two-step universal logic of world literary autonomization: in the first step, political power subordinates language and literature to the service of political autonomy and national difference. In this step, autonomy is the objective of the political project itself and literature serves as a means of difference and liberation. So in sixteenth- and seventeenth-century France, the French king seeks autonomy from the church, and in the nineteenth and early twentieth century, European states seek independence and autonomy from imperial and colonial powers, a process that repeats itself with post–World War II postcolonial movements in Asia and Africa. In the second step, autonomy shifts from political power to literature. Individual writers "reverse the polarity of the field"[114] by inventing a literary language that adheres to its own law rather than being subservient to political powers. I note in passing the asymmetry, going unnoticed in Casanova, between the fact that the autonomy of the political is to be made in the social itself, out of social struggles, and the fact that the autonomy of literature is brought about by an act of the mind that can take leave of the social ground as it pleases.

Casanova augments this two-step law with a history of the uneven development of the world literary field. Literary autonomy first developed in France in the course of the nineteenth century. At this moment the literary field, as we saw in Bourdieu, is split between what Casanova calls the heteronomous and autonomous poles. Being the oldest and most endowed with literary capital, the pole of literary autonomy in Paris provides the universal measure of autonomous literature, which quickly becomes the measure of Literature *as such*. This local development serves

---

113 I note in passing what Bourdieu but especially Casanova underplay at this point which is that however "restricted" the market of autonomous producers is, it is a *market* nonetheless to which autonomous writers must submit if they are to exist.

114 Casanova, *The World Republic of Letters*, 193.

as a model for imitation for writers interested in literary autonomy in the rest of the world, especially in newly established states bereft of literary capital. So while the heteronomous pole in such states is comprised of writers who submit their writings to national political causes, the autonomous pole develops when writers look (or literally travel) to Paris and borrow/invent autonomous styles. Eventually, through struggles and symbolic ruptures not following any linear trajectory, each state replicates the original split in France and eventually the world republic of letters is itself split between the autonomous and heteronomous poles.

At first sight this model seems very similar to Bourdieu, keeping as it does with the notion that styles and positions should be understood only relationally, and that autonomy is not an eternal property of literature but one that has a history. It takes Bourdieu's model several steps forward by showing that first, we should understand writers and styles not only internally, in relation to their position within their own national field, but also in relation to the position of their country in the world republic of letters. Second, it allows us to see, justly I believe, the similarities that connect writers from different national traditions by pointing our attention to the structural position they hold within their own countries and vis-à-vis Paris. But when we take a closer look, the models are quite different, a difference that conceals a fundamental elision.

The first obvious difference concerns the manner Casanova conceives of the emergence of "autonomy": while Bourdieu argues that the position of autonomy emerged in France through a series of *dual* negations —of political power and the market—in Casanova, autonomy emerges through a *single* negation of political power only; the position of the "bourgeois" and commercial literature does not make an appearance in Casanova until the 1970s, with neoliberalism. So to give one example, if, according to Bourdieu, Flaubert's style emerges as a negation of the logic of the market on the one hand, and the logic of political art on the other, Joyce's style, according to Casanova, is a negation of two political positions: the symbolist idealism of Yeats, written in English, and national Gaelic literature. While Flaubert's style negates two qualitatively different positions, Joyce's style negates two positions belonging to the same category (politics).

This shift from dual to single negation is only a symptom of a far more important difference. The second alteration in Casanova's study lies in the historicization of the social conditions of the market for literary goods both within Europe (outside of France) and the rest of the world. If in Bourdieu the autonomy of writers such as Baudelaire, Flaubert and others was first enabled by the influx of young people into literary professions, creating a "bohemia" and an anonymous market of cultural goods, no such social account exists in Casanova. She in effect drops the quintessential condition of possibility of literary autonomy, i.e., the social condition that allows for a shift from direct to immanent determination, or to "structural subordination" in Bourdieu's account. In other words, between the nineteenth and and the last third of the twentieth century, the literary fields of the periphery are still determined from the outside, by direct political powers, a situation not dissimilar to the field of literary production in France prior to the nineteenth century. In Casanova, then, aesthetic autonomy is not preconditioned by any social process but is strictly an act of the mind by individual authors who are influenced by Paris.

These two differences point to a central lacuna: by focusing exclusively on the state and political power, Casanova's model not only bypasses the development of capitalism in France and its significance for the historic emergence of the concept of autonomy, it also disregards the differential development of capitalism in Western Europe and the rest of the world in the nineteenth and twentieth century—a difference that produces the unevenness of the world system and therefore the unevenness *within the category of autonomy and its forms.* As my study on Israeli and Palestinian literature shows, the kind of autonomy possible in the periphery—before the neoliberal moment, where capitalist immanent determination is not yet possible precisely because of the binding power of the state—is qualitatively different from the autonomy possible in Western Europe where such development has already occurred. This qualitative difference in social forms is displaced in Casanova into the quantitative categories of literary capital and age.

To elaborate: Casanova's model obfuscates the difference within the category of autonomy, and equally between France and the rest of the world outside Western Europe, by displacing real social difference into the abstract category of international autonomy. To be sure, Casanova does admit the unevenness of the world into her model but she does so via an elaborate displacement of the social world into the literary world where structural inequality is reduced to the "age" of literature, i.e., where quality is reduced to quantity. As of the nineteenth century, Casanova argues, states such as France and England and a few others gained literary advantage because literary autonomy has had a longer history there than in other states that have just recently began accumulating literary capital. States "rich" in literary capital are thus "older," more autonomous and more modern than "poor" states whose literary capital is "young" and thus still heteronomous and non-modern.

Casanova acknowledges, albeit minimally, that there is a correlation between military and monetary power and the ability to accumulate literary capital; that is, she acknowledges the correlation between real social conditions and the possibility of autonomy, but she also argues that writers from the periphery, exposed to literature deemed autonomous, whether French or otherwise, can somehow "accelerate" the "age" of their states and bring them into "modernity" by emulating or inventing styles that are in line with Paris's literary modernity. Casanova calls this "literary alchemy" but she does not consider what gets lost in this literary transmutation.

While autonomy in France, as Bourdieu argues, is conditioned by the development of certain social conditions, in the rest of the world, as Casanova argues, it is either a matter of appropriation of styles or an affiliation with a category of Literature as such that occurs somehow independently of the social conditions of possibility of autonomy in these states. In Casanova, the shift from France to the rest of the world is actually a conceptual shift from diachronic development, grounded in social conditions, to a synchronic map, based on the dissemination of styles that lost touch with their ground. At this moment, Casanova's sociological history is transformed into literary history, moving as it is in a pure field of literary styles. Thus, writers in "impoverished" states, including Juan Benet, Octavio Paz, Rubén Darío, Georg Brandes and Danilo Kiš, and many others make literary autonomy possible in their respective states by simply importing French (and American) styles and techniques. All of them are thus aggregated into the "international pole" of literary autonomy that does not distinguish adequately between autonomy on the periphery and autonomy in Western Europe.

What truly differentiates the periphery from Western Europe is not the "age" of literary capital but the structural difference in the field of literary production, which in itself is a symptom of capitalist social relations not reaching the point of immanent determination. One can accelerate literary time no more than one can accelerate physical time; the "alchemy"—what I call abstraction—performed in such works on the periphery tries to invent autonomy on the level of language that has yet to occur in the real and for this reason it carries into its form this impossibility, this limit. If Moretti's formalism is corrected by Casanova's crucial emphasis on autonomy and freedom as the objectives of literary innovation, then we can also say that Moretti's attentiveness to the structure of capital serves as a correction to Casanova, one that reveals the qualitative difference between peripheral and core modernisms.

By shifting back from the quantity of literary "age" to the quality of social form as a marker of difference between core and periphery, we discover two limits in Casanova's model. First, if we follow Casanova's model the history of the world would end in the nineteenth century while the history of literary fields, everywhere, ends with the invention of the category of autonomy. It is no accident that postmodernity on the one hand and neoliberalism on the other are not considered legitimate phases of development but aberrations, developments that neither Casanova and Bourdieu's models can account for adequately. Let us look at one paradigmatic formulation in Casanova:

> As a consequence of the Herderian revolution, then, international literary space has come to be structured and lastingly so, according to the age and volume of its constituent literary resources and the relative degree of autonomy enjoyed by each national space. World literary space is now organized in terms of the opposition between, on the one hand, an autonomous pole, composed of those spaces that are most endowed in literary resources, which serves as a model and a recourse for writers claiming a position of independence in newly formed spaces . . . and on the other, a heteronomous pole composed of relatively deprived literary spaces at an early stage of development that are dependent on political—typically national authorities.[115]

This is to say that for Casanova, since the nineteenth century, political autonomy has arrived first, in the form of the nation; aesthetic autonomy then follows in opposition to it. In other words, national autonomy is a historical event happening *first and once*. From that point on, the political form is assumed to be constant and history is displaced onto the axis of aesthetic autonomy that each national field achieves. This means that Casanova is historicizing only the axis of aesthetic development, leaving unattended the change to the political form itself.

I propose to re-insert history into the axis of political autonomy and see that with neoliberal globalization, especially in the periphery, we have a second and different moment of autonomization. It does not involve the autonomy of the literary field from the political pole, but of civil society from the state, the private from the public, which has

---

115 Casanova, *The World Republic of Letters*, 108.

dramatic implications for literary production. It is an autonomy occurring within the *political axis itself*. If we again conceptualize the political form and aesthetic production as "ground" and "figure," it will become clear that by leaving the "ground" unattended, Casanova historicizes changes in the "figure" only, while neoliberal globalization means that the very "ground" is changing under the figure. Today, the most significant change in Israel, Palestine and other states undergoing similar neoliberal changes is not the invention/borrowing of modernist styles— this has happened since the 1960s—but the change in the conditions under which literary production (and hence literary imagination) is made possible. To stress this point, Casanova considers Beckett's autonomous and abstract style as the "end point" of the aesthetic development of the Irish field. Beckett's earliest novel was published in 1938.[116] What are we to make of the history of Irish literature since then? Is it simply a series of variations on autonomy? Casanova does admit historical events into her model—wars, for example, or the rise of authoritarian regimes that have the capacity to change the arrangement of positions—but she is silent over less-obvious changes in forms of social life. It will be accurate to say that Casanova is working with a concept of eventmental history, while neglecting long-term or structural changes. In the absence of such considerations, we discover that a sociological study like Casanova's is ultimately a taxonomic science, helping us slot this or that style in the categories of "heteronomy" or "autonomy."

Second, similar to Moretti, Casanova's "scientific" approach can result in taxonomy because it involves a preliminary amputation that occurs before the study has begun: this Freudian "foreclosure" is the exclusion of the *relation between the literary text and the real*, which is substituted by the synchronic relation between literary texts and positions. But this exclusion of the real is precisely the condition of possibility of autonomy. While Bourdieu is more critical of autonomy, Casanova replicates it uncritically in her own study, which sides with autonomous writers.[117] Thus this inquiry seeks to bring back the text's relation to the real, what I call causes or conditions, and examine the process by which autonomy is accomplished by a process of abstraction or concealment. This abstraction works in a differential manner in the core and in the periphery: in the core such abstraction has already taken place in social life and thus the literary artwork is autonomous by default, while in the periphery,

---

116   Ibid., 318.

117   For a brief elaboration of this point see Jonathan Arac, "Literary History in a Global Age," *New Literary History* 39.3 (Summer 2008): 747–60, but see especially, 752.

where, until the neoliberal moment, the literary artwork is heteronomous, autonomy is accomplished as an act of language, i.e., through a
radical abstraction of the real as in Beckett and Kafka.

I argue that what needs attention is the way that literary abstraction
works within literary worlds, especially modernist ones. Although it is
somewhat overlooked in studies of world literature, abstraction is in fact
at the very heart of these debates. For example, David Damrosch's account
of the qualities that made P. G. Wodehouse's novels into world literature
include Wodehouse's "abstraction from reality," where realist description
is turned more and more into a system of conventions that allows infinite
variations.[118] Damrosch further ties between stylistic abstraction and the
fact that Wodehouse, due to his constant travels, became an outsider
in both England and the United States, a condition that is common to
many other modernists including Kafka, Joyce, Beckett, and Nabokov.
Damrosch argues that abstraction is a major technique that enables circulation and "literarization," as Pascale Casanova would put it, though
he does not develop the argument further.

Let us take another step and see how "abstraction," although unstated,
underlies much of Damrosch's understanding of world literature, especially in its modernist idiom.

> In the twentieth century . . . a variety of writers broke with the norms of
> realism and began to set their stories in mysterious, emblematic locales.
> Franz Kafka's Castle and penal colony, Jorge Luis Borges's circular ruins,
> and the stark landscapes of Samuel Beckett's plays could really be set
> anywhere, or at least in any country peopled with arbitrary authorities
> (Kafka), melancholy linguists (Borges), and senior citizens in garbage
> cans (Beckett). Authors anywhere might choose this approach, but it
> is notable that the three writers just named were all born in peripheral
> cities (Prague, Buenos Aires, Dublin) traditionally overshadowed by the
> imperial powers that had long dominated their countries. All three chose
> to move beyond a provincialism they found stultifying.[119]

By suggesting that Beckett, Borges and Kafka's novels and stories could
take place "anywhere," Damrosch is here generalizing the meaning of
abstraction without necessarily calling it that. He takes another step,
however, by connecting aesthetic abstraction to the position of the

---

118   Damrosch, *What Is World Literature?*, 217.
119   David Damrosch, *How to Read World Literature* (Oxford: Blackwell, 2009),
108.

periphery and domination in the world system, an argument not dissimilar to that made by Casanova in her own account. Both Damrosch and Casanova identify aesthetic abstraction, then, with a desire for freedom from political powers, or in Casanova's terms, a desire for (aesthetic and political) autonomy. However, what Damrosch accentuates and Casanova underplays is that such a technique goes hand in hand with a gesture of epistemological occlusion, i.e., the fact that these stories transform the social into "mysterious" settings.[120]

I note that the co-existence of abstraction on the level of form and mystery on the level of content is not accidental, and in fact abstraction and mystery are two faces of the same phenomenon: both revolve around a gesture of concealment not so much of origin per se—i.e., of local detail—but of historical conditions. The important point here is to see that such concealment is precisely the defining characteristic of the philosophical principle of the "aesthetic" we saw in Kant and Adorno. In other words, these peripheral works achieve autonomy by projecting inward the principle of the aesthetic, by thematizing it and creating a world whose own causes are occluded. In this way, as Casanova argues, peripheral writers reject the demand, made by national political powers, to serve an "external" function and in this gesture of refusal gain their autonomy. What is missing in Casanova, and makes up Adorno's central problematic, however, is that such a gesture of refusal always comes with a price, what Adorno calls hermeticism, and I rewrite here as abstraction: a technique that occludes the causes of the social world and as such hinders our critical understanding of it. To be sure, Casanova is aware of the epistemological consequences of autonomy. She argues indeed that the process of autonomization "tends also to obscure the political origins of literature," leading to the belief in a concept of literature unburdened by history.[121] However, since she affirms and valorizes literary autonomy, this critique is not directed at writers whose imaginary worlds obscure their relationship to history, but rather at scholars and other literary agents who truly believe that literature exists in its own unique time and thus prevent us from seeing the sociological origin of autonomy. Casanova's study, as a sociological account, is not interested so much in the relation between the imaginary world and the real world, but only in the

---

120　Casanova makes a similar passing remark on the connection between aesthetic freedom and mystery when she mentions that Juan Benet's literariness is bound up with the production of "enigmatic" worlds. Casanova, *The World Republic of Letters*, 335.

121　Ibid., 86.

historical genesis of autonomy as a social practice. She also recognizes another site in which literature is cut off from its locale, which is the process of reception in the autonomous spaces that "denationalizes" and "depoliticizes" writers from the periphery as a condition of entry into the pantheon of Literature. What Casanova misses, however, is that the same obfuscation operates in the imaginary worlds themselves.

Now, if we stay with Casanova's axis of aesthetic development we might assume that such aesthetic abstraction on the periphery needs to persist to achieve recognition in the world republic of letters. But if we shift to the political axis and acknowledge the historical changes that come with neoliberal privatization, we will see that private life itself has become autonomous from the political, has turned purpose-less, such that the raw materials of the literary artwork are now abstract by default, and the concept of literature has lost its heteronomous character. Thus, if in the 1960s Koren and Oz in Israel and Kanafani in Palestine had to turn to abstract and mysterious styles (read: modernism) to achieve autonomy, now, since the 1990s, Israeli and Palestinian literary worlds are released by default from their political purpose such that there is no need to erase locality, and realism too can very well serve as a technique of "universalization." At this moment, Israeli and Palestinian literature, together with other peripheral literature, become what I call global literature, a transformation I discuss in more detail in the Conclusion.

1

Heteronomy, Inequality, and the Poetics of Making: Israeli Literature of the Statist Period 1940–1985

1.

Beginning *in medias res*, we arrive in Mandatory Palestine in the early 1940s, at the moment when Zionism, reaching the peak of its political ambitions, is on the verge of establishing a sovereign state and turning Hebrew literature into a literature of a sovereign people henceforth called "Israeli." That we begin in the 1940s and not squarely in 1948, the year Israel was established, has to do with the fact that at this point the historical conditions that will underlie literary production until the 1980s are already in place, distinguishing this period from those before and those after it. These conditions already emerged in the early 1930s when the leading Zionist labor party, Mapai,[1] was able to establish and control a centralized social structure that fuses together political and economic organization, state and civil society, private and public spheres. As we shall have occasion to see, this statist structure, far from being inertly reflected in literary form, will act as a "limit" or condition of possibility from which diverse and sometimes opposing imaginary worlds will emerge as political responses.

---

1 The acronym means Mifleget Po'ale 'Erez Yisra'el (The Party of the Laborers of the Land of Israel), which later became Mifleget Ha-'avoda (The Labor Party). MAPAI won the majority of seats in the most important labor institution (Histadrut) in 1933 and became the leading political force in the pre- and post-state period until it was ousted from power by Likud in 1977.

In contrast to current literary studies that read Hebrew literature in light of the general ideological tenets of Zionist nationalism, this inquiry emphasizes specific historical conditions underlying social and cultural life in Israel.[2] This shift in explanatory grounds stems from the fact that "Zionist ideology" is an abstract construct that is simply not subtle enough for the task of explaining and interpreting literary form let alone historical developments in Israel and Palestine. I already noted that an appeal to Zionist ideology will be hard-pressed to explain the disjunction between, on the one hand, the persistence of a robust Zionist nationalism, and, on the other, the complete transformation of cultural production in Israel since the mid-1980s. The absence of historical perspective in contemporary studies is even more damaging when we consider their central concern—the separation of Arabs and Jews—a moral condemnation turned into a humanist and multicultural research program that pushes the literary critic to work with a synchronous model, distinguishing between those writers and texts that support or at least presuppose this separation as legitimate, and other writers and texts that criticize it and imagine a more multicultural, hybrid and bi-national coexistence.[3] The limitations of such a conception become apparent when we consider, first, that the separation of Arab and Jew will be as true in 1914 as it is in 2014, which is to say that it is a static conception that explains very little about the historical specificity of Zionism over time and the way it conditions literary forms and their political import. Second, the binary division of the literary field into a Zionist position on the one hand and non-Zionist position on the other results in a peculiar asymmetry. If Zionist texts are seriously read at all, the merit of the reading rests either on demonstrating how Zionist ideology is reflected in the literary text, or on uncovering the gap between Zionist ideology and colonial violence. Conversely, when we shift to non-Zionist texts, the latter are

---

2   The postcolonial/post-Zionist position is today the central position in liberal academic circles in Israel and the US. Its main statements regarding literature can be assessed in the studies of Hannan Hever, *Producing the Modern Hebrew Canon: Nation Building and Minority Discourse* (New York: New York University Press, 2002), but see also the enlarged Hebrew edition of the book, *Ha-sipur veha-le'om* (Tel Aviv: Resling, 2007); Hannan Hever, Yehouda Shenhav and Pnina Motzafi-Haller (eds.) *Mizrahim be-yisra'el, 'iyun bikorti mehudash* (Yerushalayim: Ha-kibuz ha-me'uhad/Van Lir, 2002); Hannan Hever, "Sofer yehudi-'aravi." In Shimon Ballas, *Tel-Aviv Mizrah—Trilogya.* (Tel Aviv: Ha-kibuz ha-me'uhad, 2003), 517–25; Gil Hochberg, *In Spite of Partition: Jews, Arabs, and the Limits of Separatist Imagination* (Princeton: Princeton University Press, 2007); Lital Levy, *Poetic Trespass: Writing between Hebrew and Arabic in Israel/Palestine* (Princeton: Princeton University Press, 2014).

3   This is a widespread tendency, but see especially Hever, Hochberg and Levy in footnote 2.

usually presented as pure presence, having no unconscious of their own, no *non-dit* arranging their own disavowals and lacunas. Arguing that a text resists Zionist separatist ideology without spelling out the position from which this resistance springs to life, how it conditions its form, or what it can (and can't) think politically, collapses the distance between critic and text and forfeits the critical value such a method claims to have. The latter approach, dubbed literary postcolonial or post-Zionist studies, developed in Israel and the US beginning in the late 1980s. In its practice, critics subordinate Hebrew literature and literary criticism to a liberal and moral stance that privileges the Israeli-Palestinian conflict and reduces literature to a container of ideology, and Zionism to nationalism. Thus, however timely, the position defining Zionism solely as a separatist ideology is a narrow and eventually uncritical conception of what I suggest understanding more broadly, and more subtly, as a social form that evolves over time and acts as a historical "limit." What follows is a short analysis of the social form of the first period and especially of its key feature, the construction of state autonomy, a condition that will help us then read several literary texts and explain the different political responses they encode.

2.

Emerging towards the end of the nineteenth century as a response to both anti-Semitism and economic crises in the Russian Empire and eastern Europe, Zionism was a politically heterogeneous national movement seeking a solution to the Jewish question. The attempt of eighteenth- and nineteenth-century European Jews to move out of their "traditional" religious communities and integrate as equals into their respective European civil societies ending in failure, Zionist Jews began colonizing Ottoman Palestine as of 1882 with the intent of making it their national home. As one Zionist leader put it, as early as 1904, the aim was "to establish autonomous Jewish community," or, more specifically "a Jewish state."[4] How such autonomy was accomplished, how it made the Zionist entity and then Israeli life in this period different from Western Europe, and finally, how it conditioned aesthetic autonomy and literary form, will be our immediate objects here.

---

4   Menachem Ussishkin, 1904. Quoted in Gershon Shafir, *Land, Labor and the Origins of the Israeli-Palestinian Conflict 1882–1914*. Second Edition (Berkeley: University of California Press, 1996), 42.

Critical historians divide the pre-state period between 1882 and 1948 into several waves of colonization (in Zionist parlance these are called *'Aliyot* or immigration ascents). In this period, we observe a general shift of political solutions moving from heterogeneity to homogeneity, where one political program, that of labor-Zionism, won over others. Accordingly, we will comment briefly on labor-Zionism during its formative moment in the second wave, 1904–1914. For, according to Gershon Shafir's seminal socio-historical study, in this period the future statist structure of Israel was established, setting the collision course for the 1948 war that culminated in the establishment of the Israeli state and the Palestinian refugee problem.[5]

Shafir's detailed study of the period between 1904 and 1914 rejects one of the principle myths of Zionist history, namely, that the collectivist social forms established by labor-Zionism were not a matter of imported socialist ideas and values from eastern Europe, but rather an outcome of the harsh reality of the labor and land markets in Palestine in the beginning of the twentieth century. Arriving in Palestine with the hope of working in the agricultural sector, the second-wave colonizers soon discovered that the landowning Jewish farmers of the first wave, contrary to their "national duty," refused to hire Jewish workers on their farms as they were under-skilled in comparison to Palestinian workers and demanded higher wages.[6] As Shafir explains, faced with a crisis of employment that threatened the viability of its political project, labor-Zionism begins to supplant the individual Jewish farmers and to alter the divisions within the labor market.[7] This conflict indicates first that the Zionist separatist structure evolved also out of *internal* Jewish conflict. Second, we can see that the encounter was not between Jews and Arabs *in general*, but rather a specific encounter between Jewish and Arab workers who met each other through the mediation of a capitalist labor market. According to Shafir, this crisis led labor-Zionism to pursue two strategies that would set the social form of the Jewish polity to come: First, labor-Zionism raised capital through the World Zionist Organization for the purpose of purchasing land and establishing Jewish-only collectivist settlements (*kibbutzim*). These efficiently secured the livelihood of the workers by subsidies that shielded them from the realities of the labor market. Second, labor-Zionism sought to secure work for Jewish

---

5   Ibid.
6   Ibid., 58, my emphasis. See also Yonatan Shapira's description of this moment, *Ha-demokratyah be-yisra'el* (Ramat Gan: Masadah, 1977), 52.
7   Shafir, *Land, Labor*, 45–90; Shapira, *Ha-demokratya be-yisra'el*, 52.

agricultural workers by excluding Palestinians as much as possible from the Jewish labor market and creating a de facto split labor market. The separation and eventual control of the Jewish labor market, the purchase of land, the mobilization of Jewish capital from Europe and elsewhere, and the establishment of unique labor institutions,[8] led over time to the centralization and collectivization of the conditions of Zionist life and to their almost exclusive control by the dominant labor party, Aḥdut ha-'avoda (which, uniting with another party, Ha-po'el ha-ẓa'ir, became Mapai in 1930). According to Shafir, the statist structure, in which it is the state rather than the market that organizes all public resources, was deemed necessary given the relative scarcity of Zionist resources (money and military power) and the demographic superiority of the Palestinian population.

Before moving on, it is important to acknowledge the place of the bourgeoisie which did not necessarily share the state-making interests of Mapai. From various reasons, this urban petty bourgeoisie, which grew significantly during the fourth wave of colonization starting in 1924 and eventually comprised most of the economy in Israel, was not taken over by Mapai. However, it was controlled from the outside through the allocation of credit.[9] Thus, contrary to "advanced" liberal-capitalist states in which land, labor and capital are in private hands, in the Zionist social form of the first period they were controlled by political parties and then, after 1948, officially by the state. Michael Shalev effectively summarizes this period as follows:

> The privileged position characteristically enjoyed by the bourgeoisie in Western societies is not only the product of its technical indispensability to the economic fortunes of society as a whole, but also reflects capital's hegemony at the level of ideas and consciousness. However, in the new-born state of Israel by far the strongest political force in society was the labour movement, which espoused a blend of labourist and statist ideologies. Moreover, it was the state rather than capital which was most readily identifiable with the collectivity's most urgent and

---

8   The central economico-political institution established at this period was the General Organization of Workers in the Land of Israel (*Histadrut ha-'Ovdim*). It was a workers' union, an owner of economic institutions, and a provider of social services such as health care, loans and pensions. The different Jewish parties in Mandatory Palestine and later in Israel sent representatives to this organization but it was effectively controlled by Mapai as of 1933.

9   Gershon Shafir and Yoav Peled (eds.) *The New Israel: Peacemaking and Liberalization* (Boulder: Westview Press, 2000), 8.

universal interests. The government, the bureaucracy, and the military had accepted responsibility for an extremely broad and fateful agenda—populating and defending territory in the face of external hostility, attracting and absorbing masses of immigrants, and so forth . . . . To this must be added a cohesive political party apparatus [Mapai] in control of all of the society's key institutions, with little to no obligation to private capital . . . and with its own internal networks of élite recruitment and interchange.[10]

This structure, in which capital and the private sphere are tethered to the project of state-making, points to several key differences between Western Europe and Israel in the first period which I now turn to elaborate.

I have mentioned that the historical marker of capitalism as a new form of social relations hinges on the emergence of abstract labor. This is the moment when work no longer receives its meaning from, or is embedded in, what Postone calls "overt social relations," and becomes abstract labor power that underlies social relations. This process, as we have seen, occurred alongside the rearticulation of the political and private spheres in which overt political relations are lifted from civil society and deposited in the state proper. Further, the abstraction of overt social relations, the previous anchor of a naturalized and theological order of inequality, allows for abstract social equivalence that serves as the condition of possibility for the democratic notion of civil equivalence.

It might already be clear that by plunging its political roots into civil society, labor-Zionism invests social relations with an overt political content. By subordinating public resources to the project of state-making, labor-Zionism fuses the private and public spheres, and, although it establishes a democracy underlined by formal civic equivalence, relations of inequality, because embedded in direct political relations, persist as constitutive relations in Israeli society. Thus, unlike postcolonial critics who stress the European imaginary of Zionism, the desire to join the "civilized" "cultured" nations, the real structure of Israeli statism is markedly different than capitalist Western Europe. It is this structural difference that can explain why, between the 1940s and the 1980s, despite imaging itself as Western, Israeli culture failed to "pass" as European.

---

10   Michael Shalev, *Labour and the Political Economy in Israel* (Oxford: Oxford University Press, 1992), 293–4. It is important to note that this argument is not new or limited to positions critical of Zionism. See for example Amitai Etzioni, *Studies in Social Change* (New York: Holt, Rinehart and Winston, 1966), 185.

And, conversely, why these days, due to neoliberal transformations that make Israeli social life more private and hence more like the US and Europe, artworks produced by Israelis can become as "universal" as any American or European ones. This remarkable transformation in the value of Israeli culture in the world, and more specifically in the position of Israeli literature within world literature, goes unattended by contemporary scholarship focused on the category of nationalism alone.

It is important that we grasp the relation of the statist project to its "others": the statist project is not simply one force among others. Not only is it the most dominant political program whose interests are encoded in the law, it also appears in the world as a form of universality, a measure with which all other political programs are either recognized or not. In addition to subordinating or repressing all other political projects, this universality conditions or limits all other political claims. Hegel's concept of "limit" can help us grasp this condition.[11] As we saw previously, for Hegel a "limit" is not a border the subject confronts outside itself (external limit; quantity), but it is that preliminary condition that makes the subject what it is (internal limit; quality). Following Hegel, I claim that not only those writers who endorse the statist project are conditioned by its concept of collective autonomy and freedom, but that the statist state, as a historical limit, inheres in those writers that resist it as well. The reason this is so stems from the fact that in this period the state controls the conditions of possibility of society and does not allow any other political project to establish its law. To wit, the literary themes of Palestinian literature are markedly different than those in Israel, especially after 1960, and this is because only Palestinian writers directly resist the Israeli state rather than presuppose it.

The misconception of contemporary Hebrew literary studies is that they consider Zionism as what Hegel would call an "external" limit—as an ideology or even literary form—that non-Zionist works simply transgress or surpass. In their account, such writers would be self-grounding, or self-legislating, conditioned by no pre-existing social condition, which is another way of saying that they are abstract or ideal. This fallacy is not limited to the critics alone. Imagining a self-legislating world/character, a poetic tendency not too different from Kant's concept of the aesthetic/reflective judgment, was the manner writers themselves attempted to think freedom and autonomy in a period that denied it.

---

11   See also my earlier discussion of Hegel's concept of limit on pp. 11–12.

3.

How does the statist structure condition the preliminary semantic materials of the literary artwork? Here we need to translate the historical social form into, conceptual and poetic terms. The deepest meaning of the statist structure concerns the fact that the autonomy of the state is a collective object *to be made*. What I call "state-making" is a collective act into the conditions that provide its existence. In a manner of speaking, it is a self-referential act because by acting collectively on such constitutive conditions the collective itself is made possible. It is this social making that aspires to subordinate all spheres to its concept of finality or end, making the individual heteronomous. If statism could be put in linguistic terms it would take a conditional modality: Not until the collective is free can the individual be free. Hence, the category of the "political" (state) subordinates the "personal" category (kinship), and especially the body. The key category of state-making is antagonism, through which the conditions of possibility of the community are made. This antagonism is always in the open and hence makes explicit the causes of the self and the community. State-making generates national, social Time— itself an object of making—and it accordingly localizes, particularizes or otherwise completely represses any other times and histories. Here is how Shula Keshet discusses the culture of the kibbutz in the 1930s, the cornerstone of Zionist state-making efforts:

> The new [land] was all man-made. The intensive work performed by the pioneers expropriated the "naturalness" of the geographic terrain and emphasized the constructive act, that is, the human labor invested in nature.[12]

To be sure, like many such Zionist accounts, the colonial project disavows the existence of Arab villages and considers the land "virginal." Yet, this disavowal does not alter the fact that Zionist work made itself by transforming nature and pre-existing social relations.

Given that the state is rooted in civil society it also lends its relation of generality, investing work, land, capital and the body itself with a spiritual, at times even sacred, meaning, providing each particular instance

---

12   Shula Keshet, "'ketav hitkashrut hamur l-Erets-Yisraʾel'. Tarbut ha-kibutz: The Formative Years." *'Iyunim be-ḥeker ha-tarbut* 1 (2012): 189. The same conception appears also in the literature of the early 1930s and is expressed explicitly: "We create life with our own hands. Do you have a greater creator than that? Do you have a more sublime creation?" Aharon Ever Ha-Deni, *Ẕerif ha-ʿeẕ*, 101.

of society with a universal or symbolic meaning. The body in the statist period is then always spiritualized, always-already claimed by the state and its history, and thus even when the body deteriorates and dies, its meaning still "lives on" in the collective spirit.[13] The famous Zionist virility coupled with a return to the land is then not simply a return to the body (going against the *luftgescheft*, the "airy" business of Jewish peddlers and merchants in Europe), but an investing of the body with a new kind of generality and universality underlined by sovereignty. A Zionist body is never concrete, and work is never limited to its object—they both stand in for a universal, abstract meaning. This condition serves as the basis for the default allegorical mode of Israeli literature in the first period. Here the signifier is always subordinated to the master signified. Finally, the field of literary production in this period is heteronomous: as Casanova would say, the field is conditioned by political power and the social relations it generates. The field is divided accordingly between those writers who endorse the statist project (what I call statist writers) and those who try to resist by imagining other forms of autonomy and freedom (mainly humanist and liberal writers). But here, unlike in Casanova, such attempts would ultimately fail precisely because the historical conditions for such a liberal stance are not yet possible.

4.

In the 1940 and 1950s, the dominant literary form was what I call the "poetics of making" and it was practiced by those writers I designate as statist.[14] Statist novels of making, as I have mentioned, had appeared in

---

13   The theme of the "living dead" (*ha-met ha-ḥay*), in which the spirit of the dead lives on and transcends material decay played an important role in the poetry published just before and around the 1948 war, especially in Nathan Alterman's well-known 1947 poem "Magash ha-kesef" (The Silver Platter) and Hayyim Guri's 1949 poem "Hineh mutalot gufotenu" (Here Lie Our Bodies). In these poems the dead, who sacrificed or are about to sacrifice their lives in war for the nation, address the reader to explain the national significance of their death. It is important to acknowledge however that the transcendence of the individual body by the national project of making was already present in the early 1930s. See for example the novel by Aharon Ever Ha-Deni, *Zerif ha-'eẓ*, 11. Poets, especially women, critical of this national rhetoric, expressed their criticism by breaking the subsumption of the body by the national spirit, emphasizing the flesh and blocking its redemption by a greater spiritual meaning. I elaborate on such aesthetic techniques below. For a discussion of this aesthetic technique by women writers, see Hannan Hever, "Shirat ha-guf ha-le'umi: Nashim meshorerot be-milḥemet ha-shiḥrur," *Te'orya u-vikoret* 7 (1995): 99–123.

14   For examples of statist writers, see footnote 61, page 33.

the early 1930s, but they were not the dominant style. As Gershon Shaked himself argues, the style of the 1940s and the 1950s, attributed to the so-called "Palmach Generation," is not original or new, but rather continues the style that emerged in the 1930s.[15]

In its most elemental form, the imaginary world in such novels is constructed around a constitutive antagonism cast in terms of absolute difference through which the fate of the characters will be determined. The reason for the antagonism stems from the inequality between the sides that cannot find a mediary third term, or a common measure. The unique aspect of the statist novels of the 1940s and the 1950s is that in them the state itself is made during the time of the novel usually through war or settlement. Here "making" is a life-and-death encounter which subordinates all other literary materials to its unfolding.

One way to translate "state-making" into literary terms is to see that social making resembles *poiesis*. At the heart of both acts, social and poetic, stands a concern with universality. State-making is an antagonistic intervention into conditions of possibility through which the dominant group manages to impose its particular form of life as universal, while *poiesis*, as Aristotle argues, is an imaginary act of selection and combination of materials for the purpose of making visible a universal truth. We need to look closer at Aristotle's conception of universality, however, and alter it to our purposes. As is well known, in the *Poetics* Aristotle notes that the pleasure we derive from tragedy is inherent in the fact that when we watch this or that (particular) character we learn a more general (universal) truth. However, Aristotle is also known for being very specific about the meaning of universality, and the way the poet should bring it about. The heart of the matter lies in the relation between nomination and time, discursivity and temporality. Aristotle discourages his poet from writing character-revealing *speeches*, that is, revealing the character in conceptual language, and instead argues that the truth of the character, its name and identity, should be revealed in necessary *acts*. Similarly, Aristotle tells us that the heart of tragedy should be in the mimesis of action, given in necessary and meaningful events. In other words, the events (unfolding of time through necessity) reveal the true name of the character (nomination).

Using Aristotle for my discussion here, I would like to affect a displacement and claim that the *poiesis* of state-making is concerned less

---

15   See Gershon Shaked, *Ha-siporet ha-'ivrit 1880–1980*, Vol. III (Yerushalayimm: Keter, 1993), 216, 223. The logic behind this claim is that the transition from Europe to Palestine and the establishment of a new Hebrew social life was completed by the 1930s.

with the name of the characters, and more with the name of the state itself. In other words, if in Greek tragedy we are made privy to the transformations of Antigone or Oedipus through their acts, in statist literature what is put on display is the making of the state itself, its universality. The "character," as it were, is the state itself or its conditions of possibility. This can go a long way toward explaining the usual complaint made by critics that characters in statist literature are static, especially in writers such as S. Yizhar.[16] This is most definitely true, but only because the critics' eyes are trained at the wrong object. It is not that temporal transformation is absent; it has been moved to the axis of the state, which through antagonistic events becomes what it is. This does not mean that statist novels cannot depict characterological change, but rather that many of them did not.

Now, the statist poetics of "making," in which the novelistic world is centered around a constitutive antagonism, dominated the literary field only between the 1940s and the mid-1950s. During the mid-1950s and the 1960s, a period in which writers tried to imagine a different concept of autonomy, two important developments took place. The first is the emergence of a poetics of what can be called "iconoclastic shattering" in which the values, ideals and goals of Zionism are rejected.[17] In the second, we see what I call split imaginary worlds. We still have the poetics of "making" in which inequality reigns, but it is rivaled by the poetics of "reading" or "textuality," akin to Kant's concept of the Aesthetic, in which equivalence is imagined.[18] This poetics, advancing humanist or liberal ideology, opposes or negates the poetics of statist "making," especially by substituting its developmental time with synchronous time, or, in Aristotle's terms, replacing the necessary "act" with figures of reflection or thought.[19] If in the statist worlds the causes and conditions of the world are on display, in the liberal or humanist worlds these causes are concealed, an aesthetic gesture that brings about

---

16   See, for example, Dan Miron, "Introduction." In S. Yizhar, *Midnight Convoy and Other Stories,* translated by Reuven Ben-Yosef (New Milford: Toby Press, 2007), ix-iv.

17   The most obvious works here are those of A. B. Yehoshua, *Mot ha-zaken* (Tel Aviv: Ha-kibuẓ ha-me'uḥad, 1962), and Amos Oz, *'Arẓot ha-tan* (Tel Aviv: 'Agudat ha-sofrim be-yisra'el le-yad hoẓa'at masadah, 1965).

18   For examples of this mode of writing, see footnote 68, page 35.

19   This tendency is upended in the literature of the 1980s which returns to the act, although it is no longer constitutive of the world itself. Dan Miron notices this change in the 1980s, without, however, offering an explanation as to why this happens, or comparing between the "act" in the literature of the 1940s and 1950s and that of the 1980s. See Dan Miron, *Pinkas patuaḥ: siḥot 'al ha-siporet be-tashlaḥ* (Merḥavyah: Sifriyat po'alim, 1979). See especially the discussion of Yitzhak Ben Ner and the concluding discussion.

the (imaginary) freedom of the characters but also creates a mysterious world whose cause and reason are absent and consequently become the implicit object of a search. If in statist worlds the world and the characters are made through acting, in the liberal and humanist one, the world is ready-made and characters are involved in a search for self-recognition, usually via an encounter with a violent political act, rather than being a constituent agent of it. To put it another way, since the statist project, in which the public sphere dominated the private one, blocked any other political alternative, the only way out was by imagining a negative project in which literary works broke or split the bond between the individual and the collective, the private and the public, body and spirit, signifier and signified. This aesthetico-political technique explains both the modernist aesthetics of Israeli literature in the 1960s and the 1970s as well as its affinity with (and its difference from) European modernism, or what Pascale Casanova calls the international autonomous pole of the republic of letters and Franco Moretti identifies as the aesthetics of "core" states.

5.

Let us now look at four examples of varying ideological stances: Yonat and Alexander Sened's 1953 *A Land without Shadow* (*Adama lelo zel*). S. Yizhar's 1949 *Midnight Convoy* (*Shayara shel ḥazot*). Yeshayahu Koren's 1967 *Funeral at Noon* (*Levaya ba-zohorayim*), and Ronit Matalon's 1981 "Wedding at the Hair Salon" ("*Ḥatuna ba-mispara*").

Moving from the simple to the complex, the first novel by the Seneds will serve as an example of a statist novel, in which we see the most explicit example for the poetics of "making." The second, by Yizhar, will shift us to a humanist stance in which the world is split between nature and politics, while the third and fourth by Koren and Matalon will allow us to examine the implications of the liberal stance in a statist world, one posted from an Ashkenazi position, the other from a Mizrahi point of view.

Although mostly unknown today, Yonat and Alexander Sened's *A Land without Shadow* was an important Zionist-socialist novel at the time of its publication.[20] Despite the fact that it is in full accordance

---

20   Yonat and Alexender Sened, *Adama lelo zel* (Tel Aviv: Ha-kibuẓ ha-me'uḥad, 1953).

with Zionist ideology, the novel offers in fact one of the most realist renderings of the encounters, through the 1940s, among Zionists, the Bedouins of the south of Palestine (the Negev) and officials of the British Mandate.[21] By "realist" I do not mean the degree of the verisimilitude of the linguistic register or the roundness of the characters, for the first is elevated and the second idealized, but rather that the Seneds depict Zionism through its conditions of possibility, i.e., control over resources through a struggle with the local community and the law.

A *Land without Shadow* tells the story of the establishment of Eilata, an imaginary settlement in the south of Palestine, in July 1943.[22] The novel opens with the departure of the settlers from a more-established settlement and the initial encounter with Bedouins (mostly landowners) and British officials. After presenting the Bedouins with title deeds to the land, which we understand were acquired before the story begins, the novel moves to sketch the efforts of the settlers to secure water resources and other bare necessities. "People will have to get to know the conditions of the place, the quality of the land, the climate, its fauna and flora, and seek out solutions for water supply, which is the most important."[23] In a series of anecdotes, the novel continues to describe the daily obstacles and challenges of the settlements and, as it does so, the characters reveal their different attitudes towards an array of issues, attitudes that remain quite constant and unchanging. The novel's realist energies are then spent not so much on the characters as on the creation of the settlement itself: on the one hand we follow the changes made to prepare the landscape for large-scale habitation, and on the other we are made aware of the evolving political relationships with the Bedouin landowners, the Zionist central administration, and British officials. The settlers learn how to deal with the Bedouins, i.e., how to appear both threatening and friendly to make sure they do not interfere. They also learn to imitate the Bedouins' ways of life when it is most profitable to them. Similarly, the relationship with the Zionist central administration is also in constant tension. With desert conditions making habitation so difficult, the central governing body prefers to restrict the settlement to a small-scale reconnaissance and research post, with no more than eight to twelve individuals, while the leaders of Eilata demand the establishment of a

---

21   As I mention in the Introduction, we should not confuse political ideology with historical insight. Writers can support the Zionist project and yet depict quite real historical processes.

22   Eilata is understood to be the kibbutz Revivim.

23   Seneds, *Adama*, 27. All translations are mine.

full settlement. But by far the most dynamic element in the novel, the one fused with time and change, is the land or nature itself:

> Heavy and cumbersome, the tractors slowly closed in on the northern horizon with a rampart of dirt. Steel bulldozers pierced the dry, apathetic land with firm and secure blades . . . Every day pools of dirt . . . [to capture rain water] became more and more visible . . . taking form. Changing the landscape! . . . Does this young man with the round and childish face have any idea what change he creates in this wilderness.[24]

Or again,

> The path to Eilata turned into a road. It was formed by the mules' horseshoes, by Hamouda and Macabi [the cows] that pulled the water container to the experimental plantation, by the car wheels of Kamti, by the pickup truck of the British who came to examine the official dozen rifles, but mostly to snoop around, by Isralik's new Ford which transported supplies and crushed ice. [The road] was eroded by the camels of the desert police and the donkeys of Sheikh Hassan Abu Samera . . . It was expanded by the old yellow Caterpillar.[25]

Before moving forward, I want to stress the difference here between the object of thought of this inquiry and that of current studies of Hebrew literature. For the latter, the first passage would exemplify the masculine, penetrating nature of Zionism, its violent tendency to change its environment to fit its needs; and it would point out that the land is depicted not only as virginal but also as inert, devoid of time and history of its own. Current critics would then turn their attention to examples of the opposite number in texts critical of Zionism, and ultimately seek to establish a rivaling canon.[26]

This kind of reading is useful for understanding Zionist ideology, yet it is quite insufficient for understanding literary or symbolic texts as they relate to history. Since the transformation of the land is a historical fact, such readings collapse the text's *stance* towards this change (affirmation,

---

24   Ibid., 178–9.
25   Ibid., 102.
26   For the most current attempt see Hannan Hever, *Producing the Modern Hebrew Canon: Nation Building and Minority Discourse* (New York: New York University Press, 2002).

glorification, etc.,) with its epistemological or critical aspects. What such a reading would miss, then, is the desire lodged at the heart of this imaginary world: since we are given an account, however biased, of the making of the Zionist collective project, it is crucial to observe that this kind of writing is invested in showing time and change, in showing how Zionist life was made. Although the novel most definitely presents the Bedouins in an orientalist manner and disavows their rightful claim to the land, it does not shy away from showing the encounter for what it really is: a struggle for land and labor. And, in conceiving of Zionism as a political movement that makes its own world, it offers us an account of this making, which is mostly absent from other more liberal novels, especially those written in the 1960s. (I return to this point in my reading of Yeshayahu Koren.)

Corresponding to the emphasis on showing the making of historical time and the political community is a notion of an overarching political necessity, which locks together all spheres of life (political and personal; community and family). The novel is riddled with such statements:

> The commune is dynamic, raging, and this is what we need here . . . The commune does not have any other wind in its sails than self-reliance and self-initiative. A full settlement [*meshek*] includes wives, children, crises, everything.
>
> We must be natives here [*bnei-bayit*], and free to use any initiative. Clerks won't do it, and neither will hired workers . . . Being native means that the entire commune lives here, here the children live, here we lay with our wives."[27]

Correspondingly, romantic, private relationships, if they exist at all in this world, are subordinated to the project of the state in two important regards. First, since political life is total, not allowing any separation of spheres, love, even if it begins in secret, cannot be kept secretive very long. Here is how Hannah thinks of her first meeting with Menashke: "For now, her first *rendezvous* with Menashke is spiced up with a pinch of secretness which will soon evaporate. In an hour, maybe two, the secret will cease to exist. It will be revealed by the guards or simply by their habit of sitting together for Sabbath dinner."[28] Note how the foreignness of romantic love is here indicated and slightly mocked both by the French

---

27 Seneds, *Adama*, 183–4.
28 Ibid., 84.

phrase ("*rendezvous*") and the culinary metaphor ("spiced up"). And as any foreign body, love is an object of surveillance (by the guards; other people at dinner). Second, the time of the romantic encounter is always subordinated to the time of the political encounter in the same manner that the "life" love represents is always threatened by the possibility of "death" implicit in the encounter with the Bedouins. When love demands a separate time for itself it must seek out a *place* away from the community and as such it is considered illegitimate. No sooner than Hannah and Menashke do manage to meet away from the rest of the settlement, they hear the alarm, calling them to return to the settlement where they are reprimanded for their absence. "Where the hell were you!" "What happened [Hannah and Menashke ask]?" "The Arab Legion . . . they are conducting drills in the area."[29]

The significance of such personal relationships is not limited to their non-political content, but to their place within the time of the political. Since the personal relationship is subordinated to the political project, they cannot intervene and alter the time of the political project, and because of that they are reduced to mere ancillary "content" within the world.

And yet, even in this kind of political totality, criticism does manage to sneak in. The 328-page novel is divided into five chapters, but while four are written in the third person, one of them, taking up merely thirty pages, is written in the form of a diary. It is a rather odd chapter as it is the only one written in the first person and its insertion in the middle, dividing the first half of the book from the second, seems quite arbitrary. Here we are allowed to hear, albeit very briefly, that Jewish socialism grounded on the exclusion of the Arab is a contradiction, and that the presence of the Arab is tolerable only because he can provide cheap labor.[30] Similarly, in other chapters, criticism is allowed a fleeting appearance through those "inessential" elements, through the voice of a woman, Bracha, who makes a male Zionist notice how imperfect and oppressive the commune can be.[31]

I would like to pause here and reflect on the form of these moments of resistance and difference. Although the elevated idiom in which Shraga's diary is written resembles the idiom of the third-person narrator in the other chapters, it is still of course a personal account of

---

29 Ibid., 88.
30 Ibid., 151, 165.
31 Ibid., 217–18.

the events. And yet, the significance of this account and the reason it is written in diary form has to do with the different literary time of the diary. Contrary to the "showing" of the four chapters, in which events unfold, as it were, in real time, the diary provides a time of "telling," a report given after events have taken place, and this temporal lag provides the space for fragments of criticism and dissent. The splitting of literary time into showing and telling, into unfolding antagonism in the form of events and discursive (reporting) language respectively is the key compositional structure of novels whose aim and wish is to think of freedom and autonomy away from antagonism. The cardinal aesthetic feature of this attempt, which always ends in failure, is the spatialization of time, the creation of a sphere of ready-made imaginary autonomy and freedom that does not struggle against the state, but rather exists alongside the scene of antagonism. To reverse the order of presentation: only by positing a separate and ready-made sphere of autonomy and freedom, one that is not made but given whole, can novels, in this period, think of alternatives to the state. But this is precisely their limit, for their condition of possibility—born whole outside of antagonism—is impossible.

To conclude: understanding Zionism as a life-and-death antagonism that seeks to establish its own law and rule, the Seneds' novel constructs a world in which this political encounter subordinates all other materials, both on the level of content and time. The "political" here is not simply collective but total; it mediates and provides legibility (or illegibility) to all other materials. In this world, no other sphere can really compete with the total nature of the political and thus even the "personal" sphere as well as the "other" (Shraga's diary; Bracha) do not constitute their own law from which the time and content of the political could be challenged. For this reason, *A Land without Shadow* is an example of a unitary world, while the texts I will examine now will contend with the totality of the political and the price it demands (life itself) by splitting the world into two times and two laws/spheres.

6.

S. Yizhar's *Midnight Convoy* will move us to a different imaginary world in which we see an attempt to establish an independent sphere of freedom alongside the project of state-making.[32] Since Yizhar's schema is fairly basic, my discussion of the novella will be shorter than the previous reading, emphasizing only the essential.

As the title suggests, the novella revolves around the attempt of a small group of soldiers, during the 1948 war, to secure passage for a military supply convoy to the south of Palestine and in this way to break the Egyptian blockade. As in the Seneds, here, too, the imaginary world revolves around a constitutive antagonism, a life-and-death encounter. "Our road, begun only tonight and already done with—the last chance of an opening has been closed. Now there's no way but war. No escape . . . You can't occupy territory with convoys, you can't break a siege or win peace. To do that you have to die, over and over again."[33] As with the Seneds, the encounter with the enemy is the condition around which all characters are defined as "attitudes" towards necessity, attitudes that are supposed to ensure (or not) the freedom of the Zionist statist project.

Although he opts for a military campaign rather than the establishment of settlements, Yizhar depicts the constitutive act directly, making it into the generator of narrative time. The world of the text is one emerging around a central act such that its duration constitutes the source of time of the social world in its entirety. It is the novella's governing poetic principle, which at some moments floats to the surface of the text and receives direct expression. Here are two examples:

> This led to a spontaneous desire to be at the heart of all acts that were now going to be done. To take, to organize, to do. To put forward some project.[34]

> The numbers on the clock were reaching their peak only to grow smaller, then not so slowly to run back up into the coming light of dawn. It was already time to be getting up and racing in front of the heavy trucks, clearing their path of every obstacle, ensuring them a smooth road . . . But everything was dependent on time, treacherous time.[35]

---

32   S. Yizhar, "Midnight Convoy." In S. Yizhar, *Midnight Convoy and Other Stories*, translated by Reuven Ben-Yosef (New Milford: Toby Press, 2007), 89–205.

33   Ibid., 202.

34   Ibid., 129.

35   Ibid., 173.

And yet, unlike the Seneds, the narrator is wavering between a deep fascination with the heroic act, and a more alienated and ironic position that observes these acts as if from the outside. The main character, Tzvialeh, goes through all the manifestations of this dual desire: he admires his officer, Rubinstein, as a father, but also wants to disobey him as a petulant son; he enjoys the comradery of men but yearns to get away from it all and be with his secret love, Dali; at times he is yearning to take part in the dangerous act of war, at others mocking it. This double movement underlies the novel's two-note compositional principle.

More important than Tzvialeh's thoughts about the act of war is the overall split in the literary forms themselves. If the state's political concept of freedom takes the form of the military act, of doing and making whose time is bounded and limited, the alternative moral concept of freedom, seeking a way out of antagonism, is pressed into forms of *reflection* whose novelistic materials are nature and its eternal time.[36]

> Of them all, only Tzvialeh lay still, warming his belly on the soft, dusty, scented earth . . . keeping himself withdrawn from the conversation, and from the business of standing up and everything, going out by himself, slipping away with pleasure, silently escaping to the expanses of the great universe that gradually opened up all around as the sunset became a reality . . . That friable soil, made up entirely of small, pea-like clods which were nothing but fine dust burnt by the sun and wind into flour of granulose clots . . . which would disintegrate instantly into dusty powder, dissolved and dispersed. This is what went shooting out from under the wheels in streams of dust, this is what was so easily seduced by every riotous and licentious gust to dance off, capering higher and higher, in wide frolicsome circles, with chaff and thistles, twirling faster and faster like a top in the fields, and then becoming one big living thing in the empty expanses . . .

The narrator continues vigorously to imagine reapers, sheep, and various flora and finally ends with an explicit invocation of the pastoral as a substitute for the convoy's path:

---

36   Generally speaking, as of the 1960s the direct depiction of the constitutive "act" is associated in Israeli literature with commercial literature while literary value is placed on the suppression of the act and its substitution with reflection. As the Israeli literary field moved from the state into the market, the "act" regained its central position.

and together with the gold of curly St. John's wort, [the acacia] proclaims the nature of summer, so that you have a hankering to walk here, to walk in these straight tracks, and to leave the [Convoy's] path—any path—for the bare, naked fields . . . to walk and sweat and rejoice and raise your arms to the full breath of the wide expanses, and to be ever smaller, an invisible ant within the broad, empty fields. Oh, how many fields there are to walk in![37]

I note the romantic overtones of this passage. First notice how this alternative natural world is made possible only when the individual is breaking away from the collective. No other character joins Tzvialeh on his hike and even in a later moment when his thoughts turn to a potential partner, Dali, she remains a pure object of desire rather than a political partner. As I said earlier, the alternative to the state must take place away from the antagonistic act, in a sphere of abstract thought, associated with leisure. Second, and most importantly, the infinite expanse of nature is opposed to the finite character of the military mission and thus gives the sense that the pastoral is here understood as a site of freedom posited against the site of necessity. Third, since this pastoral alternative to the historical political project of Zionism cannot imagine any alternative political community, its materials are comprised of the general and abstract category of "life" itself. Fourth, since nature-as-life is opposed to the political, very quickly we sense that the company of soldiers trespasses and corrupts the purity of virginal, prelapsarian nature. Fifth, in contrast to the political whole (the state) that is being made and whose *causes* are laid bare during the military act, Yizhar's nature is a world already-whole whose causes are absent, or most specifically, obscured. Here lies both the limit of Yizhar's political imaginary and its utopian aspect, for in this living nature one can imagine oneself "whole" but without being made aware of the conditions of this wholeness.

Let me give one more example of the opposition between the political and the natural. Recall that the unique aspect of the Seneds' novel was their sense that the political project intervenes in its surroundings and thus even nature is never natural and static. In the world of *A Land without Shadow* everything moves as it were and the sources of change are laid bare. Here, too, the act of preparing the path for the convoy involves intervention in the terrain itself, the transformation of nature

---

37   Ibid., 104–6.

into man-made-nature. It involves planning and putting work into changing the terrain:

> Some time passed before they had learned what sort of place this was . . . and had set up not a few piles of stones, and had rolled away some boulders, while arguing about the arc of the curve which a good-sized truck could make without turning around completely or slipping down the slope; and they unrolled the paper stripes, dug here and there with their little spades, and made a trial trip with the Jeep to demonstrate various principles of road engineering.[38]

Now, while this kind of act represents purposive human action, collective decision-making and collaborative work, it is nonetheless associated with a preparation for a life-and-death encounter for which the narrator is trying to find an alternative. For this reason the solution takes the precise opposite of action and the language of action and imagines not only nature, as we saw, but static and eternal nature whose cause is unknown and in which man is *embedded* in nature rather than transforming it.

> After some time, the lost track was found awaiting them by the edge of the patch of waste. As soon as they reached it, it smiled at them and continued along its ancient path, a path of asses and plough-oxen, and silent tillers of soil, who walked barefoot, rose early in the morning and labored late into the evening.[39]

> But if a man and his beast could easily make their way along a path like this, skipping here and deviating there, without even noticing the unevenness of the way, not so tonight: you're going to have to bring through five- and ten-ton trucks, without lights, as rapidly as possible.[40]

The opposition of the natural to the political continues and finds more and more materials, especially in the female body of Dali, which, like the images of bare nature, is imagined naked, a passive object of a male gaze. I should also add that as the alternative to the political, community remains abstract: Tzvialeh never moves beyond fantasizing about Dali, and their relationship remains unfulfilled.

---

38   Ibid., 115.
39   Ibid., 106.
40   Ibid., 107.

Although the romantic and humanist conception of nature and the organic as a sphere of freedom provides an alternative to the political act, it is important to remember that in actuality nothing interrupts the military action. Not only does Tzvialeh rejoin the company, he also excels in many of its missions. Yizhar's humanism and his inability to imagine a real political alternative to Zionism have often been noted and my intention is not to repeat these observations.[41] Rather, I want to stress that the binary division of the imaginary world between the "political" and the "natural" is not a consequence of any particular writer, but rather that it is a characteristic of the historical limit in which the statist project is the determining principle, underlying the literary forms even of those writers who do try to seek an alternative.

7.

In Yizhar we begin to see the emergence of a formal principle that will be common to Israeli literature from the mid-1950s to the late 1960s. In this period, the robust Zionism, an imaginary world completely under the spell of state-making, is ceding its dominant place to a position that attempts to shift autonomy from the state to the private individual. This claim is not new; such attempts are associated with what in the received tradition of Israeli literary history is labeled existential aesthetic, especially in the 1960s, in which writers rejected the project of state-making for the psychic lives of its protagonists.[42] The same tendency also characterized a style of cinematic production at the time that came to be called the "New Sensitivity" (ha-regishut ha-ḥadasha). What is not stressed enough, however, is that the so-called "turn towards the self" fails miserably and, unlike the European models they mimic, these novels cannot in fact create a world that is fully shaped and organized by the mind's activity or the libidinal desires of the protagonists. Such attempts usually end in catastrophe, tragedy, alienation and death and their lurid or sickly tones only reassert the priority of the state as the dominant political and cultural project. I claim then that the failed attempt to establish an aesthetic independent of the state is not a matter of stylistic deficiency but rather concerns the historical limit of the overall period—the fact that

---

41 See, for example, Hannan Hever, *Sifrut she-nikhtevet mi-kan: kiẓur ha-sifrut ha-yisra'elit* (Tel Aviv: Yedi'ot aḥaronot, 1999),19; Hever, *Ha-sipur veha-le'om*, 221–223.

42 See Gershon Shaked, *Ha-siporet ha-'ivrit 1880–1980*, Vol. 4; Dan Miron, *"Hirhurim be-'idan shel proza;"* Dan Miron, *'Im lo tihiyeh Yerushalayim.*

the social conditions of private life in Israel of this period are not yet possible. As we shall see momentarily, this impossible wish for autonomous private life engenders new literary languages whose signature is a radical gesture of negation on all textual levels. Put differently, since, in this period, no other political project can compete with the concept of state autonomy and freedom, no other group can propose what I call a new principle of generality (in Hebrew: *klaliyut*) with its own authentic political and cultural content. And thus the only possible way out is sheer negation, which usually leads to abstract formalism and varieties of the obscene: incest, madness, violent death, apathy, extreme self-interest and so on.

Understanding these literary forms as the result of an underlying political failure corrects the received reading of these novels. In the received tradition such novels are tagged as "critical" of Zionism, as embodying, as they indeed do, a gesture of a generational revolt directed at the "fathers" who established the state in 1948 by the "sons" who now, in the 1960s, no longer feel indebted to state ideology. Beyond the fact that the organic metaphor of the "family" obscures political and social relations, such accounts miss what Slavoj Žižek would call a fundamental irony—if they do not utterly fail to imagine a new political principle, these novels eventually obey state logic. We can see this irony best in the widely read short story "Navadim ve-zefa" ("Nomads and Viper"] by Amos Oz.[43] There, the younger generation of the kibbutz revolts against the elders and refuses to accept their leadership. But what is the object of revolt? Confronted with repeated acts of thievery presumably by the neighboring Bedouins, the elders seek to come to terms with the Bedouins, while the younger generation sees this negotiation as a weakness and proceed to attack the Bedouins and protect Jewish property. Thus, read in formal abstract terms, Oz's story surely represents a "revolt," but in actual terms it is a revolt to make sure violent state logic prevails rather than be challenged.

Oz's story represents only one modality of the historical limit in this period. Other novels opted for abstract negation, or what can be called "novels of disillusionment," in which state ideology is revealed to be empty and false but no positive form of life can take its place. We see this in Aharon Megged's 1959 *As It Happens to a Fool* (*Mikre ha-kasil*) but its most celebrated variant is surely Yaacov Shabtai's 1977 *Past Continuous* (*Zikhron devarim*). Other more subtle and complex novels (Oz's

---

43   Amos Oz, "Navadim ve-zefa," in *Arzot ha-tan* [*Where the Jacks Howl*], 25–41.

included), tried to imagine autonomy on the side of private life, but since this was historically impossible they ended up with a split imaginary world. Oz's 1968 *My Michael* (*Micha'el Sheli*) and Aharon Megged's 1965 *Living on the Dead* (*Ha-ḥay 'al ha-met*) are good paradigmatic examples here. To my mind these novels and others are among the most interesting literary experiments of the period for two important reasons: First, the philosophical principle underlying these attempts at individual auton- omy is none other than the Aesthetic itself as it is conceived by Kant. In these novels, as I will show, the principle of indeterminateness (or reflecting judgment) is projected into the imaginary world and shapes one of the main protagonists and their sense of time. In other words, since real political content is impossible, Kantian aesthetic itself becomes the stuff or the material from which autonomy can be made. Second, noticing the principle of indeterminateness will allow us to historicize and explain literary forms in the second period (1985–) when capital is able to compete with state-making and therefore make private life a positive and universal form rather than mere negation.

I move now to discuss Yeshayahu Koren's 1967 *Funeral at Noon*, one of the most complex attempts to imagine individual freedom and autonomy.

8.

Yeshayahu Koren finished writing *Funeral at Noon* in 1967, significantly before the onset of the 1967 war, but the novella was published only in 1974.[44] Although somewhat neglected at the time of its publication it has been recovered and is hailed as a major modernist work by today's leading Israeli literary critics.[45] The novella tells of a childless couple,

---

44 Yeshayahu Koren, *Levaya ba-ẓohorayim* (Tel Aviv: Ha-sifriya ha-ḥadasha/Ha-kibuẓ ha-me'uḥad, 2008).

45 Maya Sela', "Levaya ba-ẓohorayim," *Haaretz*, December 5, 2014. The novella received scant attention at the time of its publication due to the fact that critics con- sidered it a "minor" work that ignores larger political matters for the sake of minute description of daily life. One of the leading literary critics at the time, Gershon Shaked, exemplifies this general attitude when he notes, although favorably, that Koren shifts attention from grand spiritual matters concerning Zionism and Israel to the daily and mundane lives of Israelis. Gershon Shaked, "Rikmat ha-ḥayim ba-seter," *Siman kri'ah* 5 (February 1976): 455. For more recent discussions of the novella see Ayman Siksek, "Ta'atu'ay ke'ilu," *Haaretz*, May 8, 2008; Yosef Oren, *Ẓav-keri'ah la-sifrut ha-yisra'elit* (Rishon le-ẓiyon: Yaḥad, 2009), 144–64; Gil Hochberg, "A Poetics of Haunting: From Yizhar's Hirbeh to Yehoshua's Ruins to Koren's Crypts," *Jewish Social Studies* 18.3

Hagar and Tuvia Erlich, who live in a small *moshava* (farming community), located right on the border of the West Bank. We are also introduced to their neighbors, Sarah and Simcha Strauss, and their child, Yiftah. From time to time Sarah, who needs to attend to her mentally ill second baby, places Yiftah in Hagar's custody. Playing "mother and child" Hagar takes him with her to the ruins of the Palestinian village nearby with the intent of meeting one of the Israeli soldiers who trains there. As the story unfolds, Hagar develops an illicit erotic relationship with the soldier and a motherly attitude towards Yiftah. At the climax of the novella, as Hagar finally sleeps with the soldier in the Palestinian village, Yiftah accidently sees them in the act. Frightened, he runs away and cannot be found. The Strausses hold Hagar responsible for their son's mysterious disappearance but cannot prove anything. After a while, Yiftah is found dead close to the Palestinian village but it is not clear how he died. Confronted with the dead body, Hagar brings herself to tell the Strausses what happened that day, which leads her to break up with Tuvia and leave the *moshava*.

It is obvious from the title and the suggestive relationship between Yiftah and Hagar that the former's death is the key to the novella. A moral reading would identify Yiftah's death as a form of punishment for Hagar's illicit affair; Hagar seeks to somehow escape the suffocating life of the *moshava* through a personal affair and this attempt to go against the collective (in Hebrew: *klal*) results in violent death that necessitates the removal of the transgressor. However commonsensical this reading might be, it nonetheless misses the mark. Although such a reading affirms my argument that novels that try to imagine private forms of life in this period fail, conceiving of Yiftah's death as a form of "punishment" presupposes that the novel is written from the point of view of state-making. But our key assumption must be precisely the opposite, i.e., that the novel is written as an attempt to affirm private life. The death of Yiftah, however troubling, must have then a political rather

(Spring/Summer 2012): 55–69. Siksek offers a brief review of the novella, which is in agreement with the reception mentioned above. Oren offers a long and detailed discussion but he, too, continues the line of previous critics, seeing in Koren's style an attempt to stir away from direct commentary on Zionism. Hochberg's account offers a brief discussion of the novella (64–6), noting the narrator's silence over the description of the ruins of the Palestinian village. All critics mention the riddle-like nature of the writing but do not explain its aesthetic, epistemological or political significance, nor its relation to European literature as I attempt in these pages. For other brief discussions of Koren's style, see Avner Holtzman, *Mapat derakhim: siporet 'ivrit ka-yom* (Tel Aviv: Ha-kibuẓ ha-me'uḥad, 2008), 101–102; Batya Gur, *Mi-beli daleg 'al daf: mivḥar masot u-ma'amarim* (Yerushalayim: Keter, 2008), 340–2.

than moral significance, a positive and affirmative content rather than a negative one; but to achieve this reversal of valences we will first need to examine much of the formal and thematic materials of the novel through which Hagar's autonomy is constructed.

First let's look at Koren's style, which is the main reason this text has received the attention of Israeli literary critics. Here is a typical passage:

> It was noon time. She [Hagar] entered the kitchen, opened the refrigerator, and took out an apple. She picked up a knife and started peeling it. The pots in the sink weren't washed. "I need to prepare lunch," she told herself, got up and walked to the shower. She looked in the mirror and did her hair. Her face was narrow, her eyelashes sparse. Only in her green eyes there was a faint streak of restlessness.[46]

A few patterns catch the reader's eye: first, there is the skewed ratio between the large number of verbs and the short duration of action: Hagar entered, opened, took out, picked up, peeled, got up, walked, looked etc.—all to describe the minor actions of eating an apple, looking in the mirror and taking a shower. Another example of such a ratio is evident in the fact that heightened attention is given to small and routine details that have little meaning. Second, Koren writes in short sentences, usually without subclauses, to describe a single action or a single object: "it was noon time;" "she got up and walked to the shower." And finally, the narrator's gaze, for the most part, overlaps with Hagar's; only in rare moments does the narrator gaze at her as if from the outside ("a faint streak of restlessness"). These formal characteristics justify critics' observation that Koren's style is "minimalist" and "concrete" (in Hebrew: *muhashi*), a style that produces the riddle-like nature of the novella.[47] However, despite this useful observation, critics do not elaborate on the significance of this style or its relation to literature written outside Israel, other than to acknowledge that it is a rare style that did not fit with the more explicit political narratives of Israeli literature at the time. What is needed then is an account of the political significance of "concreteness" which will tie it also to certain currents in European modernism, as well as to debates surrounding world literature.

One way to understand what is happening under Koren's concrete gaze and to tie his work to world literature is to say that it is a style

---

46   Koren, *Levaya*, 7. All translations from Hebrew are mine.
47   See footnote 48 for bibliographic details.

invested in delaying or even impeding the movement from the "material" signifier (this or that action or object) to its abstract signified, or, in other words, to its significance and allegorical meaning. While Koren's concrete style is quite rare in 1960s Israel, we can find similar attempts in Europe at the same time, especially in the young Alain Robbe-Grillet. Writing the manifestos that came to define the "nouveau roman," he argues:

> Anyone can perceive the change that has occurred. In the initial novel [taken as the bourgeois novel whose typical representative for Robbe-Grillet is Balzac], the objects and gestures forming the very fabric of the plot disappeared completely, leaving behind only their *significations*: the empty chair became only absence or expectation, the hand placed on a shoulder became a sign of friendliness . . . instead of this universe of "signification" (psychological, social, functional), we must try then to construct a world both more solid and more immediate . . . In this future universe of the novel, gestures and objects will be *there* before being *something*; and they will still be there afterwards, hard, unalterable, eternally present, mocking their own "meaning" . . . No longer objects be merely the vague reflection of the hero's vague soul . . . if objects still afford momentary prop to human passions, they will do so only provisionally [in order to show] how alien they remain to man.[48]

Although Robbe-Grillet's writing is not identical to that of Koren, both share the same philosophical principle: both writers seek to block the symbolic and allegorical levels of the text that would rob the textual object of its concreteness.[49] If we follow Jameson and Moretti in the pre-

---

48   Alain Robbe-Grillet, *For a New Novel: Essays on Fiction*, translated by Richard Howard (New York: Grove Press, 1965), 20–2.

49   I appeal to Robbe-Grillet and the nouveau roman, and not to earlier modernist writers more "intrinsic" to Hebrew literature such as U. N. Gnessin or Y. H. Brenner (or even Kafka), because Koren's "Israeli modernism" seems to me to be different from the earlier "Jewish modernism" of the early 1900s. The similarity and differences between these two modernisms merit a deeper and broader inquiry, but for now I will say that Brenner and Gnessin's modernism differ from Koren's precisely in Koren's main element, i.e., psychology. Both Brenner and Gnessin center the plot around intense psychological states whereas Koren attempts to avoid such psychologization at all costs, and in this his style resembles the stern and minimalist prose of Robbe-Grillet. Kafka's riddles are in a way closer to Koren, and I note this fact in my discussion of Adorno in the next pages, but here, too, Koren is distinct. As Adorno argues, Kafka stresses the literal meaning of words, but he never fully gives up on the metaphysical or allegorical levels of the text (especially in the longer works), while Koren avoids the latter altogether, a style that results in extreme literality.

ceding discussion, what we see in Koren could be taken as an example of traveling European form that would be domesticated in the periphery. The political and epistemological significance of this form needs further elaboration which we can find in Adorno.

Consonant with Adorno's thought after World War II in which social domination is understood as the "abstract concept," that web of categories that covers the world and denies the specificity of the object, the "concrete" is an attempt to resist the logic of subsumption of myth and the idea. Concreteness is meant to keep at bay abstract meaning, or "generality" that for Adorno comes to signify the repetition of the "ever-same," against which the concrete object is posited as the new, the non-identical, and the irreplaceable. Adorno sees this technique operative in Kafka (and then differently in Beckett),[50] but goes further and generalizes the philosophical usage of concreteness in a piece dedicated to the Homeric epic:

> The narrator's rational, communicative discourse, with its subsumptive logic that equalizes everything it reports, is preoccupied with myth as the concrete, as something distinct from the leveling ordering of the conceptual system . . . In comparison with the enlightened state of consciousness to which narrative discourse belongs, a state characterized by general concepts, this concrete or objective element always seems to be one of stupidity, lack of comprehension, ignorance, a stubborn clinging to the particular when it has already been dissolved into the universal . . . Naiveté is the price [the narrator] pays for that.[51]

> The attempt to emancipate representation from reflective reason is language's attempt, futile from the outset, to recover from the negativity of its intentionality, the conceptual manipulation of objects, by carrying its defining intention to the extreme and allowing what is real to emerge in pure form.[52]

Later on we will see how concreteness blocks narrative time (and eventually history), turning it into landscape and space (as Adorno notes in the case of Homer's description of a shield),[53] a transformation that will

---

50 Theodor Adorno, "Notes to Kafka." In *Prisms*, translated by Samuel and Shierry Weber (Cambridge: MIT Press, 1983), 243–71; "Trying to Understand *Endgame*." In *Notes to Literature*, Vol. I, translated by Shierry Weber Nicholsen (New York: Columbia University Press, 1991), 241–75.

51 Theodor Adorno, "On Epic Naiveté." In *Notes to Literature*, Vol. I, 25.

52 Ibid., 27.

53 Adorno notices that Homer substitutes the temporal depiction of the battle in

help us locate the political implications of this technique; but for the moment I take from Adorno and Robbe-Grillet the following: concreteness is an act of negation, and specifically a negation of generalization and universality, of abstract rules/concepts. This negation works on three interlocking levels. To see this it will be instructive to turn to the meaning of "rule" in Hebrew. In Hebrew, a language based on a system of roots and patterns of conjugation, "generality" and "rules" are connected in the root k/l/l. "*Klal*" and "*klaliyut*" can mean "rule," and "general meaning" but significantly it also has a strong political meaning which refers to "all" as in the "general public," or "society" at large ("*klal ha-ẓibur*;" "*ha-klal*" respectively).

Hebrew then ties neatly between generality, the abstract law and the political body who makes laws. What I propose then is that concreteness is a triple negation of universality in terms of general meaning, law and the authority of the governing political body. We see this in Robbe-Grillet quite clearly. First, Robbe-Grillet seeks to negate the aesthetic rule of realist writing, which he associates with Balzac. Second, his technique seeks to block the general meaning of objects and gestures such that they will be left literal. Third, and most importantly, concreteness seeks to block the relation between objects and gestures and their place in French history, for it is very difficult to tie between Robbe-Grillet's stories and their relation to French society.[54]

Robbe-Grillet's type of negation operates in Koren as well. We already mentioned that Koren's concrete style makes it difficult to shift from Hagar's actions to their broader or allegorical meaning; and as for the negation of the aesthetic rule, we can add that for Israeli critics Koren's style was a negation of a dominant allegorical style, one associated with S. Y. Agnon.

[You need to understand Koren] in the context of Hebrew literature of the 1960s. It was then held captive in the confines of Agnon. Writers wrote in ironic, self-aware styles, making up puzzles of meaning. Everything was an empty skeleton, a sign for something else.[55]

---

the *Iliad* with the spatial description of a shield that blocks narrative time. "The impulse that drives Homer to describe a shield as though it were a *landscape* and to elaborate a metaphor until it becomes action, until it becomes *autonomous* and ultimately destroys the fabric of narrative—that is the same impulse that repeatedly drove Goethe, Stifter, and Keller, the greatest storytellers of the nineteenth century, at least in Germany, to draw and paint instead of writing." Ibid., 26, my emphasis.

54   On this matter see Fredric Jameson, "Modernism and Its Repressed; or, Robbe-Grillet as Anti-Colonialist." In *The Ideologies of Theory: Essays 1971–1986*, Vol. I: *Situations of Theory* (Minneapolis: University of Minnesota Press, 1989), 167–80.

55   Menachem Peri's comment in Maya Sela', "Levaya ba-ẓohorayim."

Lastly, Koren's style is an attempt to negate a certain political principle: the Zionist conception of the state. At this point in the argument it is difficult to see the relation to Zionism, but I would like to place this difficulty not in the reading Subject but in the textual Object, for the concrete style seeks to block the allegorical meaning that I will propose here, and this is precisely its political meaning.

To elaborate on Koren's formal negation, it is important to see that the novella revolves around an unspoken circumvention, i.e., around Hagar's implicit abstention from becoming a mother. Koren postpones this issue and brings it up explicitly only in the very last moments of the novella when Tuvia, Hagar's husband, visits his sister in the hospital after she gives birth. The family discusses the name of the newborn baby and the conversation unfolds as follows:

> "What will you call him?"
> "Yehiel," his mother said, "as was the name of your father."
> "Your father who didn't like Hagar," Edna [Tuvia's other sister] said, as if to herself.
> "What do you have against her? What did she do to you?"
> "To me?" Edna said. "To me she did nothing. The problem is that to you too, to you too, she didn't do anything [*lo 'asta khlum*]."[56]

Although elided, the object of the "doing" or more properly "making" here is obviously a "child." For although English speakers say "having children," Hebrew speakers say "making children" (*la'asot yeladim*). It is important to see that Edna's anger is not hers alone and that it is weaved into a more general complaint that Hagar avoids fulfilling her social role as a mother. Here is an earlier moment in the novella where Tuvia associates his wish for children with a sense of a greater purpose in life. I note in advance Hagar's naiveté, her "ignorance" of Tuvia's implicit meaning as Adorno called it:

> "I have a lot of plans," he said, "but it's not at all clear to me for whom I am doing all this work."
> "What do you mean for whom?"
> "What will I do with all this?"
> "I don't understand you," she said, "for what people work?"
> "My father, for example, had something to work for."

---

56   Koren, *Levaya*, 164.

"For what?"

"For me, for all of us."

[...]

"Maybe one day you will find what you seek." [Hagar says]

"That what you wanted to tell me [earlier] today?"

"Not exactly, but it's relevant."

Tuvia held her arm and pulled her to him. "Look at me," he said.

Again they were in the main road. Children on bicycles passed by them and stopped by the bulletin board. The wind stopped, and only the clouds continued taking over the sky, covering the stars.[57]

To continue and sharpen the political significance of bearing children it will be useful to go back to an earlier moment in Hebrew literature, to Moshe Shamir's *He Walked in the Fields* (*Hu halakh ba-sadot*), one of the most important and defining novels for the Zionism of the 1950s and much after.[58] Here the relation between children and Zionist collectivity takes up the heart of the political problem of this imaginary world. After one of the children in the kibbutz dies from illness and maltreatment, Rutka, one of the main characters, leaves the kibbutz and her husband, Willi, and attempts to live a safer life in the city with her baby, Uri, and the painter Yosel Brumberg. This fleeing attempt fails and years later, when she remembers this moment of doubt, she offers us one of the most chilling Zionist confessions:

There is something in the flesh and blood [*basar va-dam*] of the kibbutz, in its inner essence, that will never forgive you running away with Uri to the city to save his life. This act, if it could be justified, even less than that, even if it could be explained as a human weakness—this act would undermine the very foundation of the kibbutz. The kibbutz is not a cooperative for this or that matter of life, not even for all matters of life. It is something rather that melts together its members and turns them into a new essence, a new quality, a new order of life. Therefore: in the kibbutz a man must accept not only life but death itself. The kibbutz leads man from ashes to ashes ... There is no way out; there is no way out for those who seek to be saved from elsewhere. The kibbutz has the duty to raise children—will it approve then of those who will take their children out

---

57 Ibid., 158.

58 Moshe Shamir, *Hu halakh ba-sadot* (Tel Aviv: 'Am 'oved, 2006).

of this collective [*lemi sheyoẓi 'et yaldo min klal zeh*]? [The kibbutz] has the duty to raise children at its home, with its own means, with its maids, with its own mistakes, with its own tragedies; and the first children must pave the way for future generations who will necessarily follow.[59]

In Shamir, the Zionist political principle is then raised to the highest universal level—the political is the body itself, biological life itself—and this universalization subordinates every other principle, even kinship. I note again how Rutka, through the phrase "*lemi sheyoẓi 'et yaldo min klal zeh,*" ties between the meaning of "*klal*" as "all," (*ha-klal ha-ẓiyoni*) and its meaning as a "rule" to be followed (*ha-klal shel ha-ẓiyonut*), the rule, that is, that demands that children be raised into a life of collectivity. In Hebrew, "*laẓ'et min ha-klal*" designates both "to leave the collective" and "an exception to the rule."

Going back to Hagar, we can now see that first and foremost Koren's novella is about a woman who tries to find, as Rutka and Yizhar would say, "a way out" and leave the collective/be an exception to the rule. The "way out" is first Hagar's passive abstention from making children and avoiding fusing her literal body with the spiritual body of the Zionist collective. Two additional abstentions can be discerned: the first is the fact that she avoids Tuvia (both sexually and in terms of their daily routine) which eventually leads to their separation. The second abstention has to do with the fact that she does not take up the place of the school teacher that died and thus abstains from taking up her role as an educator of the next generation of the *moshava*. Hagar then avoids being a mother, a wife and a teacher,[60] and in this way challenges collectivity that in this novella is expressed implicitly through the political function of children.

Once we understand Hagar's actions, the structural similarity between her abstentions—her attempt to refuse the incorporation of her *body* into that of the national collective—and Koren's *concrete* formal style becomes evident. For, can't we say that Hagar's refusal to be subsumed by the political whole through pregnancy and motherhood resembles the way Koren blocks the subsumption of the concrete signifier—the body of the word as it were—by its general allegorical meaning? Can't we say that

---

59   Koren, *Levaya*, 180.

60   I deliberately put these three roles in one sentence in order to designate a combination of two fixed idioms in Hebrew that refer to the political roles of women in Israel. The first is "*'em u-re'aya be-yisra'el*" and the second "*meḥanekhet be-yisra'el*" which mean: "to be a mother and a wife in/for Israel" and "to be an educator in/for Israel" respectively.

Hagar's body and the concrete body of the word are the twin faces of the same strategy, one on the level of content, the other on the level of style?

To recall the previous discussion, according to Adorno this attempt at concreteness stands in contrast with reflective reason. By contrasting concreteness with self-reflection, Adorno allows us to see that the opposite of the concrete body is spirit, in two modalities: in Adorno (and German Idealism in general) spirit is that conceptual movement that allows for introspection and self-understanding; in our modality here it is the spirit of the political project of state-making (also in line with Hegel's concept of the state). If we conceive of political forms such as the state as an abstract "spirit" that enters as it were and animates the "body" of the citizenry, it will be possible to see even deeper into the relation between the political significance of Koren's concrete style and its aesthetic properties. For, as we saw previously, while Shamir understands Zionism (as it understood itself) as full union between the political spirit and the body of Rutka, Koren blocks the political (allegorical) spirit from entering both Hagar's body by refusing pregnancy, and his own concrete style. Similarly, but not identically to Yizhar, this blocking splits the imaginary world. In Yizhar, we saw a split between, on the one hand, the political spirit embodied in the military act of constructing (or making) the convoy's path, and on the other, a humanist spirit embodied in nature. What was unique in Yizhar and makes his imaginary world different from Koren is that in Yizhar, both spheres embody the union of body and spirit. For him, nature is not something concrete and devoid of spirit, quite the contrary; it is an animated nature whose "life" competes with the life of the nation. And conversely, the political act is not blind necessity; it is animated with a deep sense of political freedom in the name of Jewish autonomy. In Koren, we have a different kind of split. Here the political spirit and Hagar's body have been detached from one another and Hagar's world is strictly corporeal. We see this in three ways: first, she is mostly alone and is looking for company; second, the language of the narrator avoids psychologizing her and remains only on the surface, detailing her external, routine acts; third, the narrator is attracted literally to her body for we keep reading about her thirst, her fatigue, her response to the heat—all bodily reflexes that take the place of her interiority, into which the narrator is barred from entering. We will later track the place and time to which the political spirit has been relegated, but for now it is important to stress the affinity between Adorno's concept of concreteness as a negation of universal spirit/generality, and the political spirit of the state.

Finally, Adorno also argues that the attempt to bar conceptuality results in blindness, ignorance and naiveté. This allows us to comment on Hagar's psychological makeup and eventually to understand the underlying structure of her movements in the *moshava*. Again, a comparison with Shamir's Rutka is useful here. As we saw, Shamir's Rutka is a character actively looking for a way out of the Zionist project of state-making. Even though this attempt fails, her character is guided by an explicit and conscious will to create her world, to seek out erotic and political partners, and even if she is finally unable to do so, she willfully accepts her fate. Conversely, Hagar's libidinal energies are far more unconscious and implicit, motivated as they are by an unavowed but powerful desire for sexual gratification. She is passive in almost all her interactions; she does not pursue the soldier but is pursued by him; she does not avow her knowledge about Yiftah's whereabouts the day he disappeared until actively forced to do so. This psychological naiveté is then manifested in the fact that she is constantly looking for something, a search that is manifested in her daily walks that always end, unsurprisingly, in the ruined Palestinian village where both the libidinal and (unavowed) political drama reach their climax. What Hagar is eventually looking for is of course the political spirit her impoverished body is missing, but to see this aspect of the story we will need to take a few more steps.

I propose the following: Hagar's abstention from participation in the collective can be grasped as her wish for freedom, or more precisely her wish for individual autonomy. Hagar's body is the manner Koren thinks autonomy and freedom in a time and place where this kind of freedom is not yet possible and is considered illegitimate. If we make an appeal to Casanova's study on the emergence of autonomy in the periphery, Hagar's wish for autonomy is then the appearance, within the fictional world, of Koren's own aesthetic wish for autonomy in the literary field (one expressed through his concrete style). And this in turn—if we want to push this reading further albeit a bit abstractly—is the symptomatic appearance of a political wish for autonomy of the Israeli bourgeoisie that in this statist period, as I claim, is impossible. To reverse the order of presentation: the statist project which blocks the autonomy of the private sphere is the condition of possibility for the emergence of Koren's concrete style, which tries to think this impossible autonomy in aesthetic terms. This stylistic form/wish is then projected inward, into the novella, and appears both as Hagar's psychic character—her passivity and naiveté—and in terms of the thematic content, i.e., her abstention from childbearing.

Now that Hagar's character and its concrete style have been eluci-dated, we need to account for those elements into which the political spirit has been relegated and to its aesthetic forms. This discussion will allow us to develop the temporal dimension of both Hagar's body and the political spirit. I begin by observing Hagar's class as well as that of her neighbor, Sarah. Although the text does not directly take this up, Sarah is in fact the poorest character in the novella. Contrary to Sarah who marries wage laborers, Hagar marries Tuvia who owns the garage. Tuvia's father, Yehiel, owned a soda factory and had enough money to send Tuvia to a university in England. Last, while Yehiel builds a home for Hagar and Tuvia, Simcha (Sarah's husband) is an electrician hired to set up their house. In short, while Sarah and Simcha are working class, Hagar and Tuvia are squarely in the petite-bourgeoisie. Based on these preliminary facts it is possible to locate Hagar's wish for autonomy—it is somehow related to a certain freedom that is allotted her thanks to her class. The Israeli petite-bourgeoisie is then the underlying social subject of Hagar's desire for freedom, which happens to appear in this novella as thematic content. I say "happen" because there is no real need for class to appear as such in literary works.

Unsurprisingly, class appears here through the relation to work. What becomes clear is that all other characters are described through or during work, while Hagar is the only character who does not have to sell her labor. What characterizes Hagar then is the fact that she takes long walks in the ruined Palestinian village and that she is "playing mother" to Yiftah when they go out together. In addition to these trips, the only action she takes is a trip to her parents and then a stroll on the promenade in Tel Aviv. In other words, Hagar's class appears here through a category of social time which we can label as "leisure." This time is not only represented as a phenomenal object in the novella (her "morning walks"), it also structures the novella as a subject, i.e., as form.

We have mentioned that Koren is understood as a "minimalist" or "stern" writer, but now it should be considered that in fact only Hagar's story is told in this concrete fashion. There are a few other embedded stories, those of the secondary characters, that are written in a very dif-ferent style. To tell these stories, the narrator stops the flow of narration in the present and returns to events in the past. Here, the narration is not concrete at all, but quite conventional third-person narration. Further, with the temporal shift, the novella also shifts narrative modes—in these parts the narrator is breaking Henry James's edict and instead of "showing," which typifies Hagar's story, the narrator is mostly "telling." Here is how Sarah is introduced to us:

> [Sarah was married] at the age of thirty-seven. Until then she lived in the shack behind Kasus's café; she would clean his restaurant once a week and sometimes cook. She also cleaned and did the laundry for Zemah's parents, whose father was a clerk in city hall and his mother too old to do these kinds of jobs. For a while she even worked in the school as a cook in the children's kitchen. Her [original] name was Soreeka.[61]

Here, the narration is not concrete at all, but appears in the conventional third person, and sentences are quite long. Further, events here are not only in the past but also in what Jean-Paul Sartre, and Jameson after him, call the "preterite" in which events have already been completed, while in Hagar's story events are told in what Sartre calls "open present" in which the fate of the characters is yet to be decided."[62]

In context of our discussion about world literature, I propose that the temporal difference is the first sign of the "break" between the traveling European form—the concrete narrative mode of Hagar's story—and the local raw materials—the narrative mode of the secondary characters. The "break" is exemplified by the fact that, differently than Robbe-Grillet, Koren cannot make the concrete style and its time of "showing" cover the entire story; the local materials and their time of telling somehow resist this abstract form and cannot be shaped and refigured by it.

Now the question is how to connect this temporal difference to the specific reality of Israeli society in the 1960s. First, the distinguishing factor between these two modes of narration and time is the relation to necessity and "making"—it is not enough to say that Hagar is a subject of leisure and the secondary characters are subjects of work, but that the latter are described so that we see how they make their lives and become who they are thorough the struggle with necessity, while Hagar is already who she is without needing to make herself. This different relation to necessity leads to a different relation towards the concept of autonomy—while the secondary characters, but mostly Sarah and Yehiel, can become autonomous by overcoming (or not) their social conditions, Hagar is already autonomous before and without acting in the world. Put differently, when we read the tales of the secondary characters we witness

---

61   Koren, *Levaya*, 33.
62   Fredric Jameson, *Antinomies of Realism* (London: Verso, 2013), 1–26.

the manner in which they become who they are, the reason for and cause of their social character, which is also their history, whereas the reason and cause of Hagar's life, her history, is absent. One of the most remarkable aspects of this novella is that we know more about the secondary characters than we do about the main protagonist, for the latter exists only in the present and pursues mostly routine activities.

Second, now that we see the relation between "making," time and character we can see that Hagar's autonomy is enabled through a certain removal of antagonism, or necessity—the removal of the causes of social things. But what is this cause? To see this removal in the text, I compare two moments that refer to the Palestinian village. Here is the depiction of a Palestinian house narrated in Hagar's concrete narrative mode:

> They entered the house through a curved pathway. The floorings of the entrance room were made of concrete and piles of dust and sand covered the floor. Out of that room other pathways opened everywhere. Some of them were rectangular and straight, others curved. To their left was a wide door and above it arched a chain of dark stones. Leaves and ewers were carved into the stone. In some of the slits there remained a little black color. The rest were colorless, pale. The stone arch stretched to the floor and created a figure of a horseshoe. It smelled of moist, but Yiftah put his hand on stone arch and said "it's cold, this horseshoe."[63]

And now compare this passage to another moment where the village is mentioned in the tales of the secondary characters:

> In the meantime new houses were added to the [moshava], and new people were seen in the movie house. They cut down the eucalyptus grove next to the main road, and instead they built a hospital whose construction ended at the same time they conquered the Arab villages nearby, and it was used to service the first wounded. They added a high fence to the school and a playground. Noah Bolokin built a modern coop in his back yard.[64]

Taking the second passage first, I note the large number of verbs and the more important fact that it is written in the third person impersonal (in the form of "stami" in Hebrew). Most importantly of course is that we

---

63 Koren, *Levaya*, 25.
64 Ibid., 37.

see how the *moshava* was built, how it was made, and that its making was directly related to the 1948 war. In comparison, in the first passage, not only do we move from the "many" to the "few," we also now note that the ruined house stands detached from the historical acts that made it look this way. And, in this way, the minute Koren disconnects the house from the reason for its social being, there is no escape from noticing that the house has become an aesthetic object: Hagar and Yiftah's eyes fall again and again only on the aesthetic aspects of the house, or more precisely, on its geometrical and concrete features.

We can now say that in addition to the stylistic, psychological and class aspects of the novella, we may observe a historical dimension whose removal provides the autonomy of the aesthetic—for as we just saw, the minute you subtract the 1948 war the Palestinian house becomes no more than an aesthetic and autonomous object, autonomous, that is, from the reason and cause that made it so. Since Hagar takes long strolls through the Palestinian village it could be argued that for her, history has become nature and scenery.

With all the levels of the text in front of us we can make a few more general comments about the appearance of time and history in this novella. First, the break between Hagar's time of showing and the secondary characters' time of telling is not simply the appearance of the opposition between the working classes and the petit-bourgeoisie. Rather, given that in this statist period, different from Western Europe, the Zionist labor movement is folded into the project of state building, the break is between the subordinated petite-bourgeoisie and the state itself and for this reason the times are mapped unevenly into the time of a particular class and the time of history, or universality. In this last temporal modality we see how the body politic (*klal*) is made, how the *moshava* was established and the border came to be drawn. In comparison to this history, it is clear that for Hagar the body politic is imagined only as a past event, as a great deed that already happened and as such it appears, to her mind, as a *synchronic* law (*klal*) without cause, that is, imposed on her in the form of a collective edict ("you must bear children!"). Second, the absence of the cause of the body politic can explain why Hagar is always wandering around, for while the secondary characters are bound up with the cause of their lives, she is free of it and for this reason must search for it within the world as if it were an alien thing. And it is not coincidental that she finds it, in a displaced manner, in the Palestinian village, the soldier and the Arab worker, Halmi. Following Jameson, it is possible to argue that Hagar's libidinal energies are exactly her political unconscious: she is drawn back to her own cause, which was obscured by the concrete style.

Going back to the aesthetic dimension, I have argued that since in this period there is no political alternative to the state and its concept of freedom, Kant's philosophical principle of the aesthetic is projected inward and made into the very stuff of the imaginary world. I would like to show now the relation between the removal of the historical cause and the concept of the aesthetic in Kant:

> Now art always has a determinate intention of producing something . . . If the intention were aimed at the production of a determinate object, then if it were achieved through art, the object would please only through concepts . . . It would not please as beautiful but as mechanical art. . . beautiful art must be regarded as nature . . . A product of art appears as nature, however, if we find it to agree punctiliously but not painstakingly with rules in accordance with which alone the product can become what it ought to be, without the academic form showing through i.e., without showing any sign that the rule has hovered before the eyes of the artist and fettered his mental powers.[65]

I will approach this passage by comparing the similarities between the binding power of the rule (*klal*) in Kant and the binding power of history.

Kant understands the beautiful through an opposition with rules, laws or concepts more generally. If the beautiful object is produced by rules and concepts it will seem mechanical, i.e., unfree. Thus, although the beautiful object is guided by rules, it needs to produce the appearance that it is free of them. Now, making the shift to our own discussion—if, according to Kant, the aesthetic object becomes autonomous by concealing the rule that created it, then I propose that a subject becomes autonomous by concealing the political rule (*klal*), or antagonism. Therefore, in Kant's understanding, the aesthetic involves disavowing the rules that bind and fetter the aesthetic act as well as the subject. Let me tie this argument to the appearance of the Palestinian house: if for the secondary characters (in the time of the preterite), the Palestinian village is subordinated, fettered, to its historical and public meaning, then for Hagar (in the time of the present) it can become an aesthetic object only

---

65   Immanuel Kant, *Critique of the Power of Judgment*, translated by Paul Guyer and Eric Matthews (Cambridge: Cambridge University Press, 2000), 185–6; emphasis in original removed.

if Koren conceals the historic cause, which always, as I claim, involves the general public (*klal*) and its making.

To see the affinity between Kant's concept of the aesthetic and the concept of textuality (and with this affinity to anticipate my discussion in the next chapter), we may examine the way that Jacques Derrida defines a text:

> A text is not a text unless it hides from the first comer, from the first glance, the *law* of its composition and the rules of its game.[66]

The Kantian aestheticization of Koren's world (as with all other attempts to find alternatives to the autonomy of the state), is akin to Derrida's textualization of the imaginary world, a technique that operates by hiding the determining principle of the world, and through this concealment achieving freedom, or in Derrida's language, "free play." What Derrida does not see, although it is implied in his qualification, is that the "hiding" of the law of composition is a not a property of texts in general, but of particular groups of texts. In the current inquiry, these texts thematize textualization by removing antagonism, or necessity, from their world. More specifically, they remove the process of "making" that reveals both the law of the political body and the law of aesthetic composition, i.e., explicit ideology (as we find in the Seneds and in Shamir). As I will show in the next chapter, that which will do the "hiding," that which indeed succeeds in challenging the state, will be the process of capitalist privatization. Through privatization, textualization and aestheticization will take place on the grounds of social life itself (rather than simply in novels).

Back to Koren: differently than other critics who claim that Koren is the only one who writes in this way, I argue that writers who do not completely identify with Zionism make use of the same technique. Following Jameson (and Lévi-Strauss before him), all such writers are trying to "solve" the same problem of freedom and autonomy by concealing the political rule.[67] Here is, for example, how A. B. Yehoshua explains how he

---

66   Jacques Derrida, *Dissemination*, translated by Barbara Johnson (Chicago: The University of Chicago Press, 1981), 63.

67   Jameson, discussing Claude Lévi–Strauss, gives the example of the Caduveo Indians in *Tristes tropiques*. Unlike their neighboring tribes, the Caduveo were unable to develop social institutions that would dissimulate social hierarchies. Hence, they began dreaming this solution. "We must interpret the graphic art of Caduveo women," argues Lévi-Strauss, "as the fantasy production of a society seeking passionately to give symbolic expression to institutions it might have had in reality, had not interest and

tried to differentiate his style from the dominant Zionist style prevalent between the late 1930s and 1950s (a literary period dubbed the "Palmach generation," which included the Seneds, Shamir and Yizhar):[68]

> There was a sense that the generation of the Palmach was not writing good literature; it was not deep enough, not thick enough, not sophisticated . . . I could not write in this way, in a way that was not sophisticated in terms of the concealment [hastara] . . . There was the assumption that an opening [of a story] had to conceal [le-hastir] something. And [then] when I read Agnon . . . and Kafka . . . something lit up. It was like a puzzle that made sense, I liked it.[69]

What I have up until now called "abstention" or "concreteness" could also be called "concealment," and we may note how it operates not only in terms of Koren's form and Hagar's actions but also how it also explains Hagar's concealed affair with the soldier. And indeed, if concealment is what enables Hagar's desire for autonomy, it is appropriate that the moment of unveiling and "fettering," as it were, catching Hagar in the act, is carried out by the "historical" characters (Halmi, the Arab, and Bolokin the Communist) that were made inessential to the present-time of the story. Here is the last conversation between Hagar and the soldier in the ruined Palestinian house:

> "Quiet," she said all of a sudden.
> "What happened," he whispered.
> "I heard something," she said.
> He left her and left the room.
> "I heard something," he said, "but I didn't see anything."
> "I'm afraid," she said. They could not see each other in the dark room. Invisible mosquitoes buzzed. Hagar clung to the wall. And when the

---

superstition stood in the way." See Claude Lévi-Strauss, *Tristes tropiques*, translated by John Russell (New York: Atheneum, 1971), 179–80, cited in Jameson, *The Political Unconscious*, 78–9.

68   "Palmah" is an acronym for a Jewish commando unit that participated in the 1948 war. In his influential history of Hebrew literature, Gershon Shaked divides the different styles of writing as well the different ideological positions vis-à-vis Zionism into "generations" usually lasting no more than a decade. The "Palmach generation" (1938–1950s) is supposed to be comprised of those writers whose novels were closest to Zionist ideology.

69   A. B. Yehoshua's statement in Nurit Gerts, *Ḥirbet Ḥiz'ah veha-boker shela-moḥorat*, 43, my emphasis.

floor under her back was cold, rough sounds of footsteps were heard in the building.

"The old guard?"

The soldier didn't answer.

"Come to this corner," he said. "No one will see us."

"I will see you, I will see you," the voice was heard.

"I will see you." His face bore a terrifying countenance. His eyes big, his hair cropped. His face unshaven.

"So you are here?" Halmi [the Arab worker] entered the room, into the darkness.[70]

After this encounter, Halmi and Bolokin take Hagar to see the dead body of the child, as if the historical time that was pushed to the past finally coincides with the private and present time of Hagar. I will say in passing that if the Arab appearing as a faceless voice out of the darkness reminds us of the appearance of the Hebrew God who sees and judges all without being seen, then we can understand how Koren links, albeit in a displaced manner, the historical unconscious, the aesthetic of concealment and the underlying biblical allusion running through the novella. Further, it is important to see that the Arab can only be imagined as a judge rather than a dominated subaltern when the narrative conceals the historical act of dispossession. That is, only from this position can the Arab turn from a political adversary to a moral witness asking the master (Hagar) to recognize herself. As we shall see, once privatization has secured its ground the character and political tenor of the Arab will change as well.

Finally, we need to return to discussion I have hitherto postponed: the political meaning of Yiftah's death, which is conveyed through a biblical allusion. It is easy enough to see that by naming his main characters "Sarah" and "Hagar," Koren offers us a parallel with the biblical story.[71] This allusion is strengthened when we follow the motif of water and heat. We read several times about Hagar's thirst, her preoccupation with the soldier's canteen which, in her imagination, is transformed into an "ancient ewer" (*khad mayim*).[72] These types of details allude to the biblical Hagar's thirst when she was lost in the desert after being banished by Sarah. The story of Hagar and Sarah deals primarily with the political question of the continuity of the Jewish people (*ha-klal ha-yehudi*), through the figure of childbearing: Will Sarah be able to bear children to Abraham and fulfill the divine promise for

---

70   Koren, *Levaya*, 166–67.

71   *Genesis* 16 and 21.

72   Koren, *Levaya*, 54.

Jewish nationhood? But it seems Koren upends the terms. If in the biblical story it is Sarah who is barren and it is Hagar, Abraham's Egyptian second wife, who gives birth to Ishmael, here it is Hagar (now Jewish) who is barren and Sarah who has children. Further, in the biblical story it is Hagar who leaves Ishmael in the desert bushes so as not to see him die of thirst and it is an angel of God who saves him, while in Koren it is Sarah's child (Yiftah or, to complete the allusion, "Isaac") who dies in the bushes and it is significantly not the agent of the Hebrew God who finds him but the Arab, Halmi. What is the meaning then of Koren's "Binding of Yiftah," the fact that Abraham/Simcha's child finds his death in the bushes rather than being saved by God? What kind of wish do we find here if not the wish to break the divine promise for nationhood? In other words, through the upending of the biblical story, the death of Yiftah is not a moral punishment for Hagar's affair with the soldier; on the contrary, it is the event that allows her to break free from the chain of the generations, from Jewish collectivity.

This liberatory reading of Yiftah's death affirms my claim that, in this period, autonomy and private life do not have a positive and affirmative content; rather, they are a privative project accomplished through a radical, usually catastrophic gesture of negation. Thus, though past commentators have seen in Koren's novella a minor story about the mundane existence of Israelis, *Funeral at Noon* advances a political commentary of Zionism that is similar to many others in this period, but presented in a different modality.

9.

For my next example, I move to discuss a "Mizrahi" text, a 1981 short story by Ronit Matalon. To understand the specificity of Mizrahi writers, a few words of introduction are needed about the political predicament of Mizrahim in Israel. To be sure, a more comprehensive study is required in order to account for literary production by Mizrahim, and what is offered here is only an outline of the argument.[73]

In the same manner that the global public sphere imagines Israel only through the category of the "nation-state" to the exclusion of its social form, Zionism is mistakenly taken to represent the interests of Jews in general rather than Ashkenazi Jews, a conception that obscures Israel's ethnic and class structure. Jews of the Muslim and Arab world (grouped

---

73 My study on this subject—*From Subalterns to Subjects: The Development of Liberal Subjectivity in Mizrahi and Beur Literature*—is in progress.

together under the term "Mizrahi"—meaning literally "orientals") were considered by Ashkenazim (Jews of eastern European provenance) to be inferior: base, vulgar, greedy, lustful, backwards, incapable of abstract thought, in short bearing all those anti-Semitic traits that were attributed to Jews in Europe.[74] This attitude was already in place during the early twentieth century when Yemenite Jews were lured to immigrate to Palestine on religious pretexts, and once there, were made to take over the menial work not fit for their Ashkenazi masters:

> The ashkenazim cannot compete with the Arabs and work for the farmer under difficult conditions. The ashkenazi worker that comes from abroad will not remain a lifelong worker and will not work for ever for the farmer. The reason is that he aspires to become free and refuses to be enslaved. The above-mentioned role [i.e., being a slave] will devolve on the mizrahi Jews who after a year of learning, will stay in the moshavot and do all the "inferior" tasks.[75]

This internal Jewish oppression developed into a full-scale separation system when, in the early 1950s, hundreds of thousands of Jews from Muslim and Arab countries immigrated (or were pushed to immigrate) to Israel. In these years, the immigrants were forcefully proletarianized: state authorities placed them in poor, underdeveloped towns, distant from metropolitan areas, broke their political leadership, and "tracked" their children into technical schools. And thus, within a few years, they were transformed into the cheap labor force needed for Israel's industrialization in the 1950s and 1960s. To this day, most Mizrahim remain in the lower rungs of society, blocked from entry into institutions of social mobility; and while the world's eye is trained on Jewish-Arab separation, Ashkenazi-Mizrahi separation (which now includes many other ethnicized subjects), goes unnoticed and unabated.

In more conceptual terms, the statist structure built to ensure the freedom and autonomy of Ashkenazi Jews was predicated, in part, on the un-freedom of Mizrahim. Here we see the contradiction between the abstract concept of national and civil equivalence and the concrete concept of class inequality. To put it in stark terms, the claim for freedom

---

74 Mizrahi critique of Zionist racism and class structure has existed alongside Zionism since the early twentieth century, with the first contact with Yemenite Jews. In the US, this critique was made popular by Ella Shohat. See her "Sephardim in Israel: Zionism from the Standpoint of Its Jewish Victims," *Social Text* 19/20 (Autumn, 1988): 1–35.

75 Joseph Bussel, 1912. Quoted in Shafir, *Land, Labor*, 114.

of the Mizrahi working classes cannot be represented in a democracy (statist or neoliberal) that is based on capitalist social relations.

In his groundbreaking 1981 study on ethnic-class relations in Israel, sociologist Shlomo Swirski understood the predicament of the Mizrahi working class and argued that the Mizrahi could only end their domination by establishing an autonomous economic infrastructure on the national level.[76] However, such an organizational form never materialized, and not only because it could pose a real threat to the statist structure. In his study of Mizrahi history and political organization, Sami Shalom Chetrit shows that in fact such an independent organization, challenging the very division of labor, was never supported by Mizrahi leaders. Although Mizrahi subalterns did organize the first radical civil disobedience protests in Israel, directly challenging state power, Mizrahi leaders opted for cultural or religious organization with the intent of expanding the inclusiveness of the Zionist subject.[77] Thus, Mizrahi history is underlined by a split between the subject of inequality, generated on the level of the economy, and the subject of equivalence, generated on the level of civil society, such that the former is displaced onto the latter. In other words, in the first period, given the foreclosure (the impossibility) of establishing an autonomous Mizrahi organization grounded in equality, Mizrahi politics had to seek solutions within the form and language of the state—a political position that differs markedly from the liberal Ashkenazi position seeking to break away from the state. The literature of the time, written mostly by the educated and not by the Mizrahi subaltern classes, exhibits this split and this displacement. For example, in the novels of Shimon Ballas and Sami Michael, written during the poetics of "making" between the 1950s and the 1970s, the imaginary world is split between relations of inequality, encoded in one kind of time/plot, and relations of civil or republican equivalence, i.e., democratic elections or military service, encoded in a second kind of time/plot. By the early 1980s, in Ronit Matalon's writing, these attempts at collective solutions shift to a (yet impossible) liberal imaginary cast in a modernist idiom. Similar to the Ashkenazi styles of the 1960s discussed previously, Matalon tries to release the Mizrahi individual from

---

76   Shlomo Swirski, *Lo neḥshalim 'ela menuḥshalim: Mizraḥim ve-ashkenazim be-yisra'el: nituaḥ sozyologi ve-siḥot 'im pe'ilim u-fe'ilot* (Ḥaifa: Maḥbarot le-meḥkar ule-bikoret, 1981), 343, 354, my translation. See also the shorter English edition: Shlomo Swirski, *Israel: The Oriental Majority*, translated by Barbara Swirski (London; Atlantic Highlands, NJ: Zed Books, 1989).

77   See Sami Shalom Chetrit, *Intra-Jewish Conflict: White Jews, Black Jews* (London/ New York: Routledge, 2010), 228.

heteronomous relations, and free Mizrahi aesthetics from the poetics of making.

To understand Matalon's aesthetics, it is important to articulate the similarities and differences between Ashkenazi and Mizrahi writers in the literary field. We have seen that the question of autonomy is played out on two levels: political and aesthetic. From the point of view of the writers of the 1960s, the previous (Palmach) generation is criticized for subordinating literary style to the project of state-making, thus diminishing aesthetic autonomy. The modernist endeavors of the 1960s were an attempt to think liberal freedom through literary style and thus gain aesthetic autonomy. Mizrahi writers, being of the dominated group, share a position with the writers of the 1940s and 1950s. The mere fact of writing about Ashkenazi-Mizrahi relations, not to mention directing criticism at the state, was immediately labeled as non-aesthetic writing, for the autonomy of the story was perceived to be subordinated to "political protest," as one critic put it.[78] Thus, "Mizrahi literature," locking together ethnicity and literary topic, became a label for inferior, heteronomous writing, an aesthetic category created out of relations of domination. Where it concerns aesthetic autonomy, relations of domination effect double heteronomy: they subordinate the body of the Mizrahi subject to its social symbolic meaning ("inferiority") and subordinate the Mizrahi literary signifier to its social signified ("referentiality"). The marked and particular category "Mizrahi literature" within the unmarked, universal category of Israeli or Hebrew literature is the immediate effect of racial and class relations of domination. Relations of domination appear then as heteronomy and referentiality—both deny the autonomy of the Mizrahi subject and the Mizrahi writer.

This politico-aesthetic domination is already a social fact for Matalon, who becomes interested in overcoming it as early as 1981. Since political recourse is foreclosed to Mizrahim (as was any alternatives to Zionist statist structure for the writers of the 1960s), Matalon opts for abstract negation, severing signifier and signified, individual and collective. This was labeled as a style of "restraint" by Nili Mirski, the editor of Matalon's first collection of short stories.[79] As Mirski puts it, Matalon's "lack of sentimentality . . . stands in vivid opposition to the folklorist 'colorfulness,' to the pathos and sentimental abundance . . . that characterize many a work of writers that deal with the Mizrahi experience; Matalon only seemingly

---

78   See Gershon Shaked, *Ha-siporet ha-'ivrit*, Vol. 4, 163.
79   Ronit Matalon, *Zarim ba-bayit* (Tel Aviv: Ha-kibuẓ ha-me'uḥad: ha-sifriyah ha-ḥadashah, 1992).

belongs to their ranks."[80] She writes that with Matalon "no protagonist 'represents' anyone nor does it characterize anything beyond itself. Every [character] is shaped with an aim to extreme individualization, and the combination of characteristics of every character is unique and singular."[81] The bifurcation of Mizrahi writers to folklorists (associated with the categories of nature, heteronomy, the body and the popular) and "real writers" (associated with modernity, autonomy, mind and high literature) is again an effect of domination to which the Mizrahi writer, bereft of political autonomy, must agree even before entering the field. Thus, Matalon's aesthetic style is a displaced gesture of political autonomy and bears the mark of its political impossibility in the real. But Matalon is not simply a passive subject here; she in fact adopts Mirski's position and reproduces the split operative in her reading.

In a 2001 interview Matalon is asked if she is "terrified of any stereotypical conception of Mizrahim." Matalon, offering her gesture of negation, answers, "terrified is the exact word . . . I always felt that: here I recoil from folklore, from hyperbole, from colorfulness."[82] We note already the split in the field, the need of the Mizrahi writer to identify herself when confronted with practices of literary identification. Also implied here is the division between the unruly nature of the folklorists and Matalon's civility appearing as an act of "recoiling" from nature's excess. The interviwer continues:

> So actually you are saying something like: "if I am a Mizrahi writer and am expected to write in arabesques, I will write in the strictest manner, according to the strictest conventions of the European realist novel?
>
> Matalon: it is not an arbitrary decision; I did not convene a committee and decide that. It is a matter of temperament, and as I said before, of a real, almost bodily, recoiling . . . "[83]

I note how the East/West division is mapped onto heteronomy and autonomy. In the classist-orientalist imaginary dominating the field of possible aesthetic strategies, Mizrahi writing is identified here with "arabesques," a code for the lush plenitude of the East that provides an antithesis to

---

80   Mirski continues to conceptualize Matalon's writing with all the clichés of the enlightened European critic, namely with the precision of a clockmaker, with "suggestion" that reminds one of Anton Chekhov, and finally as an example of "masculine" writing that bears no relation to the (then) fashionable discussion of feminine writing. Nili Mirski's Afterword to *Zarim ba-bayit,* 149–152.

81   Mirski, Afterword to *Zarim ba-bayit,* 151.

82   *Mikan* 2 (Summer 2001), 244.

83   Ibid., passim.

conceptually rigid Western thought. Matalon's response does not undo the binary or identify it as an effect of domination, but instead rejects the East for the West, and opts for the European novel as an act of freedom from expectations. Note the irony that the gesture of freedom ends in strict literary discipline. The appearance of the European novel as a standard is not accidental. By acquiescing to the Eurocentrism typical of Israeli literature, Matalon can "pass" the censor. The European novel satisfies here both the desire for recognition in the field and the need for a universal measure ensuring equivalence.

At one point in the interview the question of women's writing comes up. In an explanation of her refusal to be labeled as a woman writer, Matalon says, "it seems to me that Israeli sociology quite often assigns 'natural' places from which people speak . . . when I speak, I ask myself what my natural voice is, if I have one at all." She continues, as I have suggested, with the gesture of negation. "Sometimes it seems to me that my 'naturalness' is a series of negations [lavim]: what not to be, and again what not to be, and how not to be locked into a label, whether it was forced on me or I forced it on myself." And now that this social condition is explicitly in the open, an aesthetic is called for to resolve it.

> It seems to me that ever since I started writing it was a kind of an internal project: how to escape from the rain of labels that was breathing down my neck, and wanted to catch me; how to move from the personal and political, to mix them and be mixed with them. In all of those there is an announcement of freedom [herut], like saying "here, I am sovereign, the landlord."[84]

Important here is the affinity between the emergence of subjectivity and interiority ("internal project"), aesthetic autonomy, and political position. Again, confronted with social domination, the self is invented as interior autonomous space, a place that imagines itself free through a negative gesture of self-legislation.

Let us now see how the aesthetic of negation as a technique of freedom plays out in one of Matalon's earliest stories, "Wedding at the Hair Salon." In a remarkable scene where the narrator's (Margalit's) father speaks at a family wedding about a successful Mizrahi working class strike, one can literally see how the father's voice narrating the strike is moved slowly from the center of events into the background and, as this backgrounding

---

84   Ibid., passim.

of the "political" occurs, strange objects begin to emerge in the narrator's mind. I quote this in some length so to have the full effect of this technique:

> "Gentlemen . . . is there a solution to the problem of our brothers the Mizrahim . . . For years you were deceived, and in every election they approach you and promise to take care of your concerns and to improve your living conditions, and yet you remain in the same filth and they never move a finger. Since the establishment of the state until this day, they have never made good on their promises . . . " A dim light filled the salon and two long florescent fixtures above the mirrors gave off a uniform sound. "Look what happened in Ashdod! The beloved Ashdod . . ." emphasized father Goweta. Droplets of perspiration . . . half empty bottles of beer and orange juice as well as stained napkins appeared in the smooth mirrors. *A sobbing baby was hushed.* "If it weren't for the intervention of a few workers' wives much innocent blood would have been spilled . . . " *Sleeves and dresses were rolled up, exposing brown arms and thick feet stuffed in spiked high heels.* "How do you expect them to sit silently while seeing that their husbands, brothers or fathers are starving, how can they be quiet?! . . . " *A flat bare foot on the cold tiles that drain the smell of ammonia into their black cracks in front of the symmetrical rectangles of the window, blue and red squares of a mattress-cover bordered in white . . . Green surfaces covered with pink stains are opened in the crude pull of zippers.* "On that miserable day Ashdod the city of workers, Ashdod, the city of immigrants, looked like a battlefield, an army of police facing an army of workers, both are brothers! Both are Jews!" Margalit drew a straight line on her forehead, putting the back of her hand on her burning cheek. "Are you alright, are you feeling well?" Madeleine hugged Margalit . . . "To force the workers who didn't strike inside. But exactly then came the disappointment! When they saw the tragic appearance of their brothers and wives." *[Madeleine] led her behind the screen, put her head over the salon sink and pressed a wet towel to her temples . . . From behind the screen father Goweta continued . . .* "Will he finish already," Madeleine got up from her place, holding back her orange hair that was burned at the edges: "what's better, putting my hair up or down?"[85]

In a rare moment in Hebrew literature, father Goweta narrates the

---

85   "Ḥatuna ba-mispara," in *Zarim ba-bayit*, 130–4, my emphasis.

unfolding of a strike by Mizrahi workers in the city of Ashdod. Similar to the poetics of making that we have observed, the narrative revolves around a life-and-death antagonism between unequals (workers and the police). It is framed by a brief history of Mizrahi subjugation, a political narrative recounted by father Goweta at a wedding, thus maintaining the overlap of the private and the public typical of such narratives. The short story seemingly keeps with the poetics of "making," but in fact such poetics is brought in only to be negated, and through its negation allows for the emergence of an autonomous poetics of Mizrahi textuality. Note first that Margalit's consciousness brings in the historical event only as text, as speech removed from the actual events that already occurred. The occurrence taking place in this moment is not the unfolding of Mizrahi collective fate, but rather the framing of such events and their mode of narration as démodé, a string of empty words uttered by a tiresome old man ("will he finish already"). At the same time, we are directed away from the speech by a description of colors and surfaces, a riddle of interiority that turns reality into a fantasy of symmetry and concrete details whose meaning we cannot fully fathom. The collective pathos of the strike rooted in inequality is juxtaposed with a series of concrete details whose equivalence as signs is achieved through their alienation from the real. The two styles can be distinguished from one another in the following way: The first poetics follows heteronomous Mizrahim as they try to achieve autonomy and freedom through struggle, which in turn subordinates narrative language, turning it into a heteronomous testimonial. The second poetics achieves poetic freedom by detaching itself from the struggle and the testimonial, resulting in a mystified narrative language whose literariness is secured by obfuscating its grounding in the real. Finally, the subject of heteronomy and the subject of autonomy are literally separated by the screen that closes the scene. Similar to Koren, the feminine body plays a key role here: the fact that Margalit, the protagonist, is feverish is the "motivation" for her distorted optics, for her "not understanding" what she is seeing. What in Koren was accomplished throughout the duration of the novella is here condensed into a paragraph where we see the split taking place line-by-line.

Matalon's work, and literature written by Mizrahi writers more generally, deserves much more attention than I can give it here, but I stress the point that its specific attempts to think autonomy and freedom are conditioned by the same historical limit of statism that affect other writers of the same period.

10.

Now that we have discussed the three aesthetico-political relations to the historical limit (Statist: Seneds; Humanist: Yizhar; Liberal: Koren; Mizrahi-liberal: Matalon) I can offer a few broad concluding remarks.

I argued that the first statist period is dominated, politically, by the statist project that supersedes or subsumes any other (internal) political project for which Zionism appears as an unsurpassable historical limit. This kind of thinking allows us to shift our conception of the state away from what Kant would call phenomenal content (read: the Zionist meta-narrative) and instead understand it as a condition of possibility with which all political positions had to contend. Only rarely did social agents refuse the state altogether and enter into direct conflict with it (a fourth unrealizable option). Such were the revolts by the Mizrahi residents of the Wadi-Al-Salib in Haifa in 1959 and the Mizrahi Black Panthers in 1971–73,[86] But their actions were suppressed precisely because of their radical rejection of the state. The Mizrahi were never able to coalesce into a subject and remained subsumed in a subaltern position, relegated to misrecognized and aleatory roles in more sanctioned novels.[87]

The state is characterized by its status as a total political project, fusing together the private and the public sphere, and by its process of self-making, creating the social world in its own image, especially by transforming the land, organizing work and waging war. This process gives rise to the spiritual nature of Zionism that aims to fuse together spirit and body, to animate the inanimate and feel at home in the world. Despite the fact that Zionist political ideology grounds its claims to the land in a divine promise, in actuality Zionist statism is a deeply secular attitude to the world in the strict sense that its subjects make and re-make their world, grasping themselves as its cause. It is for this reason that Zionists characters in statist novels such as those of the Seneds are depicted as Greek gods on earth, not so much because their oft-mentioned virility, but because they roam the imaginary world as those who make its laws.

Aesthetically, since it delivers a world whose underlying causes are in the open, antagonism creates the illusion of transparency, as if we

---

86   See Sami Shalom Chetrit, *Ha-ma'avak ha-mizrahi be-yisra'el: Ben dikuy le-shihrur, ben hizdahut le-alternativah 1948–2003* (Tel Aviv: 'Am 'oved, 2004) and the English edition, *Intra-Jewish conflict in Israel: White Jews, Black Jews.*

87   See my "Mizrahi Subalternity and the State of Israel: Towards a New Understanding of Mizrahi Literature," *Interventions: International Journal of Postcolonial Studies* 16.3 (2014): 380–404.

are gazing into the Real of social life. However, it is not truly so because Zionism does not recognize and thus does not represent the claim to freedom of those that it made into "others." Further, since the characters create their world, there is no separation between self and world. This again points to the spiritual nature of Zionist imaginary worlds in the sense that nature and the inanimate are full of meaning, reverberating back to the Zionist character its own wishes and desires. For this reason, when early capitalist privatization takes place in the 1970s, turning the spiritual into the merely material, Yaacov Shabtai's *Past Continuous* represents Zionism as a world fallen from grace, one devoid of its spiritual, utopian meaning.

As we saw in the Seneds' novel, antagonism creates the entire social world, in this case in the form of the 1948 war. This antagonism is rooted in violence and in the fundamental inequality of the two rivaling sides (in the sense that they cannot find a universal shared measure). Through this antagonism historical time is made, as is the time of the novel which follows a developmental temporality. The antagonism and its time are made into the universal against which all other events are measured. In Yizhar, we saw the same tendency to depict a constitutive antagonism (constructing the path during the war) that produces both the time of the novel as well as the historical time of Zionism; but as Yizhar is trying to resolve the problem of violence and inequality, he turns to nature. Existing alongside the antagonistic world, nature allows Yizhar to imagine a pastoral world devoid of antagonism in which all creatures (the human and the animal) are made equivalent to one another. This equivalence is the utopian element in Yizhar. Correspondingly, time here does not develop towards a finite goal, but is imagined as infinite and synchronous. Nature in Yizhar is not historical and does not change; it is very much like divinity—it exists everywhere and at all times. The uniqueness of Yizhar in Israeli literature is not so much his humanism, which typifies many other writers, but rather that in him we are able to find an alternative to Zionist statism that does not separate body and spirit. In other words, nature rivals the spiritual element within Zionism.

In Koren we found the most complex attempt to find an alternative to statism. The fundamental gesture that allows Koren to create Hagar's autonomy is the removal of antagonism from her life in the present. This gesture produces some powerful symptoms: not only is antagonism displaced into the past, giving the false impression that the Zionist collective was made once and for all, it also alters the meaning of politics. If in the Seneds and in Yizhar political antagonism constituted the world through which all characters received their meaning, in Koren politics is reduced to a displaced phenomenal object within the world. In Hagar's world, the Palestinian house is a stand-in for politics, rather than an object of political contestation. In Hagar's time, then, the spirit of the state—which in the Seneds and Yizhar covered the entire social world—is localized within a fetishized object. Locking the jinni of the state within the house, as it were, relieves the world of the curse of inequality and, as with Yizhar, unleashes a world of equivalence. But if in Yizhar equivalence was thematic—nature—in Koren it is formal; we find it in the concrete style itself where all gestures and characters, in Hagar's time, are now equivalent to one another. Koren's editor, Menachem Peri, describes Koren's style using the photographic metaphor of a "blow-up": "The dramatic plot in Koren is flooded with concrete (*muḥashi*) details and attitudes . . . Through this [photographic] blow-up, all realistic details seem equivalent to one another."[88] This equivalence underlies the textual world of Hagar, a mysterious world made of concrete signs that conceal their meaning and ask us to decipher them. The equivalence of signs alters in turn the fabric of time. For once the antagonism, as the source of time, is removed, developmental time is replaced with synchronous time. For this reason, time and change can re-enter the world of Hagar only through a catastrophe—Yiftah's death—a singular event that is needed to rupture synchrony and through which, in a displaced manner, history can re-enter the world.

Mizrahi novels, in their own way, depict imaginary worlds split between forms of inequality and equivalence in which the latter is posited as the utopian solution to the former. In Matalon, we saw briefly a variation on the liberal negation of statism where freedom is achieved through an aesthetic gesture of obfuscation.

Foreshadowing the discussion of the second period, we can say that Hagar's mysterious world, in which politics turned from constitutive antagonism to a fetishized object, synchronous and infinite time takes the place of developmental finite time, equivalence replaces inequality, and history can enter only in the form of a catastrophic event leading to self-recognition characterizes the world of private life, in which the subject no longer makes and re-makes the social world, but is left only to read and decipher it. The cardinal historic difference between the first, statist period, and the second, neoliberal one, is that Hagar's private world will no longer be bound to a sphere within the world, existing as

---

88   From the novel's back cover.

a negation, but will be released from its boundedness and will cover the entire imaginary world now as a positive phenomenon. If in the first period politics was a fetter from which liberal writers tried to break free, in the second, politics will be sought out as a remedy to re-bind and reimagine the nation.

2

Autonomy, Equivalence, and the Poetics of Textuality: Israeli Literature of the Neoliberal Period 1985–

1.

That Hebrew literature began experimenting, in the second half of the 1980s, with new poetic forms and emitting new ideological messages was immediately noticed by Israeli literary critics. It took no more than a handful of experimental novels[1] and the literary field gushed with new theories, political speculations, and, as in the US and Europe, moral condemnation.[2] The new "wave" or "generation" of novelists was dubbed

---

1   Popular examples include: Gafi Amir, *'Ad klot* [*Till the End*] (Tel Aviv: Zemorah bitan, 1987); Orly Castel Bloom, *lo rahok mi-merkaz ha-'ir* [*Not Too Far from Downtown*] (Tel Aviv: 'Am 'oved, 1987); *Hekhan ani nimzet* [*Where Am I*](Tel Aviv: Zemorah Bitan, 1990); Avraham Hefner, *Kolel hakol* [*Everything Included*] (Tel Aviv: Keter, 1987); Yoel Hoffmann, *Sefer Yosef* [*The Book of Josef*](Tel Aviv: Keter/Masada, 1988); Etgar Keret, *Ga'aguay le-kisinjer* [*Missing Kissinger*] (Tel Aviv: Zemorah-bitan, 1994); Gadi Taub, *Ma haya kore 'im haynu shokhahim 'et dov* (Tel Aviv: Ha-kibuz ha-me'uhad, 1992) There were of course others, as well as new novels by modernist (statist) writers who began writing in new styles.

2   Major and comprehensive accounts of the new postmodern style include: Avraham Balaban, *Gal aher ba-siporet ha-'ivrit: Sifrut 'ivrit postmodernit* (Tel Aviv: Keter, 1995); Orziyon Bar-Tana, *Shemonim: Sifrut yisra'elit ba-'asor ha-aharon* (Tel Aviv: Sfarim, 1993); David Gurevitz, *Postmodernizem: tarbut ve-sifurt be-sof ha-me'a ha-'esrim* (Tel Aviv: Dvir, 1997); Hanna Herzog, *Ha-kol ha-'omer ani: Megamot ba-sifrut ha-yisra'elit shel shnot ha-shemonim* (Tel Aviv: Ha-'universita ha-petuha, 1998); Dan Miron, "Hirhurim b-'idan shel proza." In Zisi Stav (ed.) *Sheloshim shana, sheloshim sipurim* (Tel Aviv: Yidi'ot aharonot, 1993), 397–427; Gershon Shaked, *Sifrut 'az, kan, ve-'akhshav* (Tel Aviv: Zemora-bitan, 1993); "Ha-postmodernizem: *Rav siah*," *Iton 77* 138–39 (July–August 1991): 26–35. For other important contributions see Dan Miron,

"postmodern" and unsurprisingly, given the identification of cultural critics with the US and Europe, American and French theories of the postmodern (mostly à la Lyotard) were imported whole cloth, without always looking into the specificities of Israeli social life. As in debates elsewhere, postmodernism, with its philosophical affirmation of the plurality of "narratives" on one hand, and its radical doubt of any stable ontological foundations on the other, was very quickly accused of being "nihilist," "relativist" and altogether a corrosive social force. Compounding the negative and suspicious reception of postmodern (sometimes called post-structuralist) philosophers and novelists was the fact that the "postmodern" arrived in Israel just as two new intellectual and cultural fronts were opening: first, the critical studies of the New Historians, dubbed post-Zionist, exposing Zionist treatment of the 1948 Palestinian refugees and other aggressions towards Arab states. These histories weakened the state's exclusive control over its historical narrative, showing Israel to be a belligerent state.[3] Second, a renewed Mizrahi critique, now dubbed postcolonial, also advanced an attack on Zionist myths of national unity, exposing the racist and violent treatment of the state towards Jewish immigrants from Arab and Muslim lands (so-called "Arab-Jews") beginning in the early twentieth century.[4] "Postmodernism" was colored then by post-Zionist and postcolonial attacks on Zionist history and national discourse, and thus the political target of Israeli postmodernism was very

---

'Im lo tihiyeh yerushalayim; "Mashehu 'al sipure Orly Castel-Blum." In Dan Miron, Hasifriya ha-'iveret: proza me'orevet 1980–2005 (Tel Aviv: Yidi'ot Aḥaronot, 2005); Yigal Schwartz, "Shulḥan 'arukh," Efes-shtayim 3 (Winter 1995): 7–15; Hannan Hever, Sifrut she-nikhtevet mi-kan. To focus on literature, I have avoided commenting on discussions of postmodernism in the arts and in theory.

3   The earliest studies include: Simha Flapan, The Birth of Israel: Myths And Realities (New York: Pantheon Books, 1987); Benny Morris, The Birth of the Palestinian Refugee Problem 1947–1949 (Cambridge: Cambridge University Press, 1988); Ilan Pappé, Britain and the Arab-Israeli Conflict, 1948–1951 (New York: St. Martin's Press, 1988); Gershon Shafir, Land, Labor and the Origins of the Israeli-Palestinian Conflict, 1882–1914 (Cambridge: Cambridge University Press, 1989); Avi Shlaim, Collusion across the Jordan: King Abdullah, the Zionist Movement and the Partition of Palestine (New York: Columbia University Press, 1988).

4   Earliest studies include: Hanna Herzog, 'Adatiyut politit—dimui mul meẓi'ut: nituaḥ soẓyologi-histori shel ha-reshimot ha-'"datiyot" la-asefat-hanivḥarim vela-keneset 1920–1984 (Tel Aviv: Yad tabenkin, 1986). Shlomo Swirski, Israel: The Oriental Majority (London/New Jersey: Zed Books, 1989); Ella Shohat, "Sephardim in Israel: Zionism from the Standpoint of its Jewish Victims. Social Text 19/20 (1980): 1–35. But see also Sami Shalom Chetrit, Intra-Jewish Conflict in Israel: White Jews, Black Jews (London/New York: Routledge, 2010); Yehouda Shenhav, Kolonialiyut ve-hamaẓav ha-postkoloniali (Tel Aviv: Ha-kibutẓ ha-me'uḥad, 2004); The Arab Jews: A Postcolonial Reading of Nationalism, Religion, and Ethnicity (Stanford: Stanford University Press, 2008).

much the Jewish foundation of the state itself and its claim on objective and total historical truth. The debates eventually subsided and it is safe to say that as of 2000, postmodernism and the periodization debates are no longer on the literary agenda, having been replaced by a liberal and multicultural discourse (which had always implicitly subtended the Israeli understanding of postmodernity).

The fact that postmodernism was reduced to a philosophical style and that the debates were later replaced with a far more positive multi-culturalism is symptomatic of the misrecognition of the new period and requires our attention before we can progress. First, postmodernism cannot be simply taken as a philosophical trend, but as a new socio-historical reality—postmodernity—whose properties and relevance to literary production are either overlooked[5] or misread in the debates I have just alluded to.[6] Reducing postmodernity to a philosophical trend situates academia and academics as the subject of historical thinking rather than the constitutive institutions of social life, a displacement that results in the inaccurate assertion that postmodernism is now démodé because academics have "moved on." Further, if we look closely at the way literary and cultural postmodernism was articulated in Israel we will notice that at least two of its main elucidators, Avraham Balaban and David Gurevitz, grasp it as a variant of philosophical skepticism. The postmodern world, Balaban explains, is a world typified by the "impossibility to decide between two possible realities and the need to live in a world that lacks certainty."[7] Gurevitz, echoing Lyotard, argues similarly that "doubt [*safek*] begins to enter into our picture of the world, [casting a] shadow on the question of absolute truth . . . on the grand myths that strive for freedom or redemption."[8] Such statements abound across several accounts and are augmented with the claim that a postmodern

---

5   Gurevitz, Bar-Tana, Herzog, and Hever do not provide an historical explanation as to the rise of postmodern thinking.

6   Balaban, Miron, Shaked and others offer "political crisis" or a "crisis of values" as an explanation for these changes in the literary landscape but these cannot account for the emergence of new genres and forms, nor, alternatively, explain why the optimistic years immediately following the Oslo Accords did not alter the forms of Israeli literature. Political crises are important and do appear on the surface of novels, but they usually do not affect broader and more structural elements of literary production.

7   Balaban, *Gal aher*, 17.

8   Gurevitz, *Postmodernizem*, 18. And see also his statement elsewhere, "The 'postmodern condition' is distinguished by skepticism about institutions, art and theory, as discourses whose existence is not necessarily legitimate." David Gurevitch, "Postmodernism in Israeli Literature in the 80s and 90s," *Modern Hebrew Literature* 15 (Fall–Winter 1995): 10–13.

world is one where the subject does not or cannot impose its order on reality and instead finds itself affirming the partial and arbitrary nature of the world. Critics then summon literary texts to exemplify this position, Orly Castel-Bloom being the most paradigmatic example.

It is important first to raise the question whether radical skepticism can be considered a historical marker given that its manifestations accompany social life and philosophy throughout what we call Judeo-Christian culture, appearing and disappearing in moments of crisis and transition that might very well pertain to the neoliberal transformation as well. Second, some might argue that the importance of postmodern skepticism does not reside in its newness per se but in its dominance in literary production since the 1980s; but even the most exemplary writer of the genre, Castel-Bloom, did not come to influence the literature that followed her, and although she continues to be a known and appreciated writer in academic circles, her style remains quite marginal.[9] Conversely, many other novels written then and today have common and dominant philosophical and political characteristics that a theory of the postmodern-as-doubt would be hard-pressed to explain. Third, and perhaps most damaging, is the fact, argued forcibly by some,[10] that even those proponents of postmodernism-as-doubt could not adopt a stance of undecidability and uncertainty towards some of the most pressing social and political questions of Israeli life, chief among them the Israeli-Palestinian conflict, and more recently the dismantling of the welfare state leading to historic levels of inequality. Last, even those postmodern critics of the oppressive and unifying aspects of nationalism as a meta-narrative (Zionist or other) find themselves affirming the redemptive qualities of Palestinian nationalism and its importance for the freedom of the Palestinian people.

These palpable contradictions point to a central fallacy in the appropriation of postmodernism in Israel: the reduction of a new historical socio-political condition—having a plethora of forms—to one of its philosophical articulations. Most accounts of postmodernism in Israel do not fully consider the historical conditions of possibility of Israeli postmodernity. Gurevitz, for example, does not ask why such accounts

---

9   If one wants to locate influential women writers in the early 1990s I would suggest looking at Irit Linur and Gafi Amir, who introduced more quotidian Hebrew language to Israeli fiction and opened the door, together with a few others, to commercial fiction.

10   See Adi Zemah's remarks in "Ha-postmodernizem: Rav siaḥ" as well as Balaban's own remarks in "What's so Wonderful about this Game? Postmodernism in Question," *Modern Hebrew Literature* 15 (Fall–Winter 1995): 3–6.

and literary styles appeared in Israel specifically in the late 1980s and not earlier. Similarly, Hanna Herzog argues that in the second half of the 1980s novelists "began writing differently" but she does not offer any explanation as to why such literary change appeared at this particular point in time.[11]

In the absence of such an explanation and given the identification of postmodernity with a strain of philosophical thinking, it is hardly possible to understand the emergence of postmodernism in Israel other than by an appeal to the spontaneity of the mind. Quite contrary to the theories of postmodernism that they borrow, critics of Castel-Bloom discuss her "arbitrary style" as if it were a consequence of pure intentionality. Dan Miron, whose reading of Castel-Bloom echoes postmodernists, argues that "Everything [in Castel-Bloom] is directed by one 'vision'; everything serves the intention of the writer and embodies her view of reality."[12] Balaban and Hannan Hever, too, grasp the emergence of Castel-Bloom's style in the idiom of intentionality, as a direct rebellion against older literary styles or as an act undermining conventions of national consensus respectively. The implicit persistence of the discourse of intentionality, taking the writer as a locus of meaning and as the very cause and origin of style, points to the disappearance of the unconscious as an analytical category, but more importantly it closes the gap between literary style and social reality, and assumes that the literary field can be explained solely on its own terms.

The contradiction between a skeptical postmodern position and a discourse of intentionality in Israel is not a coincidence. It alerts us to a tendency to shift between radical philosophical negativity (the absence of ontological foundation) and radical political positivity (plural and incommensurable political foundations). The latter returns us to a positivist discourse that reduces society to the sum total of its parts/identities, taking each part as its own self-constituting ground. The latter tendency is especially evident in those literary accounts, such as that of Balaban, where rudiments of underlying historical conditions do make an appearance. Like many, Balaban argues that a sense of uncertainty began with a number of events: the near-defeat of Israel in the 1973 war, the downfall of the Labor Party (Mapai) in 1977 and the rise of the right (Likud), and finally the 1982 Lebanon war that was perceived as unjustified and stirred the largest political demonstrations of the time:[13]

---

11 See footnote 2 for bibliographical details of Gurevitz and Herzog.
12 Miron, "Mashehu," 442.
13 Balaban, *Postmodernizem*, 31–2.

The [1982] Lebanon War prepared the ground for the Israeli postmodern condition of the last ten years. It is a condition typified by a center-less society, the absence of consensus and a stable system of norms and values, a condition of disintegration and alienation between the different social sectors [*migzarim*]. In the 1960s Israel had one central party [Mapai], one ruling ideology accompanied with representative symbols and literary forms, while the 1980s is characterized by disintegration and fragmentation.[14]

Note that, although Balaban holds to a postmodern position that doubts the mimetic relationship between signifier and signified, what he offers here is reflection theory pure and simple, one of the targets of postmodern philosophy. In Balaban's account literature mimics political fragmentation on the level of the line; and he, and others, argue, justly, that such social fragmentation is reflected in the breaking up of Hebrew literature (i.e., secular, heteronormative Ashkenazi male,) into different corpora of identity literature (Women, Palestinian-Israeli, Mizrahi, Ashkenazi, LGBT, Russian, etc.). Such plurality of narratives surely exists, but it presupposes a direct relation between the political community and its literary/linguistic representation, a relation that postmodern theory is highly suspicious of and with good reason. Note then that the reduction of Israeli society to the sum total of its political groups, each of which is assumed as its own ground and cause, corresponds to the tendency we have seen in which the writer itself is perceived as the origin of a new postmodern style.

2.

The account I offer of the new period begins with a different approach both to literature and to Israeli society. As I have argued, we shift away from the eventmental history underlying Israeli literary history in which literature is conceived as an indicator of the national mood responding as it does to political and military events, to a more structural history which attends to the long-term relation between the state and the forces of capitalism, local and global. This relation serves here as the historical "limit" that conditions both social life and the raw materials of literary production such that each individual literary artwork is both conditioned by this limit and responds to it.

---

14   Ibid., 32.

I have mentioned that in the 1960s the statist structure suffered economic crises that led to a series of privatizations, but the most significant shift came in the 1980s, and especially in 1985, with the implementation of a new economic plan backed by the United States and other global institutions. As Yoav Peled and Gershon Shafir argue:

> Since the mid-1980s Israel's economic elites had benefitted from a profound multi-step process which recast the Israeli economy from its protectionist and state-centered origins into a more internationally-oriented, neo-liberal economy. Thus began the transformation of Israel's social structure, a process that . . . while still partial and riled with contradictions and occasional setbacks, has already revolutionized Israeli society beyond recognition . . . [This radical transformation] combined interlocking changes in economic organization labor relations, social welfare and constitutional law.[15]

What characterizes the new period is the release of the forces of capital from the statist structure, a profound historical change that brings about the rearticulation of the private and public sphere and, perhaps for the first time in Jewish and Israeli history, the creation of private Jewish life. This process, well-documented in Israeli social sciences but mostly ignored in postcolonial or post-Zionist studies, is also accompanied by the aggressive entry of global corporations and global investment into Israel, which, little by little, weakens the control of the state over its own economy such that Israel's capacity for self-determination is displaced into the global economy with its demands and protocols. This is how Thomas Friedman articulated this condition to the Israeli public in 1998:

> When your country hooks up to the global economy . . . it begins to resemble, in many ways, a publicly traded company, subjected to the discipline of finance markets . . . The rules of this economy are very strict: privatization, reduction of government involvement . . . it's a very tight straight jacket. When you take it on, however, your economy begins to grow, but your politics shrink. The economy grows but political elections are reduced to Pepsi or Coca-Cola. This straight jacket comes only in one size and one form.[16]

---

15   Gershon Shafir and Yoav Peled, *The New Israel*, 2, 7.
16   Quoted in Uri Ram, *The Globalization of Israel: McWorld in Tel Aviv, Jihad in Jerusalem* (New York: Routledge, 2010), 133.

In conceptual terms, it can be said that the infinity of profit-making, where means become ends, confronts and replaces the finality and end of the statist project. As we saw briefly in Hegel, the state, or any fetishized object, (in Israel it is neo-Zionism), is called on to counter the endless accumulation of neoliberal capitalism, now cast in moral terms as a corrupting force. This is also the moment where we observe the abstraction of labor, capital and to some degree land, i.e., the moment where these categories no longer have overt Jewish/statist content; they are secularized, as it were, and become mere objects or instruments that are devoid of any "spiritual" (i.e., national) meaning. Out of these three categories, the only one that retains its overt political Jewish content and therefore its allegorical and sacred nature is land, and especially the land beyond the Green Line, in occupied Palestine, where settler life, and hence Jewish life, is still imbued with the state and does not yet see the separation of the private and the public. Processes of privatization push, yet unsuccessfully, for the secularization of the state, i.e., for the separation of the state from the Jew itself, whose new constitutive meaning could be established in civil society as a form of private (religious/spiritual) life. Finally, the gradual (but never complete) removal of the state from civil society brings about the substitution of relations of inequality with relations of civil equivalence, allowing for the notion of a multicultural Israel. At this moment, the structure of Israeli society begins to resemble Western Europe and the US, not only in the imaginary, but in the real, and indeed as the shift to neoliberalism takes place, Israeli literature and film take up a new equivalent position in world culture. Writers and filmmakers who become worldly are no longer simply Israeli; they are first and foremost private subjects who happen to work in and write about Israel.

Finally, concomitant with the processes that separate the state and its social content from civil society, we see emerging, as Moshe Postone argues previously, a social structure whose explicit causes are missing; the direct or external determination exerted by the state is now replaced with natural law-like social and ethical conventions whose origin is obscured. Similarly, referring to the development of capitalism in Western Europe, Louis Althusser identifies this structure as a structure with an absent cause, where no single branch of society holds the essence of the whole, a condition that allows for the relative autonomy of each branch.[17] To rewrite Althusser's formulation, each social branch (law,

---

17   Louis Althusser et al., *Reading Capital*, translated by Ben Brewster (London/ New York: Verso, 1997), see especially "Marx's Immense Theoretical Revolution,"

education, religion, art, entertainment, etc.) can now create the impression that it is governed by its own law, through which, as Bourdieu would say, external exigencies are refracted. Differently than Bourdieu, however, this inquiry argues that each such subfield is ultimately conditioned by the overall structure whose mediation acts as an ultimate limit. Faced with such an abstract structure, one political response, present in both social and artistic practices, attempts to embody the absence in a local fetishized agent and reconstruct a causal structure no longer possible at this time. All these social changes now condition political action and artistic response and no account can be considered critical without accounting for their significance.

Let us now briefly review the broad characteristics of literary worlds in this period: if we could point to the most salient feature of the neoliberal period, it would be the fact that its imaginary worlds are no longer made but given. If the writers of the first period, especially in the 1940s and 1950s, constructed a world, whether in the past or the present, that arises out of a constitutive antagonism, marking and making historical collective time, the worlds of the neoliberal period localize antagonism into an event within the world such that characters now live within social time rather than make it. Put more conceptually, the conditions of possibility of social life and social time are presumed to always-already exist separately from the subject. Once the world is presumed to exist instead of being made, the world appears as a sign and a text, and the characters, whether explicitly (detectives) or implicitly (private individuals), survey it and search for its origins.[18] In the most politically displaced or unconscious novels, antagonism is localized within a particular social sphere and a search is launched to find its origins. In the most politically conscious novels, the surveyed sphere tends to be the state or the economy, presumed to be those spheres that stand in for collective life, and whose logic pervades all spheres irrespective of their autonomy. Thus, if for the liberal subject, the "limit" of the statist period was the impossibility of private life, the limit of the neoliberal period is the impossibility of political life. The deepest desire in this period is not for individual freedom, as it was in the first period, but

---

182–93; *For Marx*, translated by Ben Brewster (London/New York: Verso, 2005), see especially "Contradiction and Overdetermination," 87–128.

18   This is the partly the underlying reason for the rise of detective and mystery fiction in Israel in the 1980s. The best-known mystery writers include: Ruth Almog, Esther Etinger, Uri Adelman, Batya Gur, Amnon Jackont, Shulamit Lapid, Yair Lapid, Dror Mishani and Limor Nahmias.

rather for forms of obligation and necessity that will redeem the subject from the nauseating and meaningless freedom of private life.

The second salient feature of such worlds concerns the relation between spirit and body, signifier and signified. I argued that the statist structure can be likened to a political spirit that animates the body of its citizens, making it ideal. The statist project then spiritualizes the body such that it is, as it were, incarnated in the body of the characters and the body of the land itself. In this period, the world of the statist period is "full" of meaning. For this reason, I have argued, the liberal and modernist stance in the 1960s and the 1970s was aimed at liberating the body and the character from the spirit of the state, a technique that resulted in literal and aimless bodies on the one hand, or pure mind on the other. This technique was aided by the separation of the signifier—the body of the word—from the signified—the allegorical political meaning. The reason that, in the second period, modernist forms find their end as a timely and politically relevant literary response has to do with the fact that now processes of neoliberal privatization themselves separate the body of the private individual from the spirit of the state. This social rather than poetic process gathers the political "spirit" from the surface of society and deposits it in the state proper, stripping private life of its meaning and thus making it "matter" alone. This process then vacates the signifier from the signified, making literary language literal or prosaic. Critics notice this change, but again, place its origin in the writers themselves and read it as a matter of style, or even as a political response to earlier writers, for whom language, as we said, was "full." I claim otherwise. The emptying out of literary language is not a response—as indeed it was in modernist attempts—but rather, to recall Barthes, the zero-degree of writing in the second period. Prosaic language is now the raw material of writers, a reality that confronts them as their historical limit. In other words, they cannot write in elevated language even if they wanted to, for such writing is considered obsolete. If there is a linguistic response to the literal reality of neoliberalism it is manifested precisely in the opposite direction, where a few writers use elevated or arcane language to protest the simplification of literary Hebrew.[19]

---

19   The most explicit example is the poetry journal *Ho!*, first issued in 2005, whose editors reintroduced a more rarefied and less colloquial register of Hebrew, as well as rhyme and meter, in an attempt to reinvest poetry with "high value." In prose, Alon Hilu's 2008 *Aḥuzat Dejani* brought back a more archaic Hebrew as the language of one of the main characters. The novel won the Sapir Prize, the most distinguished literary prize in Israel.

3.

Let us now look at four examples of varying ideological positions: Batya Gur's 1988 *A Saturday Morning Murder* [*Reẓaḥ be-shabat ba-boker*], Shimon Ballas's 2003 *Outsiders* [*Yalde-ḥuẓ*], Assaf Gavron's 2006 *Almost Dead* [*Tanin-pigu'a*] and, Nir Baram's 2013 *World Shadow* [*Ẓel-'olam*].

Batya Gur's detective novel *A Saturday Morning Murder*, the first in the series following Mizrahi police detective Michael Ohayon, is symptomatic of Israel's new neoliberal society in several significant ways that are important to mention at the outset.[20] What first catches the eye of readers of Israeli literature are the twin facts of genre and author. First, the novel unabashedly takes up a commercial genre, that in previous literary history would have been labeled "trivial literature."[21] Although the history of Israeli literature surely had its best sellers and popular hits, Gur's detective novel is distinct from the latter as it announces in Israel the sanctioned arrival of genre literature, a trend that has since then intensified so that genre literature holds a dominant position within the literary market today. The novelty of the book is not so much in its commercial aspect, but rather in the fact that, as of the late 1980s, the category of Literature itself has been shifting and mutating, and authors have been shedding their direct political affiliations and becoming full-blown professional writers.[22] The second distinguishing feature of the novel concerns the category of gender and the fact that in this period, with the commercial segmentation of the literary market, Gur and many other female writers[23] are taken more and more seriously and are therefore recognized both in the fields of "large-scale production" and "restricted-distribution," to use Bourdieu's terms.[24] Thus, if in the

---

20   Batya Gur, *Reẓaḥ be-shabat ba-boker: roman balashi* (Yerushalayim: Keter, 1988).

21   I am thinking here of Gershon Shaked's account. See his *Ha-siporet ha-'ivrit 1880–1980*, Vol. 4.

22   David Grossman, achieving notoriety in the early 1980s, is probably the last of the writers which we can still call political in the older sense.

23   These include, Maya Arad, Orly Castel-Bloom, Gil Hareven, Yael Hedya, Yehudit Katzir, Savyon Librecht, Irit Linur, Ronit Matalon, Dorit Rabinyan, and many more.

24   For accounts of female writers in Israel and their marginalization in the canon see Lili Ratok, "Kol 'isha mekira 'et zeh." In Lili Ratok (ed.) *Ha-kol ha-aḥer: Siporet nashim 'ivrit* (Tel Aviv: Ha-kibuẓ ha-me'uḥad, 1994), 261–349; Yael Feldman, *No Room of Their Own: Gender and Nation in Israeli Women's Fiction* (New York: Columbia University Press, 1999); Hannah Naveh, "Leket, pe'ah u-shikheḥa: ha-ḥayim mi-ḥuẓ la-kanon." In Dafna Izraeli et al., *Min, Migdar, Politika* (Tel Aviv: Ha-kibuẓ ha-me'uḥad, 1999), 49–106. For the marginalization of women in the pre-state period, especially in the period between 1882 and 1904 see, Yafa Berloviz, "Ha-'isha be-sifrut ha-nashim shel

liberal and multicultural account of the 1990s, the rise in the number of female writers on the bestseller lists is attributed to a broad notion of "civil progress," it is usually forgotten that one of the enabling conditions of this welcome change is the opening up of the horizon of commercial publishing whose business model encouraged the creation of "women's writing" as a new category of cultural consumption.[25]

The appearance of commodified culture whose fate is somehow intertwined with the category of "woman" is not limited to the so-called sociological level of Gur's book, but is in fact present in its very themes and ideology. If in the first period we saw that it is female characters who carry the burden of the wish for autonomy (Rutka in Shamir, Hagar in Koren; Hannah in Oz), here, too, we shall see that the novel revolves around two dominant women: one representing the dying statist culture, the other representing the burgeoning capitalist one. With this context in mind, we can begin reading the novel.

A Saturday Morning Murder is set in an imaginary institute of psycho-analysis in Jerusalem and opens with the murder of one of the senior analysts, Eva Neidorf. Michael Ohayon and his team of police detectives are called in to investigate, and after a few false leads, the murderer is revealed to be Eva's colleague, the young, beautiful and wealthy Dina Silver. Although the murder is the catalyst for narrative events, I should note that Dina's motivation is as important as the act of murder itself. Dina slept with one of her patients, and the details of this unprofessional relationship were accidently disclosed to Eva who intended to expose her junior colleague the day she was supposed to become a full member of the institute. Thus, despite the fact that the murder investigation catches our attention, Dina's prior violation of the professional code of the institute serves as the principle ethical preoccupation of the novel rather than the more obvious violation of state law—the act of murder. At this point, then, we can already sense the co-existence of two laws, two social systems, and two sets of novelistic concerns: one "private" (the institute), designated as a deep "interior" world, the other public (the state), depicted as prosaic and "external":

---

ha-ʿaliya ha-rishona," *Katedra* 54 (1989–90), 107–24; "Aḥarit davar." In Yafa Berloviz (ed.) *She-ani adamah ve-adam: sipure nashim ʿad kum ha-medinah* (Tel Aviv: Ha-kibuẓ ha-meʾuḥad, 2003), 319–60.

25   In the 1990s, the public face of commercial literature was the writer-attorney-journalist Ram Oren. Oren founded one of the most lucrative publishing houses in Israel (Keshet), specializing in the genre of mystery. In recent years, the Israeli literary market has seen the emergence of literary agents like Ilana Pikerski and Deborah Harris, who mediate between Israeli writers and American/European publishing houses.

The doctor, who arrived with two nurses in an ambulance, knocked on the locked door [of the institute], and Hildesheimer . . . immediately opened. Others no longer knocked or rang the doorbell. The door that always locked out the external world, the door that protected what Gold took to be the safest place in the world, was left open throughout the morning, and through it foreign entities [i.e., the police] broke in [*parzu*], entities that hitherto were no more than hallucinations and fears in the minds of the patients.[26]

Even more important than this external/internal distinction is the crucial fact, perhaps already evident, that unlike the first period in which the personal and political spheres were intertwined, here not only do we see the new emergence of the "private" (professional) sphere, the two spheres are now separated, encountering each other, thematically, as two distinct areas of social life (the institute vs. the police).

This new development deserves further attention as it conditions the fabric of this imaginary world. First, the explicit political level is all but gone for these characters. No character contributes to the making of the state, and in fact the imaginary world has changed to the degree that now the state itself—which was the outcome of all acts—is reified as one of its representative branches within the world, i.e., the police. This means that characters no longer make their political life but *encounter* it as an external fixed law rather than as an object of social making. This does not mean that characters in Gur's novels cannot stand in for Zionism as did characters in the first period. Ernst and Eva and other characters in subsequent novels are written as allegories, but the content of the allegory is now qualitatively different. These characters do not make their world like the characters in the statist novels of the first period; rather, they stand in for the imaginary *values* of Zionism. Characters are reduced to free-floating values precisely because these are no longer possible in post-1985 Israel. From here it is also possible to glimpse another division within the novel—the division between manual and intellectual labor, the pragmatic/prosaic and the spiritual that can be mapped onto the Mizrahi police officers and the Ashkenazi suspects respectively. The police force, being identified with present-tense Israel, is associated with prosaic work and duty, vulgarity, and the body (only Michael, the orientalist fantasy of Gur, escapes this fate). The character who embodies this pole is detective Blilti, who is constantly portrayed as a patriarchal man

---

26 Gur, *Rezaḥ*, 16.

with large lips and a protruding belly, an unethical sexual deviant who sleeps with people to get information. The Ashkenazi suspects, especially those identified with the now-defunct values of Zionism, are identified with intellectual labor and ethical behavior.

Second, private life is separated not only from political life but also from personal life. Autonomy within the private realm is enabled by the strict purity of this sphere and its ability to determine its own laws. In Gur's novel, the "private" is given thematic content through, on one hand, the bodily asceticism of Eva and, on the other, the professional attitude and ethics of Ernst—setting the example for all psychoanalysts.[27] Eva is portrayed time and again as the perfect embodiment of professional behavior, an "angel"[28] that people cannot imagine has any life (or desires) outside her role as a psychoanalyst. More essential to the concept of the "private" and to the central question of the novel, however, is the ethical relation between the psychoanalyst and the patient. Ernst explains this to Michael:

> [The psychoanalyst] must keep a real distance between himself and the patient and not reveal his own private life to him.[29]

Eva and Ernst are the most ethical, i.e., professional, characters, who maintain this distance while the new generation of psychoanalysts, especially Joe Linder and Dina Silver, transgress. The question of the proper distance and the strict separation of the personal and the professional is in fact the key question of the novel, and the transgression of this boundary by Dina, as I have argued, is the preliminary violation that leads to Eva's murder. By arresting Dina and re-establishing the proper distance between personal and private life, the state's role in this novel is imagined as a ready-made *instrument* in the hands of private life, an agent that is summoned to descend from the heavenly sphere of the state—law—to regulate the bodies of the earthly private sphere taken now as nature.[30]

Seeing that the novel is as occupied with the ethical law as with the

---

27   Ibid., 10–11.

28   Ibid., 62.

29   Ibid., 45.

30   I allude here to Hegel and Marx's argument that in fully developed capitalism the state becomes (Marx) or can become (Hegel) a mere instrument to sort out the matters of private individuals. See G. W. F. Hegel, *An Outline of a Philosophy of Right*, translated by T. M. Knox, Stephen Houlgate (ed.) (Oxford: Oxford University Press, 2008), 228; Karl Marx (with Friedrich Engels), *The German Ideology* (New York: Prometheus Books), 99.

murder plot will help suggest a second displacement. For although we are drawn into the novel by the lure of police detective work, with its cloak-and-dagger techniques, its hierarchies of command, and its legends of knowledge and penetration—a mythological world through and through—the novel is equally devoted to the strangeness of the psychoanalytic institute, with its "mysterious air,"[31] its own unique and arcane hierarchical structure, and its rites of initiation. This peculiar desire of the novel to penetrate not only the mystery of the crime, but the enigma of the institute itself—where a dead body lies within its sacred walls—should alert us to the possibility that the real object of our own detective inquiry should be the setting rather than the violent act at its center.[32] What will stand at the heart of this reading then is the poetic and allegorical meaning of the institute. It should come as no surprise that I will conceive of the institute as an emblem for the Israeli private sphere, striking the reading eye as an enigmatic new form of life within the very heart of Israel, an exotic existence that was hitherto reserved for the "others" of Israeli society, either internal (Mizrahim and Israeli-Palestinians) or external (Palestinians). And yet, although the meaning of the "private" is complex in itself, the institute is more multifarious than that; certain aspects of its history stand in for Zionism, as if the institute, to appeal to Adorno, is composed of sedimented materials whose interaction we will need to carefully observe.

4.

I have already mentioned at the outset that the novel's broadest historical horizon revolves around a struggle between the declining culture of the state as a project of collective making and the rising legitimacy of the bourgeoisie and private life, a struggle that finds its content in the rivalry between the senior analyst Eva Neidorf (the victim) and her younger apprentice, Dina Silver (the murderer). At the very last moments of the novel, when she is maneuvered into giving her damning confession, Dina explains the tension between her and Eva to Ernst Hildesheimer, the head and co-founder of the institute:

---

31   Gur, *Rezah*, 8. In another early instance, Ohayon asks the director of the institute, "but what exactly is this place?" Gur, *Rezah*, 19.

32   Fredric Jameson makes a similar claim in his reading of science fiction novels. See Jameson, *Marxism and Form: Twentieth-Century Dialectical Theories of Literature* (Princeton: Princeton University Press, 1972), 404–9.

I think that . . . there was a certain competition between me and Dr. Neidorf, competition over your attention . . . I let her understand that you and I have a special relationship. I think that this is what caused her to punish me.[33]

If we recall that the aging Ernst, a commanding and authoritative figure, considers the institute he himself helped build as his second home and treats the analysts he trains as a father would, we can say that the professional rivalry between Eva and Dina—whose stakes are the eventual leadership of the institute itself—has an additional layer: that of the family drama, of two bright daughters fighting over the attention of their father. This is the way Dina sees things; she translates the professional content of her relationship with Eva, a site that in Hegel's theory of the state belongs in the realm of "private" existence, into the idiom of the family, or the "personal" realm. In the parlance of the novelistic world, Dina is guilty of transference and accuses Eva of doing the same.[34]

To generalize these meanings, we would certainly retain our literal understanding of the text on its own terms, but we also need to move into a higher level of allegorical abstraction. Here we should note, on one hand, the historical content of Eva, Ernst and the institute itself and, on the other, of Dina's character. I will attend in much more detail to the institute's historical significance, so it will suffice to say here that Eva and Ernst are portrayed as affluent Ashkenazi elites of the old guard, especially Ernst. I associate them with the statist project because in them we see a pure sense of duty and sacrifice, a spiritual existence that is not marred by material concerns or bodily temptations. To be sure, they are not the real but rather idealized and nostalgic embodiment of Zionist statist spirit, the manner the state exists in the moment when such pure sacrifice and duty are no longer possible and considered naïve.

As for the institute, Gur carefully writes its history so as to echo the history of Zionism. If we look carefully at these textual moments the resemblance begins to suggest itself very quickly. First, the telling of the institute's history is entrusted to Ernst whose nickname not coincidentally is "the old man" (*ha-zaken*). Those familiar with Zionist history would immediately recognize the allusion to one of the most well-known Zionist leaders, the legendary first Prime Minister of Israel, David Ben-Gurion, nicknamed "the old man." Second, to tell the history

---

33   Gur, *Reẓaḥ*, 204.
34   Ibid., passim.

of the institute, Ernst invites Michael to his old house, located in one of Israel's most famous neighborhoods: Rehavia.[35] This neighborhood was established in the early 1920s and became the home of many prominent Zionist leaders, politicians, intellectuals, and artists and also housed many Zionist state institutions such as the Jewish Agency, the Jewish National Fund (JNF) and others. We are given to understand that Ernst has lived there since the 1930s and thus his house is charged with the significance of the historic period itself. Third, once the setting is placed, we move to Ernst's immigration history whose details echo the history of Western Europe and the Jews in the twentieth century. He was born in Vienna and decided to immigrate to Israel in 1933 when the Nazi Party came to power. Fourth, Ernst tells us of the climate in which the institute was built, how it was made by its own founders, a key feature that brings back the importance of self-making, the concept that characterizes the program of Zionist founding leaders. Last, we learn that like the hardships involved in establishing the state, the establishment of the institute was a pioneering endeavor:

> Life was very difficult . . . The analytic training was exhausting [*mefarekhet*] and we had no income. There was a pioneering [*ḥaluẓit*] atmosphere . . . There were also language difficulties. All the seminars were in German and treatment itself was conducted in a hodge-podge of languages, including very crude Hebrew.[36]

If we read this paragraph carefully, we will see how Gur invokes the same imagery that is used to describe Zionist pioneers living on a kibbutz in the early twentieth century. Pioneers were poor, worked together in communes with little income, and hardly spoke Hebrew. Thus, Gur creates the institute in the image of the Zionist statist project: it is the outcome of collective making that infuses the private and public spheres such that one's personal life is bound up with the political destiny of the group. And yet, the fact that it is a private institution that is made to be the bearer of political significance (and not, say, the establishment of a kibbutz or a frontier) suggests a certain historical limit, the meaning of which I elaborate below.

Now, at the same time that the institute is associated with Zionism, we also note that it is portrayed as a thing of the past. It is no coincidence

---

35   Ibid., 36.
36   Ibid., 41.

that its allegorical valence is given in a historical register, while in the present we are confronted with all the indications of a dying culture. Most of the senior clinicians are old men and women; the walls of the institute are covered with framed portraits of past members, now dead, and it seems the younger generation (especially Dina and Joe Linder) are not following in the footsteps of the founders. Thus, the institute is mutating and transforming internally so as to represent the broader transition in Israeli society.

Dina's character crystalizes this transition. Given that Gur seeks to draw us off her scent, the attributes that capture Dina's character are the most economical and dispersed. We get a brief glimpse of her social status only in the last third of the novel when Michael interrogates her for the first time:

> Her hands attended to her black turtleneck. She sat in an open coat, a long and soft fur coat, and had an air of indulgence and pampering [*pinuk*] about her.[37]

A moment later we hear that she drives an expensive BMW, is married to a well-known judge and takes hunting vacations in Western Europe.[38] Now, this description might pass unnoticed in affluent societies, but in an Israel that is just coming out of fifty years of socialist making-do, this description, however brief, immediately codes Dina as a wealthy upper-class woman, and as arrogant, spoiled and self-interested—all the character traits that oppose Zionist collective sacrifice.

The significance of Dina's character then is not simply in her wealth—all the psychoanalysts are wealthy, including Eva and Ernst, and in fact all those involved in the murder case are of the upper echelons of Israeli society: "It has been a while . . . since I have seen an investigation that involves so many beautiful people: judges, military governors. What else will we have here."[39] The point is that Dina is of a new kind of class that no longer shares the older statist values. The most tell-tale sign of Dina's difference comes after the initial investigation, again very late in the novel, when we find out that Dina's marriage is something altogether different than what it seems:

---

37   Ibid., 150.
38   And there is also of course the allegorical meaning of her last name, Silver.
39   Gur, *Reẓaḥ*, 157.

They sleep in separate rooms, and if you ask me this whole marriage looks like one big business.[40]

What differentiates Dina from the rest of the analysts, not least from Ernst and Eva who represent the institute's essence, is that in her, business and money infiltrate personal and sexual life and substitute quality for quantity. To generalize, from Gur's vantage point, Dina stands in for that broader process in Israeli society (and elsewhere in the world) where relations of material exchange take over and instrumentalize areas of life that were hitherto shielded from them. In Habermasian terms, Dina is that agent in which we witness how capital colonizes non-capitalist forms of life, especially moral and ethical ones.[41] Dina is then precisely the embodiment of this new class and a new dominant sensibility in Israeli society, a form of life that is utterly dedicated to material gain. This does not mean that this sensibility does not advance political ends. Rather, politics is now rearticulated from the vantage point of material gain and subordinated to its needs.

Thus, differently from static readings of the novel that coalesce all the "old Ashkenazi elites" together and proceed to argue that Gur is critical towards their practices,[42] the novel not only distinguishes between two kinds of rival dominant classes, it also wholeheartedly endorses and idealizes the older statist class—in the figures of Ernst and Eva—and lets us understand that they themselves are victims of a heinous crime.

Now we understand the novel is written from a conservative perspective that is nostalgic for Zionist statist culture, we can also make sense of other materials in this novel, namely, the dominated Mizrahi working classes and the way the declining statist class enlists them into their cause against the rising new bourgeoisie. Gur accomplishes this political cooperation through the affective and libidinally gratifying levels of the text, which are invested not so much in the crime investigation but, again, in the setting, in the warm relationship and intimate cooperation that

---

40   Ibid., 168.

41   Marx identified this process in the transition from feudalism to capitalism and noted how it appears as a process of secularization in which the former spiritual qualities of the feudal lord that covered over material concerns are evacuated to leave pure profit in the open. Karl Marx, "Economic and Philosophical Manuscripts" In *Early Writings*, translated by Rodney Livingstone and George Benton (London: Penguin Books, 1992), 319.

42   See for example David Gurevitz, *Ha-balash ke-gibor tarbut: sifrut, kolno'a, televiziya* (Tel Aviv: Misrad ha-bitahon, 2013), 290–323; Dan Miron, "Komriyeh be-yisra'el," *Ho!* 3 (2006): 99–128.

develops between Michael, the Mizrahi detective, and Ernst, the Ashkenazi co-founder of the institute. The novel literally ends when Michael and Ernst cooperate to maneuver Dina to Ernst's house for an analytic session while Michael hides in the shadows and records her answers. This key moment has several meanings. Here we see plainly how the declining Ashkenazi statist class makes use of the Mizrahi underclasses but also how they enlist the state apparatus itself to their aid. More importantly, this moment of intimate cooperation, in bringing back social order, delivers the utopian wish of the novel to make ethnic peace between Mizrahim and Ashkenazim. Of course, that peace is granted from the purview of the Ashkenazi elite. For we should say now that Michael is written as what postcolonialists would call a colonial fantasy of mimicry. Michael is a former master's student in history, studying the European Middle Ages, who was supposed to complete his doctorate in Cambridge, England, but was not able to do so because of familial complications. He is married to an Ashkenazi woman, a second generation to Holocaust survivors, and in his spare time he listens to classical music. In short, the cooperation between the Mizrahi and Ashkenazi can happen only if the Mizrahi resembles the Ashkenazi and enacts all the former's clichéd and provincial phantasies about Western Europe. Gur completes this fantasy by employing an orientalist schema whereby Michael is written as a seductive, warm, and fatherly Middle-Eastern man, while all the institute's psychoanalysts are cold and detached Germans.

The last point that needs to be stressed here is the difference in the content of the utopian wish. Recall that since the mid-1950s, the dominant literary position in Israeli literature is that of an impossible liberalism which uses the work of art or nature as a site to think individual freedom and autonomy. In Gur, the utopian wish is markedly different. Not only is Dina's individualism rejected and condemned, and a Mizrahi, rather than an Ashkenazi, is figured as an imaginary ideal of "East and West"; what the novel seeks the most is *political cooperation* between state authorities and the older statist class, Mizrahim and Ashkenazim.[43]

---

43 Gur does not always take this nostalgic position. In her third novel about a murder in the kibbutz, the text sides with the forces of privatization against the older way of life of the kibbutz. See Batya Gur, *Lina meshutefet: Reẓaḥ ba-kibuẓ* (Yerushalayim: Keter, 1991). Miron argues that this critique of the kibbutz is still consistent with Gur's identification with Zionism. He explains that Gur separates between the Western European side of Zionism, associated with high culture and civilization, which she endorses, and the Eastern European/Russian side associated with socialism, which she rejects. See Miron, "Komriyeh be-yisre'al."

5.

The short allegorical reading of Gur's novel has allowed us to identify the social conflict that underlies its materials and trace the transformation of the utopian wish lodged at its heart. But all this is surely not enough to answer deeper and more important questions as to the form of the novel, the imaginary world the characters inhabit, or, more conceptually, its conditions of possibility. Here, as promised, we move away from the alluring murder plot and take note of the setting, first and foremost the institute itself, but also the police and the way these two spheres interact and, most importantly, interpret the world. Emphasizing the setting does the important work of distinguishing between Gur's ideological position (Zionist nostalgia, orientalism) and the historical and poetic conditions that inform the novel's structure.[44] I will say in passing that contemporary Israeli literary criticism usually attends to the first element (ideology) and tends to neglect the second (conditions).

Our inquiry into conditions under which the detective plot unfolds begins with a peculiar irony: of all possible social objects, Gur chooses a private institution to stand in for Zionism, an institution dedicated to the matters of the individual psyche, and managed by professionals. It is no exaggeration to say that nothing could be more foreign to the statist Zionism of the first period, or even to the Zionist nationalism of the 1990s, than a psychoanalytic institute. The fact that an institute—whose purpose is the investigation and healing of private life—is chosen to stand in for a collective political organization—Zionism—is symptomatic of a larger challenge facing the Israeli writer after 1985: in this period no single institution, not even the state itself, can stand in for society as a whole. On the level of civil society we have an aggregate of private interests, while in terms of political organization each group is perceived as advancing its own narrow private interest without the ability to form or impose a consensus the way the statist state and its ruling party, Mapai, did in the previous period. Thus, even when Gur's other novels do take up more representative social branches like the university and the kibbutz,[45] they are portrayed as privatized (or privatizing) institutions whose symbolic power to stand in for the whole has now dwindled or is nonexistent.

Given this historical predicament we are better able to understand

---

44   See here Jameson's formulation of literary criticism as an interrogation of "conditions of possibility" in *The Political Unconscious*, 57.

45   Batya Gur, *Mavet ba-ḥug le-sifrut* (Yerushalayim: Keter, 1989); *Lina meshutefet*.

the world that the characters inhabit. I have already elaborated the broad philosophical and epistemological properties of this period, so here I will concentrate on one key point: the privatization of the state means that unlike the previous period, characters no longer make the time and cause of their entire world (the most obvious instances are war and settlement projects), and the absence of such a binding reason and cause (which would make each individual a mere instance of the whole) creates a world in which each social branch, each institution and eventually each individual is grasped as a separate self-legislating entity whose internal law needs to be deciphered. In other words, a privatized neoliberal world is a world made up of pseudo-wholes—fetishes—that give the impression that they are self-sufficient. For this reason they appear to the social eye as exotic and strange objects whose interiority we seek to penetrate. To put it differently, in the time of neoliberalism, the social world itself becomes a *text*—in the Derridean definition in which the law of the composition is absent—and the individual a *reader*.

I argue that this socio-poetic condition explains the emergence of the Israeli detective novel, for it is the genre par excellence that thematizes this social condition by mirroring, or projecting into its imaginary world—the pursuit of signs—that which characterizes the social world itself.[46] This mirroring is duplicated on all levels of the text. First, in terms of plot, the police investigation confronts two textual objects whose governing cause or law is missing: the clues that form a series of signs whose initial cause is obscured, and the institute itself whose rules Michael is trying to decipher. Second, thematically, textualization takes us deeper into the institute itself whose own objects are the internal lives of the patients which the clinicians read as a text composed strictly of symptoms. Third, in terms of narrative objects, the investigation revolves in part around a missing text—the lecture Eva was supposed to deliver the day she died, a lecture that would have exposed Dina's malpractice and ended her career.

---

46   Here I differ with Dan Miron who argues that the emergence of the Israeli detective novel is tied to collective guilt—about the occupation and the rise of materialistic life—that the solution of the plot cleanses. However interesting, Miron's interpretation confuses the plot of the detective novel with the world the characters inhabit. His interpretation will therefore encounter its limit, first, when certain detective novels do not end in a comforting catharsis or are not solved at all, and second, when we notice that the sense of guilt already existed in earlier moments of Israeli fiction, i.e., in the stories of S. Yizhar, or the novels of Aharon Megged and many others. Moreover, when we note that the sense of collective guilt can be taken up and cleansed in genres other than detective novels. Otherwise, Miron's interpretation is a precise and perceptive account of the limits of Gur's novels. See Miron, "Komriyeh be-yisrael."

The textualization of the social and imaginary world points to a key feature of novels written after 1985—the *equivalence* of all novelistic materials. In Gur's novel, equivalence is expressed in the very structure of the world. As we saw, all of the branches of Gur's world—in this case the police, the institute, the suspects and the patients—all are written as separate and autonomous worlds governed by a law that needs to be deciphered. For purposes of comparison, recall the equivalence we found in Koren in Chapter 1. There, since the social world was based on a fundamental inequality, the imaginary world was made equivalent through style, which, in turn, harbored an implicit utopian wish for a world made of equals. Here, equivalence is already the property of the social world and therefore can appear as the immediate "stuff" of the novel, i.e., its themes. In such an equivalent social world, "inequality"—the mutually exclusive interests of Dina and Eva resulting in murder—can enter the world only as violent disruption of order, as an extraordinary thing. Thus, violence that in the first period was constitutive of world-making, and is indeed the constitutive element of social life, is re-imagined in the second period as an exceptional behavior.

Once we realize that the key aspect of Gur's imaginary worlds is the law—both in its literal sense (the law of the state represented by the police) and as represented by the law of each institution (the Institute, the kibbutz, the university, the musical world, etc.)—we can observe that the energies of this novel and others by Gur are expository in nature: they seek to expose what they perceive to be the (local) governing laws of each social institution. Gur (and Michael's) investigation into the institute is then a practice of reading or mapping. Note how different this desire is in comparison to the liberal writers of the first period in which the desired autonomy of the individual pushed artists to the opposite pole, i.e., to conceal the law of the world, the social causes that make it. To be sure, I emphasize that Gur looks into only the local laws of each institution and accepts them as self-sufficient, as if Israeli society is an aggregate of wholes. Gur does not investigate the global laws or conditions of Israeli society, those that might show us the interconnection between institutions rather than their exotic differences. More accurately, Gur exposes the laws of each social institution through the immediate lived experience of its practitioners. In many of her novels, Michael says that to solve the mystery he needs to think like his suspects and penetrate the rules of their world. Gur does not defamiliarize the characters' world by exposing its underlying structural social conditions, which for this very reason must be unfamiliar and beyond the control of its members. For example, in the present novel, Gur does not examine the clientele of the institute and the manner their payments may maintain the institute's life; we know nothing of licensure, the legal relationship between the institute and the state that regulates psychological health, and so on.[47]

To conclude, in Gur we observed the historical emergence of a privatized imaginary world and the separation of the private and public spheres into distinct and fetishized subjects that encounter and decipher each other as a text. Here each individual and each social sphere is imagined as autonomous and self-sufficient, believing itself to make and follow its own local law. These are the preliminary conditions of the imaginary world, the manner in which the real of the neoliberal period inheres in the literary artwork as its elementary "raw materials." I have argued, however, that these conditions should be distinguished from the ideological stance of the novel: Gur's conservative and nostalgic desire for a Western European statist Zionism, which is in a way superimposed here on the historical conditions and attempts to "solve" the political problem that neoliberalism posits to Israeli life after 1985. In other words, the Mizrahi police detective (state) and Ashkenazi psychoanalyst of the old guard team up to cleanse the world from the rising capitalist class and its transgressions. The distinction between the preliminary conditions and the ideological stance is useful in distinguishing between two modes of reading that inhere in the very structure of the text. The object of the first is the synchronous axis—neoliberal conditions of possibility—while the object of the second is the diachronic axis, the temporal movement of plot and its social materials that arise from the historical limit and tries to resolve it. If we can say that, in a single period, all dominant literary artworks share the same synchronous axis—axis of identity—then they can be distinguished in their diachronic axis—axis of difference—in the manner their ideological stance and its relation to time reacts to the historical limit. These two are not always as clear-cut as they are in Gur's novel, but the two axes seem to be one way to go about distinguishing historical conditions from political ideology.

---

47   In the novel about the university—*Mavet ba-ḥug le-sifrut*—we again learn nothing about the political and economic relationship between the state and the university, which is the very condition of possibility of the university and is outside the control of its members. In the novel about the kibbutz—*Lina meshutefet*—we hear a little bit about the process of privatization but this is presented as if it is within the volition of the kibbutz rather than a process enforced due to structural changes forced upon the Israeli and global economy.

6.

For the next example, I turn to Shimon Ballas's *Outsiders* (*Yalde ḥuẓ*), published in 2003 as the third installment of the trilogy Tel-Aviv East (*Tel-Aviv Mizraḥ*). That I turn to a Mizrahi novelist[48] in order to demonstrate the reality of neoliberalism would surely surprise critics who do not usually think of Mizrahi literature in this vein, so the following reading will do double duty in both discussing how the novel is informed by the temporalities of private life and, at the same time, reorienting inquiries into the corpus of novels written by Mizrahi writers, which usually highlight matters of social identity and underplay the broader social structures by which such identities, let alone their literary form, are conditioned.

The trilogy Tel-Aviv East follows the lives of Iraqi immigrants from their moment of arrival in Israel in the early 1950s to the late 1990s, and is highly attuned, at least in the first two installments, to the plight of Mizrahim and their struggle against the Zionist state. The first novel, *The Transit Camp* (*Ha-ma'abarah*), was dismissed as too political to have any artistic merit by dominant Ashkenazi literary critics,[49] but since the 1990s and the rise of post-Zionist literary criticism, both Ballas and *The Transit Camp* have been rehabilitated. These days Ballas' work is read as an example of "Arab-Jewish" writing, an identity that serves liberal academic circles in Israel and in the US as a utopian alternative to the separatist logic of Zionism.[50] In the process of rehabilitation, however, issues of class and labor inherent in the very form of Ballas' work have been for the most part expunged from the record and questions of cultural identity have come to the fore. The second and third installments of the trilogy received scant attention. My reading here will concentrate on *Outsiders*, the third installment, and demonstrate how the partial

---

48   Ballas was born to a middle-class Iraqi family and immigrated to Israel in the early 1950s.

49   See for example Gershon Shaked, *Ha-siporet ha-'ivrit*, Vol. 4, 168. See also Dror Mishani's short discussion of the novel and its reception, "Lama ha-mizraḥim ẓrikhim laḥazor la-ma'abarah," *Mittam* 3 (2006): 91–8.

50   See for example, Ammiel Alcalay, "At Home in Exile: An Interview with Shimon Ballas," *Literary Review* 37.2 (1994): 180–9; Hannan Hever, "*Lo banu min ha-yam*," *Te'orya u-vikoret* 16 (Spring 2000): 181–95; "*Mi-sifrut 'ivrit le-sifrut yisra'elit*," *Te'orya u-vikoret* 20 (Spring 2002): 165–90; *Producing the Modern Hebrew Canon: Nation Building and Minority Discourse*, 140–74; Yuval Ivri, "*Moledet 'irakit be-'ivrit: Le'umiyut 'etniyut u-merḥav ba-roman vehu aḥer le-Shim'on Balas*," *Te'orya u-vikoret* 35 (Fall 2009): 57–80. See also Ballas's own remarks on the matter of his identity *Kolot Mizraḥiyyim* (eds.) Guy Abutbul, Lev Grinberg and Pnina Motzafi-Haller (Tel Aviv: Mesada, 2005), 89–91.

legitimation of Mizrahi identity in the 1990s presupposes the logic of private life and the ideology of textuality that emerged post-1985. Taking this critical route, we can see that while critics seek to distinguish between Mizrahi and Ashkenazi writers, the two share the same historical conditions of possibility and the same political limits.

Before we look into *Outsiders*, a few words on the first two installments are needed. *The Transit Camp*, written in the early 1950s but published only in 1964, is Ballas's most explicitly political novel, showing the development of a revolt among a group of Iraqi immigrants in a transit camp (led partly by Yosef Shabi) who try resist their proletarianization by the Zionist state. The second novel, *Tel-Aviv East*, written shortly after 1964 but published only in 2003, is set in one of the poorest neighborhoods of Tel Aviv, in a post-transit-camp era when immigrants were placed in poor towns or in underdeveloped neighborhoods on the periphery of major cities.[51] The plot revolves in part around the struggle of the neighborhood residents to improve their poor living conditions, and around the attempts of Yosef, now a principal of the neighborhood school, to come up with a multicultural curriculum that will acknowledge the culture of the Mizrahi immigrants.

The reason I outlined the previous two installments has to do with the fact that once we arrive at *Outsiders,* written in the late 1990s and published in 2003, the thematic landscape of Ballas's imaginary world utterly changes. Forms of Mizrahi political organization are all but gone and we are to follow only the individual itineraries of a few Mizrahi characters, mostly Iraqi, as they roam in and out of Tel Aviv's apartments. Although Ballas adheres to his multi-character plot, a generational shift now takes center stage. As much as we follow Yosef and his generation of the 1950s, we also follow his son, Doron, a young man working in a photography shop, and his circle of friends and colleagues in Tel Aviv. The generational difference is of course not static or additive, but rather coded in a historical and social schema in which Yosef and with him the state-centric, modernist Israel recede to the background as "past," while Doron's neoliberal, postmodern Israel takes the foreground and is associated with the "future." This coding is also mapped on artistic production where commercial photography is associated with the lowbrow

---

51   Ballas, "Tel-Aviv Mizraḥ," in *Tel-Aviv Mizraḥ–Trilogya,* 2003. If we follow Ballas's short autobiography, we learn that he wrote the sequel *Tel-Aviv East* during and immediately after the publication of *The Transit Camp*, in the second half of the 1960s, but due to the rejection of Am-oved, the novel was only published in 1998. See Ballas, *Be-guf rishon* (Tel Aviv: Ha-kibuẓ ha-me'uḥad, 2009).

present of daily life while painting, one of the central preoccupations of the novel, stands in for the high modernist past. Moving to the political level, the events of *Outsiders* take place between October 1994 and November 1995, beginning sometime after the signing of the peace treaty between Israel and Jordan, and concluding days after the assassination of Prime Minister Yitzhak Rabin. This period was preceded by the signing of the Oslo Accords in September 1993 and is considered by many to be a period of hope and prosperity. As Lev Grinberg explains in his study of this period, once the political conflicts of Israeli society, understood as its "outside," were seen as resolvable, all of a sudden the social ("internal") antagonism flared up and took center stage.[52] What Grinberg downplays, however, is the fact that in the 1990s these kind of internal antagonisms unfold under a very different category of contestatory politics; they are no longer direct revolts against the state—as were the acts of the residents of Wadi-A-Salib in 1959, or the Mizrahi Black Panthers in the 1970s —but spring from and are conditioned by privatized civil life and its political limits.

Since it is impossible to do full justice to the novel's movement between diverse characters and story lines, weaving in as they do the previous two installments, I will concentrate on forms of temporality, both as represented time, (time as depicted object) and as compositional principle, organizing the time of occurrences in the novel (time as subject). I argue that there are two contradictory temporalities underlying the novel whose interpretation would lead to a better understanding of the relation between the new Israeli neoliberal reality and its "other."

7.

I begin with Doron's story. At the outset, we are introduced to Doron in the photography shop, to his romantic relationship with Smadar, to his warm and familial relations with the owners of the store and to his group of friends, most of whom are artists. Another story line, however, develops in tandem when two curators, Nili and Shay Tamir, putting up a retrospective of the painter Orna Lavi, ask Doron to photograph the paintings for the gallery's catalog. After attending the opening night, Doron returns the next day to the empty gallery and gazes at the

---

52   Lev Grinberg, *Shalom medumyan, siaḥ milḥamah: Keshel ha-manhigut, ha-politika veha-demokratya be-yisraʾel* 1992–2006 (Tel Aviv: Resling, 2007), 175–204.

paintings whose themes depict Israel in the forties and fifties. I pause over the object of the paintings and Doron's gaze:

> People in gardens, a few of whom sit on benches, others stroll, and all are surrounded with green trees and a fountain. "Dizengof Square." It's the square, gone now, after being raised on pillars, allowing cars to speed beneath it. "Demonstration," is the name of another painting that represents people walking side by side, their arms raised, their mouth open; a young woman is carrying a sign at the head of the protest, saying: "bread/jobs." Other paintings carry their own names: "Carmel Market," "Café Tamar," "Herzel Street" and in the background Herzelia gymnasium in faded lines, for it too is gone now. Tel-Aviv along the years. History. Chapters in the history of the city. But there is also a "transit camp": a frizzy-haired girl next to a water tap and a bucket underneath. In the background tents and angry skies; there are also construction workers on top a building and immigrants descending from a plane, and portraits, a lot of portraits. She [Orna Lavi] is a painter from a different period, a forgotten period that is now brought back in a kind of nostalgic forgiveness.[53]

Now, as Doron says, what we see in the paintings is a representation of Tel Aviv's history in which architecture figures predominantly as the measure for historical change. At the same time we also see chapters in the history of Israel, especially the waves of mass immigration of the 1950s and the historical transit camps in which immigrants, including Doron's father, Yosef, were housed. If we look closely at the details of the paintings and Doron's thoughts it would seem that history has been gathered from the surface of the world into the canvas, on which time has now turned into space in a double sense. First, history is located in the depicted objects of the paintings in which Tel Aviv's architecture has become a measure for time. Second, the canvas as a repository of time is replicated and mirrored in the site of the art gallery itself. For it is that place in the world where the characters, as well as we readers, *encounter* history as a completed event in the past. The artwork then does not simply represent history but seems to stand in for it, as a social site individuals can enter and leave, and gaze into as a text to be deciphered privately. The first observation I would like to make then is that for Doron social time and history are no longer made but given, as a text

---

53   Ballas, *Yalde ḥuẓ*, 334–35.

to be read. Recall here Jameson's important observation about the fate of history in postmodernity. As he argues in the context of reading E. L. Doctorow's *Ragtime*:

> This historical novel can no longer set out to represent the historical past; it can only "represent" our ideas and stereotypes about that past . . . Cultural production is thereby driven back inside a mental space which is no longer that of the monadic subject but rather that of some degraded collective "objective spirit."[54]

What we see in the art gallery is precisely this symptom in which history as a process of antagonistic making is transmuted into history as popular image and text. This sense of history as time given, as text offered for a private subject, is especially heightened when we consider its opposite and notice first that most of the figures in the paintings appear in the plural as groups of people, immigrants or workers. Second, some of them are depicted as protesting, working and arriving in Israel, that is to say, in the moment of some historical collective act, which now seems to be the object a nostalgic desire. It is nostalgia not only for the past and for the collective, but also for the sense of history as making and doing. It seems then that the scene in the art gallery emits two senses of time: time made in the painting vs. time given in the art gallery. The relation between the times needs to be articulated: while the objects in the painting are diachronic events, for Doron they have turned synchronous; his thought is now placing each moment in the past next to the other in a contiguous manner. Thus, what is being staged here, in a convention of the *mis-en-abyme*, is the *synchronization* and *textualization* of time, typical of the period and the novel as a whole.

To see how the retrospective can serve as a symptom of the historical period we would do well to return briefly to the first installment of the trilogy and see how there, contrary to the painting appearing as a reified sign/text of the past, poetry springs to life from praxis and retains its relation to the present. Here is the poem Moshe the guard intended to read at the first general assembly of the transit camp:

> Rise, my friend, to the dawn and the song of the birds
> And drink from your cup in the circle of friends
> Make hast, my friend, to listen to the tune

---

54 Jameson, *Postmodernism, Or, the Cultural Logic of Late Capitalism* (Durham: Duke University Press, 1991), 25.

Before the moon will set and the sun will rise
For many a generation the Jew wandered the world
And when he arrived in Israel he was ashamed and oppressed
Our story with the Yiddish [i.e., Ashkenazim] who dominate is long
Longer than the story of Anthar, the man of many exploits
Come and we'll tell you of the bastard [the Doctor refusing to enter the
    muddy terrain of the camp]
Who was afraid to wet his head in the rain.[55]

Unlike the retrospective, exhibiting paintings as representation of the past, as sign, here the poem is a form of experience, embedded in the struggle against Zionism and scheduled to be recited during the general assembly. There is no real separation between the artistic act and social life, for the poem arises out of experience and re-enters it both as an invocation to action and as the history of the listeners themselves.

Back to *Outsiders*: the synchronization evident in Doron's gaze is tightly tied to the removal of constitutive antagonism, the key feature of the first statist period, whose time has been gathered from the world and deposited in the painting within the world. Very much like Koren's Palestinian house discussed in Chapter 1, history, that which constitutes the world, is turned into a textual fetish through which the character is able to recognize itself.

The textualization underlying Doron's gaze also underlies the world he inhabits. Using this optic, the most prevalent novelistic material that catches the eye is the sheer proliferation not only of producers of texts, but also of texts, images and works of art. If one would stop to count the professionals we meet in *Outsiders* we will see that in addition to a photographer (Doron), and a painter (Orna Lavy) we find a freelance editor and an MA student in art history (Smadar, Doron's girlfriend), a journalist (Esther), a poet (Amnon Zaks), a film critic (Yoel Raviv), an art critic (Yoel Hoffman), and a documentarist and her assistant (Lucy and Tami). We will see later on who the "other" is for this implicit "artist colony" whose life revolves around the symbolic, around the distribution of texts and signs.

What is the significance of the proliferation of texts and text producers? Considered in context of the previous two novels,—whose plot revolved, albeit in two different modalities, around a social and political struggle unfolding in the present and constituting the very axis of

---

55   Ballas, *Ha-ma'abarah*, 28.

the world—it should be obvious that something has happened to the capacity of the novel to represent the constitutive antagonism itself; some displacement has shifted us from the events, always happening elsewhere and in the past, to their representation, whether in tracts, films, paintings, or, most importantly, pseudo-political conversations. For the novel is surely "political," but it is political in this new textual manner in which the interpretation of the political act becomes the object of struggle.

8.

Now let us shift to a higher level of abstraction, moving away from the object world of the novel into its compositional principle and finally into its spatio-temporal categories which will allow us a better understanding of the relation between Israeli neoliberalism and symbolic forms. Here I note how the social relations of this world, existing in given-time, have also been textualized.

Again we begin thematically by noticing that, while it engages the lives of a few middle class Mizrahi citizens in Israel, *Outsiders* no longer casts a world divided in half, into Mizrahim and Ashkenazim; rather, it weaves these two groups into a a plural social world. So that among Mizrahim and Ashkenazim we find references to Russian immigration, women's rights, gays and lesbians, and migrant workers. Moving from this thematic plurality to its conceptual and socio-historical significance, I ask how plurality is *posited* in the world: How is it organized? Here we find not so much difference but similarity, as if the characters are underlined by a principle of *equivalent* difference. Here is how this conceptual and social ideology finds its way into the novel—significantly not as Yosef's idea, but as an afterthought of his son, Doron:

> Outsiders. Tami [a woman] is an outsider too. Of course! Torn between two worlds of both she has no real grasp. Amnon Zaks [gay] enjoys his status as an outsider. He does not hide his [homosexual] tendencies, but does not boast them either. He is an outsider in a normative society . . . [Said, the Mizrahi] is an outsider as well. Of course! Especially in the US. But he was successful and turned into a real American. Those who climb from one class to another are outsiders who made it. This is the real division. And in fact, who isn't an outsider . . . ?[56]

---

56   Ballas, *Yalde ḥuẓ*, 386.

Doron's thought continues, to include (although somewhat obliquely) the "Ashkenazi" who has turned into an outsider as well.

The categories in brackets should give the reader a sense of the process of abstraction, how the "differences" of each category are acknowledged only at the moment that they have been commonly subsumed under another (albeit still vague) category—the "outsider." It will be important to identify the "inside" in relation to which all these characters find their communality as "outsiders," but for now I would like to rewrite Doron's social observation by understanding it via Roman Jacobson's now classical definition of the poetic function. Recall that for Jacobson "literariness" is achieved through an irregular arrangement of the axis of combination (the syntagmatic level of difference) and the axis of selection (the paradigmatic level of equivalence). "Literariness" is achieved when "the principle of equivalence [is projected] from the axis of selection into the axis of combination." Now, it might be evident that, in *Outsiders*, the process of leveling off, in which we see not differences but categorical equivalence—identities—is here precisely the social appearance of the poetic function. The cardinal, and mostly disavowed, property of "identities" is not their difference but rather their equivalence, one secured by civil pluralism that is supposed to guarantee their co-existence by excluding constitutive antagonism and inequality.

If we continue with the linguistic metaphor then we could say that this imaginary world has the tendency to substitute *parole* for *langue*, resulting in a narrative that offers us a series of categorical abstractions ("identities") meeting each other not in the diachronic syntagmatic axis (the level of social antagonism embedded in time), but in the synchronic paradigmatic one (the level of private life) released from the state and its forms inequality. To dispel any misunderstanding, Doron's world is filled with political contestation, but it happens, to appeal once more to Aristotle, on the level of speech (conversation and interpretation of texts), that is, the universality of the world is no longer given in acts but in language.[57]

Once we understand the world of *Outsiders* as a synchronous world

---

57   To see this more conceptually, it will be useful to recall Jameson's early critique of the linguistic principles of structuralism, in which he articulates this problem as the inability of "synchronic systems . . . to deal in any adequate conceptual way with temporal phenomena" which, as he continues to explain, "always find their way back to the synchronic axis, but as a symptom." See, Jameson, *The Prison-House of Language* (Princeton: Princeton University Press, 1972), ix. As I have noted, the returning "symptom" in *Outsiders* will be the unexpected irruption of an historical political event into the synchrony of private life.

in which people meet each other as equivalent categories on the grounds of the private sphere, we can begin to make sense of the symptoms, those social and temporal "leftovers" from the previous statist system that live on as anomalies. But to understand the significance of the appearance of the older social forms we will need to situate the symbolic ground into which they are inscribed as "anomalies." First, since neoliberalism in Israel means historically the substitution of statist political culture by market culture, the new commodified art production based on the principle of infinite exchange is charged with moral corruption—with the sense that money can now buy anything, even politics. And indeed this historical condition turned into a moral lesson finds its culprit in the Mizrahi pragmatist who, in this world (since Yosef occupies the role of the idealist), is crystalized in his brother, Saeed. Embodying the market, he is the man who has made his fortune employing poor Palestinian workers and is now a wealthy businessman arriving in Israel on a trip to gauge business opportunities, now that Jordanian labor has been made more attractive by the new peace treaty. But if Saeed, the potent, pragmatist Mizrahi man is as inadequate as Yosef, the impotent idealist, then any real alternative must find a figure outside these two unsatisfactory poles. It is an alternative that will serve as an antidote to the moral corruption of Israeli society and uphold some kind of non-fungible value. And indeed we find such a figure inserted subtly, *coincidently*, into the second plotline of the art theft—a Holocaust survivor, an unnamed plumber-turned-artist who does not produce art for the market, and as such stands in for the absolute. It is an existence posited as outside the "outsiders" (who are actually the norm), a fixed point from which their corruption can be measured. And again it is Doron who gazes at one of his sculptures at Nili's house, the criminal art dealer:

> His gaze was drawn to a wooden sculpture of a figure slightly bent over, wearing a coat and some kind of turban or top hat. He got up to look at the sculpture up close . . .
> "Does this interest you"? [Nili] asked.
> "Yes, it is a beautiful sculpture. Who made it?"
> "It is a sad story . . . the man is no longer alive. He hanged himself."
> "And you knew him?"
> "Only by chance; he was a holocaust survivor, and all he did was out of an internal impulse, out of the world he came from."
> Then she said that the man worked as a plumber. One day he came to their house to fix a leak and when he saw that they had sculptures and

paintings, he said that he made sculptures as well, and after a few days he brought this one wrapped in an old newspaper. "I was very surprised; I could not believe that a man as shy as he was, barely speaking, who did not study anywhere, could do such work. But he was resolute about not accepting money. He left me the sculpture and left."[58]

We need to note here both the "content" of the anomaly and its novelistic temporal structure. I have noted the coupling of the Holocaust and the non-fungible, but it is as important to note the third leg of this triangle, here only implied. For in Israel the Holocaust is not only a historic event, coded as an "unparalleled" and singular barbarity; it is also tied to the centrist state, to its national memorial days, ceremonies and monuments, to national guilt and national responsibility. Thus, the figure of the Holocaust survivor is here subtly a stand-in for the state itself and the kind of selfless life it inspired in the previous period.

The formal aspect of the encounter between Nili and the artist is as important. We cannot miss the fact that if Doron's gaze at the gallery gave us synchrony then here we see its counterpart appearing as coincidence. It is offered to us twice, once in Doron's accidental gaze over the sculptures and the second time as the incidental encounter with the plumber who turns out to be, surprisingly, a great artist. However, the appearance of "coincidence" (*mikriyut*) is not a matter of chance. In fact, the novel combines two genres: the "city novel" of crossing identities, and the mystery novel involving an investigation of a stolen painting; but while the city novel unfolds in a synchronous temporality, the investigation arises, not so much a causal development of events, but by pure coincidence. If we read the novel closely we will see time and again that the main events happen by accident. Here is Doron reflecting on the way he found himself involved in the investigation of the theft, after a car accident with the curator, Shay Tamir:

> [S]ometimes coincidence creates the most interesting stories. Shay Tamir, driving like crazy, could have caused a much more severe accident. He could have been killed, or gotten his secretary hurt. But it happened that he hit specifically him [Doron], and that he always has a camera with him, and that the camera captured the woman in the car. And the next day they [happened to] meet in the art gallery and at the same time his wife, in consultation with the owners of the gallery, decided to

---

58   Ballas, *Yalde ḥuz*, 355–6.

commission him [to prepare a catalog] and then she found out that he was involved in an accident with her husband. A chain of accidents.[59]

I hope it is clear that in a synchronous world, one lacking constitutive antagonism, the only experience of time available to the characters is random coincidence of which they can make no sense. Note also that the temporal relation between the two times is not additive. Rather, they are positioned in a particular relation to one another. For if the overall city novel moves synchronously, in a spatial mapping movement of characters with no time, the mystery genre, moving coincidently, enters as a disruption of synchrony, which in this case has been represented as an accident.

Before moving on to articulate the final relationship between synchrony, coincidence and the shift to neoliberalism let me offer one more example of coincidence and the manner in which it brings to the fore the rearticulation of Mizrahi political organization. While Nili, the middle-class Ashkenazi character, meets her unconscious in the accidental meeting with the holocaust survivor, Yosef, the middle-class Mizrahi character, meets his in the Mizrahi criminal. Note how the implied Mizrahi collective, so central to the two previous installments, returns here as a lone figure appearing in the midst of the capitalist fantasy of shopping:

Sitting in café *Jbanez* and waiting for Rina [his wife] who returned to the boutique in Gan Hair to buy yet another shirt in addition to their other purchases, he noticed a dark-skinned man, heavy and with thin hair . . . The man looked at him as well and seemed to recognize him . . . Something in his way of sitting, in the movements of his head reminded him a man he knew. Often he bumps into people that his memory cannot place . . . Did they meet in the army?. . . Or maybe he is one of his students, it is difficult to guess the man's age, and after all he barely remembers the faces of his students after they leave school . . . Men with experience, fathers, merchants, realtors, garage owners, maybe this is one of them.[60]

---

59   Ibid., 366. See also "Time and again I ask myself, whether without that coincidence in which I sent the letter to 'The Family' [the section in a newspaper devoted to women's affairs] I would have stopped writing? . . . Is everything a matter of luck? Coincidence, we float on the waves of accidents, float and sink and struggle in the waves of coincidence." Ibid., See also, 390.

60   Ibid., 438–9.

As the passage continues, Yosef is able to place the man and recalls that several years ago he saw him being taken into a police car after killing his wife's lover. He turns to Rina and says: "I cannot forget his gaze; I stood in the crowd and he looked at me, as if demanding something of me, as if he was turning me into a witness to the wrong done to him. Now, too, he looked at me in the same way."[61] So again, we see that when the Mizrahi collective disappears, and with it collective political action as a constitutive element of the imaginary world, symptoms of this reification of time and politics appear as accidental traces charged with guilt. And these workers, these "men with experience, fathers, merchants, realtors, garage owners," should be understood as those who never really entered the symbolic "artist colony" Yosef, Doron and the other characters inhabit. These characters who have almost no existence in this novel, rather than the protagonist "outsiders," are in fact those who are left outside Israeli society. In other words, contrary to post-Zionist criticism that reads Mizrahi literature, post-1985, as a positive expression of Mizrahi identity that finally comes into its own, we can say that in these moments the Mizrahi collective fate has become a representational problem for Mizrahi writers, a matter of individual guilt rather than politics.

I would like to draw attention to the highest point of articulation of synchrony and coincidence in the novel and bring this reading to a close. If the world of *Outsiders* is composed of individuals living their private apolitical lives and the antagonistic political temporality has been replaced by the exchange of signifiers based on equivalence, then time and history must enter this imaginary world from nowhere, as a catastrophe, an event that for the subject living in synchrony appears incomprehensible.

Here I would like to recall that the novel ends with the assassination of Prime Minister Yitzhak Rabin in 1995 by a man associated with the extreme political right. Let me note the dual meaning of this important scene. In terms of social and novelistic content, the political assassination disrupts the dream of a post-statist world in which people are no more than consumers and symbolic exchangers of texts. In terms of form, the assassination appears as an antagonistic event in the synchronous world of the characters; it is a figure of absolute inequality (representing a political project that cannot be integrated into the forms of private life) that erupts into the imaginary relations of equivalence. In *Outsiders* then the political event returns only within the world, localized as content.

---

61   Ibid., 440.

Synchrony organizes the world of Tel Aviv while the event disrupts it, appearing as its temporal "other." Thus, I pose the question: If the subject of synchrony is an autonomous private sphere belonging to a globalized and worldly Israeli society, who is the subject of the event, of time made rather than time given? The key lies in the identity of the lone assassin, the political far right, whose life-form is still imbricated with the state. It is a heteronomous form of life for which the symbolic separation of the private and the public spheres has not yet occurred.

Now, it is customary today to articulate the tragedy and farce of contemporary Israel, at least in one of its instances, as an antagonism between the secular Israeli and the religious Jew, Tel Aviv vs. Jerusalem. However useful, this is not a precise interpretation. The antagonism is not a matter of secularism vs. religion but rather between an autonomous sphere of private life in which economic relations of equivalence dominate vs. a heteronomous form of life, heteronomous because it is still embedded not so much in a heavenly providence, but in an earthly one, the state. These two forms generate two times (reading vs. making), which should have competed at the heart of the novel. But since the world of *Outsiders* as a whole is cast from the position of private life in which synchrony is the dominant time, it then allows heteronomy and its other time to appear only as an anomaly at its seams, here at the end of the novel, and in Israel at its borders.

This reading of *Outsiders* points to two important developments in the new period: first, while fictional narratives surrounding Mizrahi identity are surely "political," such politics presupposes the forms of private life and its political limits. It is safe to say that all Mizrahi novels are written today from the position of private subjects who encounter a ready-made world whose conditions of possibility they read and interpret rather than make.[62] Second, while they may have at times different political content than Ashkenazi novels, Mizrahi novels are "Israeli" in the sense that they share the same historical and poetic limits posed by neoliberalism as any other contemporary novel.

---

62   See for example Ronit Matalon, *Zeh 'im ha-panim 'elenu* [*The One Facing Us*] (Tel Aviv: 'Am 'oved, 1995); Dudu Busi, *Ha-yareaḥ yarok ba-vadi* [*Green Moon over the Creek*] (Tel Aviv: 'Am 'oved, 2000); Shimon Adaf, *Kilometer ve-yomayim lifne ha-shki'a* [*A Mile and Two days before Sunset*](Yerushalayim, Keter, 2004); Sami Bardugo, *Yetomin* [*Orphans*] (Bene-Berak: Ha-kibuẓ ha-me'uḥad, 2006); Dorit Rabinyan, *Gader ḥaya* [*Living Fence*] (Tel Aviv: 'Am 'oved, 2014).

9.

For the third example of Israeli literature in neoliberal society, I turn to one of the more recent articulations of contemporary Israeli society and its integration into the global economy, Assaf Gavron's *Almost Dead*.[63] The author of six novels, Gavron has become in recent years one of the most successful and widely-translated Israeli writers. As do Gur and Ballas, Gavron casts a privatized imaginary world that is conditioned by the characteristics we have already specified. But differently than Gur, Gavron's ideological stance does not hark back to a lost statist culture as a political solution. Gavron trains his critical eye on privatized life itself, but unlike Gur, who embodies capitalism in one deviant character— Dina Silver—and understands her historical emergence as an ethical flaw—greed and self-indulgence, Gavron mocks the new Israeli and global corporate culture as a whole; that is to say, his gaze is a bit more structural than Gur's and signifies a different stance in the literary field. Second, differently than Gur and Ballas who erect a meaningful moral world that is violated by transgressive characters, Gavron's Israeli and Palestinian protagonists and the world they inhabit suffer from a shattering crisis of meaning that does not permit any stable ethical ground until the last third of the novel, where we shift genres to a detective investigation and the protagonists begin to change. Third, although Gavron's novel articulates an affirmative liberal and humanist stance which at its heart stands an act of recognition of otherness, Gavron does expose a new reality of Israeli social structure—commodification—that cuts across and links together social spheres that in Gur and Ballas have been kept distinct. Thus, however displaced and fascinated with the surface materials of Israeli neoliberal reality, Gavron's political narrative desire is directed against capitalist privatization and for this reason brings the very content of capitalist social relations to the surface of the text.

Almost Dead narrates the lives of Eitan, a young Israeli working in sales for a start-up company, and Fahmi, a Palestinian electrician turned resistance fighter. Gavron's ruse is to make Eitan the accidental victim of not one but three Palestinian attacks on civilians,[64] all planned by the same group, a repetition that provides the relation between the otherwise separated Eitan and Fahmi and infuses the novel with its dark humor. As we will see, the categories of time and space are one of the keys to this

---

63   Assaf Gavron, *Almost Dead* (New York: Harper Perennial, 2010). In Hebrew, *Tanin-Pigu'a* (Tel Aviv: Kineret/Zemorah-Bitan/Dvir, 2006).

64   He is also the victim of a fourth attack, but that one is directed at him.

novel's compositional principle and I will begin first by noting that as events develop Eitan and Fahmi move towards each other, beginning the novel as abstract and anonymous enemies and ending up as friends who come to recognize each other's difference. The concepts that underlie their narratives, then, are "convergence" and "recognition"—a movement from the unconscious and unknown to the conscious and known. Note again that the striving towards knowledge and (self)-recognition is a key feature of novels of this period, usually taking the form of an investigation into an absent origin. This feature was quite absent in the statist period because those characters were making their worlds and were themselves its origin and cause, while here characters are mostly readers and interpreters of signs, social objects whose origin and cause are mysteriously missing. Before we follow the route of convergence and recognition, we need to note its precondition, i.e., the fact that Eitan and Fahmi are separated from one another.

Post-Zionists routinely remind us that since its inception in the late-nineteenth-century Zionism sought to separate Arabs and Jews, Israelis and Palestinians.[65] If we follow this line of thinking we should not find the separation in Gavron surprising at all. However, what is important in this novel and requires a more accurate historical explanation is the fact that while the literature of the statist period, especially that of the 1940s and 1950s, usually placed these two populations in direct confrontation such that no search was needed—on the contrary, the Arab and Palestinian were all too present—the energies of Gavron's novel are spent on Eitan and Fahmi finding one another as if they were somehow missing in each other's life.[66]

Thus, this "separation" has a new historical content, one that may be explained by noting the difference between Eitan and Fahmi's attributes

---

65   The separation tenet is very common in the writings of Israeli liberals and post-Zionists including Moshe Behar and Zvi Ben-Dor Benite, *Modern Middle Eastern Jewish Thought: Writings on Identity, Politics, and Culture, 1893–1958* (Boston: Brandeis University Press, 2013); Hannan Hever, *Producing the Modern Hebrew Canon: Nation Building and Minority Discourse*; Gil Hochberg, *In Spite of Partition: Jews, Arabs, and the Limits of Separatist Imagination*; Lital Levi, *Poetic Trespass: Writing between Hebrew and Arabic in Israel/Palestine*.

66   See for example, Alexander and Yonat Sened, *Adama lelo ẓel*; Moshe Shamir, *Hu halakh ba-sadot*; Aharon Megged, *Mikre ha-kasil*; S. Yizhar, *Shayara shel ḥaẓot*; *Sipur Ḥirbet Ḥiz'ah*; *Ha-shavui*. But see also later works by A. B. Yehoshua, "Mul ha-ye'arot" In *Mul ha-ye'arot: sipurim* (Tel Aviv: Ha-kibuẓ ha-me'uḥad, 1968); Amos Oz, "Navadim u-ẓefa." For an account of the representation of the Arab in Hebrew and Israeli literature see Yochai Openheimer, *Me-'ever la-gader: yiẓug ha-'arvim ba-siporet ha-'ivrit veha-yisra'elit 1906–2005* (Tel Aviv: 'Am 'oved, 2008)

and their counterparts in the statist period. In the previous period, if the Israeli and Palestinian encountered one another directly they usually met through the mediation of direct political antagonism—settler vs. Bedouin, soldier vs. soldier, soldier vs. refugee, etc.[67] In Ashkenazi liberal and humanist novels, the political mediation was sometimes augmented or replaced by more personal (so-called universal) encounters,[68] and Mizrahi literature of this period usually portrayed the Arab in a more positive light.[69] It is clear that Eitan encounters Fahmi neither as a political subject nor as a universal personal subject; rather, they meet each other at work, in Eitan's hi-tech firm in the suburbs of Israel. But more importantly, before this meeting, Eitan is primarily an object of Fahmi's attacks as a private subject whose life is unexpectedly disrupted by the eruption of political violence. Once we realize this new historical content, we can say that what is separated here is not so much the Israeli and Palestinian as two national and political subjects, but rather the private sphere from the political one, a private form of life (Eitan) that now only encounters politics and political subjects (Fahmi) accidently. As far as Eitan's world is concerned, political acts and political antagonism no longer constitute the imaginary world and its time as they did in the previous period, rather they are now, first, provincialized, reduced to mere content within the imaginary world, and second, appear as a disruption of social time rather than its constituent. This means that while the surface materials of the novel emit all the signs of humanist and liberal ideology seeking to bring together the Israeli and the Palestinian, the deeper level of the novel seeks the *re-politicization* of the private sphere (Eitan's life); it casts the Palestinian not simply as an enemy (or eventually a friend) but rather as a needed corrective to the excess of neoliberal privatization that has, as we will see, sapped Eitan's life of any meaning. Thus, differently than the post-Zionist stance that considers political violence as an abhorrent phenomena that characters seek to overcome, here political violence is figured as a necessary shock to awaken the subject of private life. As such, the relation to violence here is qualitatively different from Gur and Ballas: if in the latter two novels the act of violence—the murder; the assassination—undermined social

---

67   See footnote 80 for examples.

68   See, for example, S. Yizhar's short stories and novellas; David Grossman, *Ḥiyukh ha-gedi* [*The Smile of the Lamb*] (Tel Aviv: Ha-kibuẓ ha-me'uḥad, 1983). See also Ehud Ben-Ezer's collection of Hebrew stories featuring Arab-Jewish relations, Ehud Ben-Ezer (ed.), *Sleepwalkers and Other Stories: The Arab in Hebrew Fiction*, translated by Lynne Rienner (Boulder: Three Continents Press, 1999).

69   See the discussion on Iraqi (Mizrahi) literature in Openheimer's discussion.

order and the perpetrator had to be removed from the sphere of private life, in Gavron it is precisely the opposite: the perpetrator is invited to enter its realm and redeem the subject of their meaningless life. Further, the positioning of the Palestinian as a catalyst for change is qualitatively different from the liberal and humanist desires of the statist period in which the Palestinian served as a moral witness to the crimes of colonization.[70] To be sure, Eitan is not the only character who goes through a transformative process. Fahmi, too, is changing throughout the course of the novel, but in the obverse direction, beginning as a member of a political organization for whom Eitan is an enemy, and ending up as a private individual who spares Eitan's life and takes him as a potential friend.

The diachronic axis of Eitan's plot is then a movement of politicization that involves a shift from ignorance and heteronomy to knowledge and autonomy. Our point of entry into the novel is Eitan's professional life and work before the attacks begin. Eitan is working at Time's Arrow, a small startup funded by global venture capital. The company writes and sells telephone software for call centers that automates communication between callers and the call center. The software reduces the call time and thus allows the call center to process more calls and save money:

Our business in Time's Arrow is saving time . . . We work for years to save a second or two. And why do we need to save a second from conversations to a call center? Take, for instance, these clients of ours who provide the service in Manhattan. They've got a couple of thousand operators in New York answering calls coming in non-stop—5.5 million phone calls a day in search of telephone numbers. If we can save one second from each call we save 5.5 million seconds a day, which is 63 days, or almost three working months of an employee. Our software can save a company like that around $10,000 a day."[71]

Note the level of detail of the economic logic. Such descriptions are nearly nonexistent in the first statist period and point to two important aspects in Gavron's work:[72] first, however superficial, capital here

---

70   The most obvious example is the Arab whose tongue is cut out in A. B Yehoshua's *Mul ha-ye'arot* but this moral attitude and guilt is already present earlier, in S. Yizhar's early stories *Shayara shel ḥazot* and *Sipur Ḥirbet Ḥiz'ah* as well as in Aharon Megged, *Mikre ha-kasil*.

71   Assaf Gavron, *Almost Dead* (New York: Harper Perennial, 2010), 31.

72   The only example I can give of such detailed description is Yaacov Shabtai's 1977 *Past Continuous* but here too these descriptions are ironic and used as a sign of collapse of Zionist political spirit rather than as a positive sign of the times.

is the direct object of narration, a new literary phenomenon in Israeli literature. Second, the description of work and the logic of business is not allegorical; it does not signify—as did "work" in the first period—a spiritual collective endeavor whose meaning goes beyond itself. Rather, it is literal. Literality that in the first period was a means of negation in the hands of modernists—especially in Koren and Shabtai—returns here as the positive norm of the everyday.

Other than time as a figure for capital, another layer of Eitan's characterization concerns the fact that at the outset of the novel he is self-centered and uncaring, a trait that is expressed through his insensitivity towards his girlfriend, Duchi, and their failing relationship. Accordingly, Eitan's ego-ideal is Jimmy, the CEO, an aggressive narcissist who conceives of life in terms of profit and gain and who exemplifies an extreme version of capitalist culture. As might be expected, time and the relation to the "other" will also define the form—here genre—of the novel itself, and Eitan's transformation and rejection of time-as-profit will be accompanied with a shift from a solipsistic first person narrative to a detective investigation whose object is someone other to Eitan and whose fate somehow points to the fate of Israeli and Palestinian collectivity.

Eitan's speech about the call center is then the zero point of the novel, and his world and sense of time begins to change and indeed collapse only when the "political" cuts into his life in the form of repeated attacks. But even more important is the unexpected relation between the private and the political—the fact that, as I have noted, this very menacing violence is written as the necessary condition for pushing Eitan outside the monad of his private life and into the lives of other people. We get a glimpse of this at the outset, when the news of the first attack cuts into Eitan's day at the office and provides an excuse to talk to people with whom he rarely keeps in touch. As the novel progresses and Eitan becomes the accidental victim of two more attacks, he begins to move out of his private world to look into the death of one of the victims, Giora Guetta. Eitan and Giora were both on the minibus that was bombed at the beginning of the novel, and since they had a brief chance to chat, Eitan feels a responsibility to pass along Giora's last thoughts to his family. He finds Giora's diary gadget at the scene of the bombing and tracks down his girlfriend, Shuli, with whom, however unlikely, he has an affair. During their first and meeting, Eitan reflects on the nature of time, signaling a change in his outlook:

The whole situation was so strange to me. For years I'd been continuously running, chasing time, fretting about lost seconds . . . and now I was just letting time pass without giving it a second thought, without feeling I am missing something. Or almost. And time, for its part, hardly moved.[73]

By their second meeting, the change in Eitan's experience of time is immediately accompanied by an awareness of other people:

I reached out to touch [Shuli's] hand. I was prepared to do whatever she said. It wasn't exactly because I'd fallen in love. I mean, something had happened, I'm not denying it. Something started growing there. But as much as anything else I was amazed by what had happened to time. It seems to have stopped . . . I looked at the people eating in Café Europa: who were they? How come they had all this time?[74]

In the same way that time-as-commodity stands in for capital and Eitan's initial character, Gavron uses the theme of time to mark the shift in Eitan's perspective. We see here, on a small and local scale, an "aesthetic" moment *à la* Kant—an experience of time that is devoid of any direct purpose. And yet, as I have noted, the solution to Eitan's problem will not be aesthetic—as it was in the liberal and humanist stance of the first period. For, we need to recall, Eitan's problem is not the asphyxiating burden of purpose or duty, but rather the vapid and empty sense of capitalist "purposefulness" itself that has no larger meaning. I will attend to the solution momentarily, but for now let us see how, once Eitan's begins to free himself from his corporate mentality, he is alienated from his own daily routine. (Note the emphasis on the underlying equivalence of experience):

I wasn't doing my work very well. I didn't care about another sales presentation, another meeting summary, another two-day trip to Europe with non-stop work on the plane: flying, landing, taxi, identical hotel room, identical meeting room, identical dinner, identical porn, identical breakfast. Since the euro had come in I couldn't tell the difference between the countries: everybody spoke English with the same accent . . . I wasn't really interested in the Austrian telecoms company that wanted to improve its directory enquiries service, or in saving half a second

73 Gavron, *Almost Dead*, 106.
74 Ibid., 134.

per call in Spain or in real time solutions, server efficiency . . . blah blah blah blah *blahhh*. Time's Arrow continued to streak into the future, but I wasn't on it anymore.[75]

The passage works on several levels. First, we notice the gutting of meaning and content—the purpose of Eitan's travel plans—which leaves us only with the empty form—the means of travel by which this purpose is executed. I note that differently than the "crisis of meaning" discussed by Israeli postmodernists, here the crisis is localized as a particular work experience, and more importantly it is a crisis the novel seeks to mend rather than accept as a universal property of social life. Second, note how the weight of the first part of the passage falls on the word "identical." Eitan is pained by the equivalence underlying his experience, by the ironic fact that no matter how far and wide he travels, all places take on a similar identity. Recall that in the first period, "equivalence" was the utopian form that was directed against the inequality induced by the state, while here "equivalence" turns into a nightmare from which the subject is trying to escape by, eventually, looking into forms of "difference" (inequality) that will keep equivalent and therefore meaningless life at bay. Third, the process of abstraction and alienation brings to the surface of the text the relationship between the networks of global capital and the erasure of locality, or in other words, the fact that Israel has become yet another relay-point in global space. It is important to note that the abstraction of local difference is not a result of Eitan's global travel, but comes from the new meaning of "traveler" and "destination." Eitan does not travel as an Israeli meeting other nationals, but rather as an employee of a start-up funded by global capital traveling to meet other corporations. This means that it is not global travel or movement as such that erases locality,[76] but rather the fact that the destinations and travelers themselves are already denationalized and hence abstracted. Eitan is not moving in the world of nations or places but in the globe of capital itself. Finally, the unveiling of capital brings us closer to the formal properties of the passage. It is easy to see that Eitan's experience

---

75 Ibid., 213.

76 Discussing Christine Brook Rose's novel, *Between*, David Damrosch identifies globalization through the figure of travel and the confusion of multiple languages. But it is clear that, while travel is the means by which globalization is made, "travel" is only a figure for an already abstract world of equivalents. It is not travel per se that makes the world global; it is rather the precondition—global capital and the making of private life—that allows us to grasp cultures as signifiers and as mere equivalent stations (rather than as unequal forms of life) in the first place. See David Damrosch, *How to Read World Literature* (Chichester, UK; Malden, MA: Wiley-Blackwell, 2009), 122–4.

of identity is underlined by the temporality of *repetition*. Although the collapse of temporal sequencing and meaningful progress is motivated, as the Russian Formalists would say, by Eitan's post-traumatic stress, repetition here also characterizes a larger issue: the temporality of capital released from any obligation to a collective project. Put differently, the subordination of the ends to the means restructures temporality, which is now experienced as a cycle with no outside, sometimes referred to as a perpetual present. This temporal form is then echoed and duplicated in Eitan's experience of historical, political time, in the fact that since 1948, Israelis lived in the same kind of conflict with the Palestinians, a history that from the perspective of the private citizen is experienced as an endless cycle of violence devoid of any meaning. Gavron crystalizes this sense of historical repetition by having Fahmi and his group replicate in the present the attacks on the road leading to Jerusalem in 1948.[77]

Once we note "repetition" as the underlying temporal form of Eitan's experience of both the economic and the political we can shift registers and move from theme to the governing temporal properties of this part of the novel. Here we note that repetition also underlies the structure or the compositional principle. Recall that time and again Eitan happens to be at the site of attacks, which he experiences as the repetition of the same event. If we look even closer at the way Gavron stages these events we notice that all of them are written as a series of coincidences. Eitan is the accidental victim of three attacks by the same resistance group; he happens to change places with Shuli just before the third attack, an action that saves his life; and Eitan, Duchi and Fahmi are brought together through the random encounters of their families and friends in the present and the past. These coincidences lead Eitan to a deep sense of heteronomy, to the sense that he is not a self-legislating agent and that his life is directed by a vague notion of fate. When Shuli is killed in the third attack while Eitan is saved, he reflects feverishly on all the random decisions he made that morning that could have led to another outcome. He concludes:

> An infinity of ifs. We stand at the crossroads a hundred times a day and we have to make our choices or we can never progress, and our choices determine who we are ... And yet, I can't get rid of the feeling that, for the third time, it wasn't me but somebody else who was making the decisions.[78]

---

77   Gavron, *Almost Dead*, 39.
78   Ibid., 144.

This is the culmination of Eitan's storyline, the final point in his long process of alienation, after which the novel takes a turn (a change of genre and philosophical perspective) that will reveal the possible "solution" to this debilitating state. I note two important points here: First, as I argued throughout, the second neoliberal period is characterized by an Althussarian "absent cause," an underlying reason that, while structuring appearance, remains unrepresentable as such. Here the absent cause is misrecognized and appears as an unfathomable fate. For this reason, the "cause" is often confused with an "origin" the subject is trying to locate. Second, very differently than those writers identified as postmodern in Israel—most explicitly Orly Castel-Bloom, who celebrates coincidence and randomness as a way to fend off the determining order of Zionist life—Gavron understands these temporal and experiential concepts as the new oppressive norm, an experience the subject should not submit to but transcend in an attempt to live in a meaningful way.

Before attending to the genre shift in the novel and its meaning, I will examine Fahmi's plotline and its similarities to Eitan's. Gavron, perhaps more than any other Israeli novelist, figures the Israeli and the Palestinian as equivalent. He painstakingly divides the book into two parts, alternating each chapter so that equal space is given to the Palestinian and Israeli protagonists. Similar to Eitan, Fahmi is also experiencing a crisis of identity. The Israeli occupation makes his life intolerable and he is faced with the choice of either leading a private life—going to university and trying to stay away from politics—or a political life—moving to a Palestinian refugee camp and joining the struggle. As I noted above, Fahmi moves in the other direction from Eitan, i.e., he first joins a resistance group and slowly becomes alienated from it until he finally disobeys the group's leader and spares Eitan's life. For Fahmi this is also a story of a shift from heteronomy to self-legislating autonomy, only here the determining agent is not secular fate but Allah and destiny (and sometimes a sense of duty to family or the national cause):

> I couldn't shake the feeling that Grandfather Fahmi [a resistance fighter] was somehow guiding my life from heaven . . . Meeting [Eitan] made me wonder just who it was controlling my destiny.[79]

Thus, Fahmi's decision to spare Eitan's life will be the consequence of taking control of his own life and becoming an autonomous self-legislating agent. Although motivated by different reasons, both Fahmi

---

79   Ibid., 282.

and Eitan position the "self" as the source of agency, which here stands as an answer to the heteronomy induced by neoliberal capital and political association.

As I have noted, the last third of the novel takes a turn and we move, in Eitan's story, from a first-person account to a detective investigation. The search for the identity of one of the victims of the first attack—Giora Guetta—is a way for Eitan to exit his monadic world and begin to care about other people.[80] The search, however displaced, is a political desire to connect to other people and know the world. We will later see how in Nir Baram's *World Shadow* this political desire turns conscious and its direct object becomes global capital itself, but for now I note the fact that the social unit that takes on this investigation is the "team"—Eitan, his "sidekick" Bar, and at a certain key moment, Fahmi himself. The "team" displaces both the family unit—Eitan and Duchi whose life as a couple basically collapses—and the corporation—the relationship between Eitan and Jimmy the CEO who loses all credibility as the startup loses money—and becomes, albeit implicitly, an alternative form of political organization.

Once we enter the detective investigation, we enter a "textual" world that takes on twin aesthetic figures nestled one inside the other: locally, Giora Guetta, like the patients of Gur's psychoanalytic institute, now exists in Eitan's world only as the sum total of traces—text messages and notes he left behind on his gadget which require deciphering. The figure of the gadget, a miniature textual object embedded within the world, is then enlarged and lends its form to the social world which now—as with all investigations—appears as a riddle, as a series of textual clues, pointing to a determining yet absent cause, whose displacement and concealment makes the world into a cipher that calls for an interpreter. Eitan's agency is not expressed through making the world but in reading it, and in a moment we will see what textual object this act of reading takes up. Additionally, as Eitan becomes a detective, the structure of time and the order of the world change: no longer are we in the temporality of coincidence and mysterious fate, but rather in a developmental, meaningful time, in which Eitan takes control over his life—he becomes an autonomous agent, one determined to investigate the meaning of the events that have befallen him.

---

80 The care (Ashkenazi) Eitan shows towards the dead (Mizrahi) Giora, as well as the fact that it is the (Mizrahi) Shuli who helps Eitan become less selfish, points to the idea that the Mizrahi lower classes are an essential component for Ashkenazi redemption. This allegorical level remains implicit, or unconscious.

As Eitan and his sidekick Bar follow the trail of clues that Giora left behind, they discover a connection between a Jewish-Israeli doctor and two Palestinian-Israeli brothers. But Eitan and Bar cannot figure out the relation between these three characters, until Fahmi comes to their aid. At this point in the story, Fahmi, after escaping the Israeli police and military, infiltrates Israel proper and finds himself working as a temporary custodian in the tech company where Eitan works. Although still unknown to one another, the two meet as workers. Fahmi, the electrician, fixes Giora's gadget, and goes on to help Eitan with an Arabic translation task. The two become friends of sorts and very quickly discover that Fahmi, having access to the Palestinian community at Kfar Qasim, can help uncover information about the three people in question. Before the "solution" is revealed, we should note the important transformation in Fahmi's character. For as the narratologists used to say, Fahmi seems to have shifted his characterological valence: at this point he is no longer the "adversary" but a helper or "donor": he is the only character who can help solve the mystery by mediating between Eitan and the truth. Jameson elaborates on the importance of this figure:

> What [Vladimir] Propp's discovery implies is that every How (the magical agent) always conceals a Who (the donor), that somewhere hidden in the very structure of the story itself stands the human figure of a mediator . . . We may restate the necessity for the existence of the donor in yet another way by pointing out the fact that in the beginning the hero is never strong enough to conquer by himself. He suffers from some initial lack of being . . . The donor is [then] the complement, the reverse, of this basic ontological weakness. So it is that in the folk-tale, in the hero's story, an Other is implied, but not quite where we expected to find it [i.e., not the adversary].[81]

Jameson's last sentence goes to the heart of Fahmi's significance in this story: contrary to what we would expect, Fahmi—the Palestinian—is not the Other-as-enemy (or victim) that turned out to be a friend, as a liberal-humanist reading would have it. Rather, the otherness of Fahmi is here staged as the condition necessary to face a different (yet unknown) Other. But, as I have noted, Fahmi was the "donor" all along—for the attacks woke Eitan from his self-absorbed meaningless life, and now, in the detective narrative, what was implicit becomes explicit and Fahmi appears as the "helper."

---

81 Jameson, *Prison-House of Language*, 67–8.

Now, as Eitan, Bar and Fahmi discover the relation between the three characters, the plot thickens. As it turns out, one of the Israeli-Palestinian characters—Tamer Sarsour—had an affair with the wife of the Jewish doctor—Benyamin-Moshe Warshawski, a Holocaust survivor.[82] Humiliated by the fact that his wife had an affair with an Arab, Warshawski hired Giora, an ex-military combatant, to kill Tamer—but on the day of the act, Giora died in the minibus bombing (which was orchestrated by Fahmi's group). This incredible plot, where all ends are tied up, is significant in itself; but before we attend to its meaning, it is important to say a few words on Warshawski's motivation for killing Tamer. Warshawski is portrayed as ultra-nationalist with paranoid delusions. A victim of Nazi genocide, Warshawski finds himself, ironically, identifying with the Nazi regime, and compares Israel to a defeated 1920s Germany where Arabs take the place of Jews. Three points are cardinal here: First, as it turns out, it is right-wing extremism that is revealed here as the Other—the real enemy of both Eitan and Fahmi.[83] Thus, in this story, Eitan and Fahmi are able to recognize each other as partners and cooperate against the rise of an internal Jewish adversary. Second, I have argued that Eitan and Fahmi are written under the concept of equivalence, but note that this world still needs an Other that cannot be assimilated, a spot of inequality, that is identified as deviant and must be rejected. This spot of inequality is figured here in an implicit allegorical form. I showed how Eitan lives a literal life that has no greater meaning. Conversely, Warshawski, the agent of inequality, experiences the affair of the Jew and the Arab *allegorically*—he takes it as a symptom of a greater historical political decadence. While we must reject the content of Warshawski's actions we need to hold on to their form, to his way of reading the world: however delusional, Warshawski has a way of reading that still fuses the private and the public, the body (his wife) and spirit (the state). So what the novel rejects is not only Warshawski's ideology (content) but also this kind of political allegorical relation and way of reading the world (form), which are typical of the Zionist right. More abstractly, in the world of materialist neoliberal capitalism, lacking collective spirit, the political right, or the state, is localized and finds its place within the imaginary world not only as deviant content but as the now banished, past aesthetic form of allegory.

---

82   In the Hebrew novel, the doctor's name is Otto Shneiderman.

83   Fahmi's nationalist brother, Bilal, also occupies this position on the Palestinian side of the story.

Finally, we come to perhaps the most important moment in the novel, in its last few pages. After talking to Warshawski, Eitan, horrified, takes a moment to himself and reflects:

> [I] thought about myself, how I was in a café on a weekday morning with a . . . Polish Jew who had hired a young guy to murder his wife's lover, and I was here because the young guy's girlfriend . . . had asked me to find out what her boyfriend was doing on the morning of his death by a suicide bomber on the minibus on which I'd happened to be traveling. Adultery, murder, terrorist attacks: nothing surprising about it. It happened all the time. The surprising thing . . . *was me*. It was so strange that there should be somebody who linked all these people.[84]

And the Hebrew original is even more revealing: "What surprised me was my part in the story. How of all people it is I (*dvaka ani*) who connects all the dots."[85]

Two important attitudes are revealed in this concluding statement: first, note Eitan's surprise at the fact that he is somehow related to all these people that he, ultimately, does not know. I have argued that in the statist period, the binding power of the political project was the historical limit against which private life emerged as an alternative. Here, we see the opposite, where the mere relation to other people is almost unthinkable because the subject has become isolated. In other words, the historical limit in the neoliberal period is the near impossibility to establish and advance collective political projects that will defy capitalist forms of association. Second, note the emphasis on "linking" and "connecting." If in the first period the modernist form responded to the state by an aesthetic of severing, i.e., separating the private and the political to achieve autonomy, now the postmodern aesthetic responds to capital, rather than to the state, by a form of "mapping" whose purpose it is to connect, rather than to sever, the private individual to other people who signify its political unconscious. The limit of Gavron's novel lies in the fact that this mapping takes as its object individuals rather than systemic conditions and ends up with a conspiracy plot rather than structural violence.

Three important points are worth highlighting in conclusion: first, the change in the positioning of violence and the Arab. Contrary to the

---

84 Gavron, *Almost Dead*, 325.
85 Gavron, *Tanin*, 315.

post-Zionist stance that still structures its reading around a humanist subject and hence understands violence as an aberration, *Almost Dead* is structured around a private subject whose politicization is dependent on violence. The Arab is then positioned neither simply as an enemy nor friend, but as a condition of possibility for recognizing the isolation of private life, and as a "helper" against an internal Jewish adversary. Second, capitalism, which in the previous two novels was confused as personal greed and self-interest, takes on a more structural guise. Its main form—commodification—rises to the surface of the novel in both theme and form, and allows us to see the way Israel is integrated into the space of global capital not as a nation-state but as a relay point for investment by private corporations. Third, the deepest wish of the novel in this commodified setting is politicization whose literary form is mapping and the production of knowledge. This last development leads to a key change in aesthetic priorities: if in the 1960s, in order to think freedom, the artwork projected inward Kant's concept of the aesthetic and thus duplicated itself within itself, from the late 1980s it projects inward Kant's concept of Critique in the sense of accounting for the conditions of possibility of Israeli society. In the most politically conscious texts, the literary artwork realizes itself by moving outside itself, i.e., by resembling its other—discursive knowledge. This tendency is still marginal; it receives its most developed form, at least for now, in Nir Baram's *World Shadow* about which I will say a few words in conclusion.

10.

Critically acclaimed as one of the most important Israeli novels of its time, Baram's ambitious *World Shadow* pushes forward the incipient globalism of *Almost Dead* and writes what might be the first full-blown global Israeli novel.[86] Baram sets his complex plot in three main sites— Israel, the US and England—while each of these sites is in turn intricately connected to a plethora of other states and historical times, making the art of "mapping" the main task of the reader who keeps asking, "how is it all connected?" In Israel, we follow, in free indirect discourse, the rise of a young Mizrahi character—Gavriel Mansour—a representative of an American investment firm, involved, in part, in the 1985 economic restructuring of the Israeli economy. In the US, we read emails and

---

86   Nir Baram, *Zel-'olam* (Tel Aviv: 'Am 'oved, 2013).

newspaper clips telling us of the political campaigns of MSV, a consulting firm running questionable political campaigns all over the world. In London, we witness, in a first-person plural account, the attempts of a small group of young people to organize the first global strike, taking aim at global capital and its forms of inequality. As the novel unfolds we learn that Israeli investors, involved with the American investment firm, sold arms to Congolese businessmen that were subsequently used for massacres. As it turns out, the same Congolese businessmen owned part of MSV, the consulting firm, thus implicating the firm in crimes against humanity. As a consequence of these and other questionable acts of MSV in the Congo, a consultant of the firm, Daniel K, turns against the firm and joins the youths in England who are preparing the global strike, thus tying all threads of the story together.

While the story describes real events that occurred in the Congo in the 1990s, the novel is historical not so much because of this fact, but rather due to its conception of the neoliberal form of capital in the post-1970s periphery. Contrary to Gur whose worlds are governed by rigid local laws (the psychoanalytic institute; the university; the police), *World Shadow* is a fluid world in which politicians and businesspeople can shift from field to field without any difficulty. The paradigmatic figure of this world is the entrepreneur. Here is how Gavriel, who enters this world, reflects on its members:

> When he got to know the members of the [Israeli investment] Fund, he discovered that there is no limit [*gevul*] to the flexibility of the entrepreneur [*yazam*]; he could move from textiles, to agriculture, to oil, to real-estate, to represent known global brands, to banking. The entrepreneur will find experts for any field. As for the expertise of the members of the fund themselves, it was, as they saw it, to weave all the threads needed for a deal, and especially those ties between business people and government officials.[87]

The notion that there is no limit to capital, here figured in the form of finance, is precisely the historical state in which the logic of the market can enter any field, locally and globally, even that of the state proper. Further, the "limitless" property ascribed to capital also brings about the key concept of this period, "equivalence"—for once all such fields are understood to be commodities, they are now somehow the same.

---

87   Ibid., 62.

Equivalence also characterizes the investors themselves for now there is no real difference between the Israeli and other investors. We have seen this tendency in Gavron, but in *World Shadow* it receives an even more explicit and large-scale articulation. Even more important is the description of the entrepreneur as "weaving," whose mirror image, for the reader, is "reading." For while the entrepreneur weaves, as it were, the complex network of capital all over the globe, the political task of the reader is to follow these ties and observe how discrete events and people are in fact connected. The weakness of *World Shadow* in this regard is that it implicitly understands capitalism as conspiracy—especially in the case of the consulting firm (MSV) and its ties to the Congolese businesspeople—rather than advancing a more impersonal structure. The notion that it is people rather than structures that we need to uncover receives its fullest articulation in the form of a justification for MSV's involvement in the Congo massacres. Note the "postmodern" tone of the explanation:

> We [i.e., MSV] were all groping in the dark, which becomes even darker as your business in the global world thickens. No one fully understands who they are working for, which powers stand behind the friendly delegates you meet for lunch, and who stands behind those standing behind . . . Sometimes it seems that in the multiplicity of candidates, governments, NGOs, private or government firms, multinational corporations, and regulators, it is impossible to understand anything. We all hold only a few pieces of the puzzle, and the real frightening thing is there is no one who can fully put it together.[88]

The novel, however, rejects this excuse, and its political imperative is indeed to "put the puzzle together" and show that it is possible to understand the world. What we see in addition is how claims of uncertainty, while mobilized by Israeli postmodern scholars to undermine state power, are here used to defend capital's involvement in heinous crimes. More importantly, we see how the appeal to uncertainty through the figure of infinity—numberless agents and points of view—is not simply a philosophical stance but a stance that arises out of the structure of capital that admits "no outside."

Thus, with *World Shadow* we come full circle: the poetics and philosophy of uncertainty that was conceived as the marker of postmodernism

---

88   Ibid., 204.

and characterized the entire worlds of Castel-Bloom or Heffner, returns localized within the world, as an ideology, in a novel that seeks to show us how such ideologies arise out of social structures and can be used to cover up their violence.

3

No Kant in Palestine, Or, The Aesthetic of Statelessness 1948–1993

1.

Similar to Chapter 1, this chapter will articulate the heteronomous conditions under which Palestinian literature is written in the period between 1948 and 1993, and how such conditions demonstrate the qualitative difference between Palestinian literary production in this period and the concept of autonomous art and literature developed in capitalist and liberal states. To do so, we will first discuss existing scholarship, which presupposes a Kantian concept of autonomous art, then offer the alternative concept of heteronomous art as a corrective, and finally move to readings of Sahar Khalifeh and Ghassan Kanafani. It is important to note at the outset that while the category of heteronomy allows us to compare different corpora of literature, it does not presuppose an identity between the Israeli social form and the Palestinian one: while Palestinian social form in this period is characterized by war, occupation and exile, Israeli history, as we said, takes the variant of state-making. Both generate conditions of heteronomy, which nonetheless produce different aesthetic forms.

To examine the aesthetic assumptions of Palestinian literary criticism, presupposing a concept of autonomous art, we begin with Salma Khadra Jayyusi whose scholarly work and translation projects have been major conduits for Arabic literature into the West, especially to the US.[1] At the outset of her substantial introduction to the 1992 *Anthology*

---

1 Jayyusi founded the Project of Translation from Arabic Literature (PROTA) in the 1980s and edited some thirty anthologies of modern Arabic literature.

of Modern Palestinian Literature, the most sizeable anthology to date, Jayyusi explains her position regarding art and the Palestinian condition:

> Although I have, in my study of modern Arabic poetry, given atten-
> tion to social (and political) factors as "important {external}[2] forces
> behind the changes in the mind and consciousness of the creative Arab
> talent," *primary* importance has been given to the internal evolution of
> the poetic art, an evolution determined first and foremost by elements
> intrinsic to the poetic art itself. This approach is based on the notion
> that art has its own internal laws of growth and development and that
> although these laws are influenced by external forces, social, political,
> and psychological, the ultimate determinant in the development of art
> will be the demands, needs, and possibilities of art itself at a certain
> moment of its history.[3]

Drawing a stark line between "intrinsic" poetic elements and "external" social and political factors, Jayyusi continues to quickly underplay such externalities and argues,

> because of their immediacy, political factors often tend to interfere in the
> artistic process, sometimes diverting it from its natural course in favor
> of a certain commitment or ideology. However, the history of modern
> Arabic literature, particularly poetry, and especially in the decades since
> the Palestinian disaster of 1948, shows that art has its own way of reas-
> serting its natural course of development and growth.[4]

It is easy to understand Jayyusi's position—as at least one commentator does—as conservative, conceiving of art in natural terms, and of social and political elements as almost unnatural, incidental factors.[5] Later in her introduction, this romantic conception of art as an organically devel-oping organ and the poet as "talent" is joined by an idealist conception, conceiving Palestinian history as an aggregate of "rich material for lit-erature,"[6] as if it were sensuous matter submitted to the organizing order

---

2   Brackets are in the original; Jayyusi is quoting her earlier work here.
3   Salma Khadra Jayyusi, "Introduction: Palestinian Literature in Modern Times."
In *Anthology of Modern Palestinian Literature* (ed.) Salma Khadra Jayyusi (New York:
Columbia University Press, 1992), 1.
4   Jayyusi, "Introduction," 2.
5   See Salah Hassan, "Modern Palestinian Literature and the Politics of Appease-
ment," *Social Text 75*: 21.2 (Summer 2003): 7–24.
6   Jayyusi, "Introduction," 3.

of literary forms. This conception of politics as an external corrupting force that literature transcends or refigures is not Jayyusi's alone. In his extensive study of the Arabic novel, Roger Allen concludes his reading of *All That's Left to You (Mā tabaqqá lakum)* by Ghassan Kanafani[7] by saying that while Kanafani's "life" was committed to politics, his fiction was not "marked" by the "magnified realism" that "disfigures" lesser works. Kanafani's works are rather distinguished by his "concern with form, style and imagery."[8] As with Jayyusi, the emphasis on form, style and imagery serves as an ideal mediator, as an apolitical, ahistorical prism that refigures (but does not disfigure) reality in such a way as to make it distinct from the political and in this way gain universal value.[9] If Allen historicizes the forms themselves, they are said to be derived from European and American modernism (*All That's Left to You* is justly compared to William Faulkner's *The Sound and the Fury*),[10] but at no moment does Allen examine the history of these modernist forms, or ask whether a history of forms could explain their re-articulation in Palestine.

Even in the most politically sympathetic reading of Kanafani, that by Muhammad Siddiq, we find a similar disjunction. Taking care to safeguard Kanafani's literary value, Siddiq conceives of literary value and political ideology as opposites, saying that the more explicitly political Kanafani decides to be, the more his work suffers in terms of literary form.[11] Siddiq goes on to say that since Kanafani's *Men in the Sun (Rijāl fī al-shams]* and *All That's Left to You* were written during ambivalent political times they exhibit modernist styles, while after 1967 and the change in the political programs of the PFLP, Kanafani becomes "indebted" to

7   Kanafani was a prominent member of the Popular Front for the Liberation of Palestine (PFLP) and edited its newspaper *al-Hadaf*. The PFLP, comprised of students, professionals, and educators, was established in the late 1960s as a secular, left-leaning group with ties to Marxist organizations. For some details on the PFLP and other Palestinian political organizations of the 1960s and 1970s see Ilan Pappe, *A History of Palestine: One Land, Two Peoples* (Cambridge: Cambridge University Press, 2004), 142–69.

8   Roger Allen, *The Arabic Novel: A Historical and Critical Introduction*, second Edition (Syracuse: Syracuse University Press, 1995), 153.

9   In this regard see also Hilary Kilpatrick's introduction to Ghassan Kanafani's *Men in the Sun, and Other Palestinian Stories*, translated by Hilary Kilpatrick (Washington DC: Three Continents Press, 1978).

10   The comparison to Faulkner is justified and helpful, and Kanafani himself is reported to have considered Faulkner as a direct influence. My reservations stem from the fact that "modernism" is used here not in order to explain Kanafani's text, but rather to endow it with aesthetic value. For Kanafani's invocation of Faulkner see Muhammad Siddiq, *Man Is a Cause: Political Consciousness and the Fiction of Ghassan Kanafani* (Seattle: University of Washington Press, 1984), 38.

11   Siddiq, *Man Is a Cause*, 90.

socialist realism. Since the latter style is seen as having a low literary value, Siddiq signs off by reassuring us that "[Kanafani's] overall contribution to Palestinian fiction and political consciousness is safely beyond doubt."[12] Operative in these evaluations is a mechanical logic that proceeds to imagine the Palestinian writer as applying diverse forms to content, grasping the former as belonging to art proper and the latter to life. It is not surprising then that Kanafani's literary value and "Palestinian concerns" are eventually constructed in an inverse relation: as the latter decreases, the former increases.

It is important to acknowledge here the institutional predicament of Arabic criticism and literary production during the time these studies were published. Since until very recently both Arabic literature itself and Arabic literary studies occupied, as Pascale Casanova would put it, a "peripheral" position in the world republic of letters, modernist styles operate for both writers and critics alike as a technique of *literarization* that endows Arabic texts with legitimacy and allows them more visibility.[13] While it is commonplace today to consider the 1960s as the moment of transition when modern Arabic literature moved from realism to modernism, it is important to note that critics made the same transition. For if for Jayyusi, Allen, Siddiq and others, modernism is the standard value while realism is reduced to naïve representation, for the previous generation of critics it was mimetic realism that was dominant.[14]

However, the emphasis on form is not simply an institutional effect; one can see how it underlies points of view for which the value of Arabic literature is not an immediate concern. Neil Lazarus's review of Barbara Harlow's *Resistance Literature* is a case in point. Harlow was probably among the first in Anglo-American criticism to insist on the practical nature of literature written for liberation struggles, and although I will

---

12   Ibid., 91.

13   As Allen mentions, in the beginning of his own career few considered modern or classical Arabic literature to be a worthy endeavor. The slow and uneven stream of translations into English, and the acquisition of Arabic being more difficult than European languages, are among the reasons Arabic remains a peripheral field of study. See his "Rewriting Literary History: The Case of the Arabic Novel," *Journal of Arabic Literature* 38.3 (2007): 247–60.

14   For the shift of the Arabic novel to modernist styles around the 1960s, see Sabry Hafez, "The Transformation of Reality and the Arabic Novel's Aesthetic Response," *Bulletin of the School of Oriental and African Studies* 57.1 (1994): 93–112; Stefan G. Meyer, *The Experimental Arabic Novel: Postcolonial Literary Modernism in the Levant* (New York: State University of New York Press, 2001). For M. M. Badawi's predilection for realism and mimesis see his *A Short History of Modern Arabic Literature* (Oxford: Oxford University Press, 1993).

problematize her notion of "resistance literature," it is instructive to examine Lazarus's critique of her perspective.[15] Unlike the critics discussed previously, Harlow, who is less concerned with questions of value, provides a different understanding of Palestinian literature in which our inability to distinguish between the political struggle and the literary text is precisely what makes such texts important. In this, Harlow joins Kanafani's assessment in his own study of Palestinian literature written between 1948 and 1968: "[t]he commitment of most of the resistance writers exceeded the boundaries of art; they are truly affiliated with the national movement in one way or another."[16]

In his review of Harlow's *Resistance Literature*, Lazarus offers a sympathetic and endorsing criticism, but significantly points out that by identifying literature and liberation struggles as indistinguishable, Harlow fails to consider the "problem of form" and "literary value":[17]

> The primary disadvantage of Harlow's "expressivism" is to be seen in her occasional conflation of "literary" and "social" texts . . . the specificity of fictional mediation is sometimes neglected, and no allowance is made for narrative as a *reworking* of reality. To define narrative as documentary is to specify a certain relationship between it and that represented in or by it. Documentary only seems to, but in fact does not, reduce the distance between representation and its object.[18]

Although problematizing Harlow's "expressivism," Lazarus does not do so from a poststructuralist position; he still insists on the distinction between "literary" and "social" texts, which would have been much more tenuous had he been working with the concept of discourse. Rather, his is more specifically a modern and modernist objection, where the former (modern) conceptualizes the practical ends of art as outside the sphere of the artistic, and the latter (modernist) insists on the non-referential aspect of fiction, on literature as a process of "reworking."[19] It is indeed

15   See Barbara Harlow, *Resistance Literature* (New York: Methuen, 1987); *Afterlives: Legacies of Revolutionary Writing* (London: Verso, 1996); "Readings of National Identity in the Palestinian Novel." In Issa J. Boullata (ed.) *The Arabic Novel Since 1950: Critical Essays, Interviews, and Bibliography* (Cambridge: Dar Mahjar, 1992), 89–108.

16   See Ghassan Kanafani, "*al-Adab al-Filasṭini al-muqāwim taḥta al-iḥtilāl 1948–1968*," In *al-Āthār al-kāmila*, Vol. 4 (Beirut: Dar al-Ṭalī'ah, 1977), 256.

17   Neil Lazarus, "Comparative Resistance," *Novel: A Forum on Fiction* 23.3 (Spring 1990): 321, 320.

18   Ibid., 323.

19   For a discussion of alternative modernities see, for example, Fredric Jameson's "Modernism and Imperialism." In Terry Eagleton, Fredric Jameson, and Edward Said,

the prevailing manner in which we grasp literature today, but as much as we should not forget the specificity of fiction, we should also remember that such a conception is *socially and historically specific* to certain social formations, which, as I argue, do not adequately fit the situation in Palestine.

In Lazarus, and the critics we have discussed, the modern and modernist conceptions of art have turned somewhat ahistorical. For, more than explaining Palestinian literature, such conceptions end up mediating it, standing in between First World critics and the specificity of Palestinian society after 1948. To make this discrepancy more evident, let me turn to a paradigmatic formulation of modern and modernist art. Given that Lazarus, like Siddiq, is working within and around the Marxist tradition, the following passage from Adorno (which we also examined in the Introduction) may serve as a useful example:

> Works of art owe their existence to division of labor in society, the separation of physical and mental labor. At the same time they have their own roots in existence. Their medium is not pure mind, but the mind that enters into reality, and by virtue of such movement, is able to maintain the unity of what is divided. It is this contradiction that forces works of art to make us forget that they have been made. The claim implicit in their existence, and hence, too, the claim, that existence has a meaning is the more convincing, the less they contain [sic] to remind us that they have been made, and that they owe their own existence to something external to themselves. Art that is no longer able to perpetrate this deception with good conscience, has implicitly destroyed the only element in which it can thrive . . . A contradiction of all works of Art is the concealment of the labor that went into it, but in high capitalism, with the complete hegemony of exchange value, and the contradictions arising out of that hegemony, autonomous art becomes both problematic and programmatic at the same time.[20]

Reading this passage one feels a certain uneasiness with phrases such as "high capitalism," "concealment," "autonomous art," and "labor" as they seem to miss the mark in regard to Palestine. Even if we grant Rashid Khalidi's claim that although severely fragmented into multiple sites,

Nationalism, Colonialism and Literature (Minneapolis: University of Minnesota Press, 1990), 43–68.

20   Theodor Adorno, *In Search of Wagner* (London: Verso, 2005), 71–2.

post-1948 Palestinian society is still a "society," one cannot in good con-
science claim that the production of art under such conditions is similar
to that in advanced capitalist societies.[21] Further, the commentators
discussed previously feel uncomfortable with the fact that Palestinian
literature insists on precisely the opposite principle of Adorno's conception: it constantly reveals its dependency on external conditions, and
accepts being grounded on a heteronomous and *not* an autonomous
principle.[22] The critics seem uneasy with this condition, partly for reasons
I touched upon briefly above, and therefore constantly press Palestinian
literature into a modern/modernist mold. And when this fails, Kanafani's
(and others') "political" narratives are devalued in the name of a normative aesthetic standard that does not fit them in the first place. Once we
consider that the modern and modernist conceptions of art hinder our
understanding of Palestinian literature, it becomes necessary to turn to
a different conception of art.

Although its exemplarity is somewhat exhausted by now, Walter
Benjamin's "The Storyteller" can still serve as a good alternative. Here,
Benjamin explicitly explores a narrative mode in which the distance
between the object and its representation is not reduced to zero (naiveté),
but rather is canceled out because the modern social and historical conditions that have brought about such a distance are yet to occur.

The storytelling that thrives for a long time in the milieu of work—the
rural, the maritime, and the urban—is itself an artisan form of communication, as it were. It does not aim to convey the pure essence of
the thing, like information or a report. It sinks the thing into the life of
the storyteller in order to bring it out of him again. Thus, traces of the
storyteller cling to the story the way the handprints of the potter cling to

---

21   See Rashid Khalidi, *Palestinian Identity: The Construction of Modern National
Consciousness* (New York: Columbia University Press, 2010). For aspects of Palestine's
political economy after 1948 see Pappe, *Modern Palestine*; Joel Migdal (ed.) *Palestinian Society and Politics* (Princeton: Princeton University Press, 1980). For pre-1948 see
Roger Owen (ed.) *Studies in the Economic and Social History of Palestine in the Nineteenth and Twentieth Centuries* (Oxford: Macmillan, 1982).

22   To dispel any confusion between Palestinian literature and avant-garde art
whose principle is indeed one of demystification, it is important to remember that the
latter arises in advanced capitalist societies where, as Peter Bürger explains, art has
been separated from daily praxis and the avant-garde seeks its reintegration. In this
period, Palestinian (and Israeli) literature is confronted with the opposite situation
where private life, history and art seem inextricable. See Peter Bürger, *Theory of the
Avant-garde*, translated by Michael Shaw (Minneapolis: University of Minnesota Press,
1984).

the clay vessel. Storytellers tend to begin their story with a presentation of the circumstances in which they themselves have learned what is to follow, unless they simply pass it off as their own experience.[23]

As is known, Benjamin distinguishes here between the pure and abstract sign (information) and storytelling whose embeddedness in experience prevents in advance the break between the storyteller and his "subject matter." The suggestive metaphor of the handprints on the vessel is diametrically opposed to Adorno's conception of art as a process in which work is concealed. It is an alternative understanding of the concepts of "figuration" or "concealment," as Benjamin insists that practical antecedents enter the story. Furthermore, Benjamin's formulation, "[storytelling] sinks the thing into the life of the storyteller in order to bring it out of him again" intimates the bodily relation between the narrator and his story, i.e., a state of undifferentiation between signs and their subject.

Benjamin's conception of the relation between the storyteller and the story can easily be thought of as a prelapsarian subject-object harmony, and indeed his melancholic comments about the lost art of storytelling might reinforce such an interpretation.[24] But we need to remember that the strength of his essay lies in the fact that its aesthetic observations are embedded in a proto-anthropology that offers a dialectical relation between this kind of aesthetic figure and particular forms of life. Thus, what enables this subject/object relation depends on the historical moment itself and not only on the formal properties of storytelling.

Reading Benjamin we may ask whether our understanding of representation is adequate—especially in the category of modern literature as autonomous art—when applied to societies that are neither state-governed nor fully capitalist. Let me now introduce an alternative understanding of Palestinian literature.

---

23   Walter Benjamin, "The Storyteller: Reflections on the Works of Nikolai Leskov." In Hannah Arendt (ed.), *Illuminations: Essays and Reflections*, translated by Harry Zohn (New York: Schocken, 1968), 91–2.

24   For relevant critiques on Benjamin's notion of experience related to "The Story-teller," see Martin Jay, *Songs of Experience: Modern American and European Variations on a Universal Theme* (Berkeley: University of California Press, 2006), 312–60; Neil Larsen, "Literature, Immanent Critique, and the Problem of Standpoint," *Mediations* 24.2 (2009): 48–65.

2.

Although they work with modern and modernist conceptions of literature, critics do, in fact, affirm the singularity of the Palestinian case as one that resembles neither the socio-historical condition of other Arab states nor "advanced" capitalist societies. They do not, however, explain the implications this state might have for the forms of literature and their social locations. Writing in 1992, Jayyusi explains, for example, that "Modern Palestinian experience is harsh, unrelenting, and all penetrating; no Palestinian is free from its grip and no writer can evade it." Such a social condition, affecting Palestinians everywhere, "determine[s]" Palestinian life, and no writer can escape such a situation without "bely[ing] reality and deny[ing] experience."[25] While we are used to thinking of imagined nationalisms in such a way, this experience is not simply produced by political organizations, but rather by the historical situation of war, occupation and exile that itself produces political organizations.[26] In what follows, then, while I acknowledge the importance of the Palestinian national movement on the production of symbolic forms, I suggest that the historical conditions of Palestinian life and the forms of literary production cannot be reduced to the specific "political" aims of national organizations. So, to be clear, contrary to Jayyusi's quote, I reject the notion that one can distinguish between daily experience, forms of art, and forms of political organization, because the historical situation in Palestine after 1948 does not allow for such a separation. Thus, I ask to reconsider our understanding of the "political" in this period.

Tying the condition of Palestine after the 1948 war to the general attitude of the Arab writer, Edward Said observes,

> In such a context, then, the role of any writer who considers himself seriously engaged in the actuality of his time—and few writers during that period since 1948 considered themselves otherwise engaged—was first of all, as a producer of thought and language whose radical intention was to guarantee survival to what was in imminent danger of extinction . . . Writing therefore became a historical act.[27]

25   Jayyusi, "Introduction," 2–3.

26   For the feelings of attachment to an imaginary nation, see Benedict Anderson, *Imagined Communities: Reflections on the Origin and Spread of Nationalism* (London: Verso, 1991).

27   Edward Said, "Arabic Prose and Prose Fiction after 1948." In *Reflections on Exile and Other Essays* (Cambridge: Harvard University Press, 2000), 48. For similar claims on the historical significance of the 1967 war, see statements by Saadallah Wannous in

Moving on to discuss the 1967 war, Said argues that for Arab writers and thinkers this war, unlike others, was "immediately historical" in a sense similar to the one Georg Lukács discusses in his study on the historical novel. The Napoleonic wars, Lukács argues, assembling popular armies for the first time and waging battles on a massive scale, created a new sense of history, one unfolding in the present moment.[28] Said suggests that this change in the temporality of thinking brought about by the magnitude of the events induced a new role for art:

> Hitherto wars had been distant and exclusively the affair of armies. Now everyone was involved. Everything thought or written about the war had the status of historical act; whether as a soldier, a writer or an ordinary citizen, the Arab became part of a scene . . . Therefore the only progressive role to be played was that of an activist-author forcing the Arab to recognize his role in the struggle. No one could be, or really ever was, a spectator; the present was not a project *to be* undertaken; it was now.[29]

In Said's emphasis on the leveling effect of this moment and the performative nature of any writing as a historical act, one can begin sensing how such historical conditions would unsettle the very concept of representation along with the symbolic divisions between literature, historiography and other modes of knowledge. Said's notion of the impossibility of being a passive spectator brings to mind Jayyusi's formulations, which we have already mentioned, and furthers the notion that boundaries between the subject and the world are being collapsed.

This historical situation is intensified in Palestine proper. After the 1948 war, Palestinian society was fragmented into several communities, most of which remained in refugee camps.[30] Historians describing this period talk about processes of disintegration and gradual rehabilitation

---

Friederike Pannewick, "Historical Memory in Times of Decline: Saadallah Wannous and Rereading History." In Angelika Neuwirth, Andread Pflitsch and Barbara Winckler (eds.) *Arabic Literature: Postmodern Perspectives* (London: Saqi 2010), 97–109. Questions about the significance of literature after 1948 inform also the well-known debates in Egypt about commitment literature, especially in the journal *al-Adab* in the 1950s. I discuss this in subsequent pages.

28   Georg Lukács, *The Historical Novel* (London: Merlin Press, 1962).

29   Said, "Arabic Prose," 56.

30   Of the 1.4 million Palestinians living in what was Mandatory Palestine in 1948, 160,000 Palestinians remained in Israel while over 750,000–800,000 were displaced and lived as refugees in TransJordan, the Gaza Strip, Syria and Lebanon. See Samih K. Farsoun and Naseer H. Aruri, *Palestine and the Palestinians: A Social and Political History*, 2006, 105–43.

that changed the nature of Palestine's political, social and economic life.[31] To be sure, social and cultural structures had durability that preserved them through the 1948 war and it is not the case that all structures were obliterated in one stroke. Rather, historical accounts show that within a decade there emerged a new national movement that, conjoined with other economic and social changes, redrew social spheres and transformed older social and political relations based more on elitist representation and family relations.[32] In the early stages, this national movement was integrated into pan-Arabist movements such as the Arab Nationalist Movement, but towards the end of the 1950s it crystalized into Palestinian organizations specifically, such as the Palestine National Liberation Movement. Historian Ilan Pappe explains that while only a few thousand Palestinian refugees engaged in armed struggle, this popular development "revolutioniz[ed] the social structure of Palestinian society . . . . The young generation now took precedence over the older, patriarchal one; women began playing a more central role on the public stage; and the clans lost their dominance almost totally and were gradually replaced by the nuclear family."[33] Samih Farsoun and Naseer Aruri argue similarly that while kinship and patronage served to contain the trauma of 1948, the new modern leadership enacted "a revolutionary transformation of the Palestinian people."[34]

I would like to suggest that this revolution in "traditional" forms of social and political organization could not be understood in the same way we understand the work of political parties or even popular mobilization in democratic civil societies. Given the Palestinians' liminal status as refugees and the absence of stable state structures that erect durable symbolic divisions between social spheres, such changes in political structure not only affect a longitudinal transformation, crossing diverse social spheres, they also make social boundaries more porous, potentially endowing every sphere with a public and political significance. More importantly, given that these changes happen after a catastrophic

---

31   See Pappe, *Modern Palestine*, 142–61; Khalidi, *Palestinian Identity*, 177–86; Naseer and Aruri, *Palestine and the Palestinians*, 105–22

32   Ylana Miller examines the changing political structures in rural Palestine. See Ylana N. Miller, *Government and Society in Rural Palestine 1920–1948* (Austin: University of Texas Press, 1985). See also Albert Hourani, "Ottoman Reform and the Politics of Notables." In William R. Polk and Richard L. Chambers (eds.) *Beginning of Modernization in the Middle East: The Nineteenth Century* (Chicago: The University of Chicago Press, 1968), 41–68.

33   Pappe, *Modern Palestine*, 152. For commentary on the transformation of social structures, see also Naseer and Aruri, *Palestine and the Palestinians*, 105–42; 175–206.

34   Naseer and Aruri, *Palestine and the Palestinians*, 124–5.

war that dramatically altered the geo-political reality in the Levant, these structural changes now *appear as such* throughout the region and are grasped, as Said suggests, as "immediately historical."[35] Writing in 1971, Aziz Shihadeh explains: "with the June [1967] War all previous modes of life were shattered. The whole social structure was challenged. All previous values and convictions were put to the test."[36] And in this kind of experience, it is not implausible to think that literature has a very different function and location than in "advanced" capitalist societies in which artistic writing is mostly a private and privatized affair, and where a stable differentiation of spheres, even if contested, delineates the social boundaries of art. To dispel any misunderstanding, it is not that Palestinian literature is now *recruited* for political purposes; such an understanding still maintains the symbolic differentiation between the political and the artistic. Rather, given that social structures are themselves shifting, and will continue to shift for several decades, it is difficult to determine the boundaries of both. In this context, it is important to recall that the two most important Palestinian writers, the novelist Ghassan Kanafani and the poet Mahmoud Darwish, were active members of political organizations, the former in the PFLP and the latter in the PLO (until 1993).

Pappe, elaborating on the condition of Palestinians in Israel after 1948, offers us a telling anecdote about Palestinian poetry during these years:

> Poetry was the one medium through which the *daily events* of love and hate, birth and death, marriage and family could be *intertwined with the political issues* of land confiscation and state oppression and aired in public at special poetry festivals.[37]

Here we read the same kind of habitual separation between "daily life" and "political issues." They are intertwined, no doubt, but Pappe is still able to differentiate between them. What is of import to Pappe, however, is their embeddedness in public festivals during a period of historical uncertainty. He continues:

> The Israeli secret service was powerless to decide whether this phenomenon was a subversive act or a cultural event. The security apparatus

---

35   Said, "Arabic Prose," 56.
36   Aziz Shihadeh, "The Palestinian Demand Is for Peace, Justice and an End to Bitterness—the Initiative Is with Israel—the Time to Negotiate Is Now," *New Middle East* 35 (August 1971): 22.
37   Pappe, *Modern Palestine*, 158.

would be similarly puzzled in the early 1980s, when it began monitoring festivals organized by the Islamic movement.[38]

Poetry embedded in a public practice in such historical times can begin to explain why objections to "mimetic" or "committed" representation are misleading. The Israeli secret service is not simply uncertain as to whether the event is cultural or political; the question revolves precisely around representation. Is the poetry recited there mere representation or is it an act? The significance and social location of poetry is not determined simply by its properties (political content/form), or the context (festival), but by the historical moment that renders even the most "apolitical" content political, and *merely* cultural events subversive. In other words, if in a prevalent conception of political literature, most rigorously defended by Adorno's insistence on form, the properties of the artwork itself are understood to transgress symbolic divisions between spheres (such as the private and public; the political and the cultural), in Palestine, under conditions of crisis and occupation, these spheres objectively overlap so that poems are political almost by default.

Palestinian literature, similar to the way Benjamin describes the storyteller and storytelling, cannot be easily extracted from this complex historical situation without its meaning being affected, for precisely such an extraction renders it "autonomous." The critics do just that—they extract it from its sites, and once such a procedure takes place (quite implicitly and "naturally") the conditions have been procured to regard it as "art." Palestinian literature at this moment is therefore a kind of act, but one dissimilar to those attempted in "advanced" capitalist societies. For while in these societies, as Adorno would say, great art always seeks to be more than art, to break its *Schein*, its structure of surface appearance and depth, for Kanafani and probably others, history itself makes this transgression the norm.[39]

I believe that Said understands this condition, albeit in a displaced manner, when he tries, implicitly, to deflect criticisms of the "mimetic" quality of Kanafani's *Men in the Sun*. Arguing that the Palestinian

---

38   Ibid., 158.

39   Discussions of and around *Schein* pervade Adorno's major writings and his essays on literature. See his *Aesthetic Theory*, translated by Robert Hullot-Kentor (Minneapolis: University of Minnesota Press, 1997); "On Epic Naiveté," "The Position of the Narrator in the Contemporary Novel," and "Trying to Understand *Endgame*." In *Notes To Literature* I, translated by Shierry Weber Nicholsen (New York: Columbia University Press, 1991), 24–9; 30–6; 241–76; "Notes on Kafka." In *Prisms*, translated by Samuel and Shierry Weber (Cambridge, Mass: MIT Press, 1983), 243–71.

"present" after 1948 cannot be "given" but must be "made" or "achieved," Said understands the crisis in temporal terms as a historical predicament that complicates for Kanafani the stability of temporal presentation and the inherited form of the novelistic "scene." He argues,

> This is not a matter of providing how literature or writing reflects life, nor is it confirmation of an allegorical interpretation of Arab reality; for, unfortunately, these approaches to modern Arabic writing are endemic to most of the very scarce Western analysis of the literature . . . the scene *is itself* the very problem of Arabic literature and writing after the disaster of 1948: the scene does not merely reflect the crisis, or historical duration, or the paradox of the present. Rather the scene is *contemporaneity* in its most problematic and even rarified form.[40]

Said suggests that the crisis of Palestinian temporality is not expressed in content only. Although the crisis is glimpsed in the complex temporal modalities in the fictional world, the scene itself as an artifact of European novelistic tradition betrays the fact that it cannot function for Kanafani:

> Kanafani . . . must make the present; unlike the Stendhalian or Dickensian case, the present is not an imaginative luxury but a literal existential necessity. A scene barely accommodates him. If anything, then, Kanafani's use of the scene turns it from a novelistic device which anyone can recognize into a *provocation*.[41]

The emphasis on "provocation" here remains somewhat vague, but what is more important is the manner in which Said himself attempts to break the limit of "reflection" and the gap between representation and reality by offering us a "paradox":

> A scene is made for the novel, but out of material whose portrayal in the present signifies the psychological, political, and aesthetic result of the disaster. The scene *provokes* Abu Qais [one of the characters]; when he achieves action because of it, he has made a readable document and, ironically, the inevitability of his extinction. The distances between language and reality are closed.[42]

---

40   Said, "Arabic Prose," 51.
41   Ibid., 53.
42   Ibid., passim.

I cite here Said's reading not in order to follow its lead, but rather to present it as a symptom. The interpretive intricacy of these passages and others seems to betray Said's understanding that the Palestinian present challenges our conception of the relation between history and novelistic language. However, given that he is still committed to articulating this problem as a literary symptom, his reading, although not tempted by content, ends up taking the "scene" as a literary homologue for the crisis. Said's reading then is a reading that oscillates implicitly, as I see it, between two categories: the novel as "artwork" and the novel as "act."

If we understand that the historical moment induces a spatial crisis as much as a temporal one, we will see that the changing "distances between language and reality" are not only a matter of "form," but also of the social location of literature. As Palestinian social spheres are redrawn, their symbolic boundaries having become more porous, "literature" itself is changing its meaning as much as, following Said, other modes of knowledge. It is this historical condition that unsettles literature's structure of appearance and significance, as well as our habitual understanding of the relation between readers and fictional texts.

To understand Kanafani's works in terms of political "commitment," or in Arabic "*iltizām*," is then not entirely correct. As the issue of commitment is fairly well known, and less urgent at this moment, I leave its discussion to another occasion.[43] By invoking it here, I would like to stress briefly that Jean-Paul Sartre published *What is Literature?* in 1949, and the term "engagement" received its impetus similarly, but not

---

43   According to Verena Klemm, the term "*iltizām*" was first introduced to Egypt by Taha Hussain in 1947. It was popularized by Salma Musa, Umar Fakhuri and others and at one point "dominated the Arab world," as one commentator put it. The term received direct endorsement by Suhail Idris in 1953, in the first editorial of the new journal *al-Adab*, although critics explain that the term was understood somewhat differently in the Arab world. Important to note here is that while the term loses its vitality in the 1970s, it is then that Kanafani publishes his studies about Palestinian literature, and demonstrates the relevance of the term to Palestine. As I argue in the following pages, this would suggest that the history of Palestinian literature does not seamlessly follow the main currents and trends in the Arab world. Most significantly, while critics argue that the 1960s was the decade in which Arabic literature (especially Egyptian) shifted from realism to modernism, this shift does not pertain to Palestinian literature as it has remained "realist" until very recently. See Verena Klemm, "Different Notions of Commitment (*Iltizam*) and Committed Literature (*al-adab al-multazim*) in the Literary Circles of the Mashriq," *Arabic and Middle Eastern Literatures* 3.1 (2000): 51–62; Suhail Idris, "*risalat al-adab*," *al-Adab* 1.1 (January 1953): 1–2; Sabry Hafez, "Sh'ir al-ma'sa fi al-arḍ al-muḥtalla." *al-Adab* 3.17 (March 1969): 70–6; Ghali Shukri, *Adab al-muqāwamah* (al-Qāhirah: Dār al-Ma'ārif, 1970), 5–18; 129–42. M. M. Badawi, "Commitment in Contemporary Arabic Literature." In Issa J. Boullata (ed.) *Critical Perspectives on Modern Arabic Literature* (Washington: Three Continents Press, 1980), 23–46.

identically, from the consequences of World War II. Sartre's term, to be sure, assumed an engagement with the intellectual scene in France after the war, but he, too, understood committed literature as praxis, and distinguished it from the more narrow political ends of the Communist Party.[44] He understood the term as rising from the historical moment of France after 1945, and this is how I would like to understand *iltizām*. Although critics understood it as describing the writer's commitment *to*, or adherence *to* a specific political cause, that is, as a willful relation between a subject and an object, it is useful to remember that the word comes from the root *l.z.m* (ل.ز.م), which means necessity. Necessity is the condition that prevents a clear division between subject and object, for it is used to describe situations in which subjects are *impelled* to act, not necessarily out of free will, the bedrock of liberal self-legislation. If we understand the "political" not as a political program, but, more broadly, as a historical predicament effecting all spheres of life, "commitment" would suggest a response, that could take a broad variety of forms, political organization being only one of them.

Here is how, for example, Sahar Khalifeh, one of Palestine's best-known writers, describes this situation:

> At the time [the 1970s], we didn't differentiate between poetry and politics. This "resistance poetry," as we termed it, spoke to us of humanity, revolution, ideas and dreams; it touched our daily lives with the images of the heel of the peasant, the bread of the mother . . . The new poetry and the new situation made me feel that I had to write—it was not a decision, but a need.[45]

Situated in its context, Palestinian literature becomes a practice by which one understands and engages the world. It is a mode of knowledge whose weight is secured not simply by its own properties, but by the context of crisis. Understood in this way, the question of representation is reversed: it is not that Kanafani's works intend simply to represent or imitate Palestinian history, but rather that its readers consider it a model of imitation. In other words, it is written in such a way, and in such times, that readers may read it in the same way they read a discursive text, but with the important qualification—and this is what makes it *aesthetic* or

---

44   Jean-Paul Sartre, *What Is Literature? And Other Essays* (Cambridge: Harvard University Press, 1988).

45   Penny Johnson and Sahar Khalifeh, "Uprising of a Novelist: Penny Johnson Interviews Sahar Khalifeh," *The Women's Review of Books* 7.10/11 (July 1990): 24.

poetic—that in their hands it does not turn into a source of mere knowledge (Benjamin's notion of information), but rather something with which they make sense of themselves and the world. To paraphrase Benjamin, here the novel seeks to sink its story into the Palestinian subject in order to bring it out of him again.[46]

This kind of relation between subject and object begins to suggest that Palestinian novels challenge another important precondition for aesthetic autonomy. As Terry Eagleton explains,

> The emergence of the aesthetic as a theoretical category is closely bound up with the material process by which cultural production, at an early stage of bourgeois society, becomes "autonomous," autonomous, that is, of the various social functions which it has traditionally served. Once artifacts become commodities in the market place, they exist for nothing and nobody in particular and can consequently be rationalized, ideologically speaking, as existing entirely and gloriously for themselves.[47]

If we understand Kanafani's works in the manner suggested here, then it becomes evident that they are written predominantly for Palestinians *in particular*, and only secondarily for a general and "universal" audience. As I will demonstrate, this relation begins to change with the novels of Adania Shibli in the first decade of the twenty-first century, when Palestinian literature is not simply read *by* but also written *for* a global readership.

Palestinian literature (until 1993) has something both local and useful about it, because of the particular history of Palestine. Emile Habibi, one of the most respected Palestinian-Israeli novelists, whose novels critics usually use as an example for Palestinian literariness, conveys this local relation explicitly. In an interview conducted in 1986, explaining the use of citations from classical Arabic texts in his novels, Habibi confesses,

> I want to be honest with you. First of all, I always want to give my reader something. Some new knowledge. I don't want it to be only fiction . . . I want to give information from our heritage to the new generations, in

---

46 Critics acknowledge the fact that Kanafani wrote his last finished novel *Sa'd's Mother* [*Umm Sa'd*] with this subtle intention. Through a series of daily conversations between the writer/narrator and an old Palestinian peasant, Umm Sa'd, the peasant and her son come to terms with the political and economic situation in Palestine. See Ghassan Kanafani, *Um Sa'd: Qiṣaṣ Filastīnīyah* (Bayrūt: Dār al-'Awdah, 1969).

47 Terry Eagleton, *The Ideology of the Aesthetic* (Oxford: Blackwell, 1990), 8–9.

order that they respect it. I do this intentionally, cold-bloodedly . . . This I always do because I respect my reader . . . . I know for example, in our newspaper, everybody reads my article, I know all the young [sic] are reading my article and I want to help them add to their knowledge. And the other thing is that I always want to stress, like all the writers of the Third World, that we have behind us a rich heritage. I want to defend my heritage. I do not stick to the old heritage, but I am not a nihilist. In this, I am one of many, as I understand it, in the Third World . . . We have to defend ourselves, our humanity, our equality.[48]

What Habibi intimates here is how the Palestinian novel belongs to at least two categories: practical and aesthetic. Habibi, it seems to me, understands his role not very differently from the "pre-modern" conception of the artist whose art provides pleasurable instruction. Habibi's seamless transition from discussing his novel to discussing his newspaper article suggests that he does not hold the novel as a separate aesthetic category. The purification of the practical "function" happens only when the novel is extracted from this site and assumed in advance to be "autonomous." Habibi's confession ("I want be honest with you") suggests that he is aware of the First World/Third World break between him and his interviewers, whom he assumes in advance will not think of art in this "practical" manner.

Considering these historical and political conditions as well as the aesthetic statements by Said, Khalifeh, Kanafani and Habibi, I claim that Palestinian literature written between 1948 and the 1990s cannot be thought of as autonomous art, and should be understood instead as heteronomous. It is a category at odds with the aesthetic tradition of capitalist states whose characteristics have been obscured due to the universalist nature of "Western" literary criticism. The historical, political and aesthetic categories of "Western" criticism, grounded in the problem of "private life," are ill-suited to explain the specific nature of artistic production emerging in other societies where "private life" has yet to emerge as such. To be sure, the specificity of Palestinian writing has at times been engaged through the term "political" or "committed" literature, but such attempts are inadequate as well for they mistakenly take the "political" first to be an explicit political ideology, and second to be an attribute of

---

48 "Literature and Politics: A Conversation with Emile Habibi—Interview conducted by Allen Douglas and Fedwa Malti-Douglas." In Issa J. Boullata (ed.), *The Arabic Novel Since 1950: Critical Essays, Interviews and Bibliography*, 42–3.

the literary text while, instead, the "political" should be understood as an attribute of historical conditions. In other words, previous criticisms have displaced the historical into the literary, and offered us distinctions based on formal properties rather than aesthetic categories. Thus, a history that seeks to grasp the manner in which Palestinian literature imagines and engages the world over time needs to trace the broadest historical changes, and especially the change in the articulation between the private and the public which presents both a limit and a challenge to imaginative works.

In what follows, I offer readings in two Palestinian novels, Sahar Khalifeh's *Wild Thorns* (*al-Ṣubār*] and Ghassan Kanafani's *All That's Left to You,* and elaborate further the relation between aesthetic forms and their underlying historical limit.

3.

Wild Thorns is one of Sahar Khalifeh's best-known novels, winning her recognition both within and outside the Arab world. Its events take place five years after the 1967 war, when Palestinians in the now-occupied West Bank and Gaza Strip begin entering Israel legally as day workers for the first time since 1948. The novel begins as Usama, a scion of the respected al-Karmi family, returns to the West Bank as a guerrilla fighter (*fidaʾi*) with orders to plant a bomb in a bus taking Palestinian workers to Israel to stop this new form of dependency. This plot point provides the novel with its weight and urgency, but it is interwoven with a more patient exploration of Palestinian society. Providing a complex critique of both the Israeli occupation and the Palestinian nationalist agenda— as well as an historical insight into the changing patriarchal and class structures in Palestine due to labor migration to Israel—the novel is grounded in the political and social relations in Palestine after 1967. Thus, the moral question regarding the Israeli-Palestinian conflict (captured in the opposing attitudes of Usama, the guerrilla fighter, and his cousin Adil, the humanist) has a limited significance within the larger scope of the novel. (Though it does make the ethico-political stance of the novel explicit, through which Khalifeh's "politics" can be identified.)

Before trying to understand Khalifeh's historical thinking and its relation to the previous discussion on aesthetics, it would be useful to have a sense of the novel's reception outside Palestine. Here are two examples:

Fadia Faqir writes:

The major problem of this novel is its voice and perspective. Authorial voices and those of characters overlap and fly into each other . . . In certain scenes the voice cannot be attributed to anyone but the author, despite an evident wish not to present her point of view in this particular fictional work.[49]

And Penny Johnson observes:

Khalifeh is occasionally heavy-handed and characters ruminate far beyond the scope of their world.[50]

I begin with these relatively negative judgments so as to illustrate how *Wild Thorns* brings to light implicit aesthetic norms, and to reveal its ambivalent status as a work of art from a European stance. The value judgment of the reviews notwithstanding, Faqir seems to take issue with the fact that the novel exhibits both "fictionalized" and "referential" (authorial) voices, and identifies this as a technical flaw. Although Faqir never provides concrete examples of such authorial voices or criteria for identifying them, I suspect that at work here is a normative aesthetic standard that monitors the boundary between artworks and discursive texts and deems the latter's manner of presentation to be outside of the aesthetic. We find such an understanding in Freud's account of the creative act as one of repression in which the secret desires of the author must be disguised in order to "enter" the fictional world, but also in the famous assertion of James Joyce's Stephen Dedalus: "the artist, like the God of creation, remains within or behind or beyond or above his

---

49   Fadia A. Faqir, "Occupied Palestine: The Writer as Eyewitness," *Third World Quarterly* 9.4 (October 1987): 1408.

50   Penny Johnson, "Interrupted Lives," *The Women's Review of Books* 7.3 (December 1989): 20, my emphasis. There are other, more positive readings, but the ones cited above give a sense of the difficulties the novel posed to readers. For other reviews see Peter Nazareth and Sahar Khalifeh, "An Interview with Sahar Khalifeh," *The Iowa Review* 11.1 (Winter, 1980): 67–86; Issa J. Boullata, "Review," *Middle East Journal* 42.2 (Spring, 1988): 328–9; Barbara Harlow, "Partitions and Precedents: Sahar Khalifeh and Palestinian Political Geography." In Lisa Suhair Majaj, Paula W. Sunderman and Therese Saliba (eds.) *Intersections: Gender, Nations and Community in Arab Women's Novels* (Syracuse: Syracuse University Press, 2002), 113–31; "Men Dominate Society: Sahar Khalifeh." In Runo Isaksen (ed.) *Literature and War: Conversations with Israeli and Palestinian Writers*, translated by Kari Disckson (Northampton: Olive Branch Press, 2009), 183–8.

handiwork, invisible, refined out of existence, indifferent, paring his fingernails."[51] As we shall see, in both cases the appearance of the artist's biographical details or artistic plan would be seen as "vulgar," as they violate the Kantian nature-based concept of art.

If we also consider Johnson's comments about Khalifeh being "heavy handed" and her characters "ruminat[ing] far beyond the scope of their world," we will see, however, that Faqir and Johnson's objections are not raised against "political" content as such, but rather against its aesthetic form. Such objections (present also in commentaries on Kanafani's works, found at times to be "too clear,"[52] "flat,"[53] and so forth), are leveled against the abstract, or "direct" presentation of political content, which would be more suitable for works identified pejoratively as "social documents."[54]

The challenge of this chapter is not to demonstrate that even such "documents" have literary value. I have already noted that the "value" of Palestinian literature is not to be understood as a property of the artwork but rather a matter determined within the power relations between peripheral states and dominating states, "literary value" being the route to wider circulation, recognition and eventually cultural capital. Rather, I argue that the categorical break between literature and other, more discursive modes of knowledge through which Khalifeh's novel is judged, is first a result of applying the modern/modernist concept of art (and aesthetic autonomy as we shall see), and second an effect of the extraction of Khalifeh's novel from its socio-historical context in which divisions between politics and literature, and more generally, between discursive and literary modes of knowledge do not have such a clear-cut existence. For example, providing a panoramic view of Arab women writers,

51   Sigmund Freud, "Creative Writers and Day-Dreaming." In *The Complete Psychological Works of Sigmund Freud*, Vol. IX, translated by James Strachey et al. (London, Hogarth Press and the Institute of Psycho-Analysis, 1959), 143–53. James Joyce, *A Portrait of the Artist as a Young Man* (New York: Vintage, 1993), 207.

52   See Roger Allen, *The Arabic Novel*, 147.

53   Paul Starkey, *Modern Arabic Literature* (Washington: Georgetown University Press, 2006), 132.

54   H. A. R. Gibb made this comment as early as 1926, but one can find it also in Fadia Faqir, who argues that these novels are both art and document. Citing Gibb, M. J. L Young writes in defense of Arabic novels as well. While I do not think the novels I discuss here are merely social documents, I do not attempt to defend them, but rather to re-examine the way we understand the binary division between "art" and "document." See H. A. R. Gibb, *Arabic Literature: An Introduction*, (Oxford, Clarendon Press, 1963), 161, cited in M. J. L. Young, "Modern Arabic Fiction in English Translation: A Review Article," *Middle Eastern Studies* 16.1 (January 1980): 147–58; Faqir, "Occupied Palestine," 1405.

Miriam Cooke introduces Khalifeh's novels in a manner not dissimilar to discursive text:

> Sahar Khalifah . . . has asked questions none have known how to answer: How is Palestine best defended? Is it by staying on the land, even if that staying involved collusion with the enemy to the extent that work must be sought in Israel for survival? Or is it by leaving and plotting and then returning to carry out grandiose missions that do not count the sacrifices? What role can women play? Does the nationalist agenda have any space for feminist activism?[55]

Although she does not say so directly, Cooke implies that a Palestinian novel can indeed engage these socio-political questions the way any other discursive text would.

I would like, however, to return to Faqir and Johnson's comments and read their aesthetic judgments more closely. It would seem that both critics suggest a problem of epistemological boundaries. Not only do characters' thoughts exceed the "scope" of the fictional world, they compete with the perspective of the narrator. This leads to a problem of attribution—who speaks? Let me give an example of such a moment in the narrative. Here are Usama's first impressions upon returning after several years away from Palestine:

> Nothing in the town seemed to change. The square looked the same as always; the hands of the clock still moved on slowly and silently, marking the passage of time. Only the trees and plants have grown taller. The soap factory was still there; a damp smell of crushed olive pulp still seeped from behind its huge door. In the main office of the factory the big men of the town still sat talking, but doing nothing. Everybody was out on the pavement, doing things but not talking. Yes, nothing has changed.[56]

Keeping with the novelistic free indirect discourse, Khalifeh's narrator stays very close to Usama's perspective. The imbrication of omniscience and mind takes here the subtle form of a spatio-temporal weaving, in

---

55   Miriam Cooke, "Arab Women Writers." In M. M. Badawi (ed.) *Modern Arabic Literature* (Cambridge: Cambridge University Press, 1992), 452–3.

56   Sahar Khalifeh, *Wild Thorns*, translated by Trevor LeGassick and Elizabeth Fernea (New York: Olive Branch Press, 1989), 26. In Arabic: Khalifeh, *al-Ṣubār*, 26. From now on, pagination for *Wild Thorns* will list the English edition first followed by the Arabic.

which Usama marks the temporal dimension ("seemed," "looked," "as always," "still") while the spatial mapping ("square," "clock," "trees," "factory") invokes the impersonal surveying of scenery typical of an omniscient narrator. Further, Usama's consciousness is identified by an emphasis on details, which intimates a familiarity, but more importantly a sense of his *own* time in the present. Now compare the following passage not eight lines later:

> And yet. The people no longer seemed poverty stricken . . . There seemed to be a lot of money about. There were more sources of employment and wages had gone up. Prices had risen, but people were eating meat, vegetables, and fruit voraciously, as though they were starved, stuffing their children. Those who once had not owned so much as a sweater now swaggered about in leather jackets. Those who did not even possess a scarf now muffled their ears in fur collars . . . Girls who had once been servants now worked in factories and offices. They were plumper, too. Something has changed.
>
> But occupation is still occupation . . . the servant girls were servants no more, and the class ladder was less steep.[57]

Although the previous mode still lingers on, the relation between narrator and character is markedly different. Usama is still on the street and in a moment someone will address him, but the kind of observations he makes now are out of sync with the present time of the scene. If in the previous passage his consciousness was identified by an emphasis on concrete objects in the present time, the shift to "sources of employment," "prices," and "class ladder,"[58] to choose the most obvious, assumes a quasi-omniscient perspective, existing in a different (impersonal, historical) kind of time. More interestingly, Khalifeh ultimately suggests a disjunction of times: while the personal, existential time of Usama seems immutable (nothing has changed), the historical collective time betrays complete change. What makes this disjuncture difficult to resolve is the tone and texture of the passage, intimating that these are Usama's thoughts and not those of an omniscient narrator. It would seem then that the

---

57 Khalifeh, *Wild Thorns*, 26–27/26.

58 To be sure, "sources of employment" is not an accurate translation as in Arabic Usama says simply that there is more work, or more employment. The French translation renders this phrase more accurately as "plus de travail." For the French translation see Sahar Khalifeh, *Chronique de figuier barbare* (Paris: Gallimard, 1978), 28.

received category of omniscient narration is challenged in a manner not dissimilar to the "scene" Said identifies in Kanafani.

In the first passage, Usama's sense of time, as I suggested, is inseparable from concrete objects while the second sense of time suggests conceptual abstraction. Usama is not simply shifting "number"— singular to plural—he is shifting "kind": concepts such as "sources of employment," "prices" etc., are not only aggregate nouns, they are what we might call structural indicators, identifying Palestinian society as an abstract construct, and individuals as social types. The difficulty arises due to the fact that this kind of conceptual and structural abstraction is usually reserved for the omniscient narrator of the realist variety, while here it seems that characters are taking over this role. We find another example of such abstraction, this time in a conversation between Palestinian youths, who elaborate, as would a sociologist, the rigid social structures that mold the lives of young Palestinian men—pushing them to study medicine and engineering and to immigrate to the Gulf so to pay back their tuition, a process which culminates in the dwindling of the educated classes.[59] This kind of abstraction, offering a structural and historical account of Palestinian society on behalf of the characters, unsettles a dominant principle of literary description that was famously expressed in Henry James's dictum "dramatize! dramatize!,"[60] but that received philosophical expression a hundred years earlier, in Kant's conception of reflective judgment.

As Kant's concept of the aesthetic has already been discussed,[61] we will assume a familiarity with the argument and move to its application here. I argue that what Kant understands as "concept" and "nature" in the Third Critique, the critics we have just discussed understand as "politics" and "aesthetic illusion" respectively. Given this implicit substitution, I would like to make several claims. First, if for Kant art executed according to a concept is mechanical, then for the critics a novel written according to a political program is didactic. Second, if for Kant a concept, or rule, appearing as such, foils the natural illusion of art, then for the critics, explicit political content (whatever that might be) unsettles the fictional illusion and exposes the novel as a document. Third, such "violations" shift the category under which Palestinian novels are read from art to non-art. In other words, although never admitted as such, the aesthetic

59   Khalifeh, *Wild Thorns*, 59–60/56.

60   Henry James, "Preface to *Daisy Miller*," in Henry James, *Daisy Miller* (London: Penguin, 1986), 40.

61   See the Introduction.

principles underlying readings of Palestinian literature, presented in this section and in previous pages, are grounded in a Kantian understanding of the relation between art and nature. They assume in advance the indeterminate (concept-less) relation between particulars and universals, and use this aesthetic principle as an implicit standard. If we do not want to impose a normative Kantian standard on Palestinian literature and press it to fit the critics' strictures, we will need to formulate a different relation between the universal and the particular.

Let us return to Said's aesthetico-historical observation from the previous section, but this time translate it into Kantian terms.

> Hitherto wars had been distant and exclusively the affair of armies. Now everyone was involved. Everything thought or written about the war had the status of historical act; whether as a soldier, a writer or an ordinary citizen, the Arab become part of a scene . . . No one could be, or really ever was, a spectator; the present was not a project *to be* undertaken; it was now.[62]

What I ask to do here is to map the relation between the Kantian subject and the work of art onto the relation between the Arab subject and history, and propose that once the subject-object relation between the subject and history collapses, so does the subject-object, particular-universal relation that underlies Kant's concept of the aesthetic.

Without spelling it out, Said unsettles here the paradigmatic aesthetic relation at the heart of Kant's theory of taste—spectatorship and its temporality. Kant's conception of the aesthetic does not spring so much from the site of art-making but from that of the observer, the museumgoer and art critic. The knowledge of the art observer, and indeed, as Terry Eagleton explains, the eighteenth-century European bourgeois subject more generally,[63] is grounded on a subject-object relation, the former taking the artwork, as the world itself, as an object of its gaze. In contrast, similar to Benjamin's account of the storyteller that we have discussed, Said argues that such symbolic binarism between the "Arab" and history has been shattered due to epochal events. For these events, which make it impossible to occupy a contemplative stance looking onto the theatre of history (the way Kant admits to being a non-participating spectator of the French Revolution[64]), also collapse the relation between the

---

62 Said, "Arabic Prose," 56.
63 Terry Eagleton, *The Ideology of the Aesthetic*, 70–101.
64 "This revolution of a gifted people which we have seen unfolding in our day

particular and universal such that the individual understands himself or herself as "immediately historical," that is immediately universal. Appealing to Benjamin again and recalling his well-known concept of "jetztzeit" (the time of the "now"), we notice a similar concept of time, history and epochal events. In his "Theses on the Philosophy of History," tying together the revolutionary classes, the materialist historian and the French Revolution, Benjamin argues that all of these figures break the empty and homogenous time typical of historicism that gazes over completed and past events as an indifferent subject.[65] Such objective historical conditions have direct bearing on Kant's concept of the aesthetic as well as on art production. Khalifeh breaks the aesthetic distance between the reader and world and dismantles the sense of security one has when reading a fictional text, because such an aesthetic distance between the subject and the world has already been broken in social reality.

To elaborate on this last point let me return to Shihadeh's 1971 article. I cite a passage that follows the passage already quoted, and repeat a few lines to offer continuity:

> With the June [1967] War all previous modes of life were shattered. The whole social structure was challenged . . . Never before were the mistakes of Hashemite rule [in Jordan] so obvious. Never before had the mistakes been so apparent. Now, with the other side open to visitors [i.e., Israel open to Palestinians], everyone could see the progress the Jews had been able to make. Something basic was wrong. The organization of the society, the values, the ideals were all upset . . .
>
> Not only was the social life challenged but also business life. The difference of working under a more organized system was obvious to any employer or worker . . . Thus, a change has become urgent in the mind of the majority who may rightly be referred to as a silent majority. They are obviously heading towards enlightenment, a social revolution and co-existence.[66]

Scholarship on the 1967 war agrees that it was experienced as a shock in the entire Arab world, leading to the eventual decline of pan-Arabism

may succeed or miscarry . . . this revolution—I say, nonetheless finds in the hearts of all spectators (who are not engaged in this game themselves) a wishful participation that borders closely on enthusiasm." Kant, *The Conflict of the Faculties*, translated by Mary J. Kregor (New York: Abaris Books, 1979), 153.

65   Walter Benjamin, "Theses on the Philosophy of History." In *Illuminations Essays and Reflections*, 253–64. See especially 261–3.

66   Shihadeh, "The Palestinian Demand," 22.

and Nasserism, and to a period of intense internal critique. I would like, however, to focus on the *aesthetic* side of Shihadeh's account. At this moment of historical break, past life is not only grasped as already in the past ("all previous modes of life were shattered"), but it is also *seen as such*—as a complete form of life that precisely at its moment of demise enters consciousness as a system. Hegel's idiom is pertinent here: "The owl of Minerva spreads its wings only with the falling of the dusk." The crisis befalling Palestinian society then makes the previous form of life appear as a form in itself, and consequently forces historical meaning—i.e., the universal—on the particular phenomenon and alters the relation between the two so that we no longer have two distinct poles. That is, in these moments the abstract and unconscious structure of daily life is revealed as such, so that it is impossible not to *see* at *one and the same time* the individual act and its historical significance. This historical condition unsettles the aesthetic movement, whose innermost principle is that of an indeterminate shuttling between particular and universal, surface appearance and significance. The epistemological break in Usama's perspective as well as in other characters' experience is then a symptom of the existence of historical time on the very surface of reality, as it were.

Although he had a different scale of events in mind, Fredric Jameson suggested such a relation between aesthetics and historical events:

> [T]he "appearance" of History is dependent on the objective historical situations themselves . . . Just as it is in revolutionary situations that the dichotomous classes are so radically simplified as to allow us to glimpse class struggle as such in a virtually pure form, so also only privileged historical crises allow us to "see" history as a process—and it is also in those crises that "history" is most vulnerable.[67]

Important also is the fact that the coming into existence "as such" of the existing mode of life has to do not only with war, displacement and occupation, but also with the sheer mass of Palestinians who, now working in Israel for the first time in nineteen years, can compare their form of life to another, and as a consequence grasp it as such. This social and historical abstraction, I would like to stress, both "enters" literature, putting pressure on its received forms, and as Said suggests, unsettles the distinctions between art, social science, and historiography. Thus, it

---

67   Fredric Jameson, *Valences of the Dialectic* (London: Verso, 2009), 583.

is the co-existence of these historical conditions with the narrative forms of *Wild Thorns* that provides a different concept of aesthetic, one that is usually ignored and misread.

Before moving forward to another example, it bears mention that this kind of surfacing of abstraction is not necessarily unique to Palestine, to the Third World or the "East," but is characteristic of periods of crisis and acute social change in general. Many of Balzac's novels, for example, and the period between the French Revolution and 1848 are often understood in the same manner.[68] Benjamin's "Paris" essay can provide us with such an example and help us transition to the problem of character and subjectivity in *Wild Thorns*. In a section devoted to Baudelaire, Benjamin observes the problem of individuality. He gestures to Balzac and explains:

> The typical characters [in Balzac] seen in passersby make such an impression on the senses that one cannot be surprised at the resultant curiosity to go beyond them and capture the special singularity of each person. But the nightmare that corresponds to the illusory perspicacity of the aforementioned physiogonomist consists in seeing those distinctive traits—traits peculiar to the person—revealed to be nothing more than the elements of a new type; so that in the final analysis a person of the greatest individuality would turn out to be the exemplar of a type . . . [In Baudelaire's "Les Sept Vieillards"] the individual . . . testifies to the anguish of the city dweller who is unable to break the magic circle of the type even though he cultivates the most eccentric peculiarities. Baudelaire describes this procession as "infernal" in appearance.[69]

What Benjamin describes here is the contradictory appearance in modernity of singularity, individuality and eccentricity, which have the tendency to turn into their opposite and be revealed as typicality. Again, we see here how periods of acute transformation collapse the gap between particular and universal (here in the figures of individual and

---

68   Lukács's *The Historical Novel*, which has been mentioned, is an important precedent here, but there are more recent examples such as Judith Lyon-Caen who examines Balzac's correspondence with his readers and argues that in such historical times his novels were read and used as guides to a chaotic and changing reality. Although not invoking Lukács, she argues that such a practical relation changed after 1848. See Judith Lyon-Caen, *La lecture et la vie: les usages du roman au temps de Balzac* (Paris: Tallandier, 2006).

69   Walter Benjamin, "Paris, Capital of the Nineteenth Century. Exposé of 1939." In *The Arcades Project*, translated by Howard Eiland and Kevin McLaughlin (Cambridge: Harvard University Press, 1999), 22.

type), so that it is impossible not to see the social category, as it were, underlying the most unique particularity.

Similarly, problems of individuality are tightly associated with the very possibility of poetry and art in *Wild Thorns*. Usama, now the determined agent of action whose sense of time is shot through with history, is characterized as a person who once believed in poetry and art, but can do so no longer:

> He'd never been a romantic himself. At least he wasn't any longer, or so he believed. How had he come to this conclusion? Training. Bullets. Crawling on all fours . . . Such things make you unromantic in thought and deed. Personal dreams evaporate . . . That was the logic of it all. They'd said many things and so had we; logical things, historical equations imposed on the individual, making him a single number in the equation . . . . Thus the equation takes form scientifically, rationally, tangibly. Thus romanticism fades and dreams die.[70]

And this thematic appearance of the impossibility of art in the fictional world returns also as the problem of Usama's character for us. For his sense of history also renders his character "flat," motivated only by a principle. He is unable to develop a private personal life, or interiority, and is portrayed as the most abstract and superficial of all characters. And yet, this is not only the problem of the guerrilla fighter. As crisis renders their lives abstract and palpable, other characters become unable to develop "depth" and appear to their peers as abstract types. This kind of abstraction receives one of its most spectacular, or "infernal" demonstrations as Baudelaire would say, at the height of the crisis, in which, in the very last moments of the novel, the political crisis intersects with forms of patriarchy, bringing the collapse of the latter. Basil, the youngest member of the al-Karmi family, lashes out after silently witnessing the effects of the occupation and the degeneration of the patriarch throughout the novel:

> I hate my father because he personifies sickness. I hate my mother because she's the personification of submissiveness. I hate my old grandmother: she represents man's collapse in the face of time. And Nuwar's hateful because she's spineless. She's unsuited to her role in life . . . I'm a stranger in this house, damn this house.[71]

---

70   Khalifeh, *Wild Thorns*, 5–6/7.
71   Ibid., 199/169.

The estrangement of Basil invites us to consider this moment in Brechtian terminology, understanding it as the moment when the mimetic illusion is broken and the novelistic apparatus is exposed. But this reading will miss the fact that this kind of Shklovskian "laying bare the device" takes place for the characters themselves, for whom "traditional" life in the moment of crisis is revealed in all its conventionality as mere representation. It is not then that the medium is exposed here; it is life itself that is revealed to be as conventional as a play, one that has reached its end.

As life is revealed in all its abstraction, Basil's subjectivity and interiority are affected as well, and he is gradually reduced to objectivity: his movements turn mechanical and he speaks with "the tone of a radio announcer," and "as though [he is] reading a formal statement."[72] As this kind of abstraction and conventionality surfaces, the older form of life—here explicitly patriarchy—loses its grip, and at the end of Basil's infernal speech exposing all lies and secrets, we read of the death of the patriarch and the entry of Israeli soldiers. "The father's hand clasped the table convulsively . . . His head fell forward and hit the table with a bang . . . While they were struggling through the hall, a loud banging sounded on the door below: 'Open up! Open Up!' soldiers were shouting. 'Open Up!'[73]

Finally, as the Israeli soldiers enter the al–Karmi house and discover Usama's weapons in the basement, we notice in tangible spatial terms the overlap of the private and the public spheres, i.e., the co-existence of the personal (the category of the "family") and the political (the guerrilla cell) that has underlined the entire problematic of the novel and finally finds its resolution when both poles are destroyed as the soldiers blow up the house.[74]

4.

It is impossible to say that there is a Palestinian psychological novel.[75]

—Muhammad Ayub

---

72   Ibid., passim.
73   Ibid., 201/171.
74   Ibid., 202–207/172–76.
75   Muhammad Ayyub, *al-Zaman wa-al-sard al-qiṣaṣī fī al-riwāyah al-Filasṭīnīyah al-muʿāṣirah bayna 1973–1994* (al-Duqqī [Giza]: Sindbād lil-Nashr wa-al-Tawzīʿ, 2001), 126.

Muhammad Ayub's comment about the impossibility of a Palestinian psychological novel in which the psyche (*nafs*) of the characters takes precedence over the collective fate of the Palestinian people is in line with my claim that in Palestine, until the 1990s, the interlocking of the private and public spheres blocked the emergence of autonomous private life and its attendant poetic and psychic forms. However, this historical impossibility also allows us to understand the structural limits of those modernist attempts to borrow and embed within Palestinian imaginary worlds and poetic forms grounded on autonomous private life. Understanding Palestinian modernism as poetic borrowing not simply of literary style and form, but of a form of social life that is at odds with Palestinian reality in this period, makes it possible to tie this discussion to Moretti's discussion on world literature and to elaborate on its claims.[76] My main example will be Ghassan Kanafani's 1966 novella, *All That's Left to You.*

As with my discussion of Yeshayahu Koren in Chapter One, I argue that Kanafani's modernist novella is an attempt to imagine individual autonomy and private life in a time and place where such autonomy is impossible. Following Casanova, we will see that the autonomy of certain characters as well as certain poetic relations within the imaginary world will guarantee the writer's aesthetic autonomy in the literary field. In other words, Kanafani attempts to universalize the particular experience of his Palestinian characters and make his novella more "worldly." To think this autonomy and universality, Kanafani borrows "Western" modernist forms, most explicitly those at work in William Faulkner's *The Sound and the Fury*,[77] and yet, because of the qualitative differences

---

76 Franco Moretti, "Conjectures on World Literature," *New Left Review* 1 (January–February 2000): 54–68.

77 Kanafani acknowledged the affinity to Faulkner, saying "I admire [Faulkner's] novel *The Sound and the Fury*. Many critics observe that my novella *All That's Left to You* is a manifest expression of admiration, and I agree. Faulkner's novel has influenced me greatly." Quoted in and translated by Aida Azouqa, "Ghassan Kanafani and William Faulkner: Kanafani's Achievement in 'All That's Left to You,'" *Journal of Arabic Literature* 31.2 (2000): 148n. For studies discussing the novella's modernist aspect, see Aida Azouqa, "Ghassan Kanafani and William Faulkner: Kanafani's Achievement in 'All That's Left to You,'" *Journal of Arabic Literature* 31.2 (2000): 147–70; Hilary Kilpatrick, "Tradition and Innovation in the Fiction of Ghassan Kanafani," *Journal of Arabic Literature* 7 (January 1976): 53–64; Muhammad Siddiq, *Man Is A Cause*; Barbara Harlow, *Resistance Literature*. For a few studies in Arabic see Ahmad Abu-Matar, *Riwāyah fī al-adab al-Filasṭīnī, 1950–1975* (Bayrūt: al-Mu'assasah al-'Arabīyah lil-Dirāsāt wa-al-Nashr, 1980), 247–50; Faruq Wadi, *Thalāth 'alāmāt fī al-riwāyah al-Filasṭīnīyah: Ghassān Kanafānī, Amīl Habībī, Jabrā Ibrāhīm Jabrā* (Bayrūt: al-Mu'assasah al-'Arabīyah lil-Dirāsāt wa-al-Nashr: Dā'irat al-I'lām wa-al-Thaqāfah, Munaẓẓamat al-Taḥrīr al-Filasṭīnīyah, 1981);

in forms of life between 1920s United States and 1960s Palestine, the novella is "fractured,"[78] as Moretti would say, between two concepts of time; between autonomy and heteronomy. The following reading traces these fractures and explains their significance.

All That's Left to You tells of the dissolution of a Palestinian family after the 1948 war. During the war, the Israelis kill the father, a resistance fighter, leaving behind the mother and two children, Hamid and Maryam. In their flight from Jaffa to Gaza, the children are separated from their mother who ends up in Jordan, while Hamid and Maryam stay with their aunt. In the absence of their parents, Hamid and Maryam seem to develop an incestuous relationship, although we are made to understand that they do not have sex. Eventually, Maryam meets another man, Zakaria, and bears his child. Zakaria, as we learn, betrayed a group of Palestinian resistance fighters, an act that led the Israelis to kill a friend of the family. These historical and personal events appear only as blurred memories, and the story opens with an older Hamid and Maryam in the middle of a familial-political quarrel. To avoid public shame, Hamid agrees to the marriage of pregnant Maryam to the traitor Zakaria, but, dismayed by Zakaria's acts and the prospect of losing his sister's love, he runs away to find his mother in Jordan. To do so, he must cross the desert at night, a perilous journey that brings him into contact with an Israeli soldier who he ends up killing with a knife. At the same time, Maryam has a quarrel with Zakaria who demands she have an abortion; she ends up killing Zakaraia, also with a knife. The story is told in three main voices: Hamid, Maryam and the desert.

The story has been read, justly, as a political allegory signifying the renewal of Palestinian resistance in the 1960s. Differently from *Men in the Sun*, which concludes with the tragic death of three Palestinian protagonists, here Hamid and Maryam face both the internal enemy (Zakaria) and the external enemy (the Israeli soldier) and prevail. If *Men in the Sun* ends with a critique of the passivity and impotence of the characters, in this novella Hamid and Maryam take active control over their lives and directly face their oppressors. Given that the political significance of the novella is self-evident, what needs our attention is the intricate family drama, the psychology of the characters, and more importantly, the formal properties of this imaginary world.

Following Moretti's theory, I begin by identifying the poetic "units"

Mahmoud Ghanaim, *Tayyār al-waʿy fī al-riwāyah al-ʿArabīyah al-ḥadīthah: dirāsah uslūbīyah* (Bayrūt: Dār al-Jīl; al-Qāhirah: Dār al-Hudá, 1992), 257–82.

78   See discussion of Moretti in the Introduction.

that Kanafani borrows from Faulkner's *The Sound and the Fury*. The obvious parallels are, of course, the division of the story into separate streams of consciousness, the incestuous relationship between Hamid and Maryam (echoing that of Caddy and Quentin), and the predominance of time and the wristwatch. These parallels play a significant part in the novella, but I argue that, as far as form goes, what Kanafani borrows is not so much the technique of stream of consciousness, but rather the *separation of the personal/psychological and political* levels of the text that guarantee Hamid's autonomy and by extension the literariness of the text in the world republic of letters. However, since such a separation does not exist in Palestine in this period, the interconnection between the two spheres now presents Kanafani with a narrative problem, one that produces the novella's intricate structure on the one hand and its obvious political "message" on the other. This difference between Palestine and the US, where such a separation did take place on the social ground itself, points to the differences between Kanafani and Faulkner: while the formal solution to the preliminary separation of levels is the *intersectional* structure of Kanafani's novella, Faulkner's novella flaunts the *inability* to bring together the different strands of the story, a fact that leaves Caddy's life a mystery. Further, if in Kanafani the historical events that put Hamid and Maryam in their predicament, and make them into allegories, are always evident on the surface of the story as causes, in Faulkner, the dissolution of Southern culture is revealed in its effects—Caddy's promiscuity and the poverty of the Compson family.

The separation of the personal/psychological and political levels of the text is manifested in the qualitative difference between Hamid's autonomy and Maryam's heteronomy. These two poetic and conceptual forms and the relationship between them represent the "fracture" that runs along the novella and signifies its historical signature. Similar to Koren, to achieve Hamid's autonomy and by extension the text's literariness, Kanafani separates or abstracts Hamid from his historical conditions of possibility—the Israeli-Palestinian conflict—a poetic and philosophical procedure that displaces the historical causes of Hamid's self into his psyche and makes him self-sufficient and autonomous. Now, since this abstraction is a poetic procedure rather than a historical reality, the materials that are removed or abstracted from Hamid's storyline find their way back through Maryam's character. Thus, if the characters in *Men in the Sun*, especially Abu Khaizuran, express a unity of the personal/psychological and the political—if their bodies and minds are inseparable from and marked by the 1948 war—in *All That's*

Left to You Kanafani achieves Hamid's autonomy (as Koren achieves Hagar's) through a dual separation and replacement: the mind is separated from the body and mythical time replaces historical time. These two sets are mapped onto Hamid and Maryam's characters, and onto the concepts of "land" and "home" respectively, and their reconnection becomes a political imperative. Thus, Hamid is written as a process of internal psychological deliberation that takes place in a mythic desert and in a mythic time, while Maryam's character is motivated by the needs and desires of her body, in a narrative that takes place in the home and unfolds under physical time. What complicates the story further is the fact that the novella is written as "traditional" forms of patriarchy are being challenged by a Palestinian national movement, and traditional and non-traditional social forms are also distributed between Maryam and Hamid respectively.

The narrative focuses on Hamid's impotence and his infantile attachment to his sister and mother, and accordingly, most of the novelistic materials are organized around his process of initiation and self-discovery:

> What do you really want your mother to say? It would have made better sense to slit her [Maryam's] throat over your knees, throw him [Zakaria] into hell, and wipe the blood on your face and on the walls of your house . . . But you were too cowardly to do violence. No, not cowardly! It would have been futile, as ineffectual as your desire to place your mother between Maryam and yourself . . . In your mind your mother has always been an absent protectress, ready always to take up arms in your defense . . . Why not sit down under this sky which reverts to its own depths and reflect on what you've done? Gaza's behind you now, erased by the universal blackness. The thread unraveled itself from the ball of wool, and you're no longer the person wound on to that spool for sixteen years. But who are you?[79]

Hamid's interior monologue coalesces several broader meanings, all related to his impotence. First we note the violent fantasy, meant to compensate for its opposite in the real, i.e., Hamid's hesitation and inactivity. This fantasy is underlined by the code of patriarchy that Hamid cannot uphold. He was able to prevent neither Maryam's pregnancy nor her marriage to a traitor, but he is also unable to bring himself to harm

---

79   Kanafani, *All That's Left to You*, 25. Kanafani, *Mā tabaqqá lakum*, 41. Page numbers will list the English edition first, followed by the Arabic.

his sister and clear the family name. This failure forces him to realize his childish reliance on his mother, and question his identity: "who are you?" The answer to this question is indirectly answered when Hamid manages to withstand the hardship of crossing the desert and kills the Israeli soldier, two acts that confirm his ability to do violence, and usher him into manhood.

Hamid's impotence and immaturity can be read as a psychological allegory for the political state of Palestine, as indeed was the character of Abu Khaizuran in *Men in the Sun*. Such a reading would suggest that both novellas are characterized by the same kind of overlap of the psychological and the political. However, a close reading of the two novellas reveals important differences in allegorical structure.

The principal difference in each novella's treatment of its psychological materials has to do with the distance between the protagonist and history, the Israeli-Palestinian conflict. Abu Khaizuran can stand in for Palestinian weakness because he joined the resistance fighters in 1948 and was injured by a landmine. The 1948 military defeat is then inseparable from Abu Khaizuran's mutilated body, and his impotency is tightly tied to the spiritual impotency of the Palestinian people at this time. Hamid, however, is a child when the 1948 war erupts and unlike Abu Khaizuran he is only a witness to historical events. Hamid's youth is not accidental; it provides mimetic motivation for separating him from the primal cause that made Palestinian life what it is, and allows for his relative freedom from it. Second, what usually passes unnoticed is the fact that although all the characters, especially Maryam, experience the same historical conditions, only Hamid has an identity crisis. Third, and most important, Hamid is the only male character whose manhood is put in question. These differences suggest that Hamid is an anomaly in *All That's Left to You*. Hamid's immaturity and especially his sexual attachment to Maryam are not meant to stand in for the political situation in Palestine, but instead seem to be superimposed upon it.

Since in this period autonomy can be achieved only negatively by abstracting the character from its conditions of possibility, Hamid ends up with a "lack" ("manhood") that pushes him to find the historical reason (the Israeli soldier) that the poetic technique removed in the first place. This plotline highlights the most important characteristic of this modernist technique: since the novella prioritizes Hamid's sexual maturation, it not only separates the psychological from the political, it also *subordinates* the political to the psychological; the political encounter with the Israeli soldier is merely the means by which Hamid crosses into manhood. Furthermore, for Hamid, the "political" is fetishized within the character of the soldier, a fetishization that reduces history to an encounter, and an accidental one at that. Thus, Hamid's journey into the desert (like Hagar's morning walks to the Palestinian village) mirrors Kant's conception of the aesthetic as a movement of a "particular" searching for its severed "universal," for only the latter can endow it with meaning.

As I have argued, the universalization and autonomization of Hamid is accomplished through abstraction, a poetic technique that here takes two main forms: Freudian sexuality and mythical causality/time. If in *Men in the Sun* Abu Khaizuran's sexual impotence was directly caused by the 1948 war, a particular historical event, in *All That Left to You*, Hamid's sexual immaturity is displaced from the political into the family unit and develops according to the Oedipus complex, a schema that Freud considers a universal trait.[80] As we know, Freud argues that once a male child arrives at the "third genital stage" he begins to desire his mother and considers the father an obstacle obstructing this wish. If the Oedipus complex is overcome positively, the child, threatened by castration, gives up the love-object (the mother) and identifies with the father. At this point the sexual desire towards the mother is replaced with affection and the child develops an ambivalent relation with the father. The "dissolution of the Oedipus complex," as Freud puts it, leads to the development of the super-ego, the origin of morality, religion and other social taboos.

We will see in a moment why the Freudian model does not fit easily in Kanafani's novella, but first let's see how it is used. Although the story's timeline is fragmented, what emerges when we arrange the sequence of events is that Hamid, as a child, witnesses the primal scene of his mother and father having sex, and with this event the rivalry over the mother is suggested. The Oedipus complex develops further when the love for the absent mother is displaced onto the sister. The two seem to flirt with an incestuous relationship which is blocked by a new male presence,

---

80   "[Oedipus's] fate moves us only because it might have been our own, because the oracle laid upon us before our birth the very curse which rested upon him. It may be that we were all destined to direct our first sexual impulses towards our mothers and our first impulses of hatred and violence towards our fathers." Sigmund Freud, "The Interpretation of Dreams." In *The Basic Writings of Sigmund Freud*, translated by A. A. Brill (New York: The Modern Library, 1995), 276. Freud repeats this claim elsewhere saying, "the majority of human beings go through the Oedipus complex." See his "The Dissolution of the Oedipus Complex." In *The Ego and the Id and Other Works*. Standard Edition Vol 19, translated by James Strachey et al. (London: Hogarth Press, 1961), 174. On this matter see also Freud's "Totem and Taboo." In *The Basic Writings of Sigmund Freud*, translated by A. A. Brill (New York: The Modern Library, 1995), 882–98.

Zakaria, who Maryam chooses over Hamid. Unable to confront Zakaria, Hamid runs away to his mother. This Freudian pattern allows Kanafani to suggest that the cause of Hamid's predicament is a universal human condition. However, when we look closely at the conclusion of the story we see that the Oedipus complex is not "dissolved" but transferred from the family unit to the original cause of Hamid's character, the Israeli-Palestinian conflict.

Let us follow the events. First, recall that Freud argues that the development of morality and the super-ego requires the child to give up the love-object and the aggression towards the father. Here, the point of Hamid's maturation is precisely the opposite—his journey into the desert helps him tap into his aggression and violence. Putting aside for a moment the fact that the Israeli soldier in no way blocks Hamid's sexual development nor his access to his love object, if we follow the Freudian model to its logical conclusion, the soldier's death (together with Maryam's killing of Zakaria) should now make Maryam available to Hamid and license the incestuous relationship. It is not accidental that the story abruptly ends with these dual violent acts, for it is here that the political level of the text contradicts the psychological one; it is the place where the importation of the "Western" schema fails to fit with the historical situation in Palestine. Further, moving from the end to the beginning, we cannot fail to notice that the event that puts Hamid in his predicament is the killing of his father during the 1948 war. Indeed, Maryam explicitly suggests that it is the war, and not parental sex, that functions as Hamid's primal scene. As the two siblings make their escape from the scene of war, separated as they are from their mother and father, Maryam acknowledges:

> He was only ten years old, and I was twenty, but even so he seemed to have discovered everything in one mad moment . . . Jaffa aglow with flame, slowly receded from view into the infinite expanse of the horizon.[81]

The heart of the matter lies in the fact that the Oedipus complex and the archetype of the neurotic, far from being universal, presuppose an historical bourgeois society and bourgeois family. In this type of historical society, the law—the father—is given ready-made and social forms are reproduced through the recognition of authority and the suppression of violence. In post-1948 Palestine, precisely the opposite is the case. With

---

81   Kanafani, *All That's Left to You*, 17/32.

the breakdown of patriarchal norms, the establishment of a new Palestinian society is achieved through violence and the making of new laws/ political structures. Hamid's father is very clear on the issue of reproducing patriarchal forms of kinship in a time of national crisis. When the issue of marrying her off comes up, Maryam recalls:

> My father stood in the doorway. He was angry . . . He shouted in his gruff husky voice: "Don't talk about marriage before our national cause has been decided." Whenever he expressed himself in terms of a cause, blood and danger seemed immanent . . . Hamid had probably adopted this habit [of speaking] from his father.[82]

Several issues are at stake here: first, if in Freud bourgeois sexual relations are separated from the political, we see here how the political reality of Palestine disrupts the reproduction of kinship. Second, if the Oedipus complex is the condition of possibility of the repression of violence and the reproduction of social taboos, here, it is precisely the opposite: the father endorses violence as the condition of possibility of the continuation of Palestinian society. Third, and most important, in post-1948 Palestine, the law and authority of the father is interrupted and taken over by an external law/authority—Israel. This authority cannot be accepted and internalized as superego; on the contrary, it must be challenged and removed so Palestinians may remake their own law once again. For this reason, while the struggle with the father, and his elimination, are understood in metaphorical terms in Freud,[83] in Kanafani we witness a literal struggle to the death over the reproduction of Palestinian life. For this reason, the real struggle must be with the Israeli soldier and not with the father (or even with Zakaria as Maryam's lover), an encounter mentioned at both ends of the story, for this struggle indeed determines the beginning and end of Palestinian reality post-1948.

The second poetic technique that abstracts and universalizes Hamid's historical Palestinian reality is his mythical experience in the desert. Two substitutions need our attention here: the transformation of historical

---

82 Ibid., 19/34–35.
83 Although he is somewhat ambivalent on this matter, Freud does map the difference between literal violence and imagined violence upon the distinction between primitive man and the modern neurotic, respectively. Hamid's character is fractured precisely because he seems to shift from the latter to the former as the novella progresses. Freud, "Totem and Taboo," 896–8.

and physical time into metaphysical time, and the concomitant transformation of the land of Israel/Palestine into eternal nature.

After walking for a while in the desert night, Hamid then decides to discard his wristwatch. I follow the exchange between Hamid and the Desert:

> I tried to look at my watch but it was pitch black. As I did so, I came to realize how insignificant a watch is when compared to the absolutes of light and dark. In the infinite expanse of this desert night, my watch appeared to represent a temporal fetter which engendered terror and anxiety. Without hesitation I unstrapped it from my wrist and threw it away.[84]

The Desert responds:

> [The watch] began ticking in my depths with a sad abandoned sound like a small iron heart embodied in a giant . . . [The watch], whose sole task in the universe was to guide, to instruct by its numerals, became lost in the face of that real time which had survived over eons without sound or motion.

Hamid's ensuing thought:

> I felt more at ease when I remained alone with the night. Without the contrived semblance of time, the barrier collapsed, and we [Hamid and the night] became equals in the confrontation of a real and honorable struggle, with equal weapons.[85]

In this moment, we notice the staging of the temporal substitution. It is not simply that we shift temporal scales, moving, à la Fernand Braudel, from individual daily experience to the vast expanse of geological time, the time of hills and mountains, rivers and forests. Rather, the shift from Palestinian historical time to natural time is a shift in kind, for while other characters make and are made by their unique historical time, the time of the desert is unmade ("without sound and motion"): it is eternal, and serves as the site of the "ever-same" as Adorno would put it, seeing again and again the same "honorable struggle" existing for

---

84 Kanafani, *All That's Left to You*, 20/35.
85 Ibid., passim/35–36.

"eons." Once within this kind of abstract mythical time, nothing external makes or unmakes Hamid; he is affected only by his own internal psychic deliberations.

This substitution releases Hamid, as he says, from the "fetter" of time, and allows him autonomy from Palestinian history. Recall that the passage in Kant that we have discussed also conceives of the universal (or the guiding concept) as a "fetter" limiting the hand and mind of the artist. If we substitute the "concept" with history as I suggested in the discussion of Koren, we can see again how autonomy in this period, both for the writer and for the imaginary world, can be achieved only negatively, by abstraction and the negation of the fetters of history.

Now, as I have mentioned, since the separation of the psychological and political levels of the text and the abstraction of Hamid's psychic activity are literary techniques rather than a historical condition, *All That's Left to You* still contains novelistic materials that do not undergo such abstraction and separation. I already noted that, like in Koren's *A Funeral at Noon*, the secondary characters—Hamid's father, Zakaria and Salim—still maintain a more direct relation to Palestinian history, but it is Maryam, above all, who seems to embody the historical predicament of Palestine in this period.

Unlike Hamid who goes through a mythical journey associated with eternal nature and its time, Maryam is rooted within the particular historical moment in Palestine when patriarchal social structures are contested by the objectives of a national movement. While Kanafani associates Hamid's character and his encounter with the political—the Israeli soldier—with "mind," the relation to patriarchy is expressed, not accidently, through Maryam's new control over her body. We learn that prior to the 1948 war, Maryam was supposed to be married off to Fathi. But with the onset of the war and its devastating consequences, the viability of these patriarchal social relations become more tenuous, especially after the death of the father and the exile of the mother to Jordan. To continue patriarchal control, Hamid is named his sister's guardian. But by sleeping with Zakaria, bearing his child, and finally killing him (all acts done to, or by, her body) Maryam defies both Hamid's control and their impossible incestuous relationship. What is important in all of Maryam's actions is that she is *fettered* to her body and to history, as the cause of her predicament:

> Poor Hamid, what did you really believe? That the plough should remain forbidden to this fertile earth? That I should spend all the days of my

life subservient to your manhood, conjuring out of your trousers a man from Jaffa named Fathi, who, silently and proudly, had been preparing a dowry worthy of Abu Hamid's daughter? . . . Jaffa and Fathi are both lost, forever—there's nothing left. It was you who placed that bier in front of me, to punctuate my days and nights remorselessly with this tragic truth . . . [Our mother will say] You [Maryam] were the flower of al-Manshiyya, ambitious, educated, from a good family. What misery made you accept Zakaria as a husband, with his children and wife?[86]

Note that in this key monologue, Maryam ties directly between the historical cause—the 1948 war—and the chain of events in her present. In comparison to Maryam's historical consciousness, neither Caddy nor any of Faulkner's other characters present us with the historical narrative that underlies the decline of the American South, of which Caddy's promiscuity is supposed to be an effect. In other words, Caddy can become a mythological feminine character precisely because the causes that underlie her form of life have been obscured.

The difference between Hamid and Maryam's worlds is further expressed through the figure of time. While Hamid, as I have noted, is able to detach himself from physical time by discarding his wristwatch, Maryam is doubly bound by both the physical clock in her house, which measures Hamid's progress across the desert, and her "biological clock," which pushes her towards the future as an unmarried woman:

[Hamid] hadn't yet come to see how important the passing of time was; but to me it was death announcing itself at least twice daily; I was gradually turning day by day into his substitute mother, while day by day he was becoming for me a man who was just a brother. He'd never realized that for me a moment's encounter with a real man would lead to the dissolving of our bond, and the small beautifully shallow world we'd forced ourselves to choose, a trivial world unprepared to accommodate another spinster.[87]

What we see here is Maryam's acute sense of the entanglement of biological and social time. Not only is she aware, throughout the entire novella, of the power of her sexual desire over her social choices, she is also aware of the fact that she is socially aging, becoming less and less

---

86 Ibid., 23–4/39–40.
87 Ibid., 18/32–3.

desirable to men in society. Maryam's character is then heteronomous; she cannot simply discard the fetters of social and biological time, but is made by them, becoming who she is through her struggle with and against limited choices.

Now that we see all the instances of the personal/political split between Hamid and Maryam we can better understand the significance of the supra-natural causality that is conjured to tie them together. Continuing the mythic elements that we have discussed and pushing them further into the realm of the magical, Maryam is able to sense Hamid's actions across time and space, a spiritual bond that transcends the limits of the human mind and body. Kanafani uses two techniques to bring this about: The first finds its expression in content, through Maryam's intuition:

> Without knowing why, I began to shake. I seemed to know, intuitively, that Hamid was in danger at that very moment; but if I'd awakened Zakaria and told him: "Something terrible has happened to Hamid at this very moment," he would have said I was mad.[88]

And indeed, at this point Hamid confronts the Israeli soldier in the desert and danger is imminent. Again, the importance of such a moment is the obscure nature of this knowledge: it emerges from Maryam's intuition, rather than from an objective external source, and even she does not understand its origin. It is no coincidence that this kind of intuition takes after Kant's romantic definition of genius, i.e., a form of creative knowledge whose guiding concept or origin is obscured and internal to the artist. It is a knowledge that cannot be measured, and this precise quality provides for artistic autonomy. The second technique, this time on the level of form, is subtler and far more crucial to the way Kanafani stiches up the fragmented narrative. It is common to modernist fiction, especially in works whose main novelistic material is memory, to substitute causal with associative relations. Consider the way Kanafani writes the following conversation, beginning with Maryam's memory at home and then shifting to Hamid in the desert:

> [Maryam:]
> He [Hamid] came home calm, and sat down biting his lips. He looked at me, then went to the kitchen and from there informed me, "They killed

---

88   Ibid., 39/56.

Salim . . . and it could be my turn tomorrow." [Maryam replies:] You haven't done anything wrong . . . why should they kill you?"

[Hamid:]
She probably meant to reassure me. She didn't realize she was burdening me with more shame. I could hear her question reverberate: "Why should they kill you?"[89]

Although they are in two separate places, Maryam and Hamid seem to be having the same conversation, as if they were in the same room. Such a simultaneous overlapping of memories is quite different from the stream of consciousness we find in European and American modernism. In Faulkner's *The Sound and the Fury*, for example, smells and objects that Quentin and Benjy encounter in the present trigger memories of the same object in the past; this technique allows Faulkner to connect past and present through the internal workings of the mind rather than an external omniscient narrator. These instances, however, occur within one character's consciousness, while Kanafani uses this associative technique to patch two different characters together and in this way to suggest a supra-natural bond that defies the fetters of physical reality. Further, while modernist techniques usually fragment so-called linear narrative, here Kanafani's energies are directed at uniting the narrative strands into a cohesive whole. This convergence receives its most important articulation when both Maryam and Hamid pick up a knife at the same time and, as if in unison, kill Zakaria and the soldier. Note how one action bleeds into the other to create a flow of movement in two different places:

[Hamid:]
With its long glowing blade, the knife flashed in front of me . . .

[Maryam:]
There it is, on the table . . . My fists grabbed the knife . . . The blade projected from my tightly closed hands.

[Hamid:]
I felt it plunging into him as we collided together.

---

89   Ibid., 31/45.

[Maryam:]
He gave out a long moan . . .

. . .

[Hamid:]
Suddenly the silence reverberated, as dogs began to bark furiously and continuously

[Maryam:]
Outside the window. They were only silenced by the sound of his footsteps, continuing above the noise of the bier hanging on the wall

[Hamid:]
And hammering with cruel persistence into my head. Remorseless. Pounding over him, and the bulk of his death heaped there. Pounding. Pounding. Pounding.[90]

Note that in the first sequence, Hamid and Maryam's use of the knife alternates between the desert and the house, and in the second sequence, Kanafani ties between these two locations through sound: the noise of the dogs barking in the desert bleeds through the window of Maryam's apartment, and then the sound of the clock bleeds back into Hamid's narrative.

The significance of these moments belies the Freudian notion, advanced by Siddiq, that the bond between the siblings needs to be overcome and suppressed by entry into society. Here we see clearly that the bond is cardinal both to the inter-worldly meaning of Hamid and Maryam and to their allegorical meaning. We can now say that the spiritual bond is the means by which the text brings together what it originally separated—the spheres of the personal and the political—and for this reason it is a bond the novella *affirms* rather than rejects. Through the unfolding of time, the incestuous physical bond is replaced with a spiritual bond. Here too, this substitution enables the autonomization and literariness of the text. Since autonomy, as I discuss it here, is the process of abstraction from underlying conditions, we can see how the incestuous bond, tied as it is to the fetters of bodily instincts, is superseded by a mental causality whose origin is obscure.

---

90   Ibid., 49–50/69–70.

Before moving on to another example, it is important to compare Koren and Kanafani's novellas, an exercise that should offer inroads toward a comparative study of Israeli and Palestinian modernism that has been absent from contemporary scholarship. The two novellas were written a year apart (1966/1967) from within societies that Casanova and Moretti would place on the periphery. Both Kanafani and Koren borrow modernist forms, based on negation and abstraction, to think the autonomy of their characters, as well as their own position within the national and international literary field. Both techniques separate the body from spirit/mind, and associate the latter with the sphere of political conflict. However, despite these similarities, the political import of the novellas varies considerably. Koren's novella is written from a liberal position, whose political subject is the Israeli bourgeoisie, in a time where such liberalism is impossible and private life is not yet universal. It manages to suppress direct political content and transforms constituent violence into a random local accident in which a child dies under mysterious circumstances. Kanafani's novella, however, affirms the use of violence and weaves in direct political content. Further, unlike Koren, Kanafani does not seek a way out of political collectivity, but rather a way to think individual autonomy alongside political heteronomy. These differences arise, I believe, due to the absence of a Palestinian state whose making, unlike Israel at this time, is barred and remains a project to be achieved. Kanafani's literature, then, is not written from a liberal position, and its world in not undergirded by a middle-class ideology but rather by a humanist outlook, and in this aspect he resembles S. Yizhar. In Yizhar we see the affirmation of violence and the transformation of nature—that which is supposed to provide relief from violence—into a metaphysical entity. The similarity between Kanafani, Yizhar and Koren does not seem to have been studied, but we can see that there is a basis for such a study.

Imaginary worlds written from a liberal/bourgeois position are more typical of Jabra Ibrahim Jabra, especially his 1970 novel, *The Ship* (*al-Safīnah*). Here we see a fantasmatic imaginary world in which affluent characters of the Arab world and the Mediterranean meet each other on a cruise, away from any scene of violence and war, and are free to pursue their physical and intellectual desires. As with Kanafani's metaphysical nature and Freudian sexuality, Jabra attempts to universalize the experience of his characters by displacing the concrete history of Palestine and Iraq—a history of nationalism and tribalism where inequality reigns—into an abstract space of equivalents where human emotions and language are the medium through which universality is accomplished.

However, since such liberal fantasies are impossible at this point, the narrative is repeatedly punctuated by violence and inequality: once by a long memory of the 1948 war related by Wadi Salman, a second time through a traumatic encounter between Mahmud Rashad and a person he believes to be his torturer, and finally through the suicide of Falih Haseeb, which marks the leisurely cruise with the signature of death. While borrowing poetic forms that can be traced to both the Arab literary tradition and the Western one—namely storytelling and the aesthetic-political debate—this split imaginary world affirms the claim advanced here that in this period aesthetic and individual autonomy works only by negation and is finally contradicted by catastrophe.

Beyond these local similarities and differences, it is important to grasp the difference between Israeli and Palestinian literature in this period. Both literatures can be described as heteronomous and engaged in processes of collective social making through which the conditions of social life are made visible, yet they rise out of and respond to two different social forms. The forms of Israeli literature rise from the statist structure as a historical "limit," whereas those of Palestine arise from the situation of statelessness, i.e., the war and exile, occupation and anti-colonial struggle that takes place as "traditional" social relations are being revolutionized. The end of both social forms is freedom and autonomy but it situated in opposite poles: the freedom and autonomy of the Zionist state is predicated in part on the unfreedom of the Palestinians, making its literature a literature of the dominating, while the autonomy and freedom of the Palestinians is predicated on undoing this domination, making it a literature of the dominated. With time, however, while Palestinian social life remained directly tied to defeat and to the persistence of colonial rule, Israeli freedom and autonomy were no longer solely dependent on direct struggle. Given this imbalance, Palestinian literature, written from an anti-colonial position, focused mainly on Zionist domination— that is, on the condition of impossibility of Palestinian autonomy—while Israeli literature could develop literary forms that, although rooted in heteronomy, did not arise from the struggle itself. Palestinian literature in this period is then defined by a constitutive limit: faced with Palestinian unfreedom it is impelled to imagine ways to undo it yet undoing it in literature alone would be a mis-representation of Palestinian reality.

The next chapter elaborates on the political significance of new narrative forms written after the 1993 Oslo Accords, a turning point in both the social structure of Palestinian society and the poetic raw materials that stand at the disposal of writers.

4

Palestine as Text and Sign: The Aesthetic of Private Life 1993–

Today . . . the fragmentation of the [Palestinian] body politic—externally engineered and increasingly internally driven—has now been achieved. Even the liberal Israeli press has begun to notice that the key people in Ramallah, the Palestinian Authority capital in the West Bank, no longer discusses strategies of liberation but rather the huge business deals that prey on the public imagination. Every institution or overarching structure that once united Palestinians has now crumbled and been swept away . . . There is, at this moment [2010/2013], no single body able to claim legitimacy to represent all Palestinians, no body able to set out a collective policy or national program of liberation. There is no plan.

—Karma Nabulsi, "Exiled from Revolution"

1.

With the implementation of neoliberal reforms after the 1993 Oslo Accords, Palestinian literary production began taking up new poetic forms and emitting new ideological messages. Here, too, the matter that concerns this inquiry is the autonomization of private life, which now comes to condition the construction of literary worlds and turns constitutive politics ("making") into an organizational and narrative problem. To be sure, it is not the case that the earlier mode of writing has utterly disappeared but rather that it has become marginal and less visible, especially when it comes into contact with networks of global circulation.[1]

---

1 Thus, it is more than likely that Palestinian literature in Gaza continues older forms of writing but these novels do not mark the emerging dominant style.

The burden of this chapter lies in showing how, despite the occupation, Palestinian civic institutions, mainly foreign-funded NGOs in the West Bank, rearticulate the private and public sphere and create the conditions for autonomous cultural production predicated on private life. This new articulation brings in turn a new aesthetico-epistemological relation, one turning Palestinian life into a text and the writer/character into a reader. Thus, although very different from one another in terms of daily life, Israeli and Palestinian social forms begin to share certain politico-epistemological conditions that make their literary forms equivalent. It should be apparent, however, that the shift in aesthetic categories is not clear-cut.

While the Israeli occupation and the internal political rivalry between different Palestinian political groups (predominantly the Palestinian Authority [PA], Fatah and Hamas)[2] continue to unsettle, and at times make impossible, stable forms of life, after the 1993 Oslo Accords, the nature of the "political" in Palestinian society begins to change. Although this process is highly volatile, it seems that for several interlocking reasons, previously communal-political organizations have been professionalized so that by the end of the 1990s clearer boundaries begin to separate civil society, proto-state bodies (PA, Fatah) and the sphere of private life. Rema Hammami was perhaps the first to notice this change in 1995.[3] If, as I argued, in the previous period the nature of the "political" was such that it potentially transgressed all spheres of life, Hammami explains that after Oslo, social spheres had to be demarcated.[4]

According to Hammami, after the 1977 Camp David accords, the PLO/Fatah together with rival leftist organizations such as the PFLP, DFLP and the PCP,[5] began mobilizing a mass base in the occupied territories against the accords. Organization took the form of what could be called proto-NGOs: community committees of all sorts (on women, health, students, labor, agriculture, etc.) initially working across political factions, and effectively blurring the boundaries between the political

---

2   Fatah—Palestine National Liberation Movement; Hamas—Islamic Resistance Movement.

3   Rema Hammami, "NGOs: The Professionalization of Politics," *Race and Class* 37.2 (1995): 51–63. See also her related article from 2000, "Palestinian NGOs Since Oslo: From NGO Politics to Social Movements?" *Middle East Report* 214 (Spring 2000): 16–19, 27, 48. For an important critique of Hammami, see Benoît Challand, *Palestinian Civil Society: Foreign Donors and the Power to Promote and Exclude* (London: Routledge, 2009).

4   Hammami, "NGOs: The Professionalization of Politics," 53.

5   PFLP—Popular Front for the Liberation of Palestine; DFLP—Democratic Front for the Liberation of Palestine. PCP—Palestine Communist Party.

bodies proper and their community bases. By the mid-1980s mobilization was fragmented, each political faction now organizing its own
NGOs, and quickly contradictions began to rise between national grass-
roots mobilization and narrower political aims. Hammami explains that
this first fragmentation was the beginning of the NGOs' professionalization, by which she means that their organizational forms became
more politically autonomous. However, the first years of the intifada,
beginning in 1987, blurred boundaries again, and only towards its third
year, with funds arriving more and more from foreign donors (shifting
from Arab countries to European and American sources) did the logic
of NGOs begin to change causing them to become autonomous:

> This transformation of the mass movement into an NGO community, of
> mass-based, voluntarist organizations into more elite, professional and
> politically autonomous institutions was a complex process in which a
> variety of forces were at play [but critics point predominantly] to the
> dependence on foreign funders ... Organizational leadership, in becom-
> ing financially independent of their [political] factions, were able to wrest
> a certain autonomy over setting and managing programme priorities and
> content ... and see the party as something separate.[6]

In 2005, Sari Hanafi and Linda Tabar, picking up and extending Hammami's argument, asserted that the shift from political "grass roots"
organization to a professional, externally funded NGO community
had restructured the forms of "knowledge and practices" with which
such organizations could engage Palestinian society.[7] They describe a
condition of "disarticulation" between the civic and the political.[8] It is
worthwhile to emphasize one key element that bears special notice in an
inquiry centered on the relation between aesthetic categories and globalization processes in Palestine: the "disembedding of social relations
from their local context"[9] and their re-embedment within international
organizations, whether European or North American. Put simply, if in
an earlier moment social and political organizations, such as the PFLP,
DFLP and others, stemmed locally from within Palestinian forms of life,

---

6   Hammami, "NGOs: The Professionalization of Politics," 56.

7   Sari Hanafi and Linda Tabar, *The Emergence of a Palestinian Globalized Elite:
Donors, International Organizations and Local NGOs* (Jerusalem: Institute of Jerusalem
Studies, 2005), 24.

8   Hanafi and Tabar, "Palestinian Globalized Elite," 354.

9   Ibid., 28.

new NGOs were based on activists, Palestinian or not, who "approach" the local community as professionals. This new relation is an outcome of implementation of foreign donors' policies that treat society as a set of technical problems to be fixed and managed.[10] Correspondingly, a new "development" and human rights discourse replaced the older national-political one, favoring short-term "relief" projects and effectively de-linking the political aspects of refugees' lives and their "rights."[11]

More recently, Raja Khalidi and Sobhi Samour explain that the Oslo Accords "redefin[ed] the Palestinian liberation struggle as it has hitherto been known."[12] Calling it "neoliberal liberation," Khalidi and Samour argue that the US-backed neoliberal policies, implemented through the Palestinian Authority, effectively separated Palestinian political sovereignty from economic development, or daily life more broadly. In this way economic stability—the propping up of a middle class and a hospitable environment for foreign donors—could be achieved without ending the occupation. Khalidi and Samour emphasize the fact that neoliberal economists and politicians tasked the Palestinian Authority with maintaining the "rule of law"—more neutral language for the suppression of any resistance to the occupation—as a precondition to economic development and foreign investment:

> [T]he PA statehood program must embed the discourse and practice of neoliberalism in Palestinian society. It is here where the concept of the rule of law . . . proves its institutional value. Underlying its technical, neutral vocabulary is the *desire to escape politics* and, indeed, the very political nature of the question of Palestine. The statehood program encourages the idea that citizens may have to acquiesce in occupation but will not be denied the benefits of smoother running traffic, a liberal education curriculum, investor-friendly institutions, efficient public service delivery [etc.].[13]

---

10   Ibid.," 223–33.

11   See Sari Hanafi, "Palestinian Refugee Camps in the Palestinian Territory: Territory of Exception and Locus of Resistance." In Adi Ophir, Michal Givoni, and Sari Hanafi (eds.) *The Power of Inclusive Exclusion: Anatomy of Israeli Rule in the Occupied Palestinian Territories* (New York: Zone Books, 2009), 495–518.

12   Raja Khalidi and Sobhi Samour, "Neoliberalism as Liberation: The Statehood Program and the Remaking of the Palestinian National Movement." *Journal of Palestinian Studies* 11.2 (Winter 2011): 7.

13   Khalidi and Samour, "Neoliberalism as Liberation," 15.

What Khalidi and Samour describe here is effectively the separation of the private and political spheres. I would like to develop the logical and temporal properties of this new historical reality in relation to the question underlying this inquiry: the form of freedom and autonomy. In the pre-Oslo period, the freedom of the Palestinian people not only subordinated the (liberal) freedom of the private citizen, this statist project also had a temporal character: the private citizen could not be free until the freedom of the Palestinian people had been achieved. For this reason Palestinian freedom, as its historical time, were objects to be made, as Edward Said put it.[14] This logical and temporal condition locks the freedom of the individual to the freedom of other people, and any claim to individual autonomy is perceived as invalid or simply impossible. Neoliberalism in Palestine, especially in the West Bank, means that the freedom and autonomy of the private individual can now be achieved irrespective of the freedom of the Palestinian people. More than this, confusing political freedom—collective self-legislation—with the machinery of Palestinian state bureaucracy, this new attitude seeks to convince us that the Palestinian Authority is now technically sovereign, lacking only an official stamp of international recognition. And this is why, contrary to the widely held belief that it is simply the occupation that obstructs the freedom of the Palestinian people, it is possible to observe that Palestinian neoliberalism already presages the forms of domination typical of neoliberal sovereign states, where it would be Palestinians themselves—via the mediation of the global economy—who would dominate other Palestinians.

Therefore, although the object of Khalidi and Samour's "escape from politics" is the Israeli occupation, the same "escape" can be said to be true of the subject of private life in other sovereign neoliberal states for whom constitutive politics is now a problem. In this period, politics in its constitutive, self-making form is foreclosed in the strong Freudian sense of a non-negotiable preliminary negation, and as a consequence such politics enters imaginary literary worlds as a wish only.

The irony lodged in the concept of "rule of law" is that the Palestinian Authority is unable to make its own law, and manages the life of its citizens according to the dictates of foreign powers, i.e., global investors and American and European governments.[15] This last fact crystalizes the nature of neoliberal globalization, for in Palestine we see clearly how

---

14 See Chapter 3 for a discussion of Said's argument.

15 On this matter see Adam Hanieh, *Lineages of Revolt: Issues of Contemporary Capitalism in the Middle East* (Chicago: Haymarket Books, 2013), 117–22.

Palestinian internal constitutive powers are ceded to the networks of global capital, a condition that is usually more sublimated in sovereign states (other than in moments of crisis when such sovereignty is directly contested by global institutions). In the reading that follows of Selma Dabbagh's *Out of It* I show how the novelistic world consciously takes up the problem of politics in the present, only to find that the older constitutive politics has turned into a fantasmatic wish of the private subject.

Although the particular social processes driving the privatization of Palestinian society are different than in Israel, the manner in which this historical transformation appears in literary form is quite similar. In this second period, three transformations take place: first, the private and political spheres give the impression that they are self-legislating and autonomous. Since novels presupposing this condition adopt the subject of private life, the movement of events and characters in explicitly political novels is directed towards the intersection of the two spheres. The encounter with the "political" is often figured in the general type of the investigation and is used as an instrument of self-reflection and revelation. In other words, the "other" in such novels is not only the Israeli, but, as importantly, Palestinian political characters, if not Palestinian collectivity itself. The crisis of Palestinian society under neoliberalism is that Palestinian life itself becomes a foreign object, especially to the eyes and body of the private subject. This is clearly shown in those novels and memoirs where a character returns to Palestine after many years of exile. While such accounts concentrate, justly, on the devastation brought about by the Israeli occupation, what is underplayed is the fact that the Palestinian returnee is now a private subject for whom Palestinian life has become a foreign experience, a text that they cannot relate to and need to decipher.[16] It is crucial to remember that for the local Palestinian population, in so far as the occupation goes, nothing really changed. In other words, the figure of the exiled protagonist obscures internal divisions within Palestinian society.[17] Second, with the rearticulation of the

16   See for example Raba'a Al-Madhoun, *The Lady from Tel Aviv* [*al-Sayyidah min Tall Abīb*], translated by Elliot Cola (London: Telegram, 2013). See especially, 132–4, where the misery of Palestinians at an Israeli checkpoint becomes a textual object of fascination for the protagonist.

17   Although I take exception to her position, Anna Bernard touches on this disjunction when she criticizes Edward Said's Foreword to Mourid Barghouti's *I Saw Ramallah* (*Ra'aytu Rām Allāh*). Said emphasizes the figures of exile and displacement in Barghouti's account, thus positing a unified national narrative, while Bernard argues that such an account erases the diverse points of view of the local population that are not so easily folded into a collective identity. See Anna Bernard, "'Who Would Dare

private and political sphere, the body and spirit are also severed. Private life is regarded as a bodily or material existence lacking in spiritual (i.e., political) edification, a lack that necessitates the genre of initiation. Third, if in the previous period imaginary worlds were, to some degree, "made," the worlds of the second period are given ready-made and the characters confront them as a sign and text to be deciphered. There are surely more new characteristics, but these seem to be the most salient in terms of world-construction, and provide the basis for what I call "global literature."

Before moving on to a few examples, I would like to note that contemporary scholarship on Palestinian literature does not adequately attend to this new political reality and its aesthetic dimension. Critics mostly work with the category of the "nation," and prioritize the Israeli-Palestinian conflict without noting how, due to neoliberal policies, social relations are changing, especially in the West Bank, and with them poetic form.[18] In many instances, such scholarship does the important work of elucidating how literary works, in both Hebrew and Arabic, undermine the logic of Zionist oppression and the separation of Jews and Arabs, while in other instances, debates revolve around the autonomy of the literary artwork in the face of political exigency. And yet, however important, such readings work with romantic or idealist theoretical presuppositions that posit the writer as the ground of poetic language and resistance without accounting for those structural conditions that limit and condition the construction of imaginary worlds and poetic language. Thus,

---

to Make It into An Abstraction': Mourid Barghouti's *I Saw Ramallah*," *Textual Practice* 21.4 (2007): 665–86.

18 See for example Samar H. AlJahdali, "Venturing into a Vanishing Space: The Chronotope in Representing Palestinian Postcoloniality," *Journal of Postcolonial Writing* 50.2 (2014): 216–29; Anna Ball, *Palestinian Literature and Film in Postcolonial Feminist Perspective* (New York: Routledge, 2012); Anna Bernard, *Rhetoric of Belongings* (Liverpool: Liverpool University Press, 2013); Hella Bloom Cohen, *The Literary Imagination in Israel-Palestine: Orientalism, Poetry and Biopolitics* (New York: Palgrave-Macmillian, 2016); Gil Hochberg, *In Spite of Partition: Jews, Arabs and the Limits of Separatist Imagination* (Princeton: Princeton University Press, 2007); Lital Levy, *Poetic Trespass: Writing between Hebrew and Arabic in Israel/Palestine* (Princeton: Princeton University Press, 2014); Karim Mattar, "Mourid Barghouti's 'Multiple Displacements': Exile and the National Checkpoint in Palestinian Literature," *Journal of Postcolonial Writing* 50.1 (2014): 103–15; Patrick Willimas, "No Aesthetic Outside My Freedom," *Interventions* 14.1 (2012): 24–36. For a few studies in Arabic see: Muhammad Bakr al-Buji, *Āfāq al-adab al-'Arabī fī Filasṭīn wa-shahādāt adabīyah*, Vol II (Ghazzah: Maktabat al-Quds, 2013); Nādī Sārī al-Dīk, *Ẓilāl al-qayqab wa-mabāsim al-zīzrūq: qirā'āt taḥlīlīyah fī nuṣūṣ riwā'iyah Filasṭīnīyah* (Rām Allāh: Dār al-Shīmā' lil-Nashr wa-al-Tawzī', 2013); Salīm Najjār, *Qirā'āt fī al-riwāyah al-Filasṭīnīyah al-ḥadīthah* ('Ammān: Dār al-Karmil lil-Nashr wa-al-Tawzī', 1998).

the novels that I read here can be said to be resisting Zionist oppression and questioning Palestinian nationalist priorities (mainly those related to the issue of violence), but the question I ask is what poetic form such criticism takes, what its limits are, and why we see a shift in poetic forms after Oslo. These questions are rarely asked in contemporary scholarship, which often collapses the critical distance between critic and text and ends up endorsing Palestinian literature rather than taking it as an object of critique.[19] Let us now take a closer look at a few novels written in the post-Oslo period.

2.

Adania Shibli's first novella, *Touch* (*Masās*), intimates the sensations and impressions of a small Palestinian girl, impressions that center around colors, silence, movement, language and "the wall"—which are also the titles of each of the novella's five parts.[20] In an anthology of short stories, the renowned Palestinian writer, Anton Shammas, introduced Shibli as a "writer who has turned her back on the ready-made structures and prevalent rhetoric of modern Arabic literature."[21] We receive a first sense of this shift when we compare the manner in which Sahar Khalifeh's *Wild Thorns* and Shibli's *Touch* are presented to English readers. Although "back covers" are a pure product of market forces, they still provide insight into the dominant aesthetic of the time:

> Written in the Arabic of the West Bank and first published in Jerusalem, *Wild Thorns*, with its panorama of characters and unsentimental portrayals of everyday life, is the first Arab novel to give a true picture

---

19   Exceptions to this collapse of critical distance can be found in Bashir Abu-Manneh, "Palestinian Trajectories: Novel and Politics Since 1948," *Modern Language Quarterly* 75.4 (December 2014): 511–39; Karim Mattar, "Out of Time: Colonial History in Ibrahim Nasrallah's Time of White Horses," *Journal of Postcolonial Writing* 50.2 (2014): 176–88; Anna Bernard, "States of Cynicism: Literature and Human Rights in Israel/Palestine." In Sophia A. McClennen and Alexandra Schultheis Moore (eds.) *The Routledge Companion to Literature and Human Rights* (New York: Routledge, 2016), 373–9.

20   Adania Shibli, *Touch*, translated by Paula Haydar (Northampton: Clockroot Books, 2010); Adania Shibli, *Masās* (Bayrūt: Dār al-Ādāb, Mu'assasat 'Abd al-Muḥsin al-Qaṭṭān, 2003). The novella was originally written in 1999. From now on pagination will refer first to the English translation and then to the Arabic edition.

21   Anton Shammas, "Adania Shibli." In Samantha Schnee, Alane Salierno Mason and Dedi Felman (eds.) *Words without Borders: The World through the Eyes of Writers* (New York: Anchor Books, 2007), 131.

of social and personal relations under the occupation. Its convincing sincerity, uncompromising honesty, and rich emotional texture plead elegantly for the cause of survival in the face of oppression.[22]

Published in English translation in 1989, two years into the first intifada, this introduction draws attention to the authenticity and truth-value of *Wild Thorns* by emphasizing its aesthetic directness as well as its relation to origins (written in a colloquial Arabic; published in Jerusalem). However, because it is still a work of art, these values are balanced in the last sentence with a mention of the novel's artistic qualities, here colored with an appeal to nature as the opposite of harsh social relations (emotions and texture). All in all, it seems that the "value" communicated here is that *Wild Thorns* is first and foremost a "document," and whatever "elegance" it has is secondary. The introduction to Shibli's *Touch*, published in English translation in 2010, is markedly different:

> In the singular world of this novella, this young woman's everyday experiences—watching a funeral procession, fighting with her siblings, learning to read, falling in love—resonate until they have become as weighty as any national tragedy. The smallest sensations compel, the events of history only lurk at the edges.[23]

It will not be too symmetrical, I hope, to say that we have here an inversion. The newness of Shibli's novella is expressed in an inverse relation between "self" and "history," along with an innovative and more intricate style of writing. The phrase "as weighty as" signals the publisher's anticipation of objections to a Palestinian novella that might be seen as indulging in such miniature sketches at a time in which Israeli occupation has reached new levels of violence and new levels of global denunciation, especially after the 2008 Gaza War (Operation Cast Lead). If history lurks only at the edges then surely the self has taken center stage, filtering the "referent" through the prism of its consciousness until the very arrangement of the signifier takes over the signified:

> Every night the little girl would go to bed at sleepiness's command, but this night she went to bed at the mother's.

---

22 Sahar Khalifeh, *Wild Thorns*, back cover. See a similar technique of authentication in both the original Arabic edition and French translation. Khalifeh, *al-Ṣubār*; Khalifeh, *Chronique de figuier barbare*.
23 Shibli, *Touch*, back cover.

> From time to time, she would hear bits of words: "imals," "ker,"
> "Allah," "dren," "tards," "ratila" through the door separating her room
> from the living room where the family had gathered. "Ratila" was espe-
> cially difficult. Then she heard the television set click on, though the
> sound hardly made it through the door, but "ratila" became "abra and
> tila." After more repetition, Sabra and Shatila.[24]

In case it needs to be mentioned, "Sabra and Shatila" refer to a tragic
event in Palestinian history. In September 1982, during the invasion of
Israeli forces to Lebanon, Christian militia (Phalanges) infiltrated Palestinian refugee camps (Sabra and Shatila) and massacred their inhabitants.
Israeli forces, surrounding the camps, were accused of allowing the massacre to happen.

The prismatic registering of the world (and not only of historical
events), and not least the status of the "referent" as a television image,
might suggest a shift from "realism" to a modernist or postmodernist
idiom. Such a shift, as I have mentioned, is said to characterize Arabic
literature after the 1960s, most notably in Egypt with the appearance of
the Sixties Generation (*jil al-sitinat*)—including writers such as Edwar
al-Kharrat, Sonallah Ibrahim, Yusuf Idris, Ghamal al-Ghitani, as well
as Naguib Mahfouz's own shift into experimentation with stream of
consciousness. Palestinian literature, however, cannot be appropriated
into this narrative so easily. Although Kanafani's 1966 *All That's Left to
You* might be said to exhibit such modernist tendencies, his prose never
undermined the relation to history and referentiality as one understands
the terms in the context of Western European high modernism around
the 1920s. We would need therefore to look more closely at the meaning
of the "self" here, and examine how it differs from the aesthetic principle
I discussed in Khalifeh.

"Defamiliarization" might get us a little closer to the significance of
Shibli's attention to detail. It is partly at work in the extract we have
examined, in which the historical "event" is not given immediately but is
rather delayed and deferred. The difficulty, however, arises when we consider that defamiliarization techniques are directed at the habitual and
the ordinary, and are intended to change our perception and show reality
anew. By contrast, Sabra and Shatila, and perhaps the Palestinian experience in general, already belong to the extraordinary, to that experience
that never turns habitual in the way that Jayyusi has described. Shibli's

---

24   Ibid., 56/84.

style reacts to this kind of historical predicament. Although it filters the harsh reality of Palestine through the little girl's mind, *Touch*'s energies are directed not at estranging it, but rather at weakening its "grip," as Jayyusi says, so to carve a space for language and the aesthetic itself.

The little girl's consciousness is a device that allows history to be held at arm's length. She is too young to understand the full meaning of the historical situation and consequently licenses a period of time during which events (and more generally signifiers) can be appreciated not for their meaning, but precisely for their aesthetic quality—for their color, sound and movement. When we finally arrive at language acquisition, as in the first extract, words are disassociated from their historical meaning and appreciated either as sounds or as lexemes. This hiatus from history and signification, however, cannot last forever, as the narrative trajectory moves towards it, towards language, conceptuality, and comprehension with which, at the very last page of the novel, we seem to arrive at some form of (obscure) necessity greater than the girl's consciousness. Concomitantly, as language is acquired, the novella also seems to suggest a (secular) movement through different modes and genres of texts, beginning with the Quran for children, going through the sisters' diaries and ending with the classical French and Russian novels that the girl is beginning to read.

> The once meaningless lines transformed into words that created worlds.
> Those worlds stood right behind the clean panes of glass.
> The little girl started at the beginning, with the first book on the shelf.
> Al.Alex.an.der.Dumas
> *The Three Musketeers* . . .
> "Dos.Dosto.oevs.ski.yevski.
> *Crime and Punishment* . . . [25]

In *Touch* we follow then the interweaving of the slow establishment of conceptuality with an obscure sense of history whose deferral, I suggest, allows space for the aesthetic. But I would like to offer a more specific explanation of this important process and its historical conditions of possibility.

It will be helpful to think here of Henry James's *What Maisie Knew*, and the manner James explicates its stylistic logic in the Preface. As in Shibli, James's Maisie is a "small expanding consciousness," perceiving

---

25 Ibid., 64/94.

the world in "gaps and voids"[26] such that we learn of that world through her precocious mind. James's early experiment with inwardness can be understood as a displacement in which the way that Maisie grasps events (i.e., the mundane relationships of her parents, Ida and Beale Farange) is more important than the events themselves. By initiating such a displacement from world to mind, James strikes gold:

> [These apprehensions] become, as she deals with them, the stuff of poetry, and tragedy and art; she has simply to wonder, as I say, about them, and they begin to have meanings, aspects, solidities, connexions— connexions with the universal!—that they could scarce have hoped for.[27]

Here, too, the intricacy of the fictional world is achieved thanks to the absence of conceptuality, the fact that Maisie's apprehensions and perceptions, as James explains, are far stronger than her ability to conceptualize their meaning.[28] The universal for James is not the universality of conceptuality, but rather the universality of the mind in the moment of its internal perceptions, which James's style makes visible, as it were, to the reader.

James's sense that he has found "art and poetry" in Maisie's relation to the world should bring to mind again Kant's concept of the aesthetic: that movement of the particular searching for a universal, which is at one and the same time the property of the beautiful object and the characteristic of reflective judgment. In other words, Maisie's consciousness is a figure for the aesthetic, while James's technique is its instantiation. As Eagleton would say, James, as Kant, projects upon the object (here, Maisie's mind) the very logic of the aesthetic.[29]

With this in mind, we can see that Shibli's little girl is a similar literary instantiation of this aesthetic principle, of a mind that makes sense of the world without the direct application of concepts. The cardinal question is, then, what concept is missing in the world of *Touch*? What concept, or "universal," as James and Kant would say, are we sensing, though it is never there as such? I argue that what has turned implicit is the historical meaning of "Palestine" as a universal concept capable of endowing meaning to the girl's particular aesthetic experience. In other

---

26   Henry James, "Preface," in *What Maisie Knew* (New York: Charles Schribner's Sons, 1908), vi, ix.

27   Ibid., xii.

28   Ibid., x.

29   Terry Eagleton, *Ideology of the Aesthetic*, 87.

words, what we see in the apprehensions of Shibli's girl are the moments before she becomes conscious of her subjectivity as a Palestinian girl: "the girl tried to understand the meaning of the words *Sabra* and *Shatila*. Maybe they were one word. The word *Palestine* was unclear, except that its use was forbidden."[30] But this aesthetic-psychological principle, entering the novella as "content," as a mind within the world, governs the very world of the girl, that is, it is the condition that underlies such a world in its entirety. Its significance is double for, as content, it allows an aesthetic space, in Kant's sense, one intimating "Palestine" but remaining un-subsumed by its significance, which in turn provides for the autonomy of the character's private inner life in relation to Palestinian history. As literary form, it ushers Palestinian literature into aesthetic autonomy, allowing it freedom from the national struggle that in the past imposed itself on writers in the same way a determinate judgment imposes its category on particular sense-data. I stress the point that while in the first period, modernist attempts to invent Palestinian private life ended in split imaginary worlds (as we saw in Kanafani), in Shibli the world is unitary; the private psyche takes over the entire world.

I have argued that the privatization of literary production is concomitant with the NGOization of Palestine after Oslo. Significantly, Shibli's two novels won awards from and were co-published by such an NGO—the A. M. Qattan foundation. By 1999 the foundation was fully operational in Palestine and began several projects in education and the arts. Its mission statement, though it did not make it into the English translation of *Touch*, welcomes the reader in the first pages of the Arabic edition. It states, among other things, that the non-profit foundation "seeks to support the educational and cultural development as well as the critical thinking of the Arab people in general and the Palestinian people in particular."[31] On its website, the language of the foundation very closely follows the language of development that Hammami, Hanafi and Tabar discuss in their studies. The Qattan foundation, according to their site is,

Inspired by the shared heritage of humanity and in compliance with the Universal Declaration of Human Rights' vision that "All human beings are born free and equal in dignity and rights… [T]he Foundation encourages individuals to combine their self-development with the

30   Shibli, *Touch*, 58/86.
31   Shibli, *Masās*, 5.

service of others, while keeping a balance between personal and public interests.[32]

It is not necessary, or even possible, to map Shibli's aesthetics directly onto the foundation's aims. Suffice it to note, first, that the foundation allows autonomy from the political sphere, now understood more narrowly as the proper domain of the PA, Fatah, or Hamas. Second, the differentiation of civic practices from the political sphere changes modes of knowledge in Palestinian society and consequently the status of art and literature. For example, one of the consequences of these new civic practices is the transformation of local communities into *objects of knowledge* in relation to which civic organizations are constituted as *spectators and observers*. In other words, the differentiation of the civic and the political levels has established a new aesthetico-epistemological relation towards Palestinian society. This kind of relation is quite palpable in another short diary piece by Shibli, in which she and a Finish journalist visit Balatah refugee camp.[33] Shibli accompanies the journalist as a translator and becomes a mediator, a position not unsimilar to the one Hanafi and Tabar examine. Shibli, although Palestinian, confronts a Palestinian reality that is hers, but not entirely, and by translating this reality also transforms it into an object of knowledge for the Finnish outsider. Most importantly, once this social position is created, Palestinian reality turns into a text and the narrator into a reader. Meeting Salma, a refugee in the camp, Shibli observes:

> [T]he dark rings under her eyes undoubtedly hinted at extreme fatigue that she refused to give in to, and wouldn't even acknowledge in the first place. She was behaving responsibly, trying to rein in the loss and the destruction and, on top of that, to insist that there was something worth living for. After a while, and at the request of the journalist, she took us around to see the holes that the soldiers had left behind.[34]

Note how although both Shibli and Salma are Palestinian, the latter is an object of curiosity whose signs Shibli is trying to decipher: "[T]he dark rings under her eyes undoubtedly hinted at extreme fatigue." Interpreting Salma's attitude from her bodily signs, it is clear Shibli is engaged in

---

32   qattanfoundation.org/en/qattan/about/about
33   Located in northern West Bank, adjacent to Nablus.
34   Shibli, "Faint Hints of Tranquility." Translated by Anton Shammas. In *Words Without Borders: The World Through the Eyes of Writers*, 134.

an act of "reading," which is compounded when Salma shows the visitors "evidence" of Israeli aggression.

I would like to stress the relation between Shibli and Salma. It is not simply that Palestinian daily life is observed; rather, it is observed from the point of view of private life, from the perspective of someone who is shielded from these events to certain degree and reflects on them. Indeed, Shibli's diary piece moves between moments and sites of private life and encounters with Palestinian life. This is most evident when Shibli encounters the "political."

> *March 28, 2002*
> I hadn't finished my cup of coffee, but was ashamed to say so to the girl who'd lifted my tray with the other cups and walked away toward the kitchen. My coffee!
> I came back to my senses and to the two persons with whom I was sitting, the Finnish journalist and one of the political leaders of Hamas . . . More than three weeks ago, on March 4, 2002, the Israeli government tried to assassinate him . . .

> *March 29, 2002*
> I went back to bed with my coffee, away from the kitchen and its thoughts.[35]

The differentiation between private life and the political sphere underlies the form of the diary: Palestinian life is now a series of events, or more generally "content" that the author of the diary registers. Once such a differentiation has occurred, the private subject develops an instrumental relation to its own people, seen now as an external object of knowledge.

Such diaries also appear in *Touch* and I would like to conclude this reading by returning to the novella to reflect on the new mode of knowledge it offers in a time of such social differentiation. While the girl's consciousness keeps Palestinian history at bay, understanding it mostly in its aesthetic dimensions, the movement in *Touch* is still towards necessity, that which, if to appeal to Lacan's concept of the Real, cannot be refigured or reworked by the imagination. Such necessity is given in a displaced manner when the girl, who now knows how to read, discovers her sisters' diaries and her father's work-related documents. In the

---

35   Shibli, "Faint Hints of Tranquility," 136–7.

following passage one can notice how both "others" turn into signs for the subject, and how, perhaps for the only time in the novella, the subject imagines collective life existing outside herself.

> About the sisters she read on a sheet of paper or a diary carefully hidden under a mattress or in a drawer behind a picture hanging from the wall. The father's world came from a little green box filled with papers . . . Shared events and similar feelings gathered in every diary and on every sheet of paper, transforming the single world of the house into several distinct, contradictory worlds, which the girl's eyes traversed. She read all the pages and reread them again and again. Without anyone seeing her, she came near each of their worlds.[36]

While Palestinian history is deferred, it finds its way back into the novella in the foreign world of the family. The latter stands in both as an allegory for the disjunction between the autonomous subject and Palestinian society figured as a sign, and for Palestinian history as that multiplicity of (hidden) narratives now left outside the purview of the fictional world. Note how what was supposed to be most immediate to the girl—her family, and more broadly Palestinian society—appears hidden from the private subject, a secret that can now be accessed only through the mediation of signs, through a miniature investigation, a literary type that becomes more and popular in Palestinian cultural production.[37] Further, the disjunction between the private subject and society gives birth to the differentiation between surface appearance (the "single world") and depth ("contradictory worlds") that now lies underneath the surface, inaccessible to direct experience and ready to be unearthed. As in the Israeli case, the girl's inquiry becomes a compensatory mechanism taking the form of the social fetish: social relations, now no longer made, are projected onto mesmerizing objects—here a chest of letters—that represent the world *within* the world, like a crystal ball.

Finally, the clearest disjunction between the new subject of private life and the older form of Palestinian life is illustrated in the estrangement

---

36 Shibli, *Touch*, 66/96–97.

37 See for example Sahar Khalifeh, *The Inheritance* [*al-Mīrāth*] (Cairo/New York: The American University in Cairo, 2005); Adania Shibli *We Are All Equally Far from Love* [*Kullunā ba ʿīd bi-dhāt al-miqdār ʿan al-ḥubb*] (Northampton, Mass.: Clockroot Books, 2012); Rabai al-Madhoun, *The Lady from Tel Aviv* [*al-Sayyidah min Tall Abib*] (London: Telegram, 2013); Selma Dabbagh, *Out of It* (London: Bloomsbury Publishing, 2011); Ahmed Masoud, *Vanished: The Mysterious Disappearance of Mustafa Ouda* (Cyprus: Rimal Publications, 2015).

between the child and the mother, the literate and the illiterate. Since the mother cannot write or read, the child cannot approach her:

> It was impossible to approach [the mother's] unwritten world . . . Every new book and every new day increased the distance between the two. In the meantime, the mother waited for the girl to move the books out of the way between them, and the girl waited for the mother to read these books; the only time their two languages met was in an argument that accelerated their separation.[38]

Here we see an illustration of something that many critics of contemporary Palestinian literature underplay or ignore: the more Palestinian society follows the path of privatization, the more an internal process of differentiation begins to take hold, making the Palestinian population itself into an illegible sign, an obscure world. I cannot stress the point enough that this is not a consequence of the Israeli occupation per se; on the contrary, the occupation—being always present—forces forms of legibility upon reality. The new illegibility is brought about by neoliberal global processes that profoundly transform Palestinian society and shape it according to its needs. Note that this process of differentiation betrays all the signs that it is already posited from the position of the child (private life) rather than the mother's: first, the mother's form of life is reduced to an illegible sign, and second, with this reduction the private subject posits the *inequality* of these two forms of life through the medium of reading and language rather than social reality. These unequal forms of Palestinian life are now figured as signs (a process brought about by privatization rather by than the mind) and this, I argue, is one of the markers of globalization and global literature.

3.

For my second example from the post-Oslo period, I turn to a relatively new phenomenon in Palestinian literature—novels originally written in English. Although many Palestinian writers reside in exile outside Palestine and Israel, writing in languages other than Arabic is fairly rare, but becoming more common.[39] Given the dominance of English in the

---

38 Shibli, *Touch*, 66–7/97.
39 In May 2015, the online literary journal *Words without Borders* published selections from "New Palestinian Literature" written in English, Spanish, Danish and Arabic.

world republic of letters and the fact that English is not a major language of daily life in Palestine or the Arab world, Palestinian novels written in English can be said to be written mostly for the world literary market rather than Palestinians living in Palestine. Such novels are then a good indication of the transformation of Palestinian literature and its new position in the world.

Portraying the global nature of Palestinian life on the surface of its imaginary world, Selma Dabbagh's *Out of It* is set in Gaza, London and the Gulf during the second intifada (early 2000s).[40] The story centers around a middle-class Palestinian family, the Mujaheds, and specifically around Iman and Rashid whose travels to and experiences in London and the Gulf allow for self-reflection and internal transformation, especially in matters of political action. As with Israeli literature post-1985, the introspection of private individuals and their impossible (and at times fantasmatic) relation to politics is at the heart of the novel. This question is played out most broadly on the spatio-temporal axes: the geographical setup, displacing Gaza's affairs into London and the Gulf, provides the characters with the needed distance for self-reflection, while the generational break, in which the parents engaged in direct struggle against Israel, while the children seem to be unable to do so in the same manner, sets up the difference between old and new historical forms of politics.

The father, Jibril Ali Mujahed, is presented to us as a former prominent member of the Palestinian Liberation Organization (PLO), the umbrella organization of Palestinian politics. Out of political exigency, he has taken his family to live in Paris for a period, sent his children to study in Switzerland, and now lives an apolitical life in the Gulf after removing himself from the leadership over a matter I will discuss at the end of this reading. We get a glimpse of Jibril's new life and his relationship to politics in the following recollection. Here he remembers how a messenger came to inform him that his daughter was almost caught up in a risky political action in Gaza:

Nathalie Handal, the editor of the collection, says, "for close to seven decades . . . Palestinians' rich literary production has contributed to Arabic letters, taken part in all its literary experiments, and left enduring poetry collections, novels, plays, and memoirs. Today, Palestinians write in multiple languages and have different nationalities, cultural influences, and varied aesthetics; many also belong to other literary traditions and nations." Nathalie Handal, "The Shape of Time: New Palestinian Writing," *Words Without Borders*, May 2015, wordswithoutborders.org.

40   Selma Dabbagh, *Out of It* (New York: Bloomsbury, 2011).

Suzi [his second wife] had been in her champagne negligée and they had
been having a whiskey; they had assumed it was a supermarket deliv-
ery boy bringing them up some ice and Suzi had not bothered to put
anything away, meaning that it was all there when the official from the
Representative Office had turned up in his flat, at midnight. The last
thing Jibril wanted was to be brought back into the fold by that lot again.[41]

As with her presentation of the superficiality of consumerism in the Gulf
and in London, Dabbagh's criticism of this new lifestyle clearly comes
across through the "champagne," whiskey, and the "boy" delivering ice.
But more important, here is the appearance of "politics" as a stranger
knocking at the door, an agent now external to Jibril's personal and interior life, bringing up politics as an "old past." The two characteristics
of politics, or more specifically direct antagonism—it is "something of
the past" and it arrives in the form of "news/text"—surround the life of
the characters and reappear throughout the novel. Although the story is
situated in the present, in the midst of the second intifada, the conflict,
especially in London and the Gulf, appears mostly in the form of news
on the radio and in the newspaper. Even when we are back in Gaza,
we mostly "hear" of political developments rather than getting directly
involved in them. I attend more carefully to such instances later, so here
I will concentrate on the second characteristic we observed in Jibril's
recollection—the "pastness" of direct antagonism and its appearance as
a text or recollection.

The character who embodies this important aspect of history and its
current form in politics is Sabri, the older brother of Rashid and Iman.
Sabri, who is a paraplegic due to a car bombing, was once a direct participant in the first intifada and now writes its history. He lives in Gaza and
is surely surrounded by the conflict, but now rather than participating,
he documents and interprets the past and the present. Let us take up first
an example of antagonism appearing in the present:

During the night he kept a record of the attack [on Gaza]. He kept his
notepad, binoculars and two sharpened pencils on the end of a shelf by
the window in preparation for his eyewitness accounts. He timed strikes
using a digital watch that he set against the *bip, bip, bips* of the BBC
World Service. Last night was three pages of notes. The night before
that had just been one. Documenting destruction. Chronicling chaos.

---

41   Ibid., 168.

Point by point strike. That was what he did and he liked to think he did it well.[42]

Sabri is one of the characters who turns the real of war and violence into a text. Antagonism for Sabri is then a distant and external object of observation, an event that is turned into a report that is submitted to European agents outside Palestine, among other addresses. Sabri's political act is then characterized by mediation and documentation, while direct antagonism is reserved for Palestinian characters outside the Mujahed family, some of whom serve, as we shall see, as an object of desire and fantasy. Although Sabri's involvement in the first intifada brings him closer to direct antagonism than Iman and Rashid, he is positioned on the cusp of this kind of activity and therefore he straddles the roles of insider and outsider. This ambivalent position becomes more evident when he turns to document the past:

> He put away the documents concerning his mother and arrayed the first Intifada material around him. This was history of an uprising that he lived through. He *was* that history right from the beginning. His proximity to the subject matter was what made it unsettling. He had known many of the key figures whom he was now trying to write about. Some of them had been heroes to him; some he had despised. But how he had viewed them at the time was an easier question in terms of objectivity, compared to the other problem, which was how he viewed them *now*, in the light of what they had become.[43]

The split between the present and the past is then not simply a matter of chronology and the "natural" passage of time; it is rather enabled by the political break between Sabri as "participant" and Sabri as "spectator," a split that receives its thematic and explicit expression in the figure of historical writing. Once separated from the scene of direct antagonism and "making," Sabri becomes troubled by his objective relation to the act and its significance, rather than the act itself. Further, once his body is no longer enmeshed in the exigencies of struggle, Sabri takes on the intellectual activity of interpretation, and very quickly the production of the historical text becomes a representational dilemma, where he has to decide between competing narratives, between the "official line" of

---

42   Ibid., 36.
43   Ibid., 40–1.

the PLO and what "really happened."[44] We will return to Sabri at a later point to see what comes of his historical research, a discovery that will also allow us to examine the significance of Jehan Mujahed, the mother of the family.

If for Jibril and Sabri direct antagonism was at least a real biographical past that has now became an object of recollection, for Iman and Rashid, the main protagonists, direct antagonism is figured as an (impossible) wish, one whose attainment has more to do with the satisfaction of their own private libidinal desires than the collective fate of Palestinians. Let us follow the construction of Iman's desire first.

After completing her education in Switzerland, Iman returns to Palestine and takes part in a women's committee with the intent of taking a leadership role. Before attending to her desire to engage in political action, let us first note her actual dealings with the Palestinian community:

> Iman tried not to look too eager to cross the threshold into her building. It was essential that she concealed her desire to put a gate, a path and two metal doors between her and the mess outside, out of respect for those who were forced to live there. She strained to talk to the neighbours, to ask after their children, and to find something to chat about . . . She could not offer help, she kept telling herself, because if she did, there was no knowing where it would end.[45]

It is quite clear that Iman harbors slight disdain towards the very people in whose name she purportedly wants to act as a political leader. Although fantasmatically, as I show below, Iman wishes to fuse herself with the political—the collective fate of Palestine—in actuality, she seeks to put a barrier between herself and the poor people surrounding her house. Already we can see that for Iman (and other characters of the Mujahed family), "other people" are something external that they have difficulty connecting to. A moment later, this separation is identified as a matter of class:

> And then she was through. The gate would close and she could forget them and their mile-long walks for water . . . their haggling for cement and building materials, their tempers lost on bored, hungry children.

---

44   Ibid., 45.
45   Ibid., 21.

She could close the gate behind her and walk down . . . through . . . the garden . . . and upstairs into her own home.[46]

If Iman is disdainful of poor Palestinians why is it that she seeks to become their political leader? The heart of the matter lies in the fact that Iman is first and foremost a private subject whose innermost desire is to be recognized and seen, but this desire is displaced into the political. Once this desire is fulfilled her political wish will be transformed as well. Let us follow this transformation.

As I said, we first meet Iman during a women's committee meeting. The women are skeptical of the new middle-class upstart, and put her in her place, in a way. Nothing that she suggests is taken seriously, and she develops the notion that the actions of the women's committee are not radical enough. Now, I should also mention that Iman is a virgin, and her political desire to act is interwoven with her sexual desire, which usually finds its object in militants who are willing to engage in violence as means of action. Iman's story (as does Rashid's) takes on the genre of the initiation story, through which Iman comes to recognize herself and the world around her. As I show, rather than being the objective of her actions, the "political" serves Iman as a *medium* through which she matures, both sexually and politically. In other words, the collective fate of Palestinian life serves the subject of private life as an instrument of psychological development.

Iman's political and sexual desire appears first as a desire to be seen. During the conversation with the women's committee she imagines a conversation with her first potential lover, Raed:

> She had to handle herself as though he [Raed] was watching her, she thought. "This is how I dealt with it," she would tell him if he were to ask later, if she saw him again.[47]

And a moment later, she continues this imaginary conversation:

> The circumstances would never change if they [the women's committee] didn't do anything. But do what? "We should," Raed had said, in such a simple way, as though describing how to play backgammon to a child, "fight them with what they fight us with . . . We are being too soft . . ."

---

46 Ibid., 22.
47 Ibid., 6.

Making tea during the bombardment had made her feel like she was part of a meaningful movement. And that was where it was. She was too soft was where it was at.[48]

Raed here acts as the embodiment both of Iman's physical desire, and of her more abstract political desire to take bolder actions. The adjective "soft" also plays double duty—it describes both the softness (read: inadequacy) of the women's committee and Iman's softness as an uninitiated woman ("child") who is a virgin both sexually and politically. In short, the "political" in Raed's voice is both the commanding superego (you should take up direct action!) and the unconscious driving her towards sexual gratification.

Playing on the adage "be careful what you wish for," Dabbagh grants Iman's wish. At the end of the meeting, Manar, another participant, approaches Iman and acknowledges her desire to be seen and heard. Telling Iman she was sent to recruit her, Manar externalizes Iman's inner desire:

"I have been listening to what you say in there. You are right about making a difference." The statement was delivered with significance, like a medal dropped around Iman's neck. "You *were* right to come back to Palestine, you *do* have a role here."

"And what is my role? . . . Who are you talking about when you say 'we'?"

"A group . . . " Manar replied. "We don't *meet*, not like this. It is a question of being *contacted*. It just depends on whether you are ready."

"Ready for what?"

"To make a difference. To *really* impact the situation . . . They think you are capable of it. Only you . . . They chose you."

"They *chose* me? Who did?" Exam-result expectation flushed to Iman's hands. She always did well in exams.[49]

I note first the implicit fairytale-like, wish-fulfillment tone in this scene. It is not only that Iman again imagines herself as a child being recognized by an authority figure (medal dropped around her neck; exam), the scene is keyed to the genre of the fantastic where a concealed power selects an unknown entity to perform a life-changing task that will redeem the

48   Ibid., 10.
49   Ibid., 13.

collective. Even before we attend to the way this wish is frustrated and aborted, it is important to stress again that the "political" appears here as an exotic wish, rather than as an inescapable burden whose execution threatens the life of the protagonist, as was the case in Kanafani and Khalifeh in the first period.

After Raed is killed in an Israeli attack and she is summoned to gaze at the dead body, Iman is covertly contacted again. In the same manner that Manar externalized Iman's wish, another character, Seif El Din, engages Iman and Rashid in a conversation about two forms of politics. Seif El Din mocks the actions of Rashid's friends, Khalil and Jamal, who gather evidence in attempt to build a legal case against Israel's human rights violations. Seif El Din continues to rebuff Khalil, arguing that the legal route is "virtuous" but ineffective, because the laws, international or not, justify the occupier and its interests. Khalil insists that it is imperative they continue in the documenting work and trust international law. Seif El Din comes then to his final point, justifying direct antagonism:

> If you want them to change, let me ask you this: what would alter your behavior if you are benefiting from the situation? Feeling guilty about something? The loss of money? Or the prospect of someone you love getting hurt or killed? I would say only the last two, and those are the only things we can use to get this situation to change, to get them to stop.[50]

Through Seif El Din, Dabbagh is distinguishing between what Lacan would call Symbolic politics (the Law) and Real politics (violence). The difference between these two forms of politics is lodged in the source of power and law. In the symbolic work of documenting the violence of the occupation, Khalil and Jamal become instruments of an external lawgiver—the "Europeans." It is not simply that they do not choose violent means; they also delegate their constitutive power to an external entity who now objectifies their very life as "evidence" according to legal measures they themselves did not legislate. It is this position vis-à-vis the external lawgiver that turns the Real into a "text," or a "sign" to be collected and weighed against other equivalent "texts" the Israelis will present in defense of their own actions. Seif El Din rails against the practices of documentation and political delegation precisely because they transform an inequality in power into an equivalence of evidence

---

50   Ibid., 65–6.

PALESTINE AS TEXT AND SIGN 247

(submitted to international law). Disavowing the irreducible constitutive effects of power—the condition of possibility for the emergence of
the Symbolic order—turns documentation into a farcical theatre of legal
drama. Seif El Din's speech confronts Khalil and Jamal with the Real, and
in a way with what they must disavow in order to continue their work:
"'It is essential,' Khalil [said] 'that we believe in the Western governments'
ability to change.'"[51]

In contradistinction, the significance of Seif El Din's politics of the
Real for this reading lies not so much in the idea of taking up arms but
in the political and philosophical implications of violence. By refusing
to delegate power to an external lawgiver, Seif El Din's acts fuse together
(re-fuse) the split between the subject of constitutive power ("making")
and the subject of constituted power ("reading") that the international
community imposes on Palestine. This subject is precisely Iman and
Rashid's object of desire, which they seek to attain throughout the novel.

Equally important here is the fact that this political bifurcation
(between Seif El Din and Khalil and Jamal) appears within the imaginary
world as a question directed at the subject of private life who is now faced
with a choice. We saw this bifurcation in Sabri a moment ago, when he
opted between two forms of historical writing, and here it shows its face
again. Note also the fact that Iman is again "encountering" the political
in the form of a secret message that she needs to decipher. To clarify, Seif
El Din's speech has an exoteric and an esoteric message: the former is
openly directed to Rashid and Khalil while the latter is directed to Iman;
his speech is the secret sign she has been waiting for, telling her Seif El
Din is a member of the group that wants to recruit her.[52] A few moments
later, Iman directly expresses her political wish, saying:

> She was not about to stay at home making pickles like her mother. For
> all her talk what had her mother actually done? Marry her father? . . .
>
>   Khalil had to rethink. They could do it his way but it was not for her,
> not any more. She needed to act . . . The thing was to *act* and that was
> what she was doing [by wishing to join the secret group]. Peoples Fronts,
> Popular Wings, United Leaderships—the hell with them, too. It was all
> about *action*: there was no alternative . . . Rashid's assumption that gath-
> ering evidence of these [human rights] violations mattered was flawed.[53]

---

51 Ibid., 66.
52 We are given to understand that Seif El Din is member of Hamas, which challenges the rule of Fatah.
53 Dabbagh, *Out of It*, 70–1.

As before, the desire to act is presented to us as both a political wish and as a feminist critique of patriarchy. It seems then that if Iman can fulfill her desire she will indeed reunite the political and the sexual, the personal and the political. We will see how the relation between the mother and the daughter, the past and the present, is in fact reversed. The wish, however, is frustrated, and in a way Iman's journey through the novel will take her back to the Symbolic and to the renunciation of direct antagonism. Understanding this process is important for understanding the displacement of her political desire into sexual (personal) gratification.

Iman makes a bold move and follows Seif El Din, under the assumption that he is leading her to meet the secret group face to face. However, Seif El Din is being tracked by the Israeli military at the same time. Just before Seif El Din is killed, Iman is pulled back by another man, Ziyyad Ayyoubi, who literally blocks her unification with her political desire. Ayyoubi is a mid-level leader with Fatah, the Palestinian party running the Gaza Strip at the time. With time, Ayyoubi becomes Iman's love object and she displaces onto him the fulfillment of her political wish to act. In other words, instead of joining Ayyoubi and reuniting her sexual and political desires, she turns Ayyoubi into a love object and thus both separates the sexual and political desire and gives up the latter. This transmutation takes place in London, when she happens to see Ayyoubi during a demonstration. The bifurcation of the political and the sexual is staged here in the bifurcation of genre: Iman's sexual gaze is written as romantic kitsch, while Ayyoubi's politics are described in the language of the thriller. Iman, for example, describes Ayyoubi as "surrounded by a profusion of petals and lusciousness [and] scents of blossoms"[54] while Ayyoubi talks about being followed by the police and recalls the trauma of his parents' assassination."[55] The coexistence of the two mismatched idioms continues throughout the conversation. Iman keeps thinking in romantic terms about their encounter and the fantasmatic figure of Ayyoubi, pushing aside the concrete reality of Palestine, while Ayyoubi again and again tries to bring back "the political" by explaining to her the reason he and his party arrested their neighbor, Abu Omar. With time, in contradistinction to the beginning of the novel, Iman no longer feels the need to act. She feels guilty for "skiving in exile," and for not fulfilling her political duty, and at some point she thinks she needs to apologize to

---

54   Ibid., 228.
55   Ibid., 232.

Ayyoubi for wanting to join Seif El Din because her older political wish was "stupid."[56]

Once she gives up the political wish to act through direct antagonism, Iman finally begins to advocate human rights actions. Her new realization comes after sleeping with the British official responsible for funding Palestinian aid projects. She says to an incredulous Rashid:

> We are definitely going to fund the center for the handicapped, get their offices moved, and provide facilities. Then a women's centre, maybe a crèche. There's so much, Rashid. Don't give me that look like—I know what you're thinking. That they're just palliatives, right? But every little bit helps—[sic] is important. Maybe we can do something with the Centre [run by Khalil] too. Maybe they'll fund some of the positions there?. . .
>
> [Rashid:] "Are you offering me a job or something?"
>
> "It's possible."[57]

I will return to the significance of money in the novel, but now I note in conclusion that similar to Fahmi's journey in Assaf Gavron's *Almost Dead*, Iman's journey takes her from the "political" to "the private," during which she gives up her fantasmatic infatuation with direct antagonism and adopts a more "mature" and "responsible" behavior. It is also important to note the novel's implicit position vis-à-vis Iman. While the novel seems critical of Iman's distance from poor Palestinians, it also mocks political engagement in the form of direct antagonism and brands it as an infatuation of spoiled middle-class girls. It is not simply that the novel valorizes human rights activities, it also belittles Iman's political desire by implying that once Iman was both satisfied sexually and recognized by a male political figure, she could give up her own wish to engage in direct antagonism. Thus, although it might seem to flirt with a feminist critique, the novel takes up a conservative position that disparages women's politics by sending them to satisfy their sexual desires first. Let us now look at Rashid's transformation.

Initially, Iman and Rashid's desires could not be more different. While Iman wants "in," to take part in politics, Rashid, evoking the title of the novel, wants "out of it" all. His journey "out" begins in the very first pages of the novel when his application for an academic fellowship in

---

56   Ibid., 228.
57   Ibid., 262.

England is approved and he can reunite with his British love-interest, Lisa. However, when we examine his underlying frustration, the reason he wants out, we discover that his desire is very similar to Iman's. He wants to be seen and recognized, a desire that will allow us another look at the fantasmatic nature of the "political" in this novel.

Not surprisingly, given that we are dealing with a privatized world, the object of the complaint is the family, specifically the mother who, to Rashid's mind, does not love him. So while Rashid does what he can to stay "out of it" (staying stoned most of the time, pursuing a relationship with a foreigner, traveling abroad, etc.), he secretly wants to find his way into the family, which will take him into the "political." As with Iman, the transmutation begins to take place in London and is associated with Ayyoubi, the fantasmatic political subject. The figures that underlie Rashid's change are "substitution" and "appearance." As we learn, Rashid looks like Ayyoubi, and for this reason he is mistakenly picked up by the London police. When the police officers recognize they have made a mistake they charge Rashid with possession of weed and throw him in jail.

Rashid's entry into the political and into the approving gaze of other people is staged directly through "appearance"—Rashid begins to understand this and contemplates his desire while in jail:

> Rashid wanted to remember all of this, to mentally document it. He wanted to ensure that any tale told later to Khalil, for example, would be detailed enough . . . There was something almost desirable about the drama of the situation. It was so familiar to him from films and TV that to find himself in it gave him the sense that his life had taken on a dramatic purpose, that he had actually (finally) reached the level of being able to not just feature but to *star* in a narrative of some interest.[58]

Note how again, although Rashid is the subject of "action," he detaches himself from it and turns himself into an object by "documenting" what's around him and turning it into a "text." But more important is Rashid's realization of what he had suppressed all along—his desire to find purpose, to join some act that is greater than his petty self-centered life. Again, we see that the "political" appears as a wish, something the characters truly want but cannot achieve. And yet, given Rashid's bad faith, the moment that the content of this wish finds conscious expression it is immediately displaced and substituted with its form—the representation

---

58   Ibid., 225.

of the political narrative itself. In other words, Rashid realizes that the political can alter his appearance; he can turn from a secondary character to a protagonist in the eyes of others. Thus, for Rashid, politics is first and foremost a way to solve his personal problems—the fact that he is disregarded by others—and second, politics is a representation (a film) whose most important aspect is appearance.

Rashid distorted fantasy of recognition receives its most fantasmatic elaboration when he returns to Gaza. By splitting and paralleling the storylines, Dabbagh shows how Ayyoubi's own political allies try to assassinate him, and, at the same time, how the events in Ayyoubi's storyline turn into a political fantasy for Rashid:

> Rashid had gone down to the beach, trying to find somewhere to have a smoke . . . There were trucks of armed men speeding over the tarmac . . . open trucks overloaded with men in uniforms, their guns spiked up at the sky . . . It came over him suddenly as an extended epiphany: that the trucks were only speeding so that they could find him, Rashid; that there were armed men anywhere looking for him, Rashid; that every car shadow held a man crouched with their guns readied, searching for him, Rashid . . . The dunes hid tanks and bulldozers; each helicopter searched for him with its beam; the gunships pointed at him alone, Rashid.[59]

We need to interpret what happens here on two levels: both from Rashid's point of view and on the level of the textual world itself. On the level of the character, what we observe is simply the climax of Rashid's desire to be seen within a Hollywood-like fantasy of the political thriller where the hero is chased and gunned down by armed forces. As some of these events might be taking place in Ayyoubi's storyline, we begin to see the enactment, first in the mind, of Rashid's substitution with Ayyoubi. But even more importantly, on the level of the world, this is the moment where the novel itself desires to be the political action novel it cannot be because its main characters have little to do with direct Palestinian antagonism. Thus, Rashid's fantasy of direct antagonism also rises from the unconscious of the novel itself, in the form of an embedded fantasmatic genre that is otherwise impossible to enact within the confines of private life. It is no accident that this takes place at the end, as a final attempt to break out of the asphyxiating privatized world of new Palestinian literature.

---

59   Ibid., 285.

Now, after this drug-induced political delusion, Rashid ends up at the family home only to find Ayyoubi is already there, wounded by a gunshot. Again, once the political level is separated from the private one, they can only intersect and mirror one another. So, attending lovingly to Ayyoubi's wounds, the mother of the family, Jehan, says "[Ayyoubi is] a hero you could say . . . [He] could be my own son, don't you think?" And Rashid thinks: "The son you never had."[60] Once Rashid hears this statement the relationship between the political and private life suggests itself: to win the love of his mother and be recognized by her, Rashid needs to take Ayyoubi's place. The political is instrumentalized here as a form of personal redemption. Considering taking Ayyoubi's place, Rashid thinks:

> And once he found it (his destiny) he became wired with sensitivity to his surrounding that he had never previously experienced . . . Wired with purpose. Reborn.[61]

Note that, as a privatized subject, Rashid's experience of this redemption and rebirth is not coincidentally figured as a deep wish to be connected to other people and his surroundings.

The manner in which Rashid goes about his substitution returns us to the theme of appearance. Since they look alike, Rashid borrows Ayyoubi's coat and steps outside onto the streets of Gaza, knowing he is about to be shot. Once we are in the streets, the novel slips into the thriller genre again and we are now witnessing the kind of "action" Iman was fantasizing about in the beginning. The fact that this section is written as a literary fantasy points yet again to the fact that it is not only Rashid who fantasizes about direct antagonism but the novel itself. In other words, the only way the novel can imagine the real is in the form of the imaginary.

To complete this reading, I turn to three short ancillary materials: the political development of Eva, a British medical student; the appearance of money; and finally, the identity of Jehan Mujahed, the mother of the family.

To continue on the heels of Rashid's fantasy, I begin with Eva's political transformation. Although secondary to the unfolding of events, Eva is important in two regards: her character articulates the political desire

---

60 Ibid., 286.
61 Ibid., 290.

of this imaginary world and serves as a measure to gauge the new equivalence between the Palestinian and the private subject of "advanced" capitalist states ("Westerners").

We first meet Eva in London, when Iman arrives to visit Rashid. Being a studious British medical student, Eva is written as a kind but ultimately ignorant professional whose scant knowledge of world affairs leads her to reproduce the hegemonic discourse on Israel-Palestine. Iman immediately jumps on the opportunity to chastise the ignorant Westerner, accusing her of "supporting the existing system."[62] However, as the plot unfolds, Eva is persuaded by Khalil (her soon-to-be boyfriend) to attend a demonstration, and we get the sense that she begins to be more engaged with her surroundings. A little while later when we are back in Gaza, we meet Eva again. This time she is no longer a passive spectator but engaged in attending to the sick and wounded in Palestine as a volunteer. At the very end of the novel, after helping a group of Palestinians under attack, she gives a long speech about her newfound political awareness:

> I feel completely overwhelmed, Eva started . . . I can't forget that feeling, like nothing I have ever had: the closeness, the volunteers, all felt together and with the families. We kept smiling at each other and hugging each other . . . I can never forget that evening, the memory of it will be sacred until I die; nothing I ever did before compares with that. It scares me to think that I could've lived without coming close to ever feeling that.[63]

Eva's feelings here are in line with the rest of the present reading in the sense that she, too, craves participation in a larger, non-mediated social action that could lead to real change. She stresses the relation to the body specifically, her own and that of others (the "closeness") as that which is lacking in her own life. Eva takes it a step farther: she realizes that being and acting together with a group of Palestinians, an act that put her life at risk, is something she desires, and that her own way of life indeed blocks her from this kind of social action. Ironically, she seems to be more afraid of living without this sense of shared purpose than of the attack itself. On the surface, the novel offers here a short critique of the Westerners' private life in comparison to Ayyoubi's life, for example. But if we recall Iman's difficulty connecting with the people in her neighborhood, her

---

62   Ibid., 192.
63   Ibid.,, 283–4.

own political wish to be part of a greater social action, we can see not so much the difference between the privatized Palestinian and the "Westerner" but their *equivalence*. What makes them similar is not the fact that both of them ended up supporting the Palestinian cause—but rather that they are now private subjects for whom engaging with other people is both a wish and a political problem. Iman and Eva instrumentalize politics for personal development and to reach self-awareness. It is this measure—private life—that makes Iman "worldly" in my account, the measure that reveals a communality that crosses nationalities and geographies without reducing their difference to identity.

The second narrative material that contributes to the new sense of global equivalence is the measure of equivalence itself—money and commodities. These materials appear as a faint leitmotif throughout the novel in a recurring form: several characters, but specifically Iman, overhear conversations about money and ads that cut into their stream of consciousness. I have already commented on the importance of wealth in the presentation of Iman's father, Jibril Mujahed, but more important is the way money and class are juxtaposed with Palestinian politics once we are in London with Iman. Here is a typical example:

London was babbling. The air was crossed through with questions and fragments of sentences [. . .]

. . . *could always do Ibiza if we can't do Goa* . . .
. . . *machine-washed my dinner jacket three times already* . . .
. . . *I told him about the Viagra* . . .
. . . *Her mother sang at the Sydney Opera* . . .

To get more of their lives, Iman followed strangers, fascinated by the directions that the mind's interests took when no longer consumed by fear. But then her world caught up with her and she could not do it anymore. The news became so terrible: an onslaught on a West Bank town, rumors of a massacre, of mass graves, and yet the chatter did not ease up for a second [. . .] the dead were rotting in the streets.

. . . *it was bliss, it really was. Sailing on Thursday?* . . .

Food could not get into the town and the water was dirty: medical professionals spoke of the spread of cholera and typhoid [. . .]

. . . he has the same land but better money . . .

> The chatterers that filled the streets became complicit with each missile
> that blasted the town.[64]

The novel spells out the point of the juxtaposition by emphasizing that
the idle chatter of self-absorbed Londoners (the "first world") is somehow
"complicit" with the fact that the bombing of innocent people in Palestine goes on. This is an assignment of guilt, a form of insult Iman directs
at other people throughout the novel. But we should not be taken by the
interpretation Iman offers here and should look instead at the subject
of the juxtaposition rather than the object. For we should note first that
Iman is not much different than the Londoners she so readily accuses of
apathy. For her, too, politics can appear only in the form of textual news
from elsewhere which she experiences as something external that bears
her own guilt.[65] Second, her equivalence with the Londoners is replicated
in the written lines of the novel itself, where we see how, by reducing
politics and daily city life to news and conversation respectively, Iman
makes them both equivalent to one another as text and sign. Third, since
for Iman the private and the political sphere are now two reified spheres
of life, the only way the subject of private life can bring these two together
is by "intersection."

But more important here is the appearance of money and leisure,
and through them, of capital, a global system of intersecting class interests that undercuts Palestinian national allegiance. This political critique
only flickers in and out of the plot but once we've tuned in to it, we start
hearing a coherent message. Let's begin with the past and recall Sabri's
historical study of Palestine. He is not only documenting the first and
second intifada but also the earlier years of Zionist colonialism, in the
late nineteenth and early twentieth century. His studies show him that it
was not only the Zionists and colonial powers that brought ruin to the
doorstep of the Palestinian people, but also Arab states themselves. He
then examines the larger social context in which Zionism developed and
says that it is "our stinking feudal system [that] allowed" for that defeat,[66]
i.e., the interests of landowners (present and absentee) who sold land to

---

64 Ibid., 186.
65 While here the news from Palestine is written as Iman's internal thoughts, in
other places it is quoted directly and written in italics, similar to the quoted London
chatter.
66 Dabbagh, *Out of It*, 103, emphasis removed.

Zionist institutions, leaving the poor peasants to fend for themselves. He continues to see this pattern in present-day Palestine too:

> A bunch of men wanting their own piece of the pie, yearning for cheap suits and desks with plaques. No ability to work together, to fight together; to assist each other. It was a long history of betrayal. They screwed us; we betrayed ourselves.[67]

What is alluded to here is the structure of the Palestinian Authority, put in place after the 1993 Oslo Accords, whose functions of internal policing and governance are still subject to the conditions of Israel, European and American powers. The "plaques" and "suits" simply mean that the money pouring in from global donors created convenient jobs and positions, otherwise not possible in the Palestinian economy. Thus, we see how the political form (the PA) is undergirded by global capital which, as I have noted, hollows out Palestinian sovereignty. Once we notice how capital and class interest have shaped and will continue to shape Palestinian history, we may reread a key moment in Iman's transformation. Here it is again:

> We are definitely going to fund the center for the handicapped, get their offices moved, and provide facilities. Then a women's centre, maybe a crèche. There's so much, Rashid. Don't give me that look like—I know what you're thinking. That they're just palliatives, right? But every little bit helps—[sic] is important. Maybe we can do something with the Centre [run by Khalil] too. Maybe they'll fund some of the positions there?. . .

> [Rashid:] "Are you offering me a job or something?"
> "It's possible."[68]

What we see here is precisely how the shift I have discussed—from constitutive power involving direct antagonism, into constituted power

---

67   Ibid., 103–4, emphasis removed. This accusation arises again and again against various people who are accused of "selling out," of prioritizing their own private interest over the interest of the Palestinian people. See for example Sabri's disdain for Khalil and his "profiteer" father, 106; the people's suspicion of the upper class, 47; the already discussed disapproving tone when describing Jibril Mujahed's life of leisure in the Gulf, and a few other instances.

68   Ibid., 262.

limited to social work—is enabled by the Palestinian NGOs set up by global capital. Because the novel affirms Iman's transition, it does not take up these materials directly, or explicitly explore the intersection of capital and state power that has shaped Palestinian life since the late nineteenth century. Rather, it addresses these issues obliquely through Iman's travels to the Gulf and to England, the sites that partly enable not only her own transformation (viewed as a personal journey) but the transformation of Palestine itself.

Finally, the third narrative material brings us back to Jehan and to the literary type of investigation or search I discussed in Chapter 2. With Jehan we return to the questions of gender and generation. Recall Iman's critique of patriarchy and her wish to lead a more active life than her mother. However, it turns out that the identity of the mother is not as straightforward as it seems. As the novel unfolds we are told that the separation between the mother and the father, what the children call the "divide," is a mystery. This familial history is somehow connected to a political mystery concerning a document Sabri needs for his historical research. While in England, Iman and Rashid recover the document: a British intelligence report released only now, after thirty years. The report discusses the "Sparrow," a Palestinian guerrilla fighter involved in hijacking an airplane headed to Israel in 1971. Iman and Rashid recognize their mother in the picture attached. To avoid being discovered, Jehan had undergone plastic surgery and never discussed the issue with her family, not even with her husband, Jibril. When Jehan's identity was exposed in internal Palestinian circles, Jibril, being part of the leadership, took Jehan's unauthorized operation as a personal offense and ended the marriage.

The appearance of the "political" in Jehan's past and present crystalizes the differences between the two periods that we have discussed, and brings this discussion to an end. Here again we see how the older political form (Jibril and Jehan's activity) appears in the present only as a secret text, a message delivered to the subjects of private life. This past contains an overlap of personal and political that is no longer possible in Iman or Rashid's world other than as a fantasy. Finally, the absence and impossibility of constitutive politics gives rise to a search into the origins of the present, a literary type that begins to characterize Palestinian literature and cultural production more broadly.

Conclusion

From World to Global Literature

While the situation in Israel and Palestine cannot in and of itself serve as the basis for theoretical extrapolation, the historical and analytical categories we developed throughout this inquiry and the formal properties we observed in individual novels do in fact provide a starting point for a theory of modern literary production in the transition to neoliberal globalization. Such a theory, as stated earlier, depends on bringing together explanation and interpretation, attending to social and political conditions, and giving ample time to reflect on the details of aesthetic form.

Such a theory would first distinguish between two poles, that of the Subject and that of the Object, the former designating the critic and its task, and the latter covering the twin categories of social and aesthetic form. If we agree that literature is conditioned by the social form and that the latter's end, to paraphrase Marx, is to wrest a realm of autonomy from heteronomy, then the broadest task of the critic is, as it is understood here, to inquire after the political forms embedded in the literary text which ultimately make a claim about freedom and autonomy.[1] Such an inquiry is associated more with Critique than criticism, and involves two interconnected moments of analysis: social form and political ideology. Understood from the vantage point of critique, the text is conceived as a political response to the historical social form acting as "limit." Since the social form inheres in the literary raw materials, the formal properties of the literary artwork are always mediated, or "other" than themselves, carrying within them the very social limit their imaginary world tries to

---

1   Marx, *Capital III*, translated by Ben Fowkes (London: Penguin Books, 1976), 958–9.

overcome or resolve. For this reason, we can never simply compare one political ideology to another (e.g., Zionism vs. liberalism; nationalism vs. humanism), but must understand each in the relation to the historical limit that shapes both political responses.

Moving to the Object, it was argued throughout this inquiry that we are in the midst of a non-linear global transformation in which capitalist social relations remake the social world in their image, replacing what I called here the external with immanent determination, heteronomy with autonomy, and inequality with equivalence. To be sure, the superseded term in each couple does not disappear but becomes secondary. The fundamental change between these two social forms, especially in the periphery, concerns the subordination of political ends to the endless production of value, bringing about an abstract, textual social world with an "absent cause" whose constitutive conditions are now veiled or missing. While new in the periphery, such a transformation has already taken place in Western Europe in the nineteenth century. Thus the novel elements in the "core," ushering in a new period, are the global dispersal of the capitalist production process, and the weakening of the state as a bearer of qualitative social needs (e.g., a Keynesian or developmental model). This process is not inevitable and invokes resistance, which we will discuss, but insofar as it explains the transformation of the world in the last fifty years it is a global condition that cannot be ignored in any investigation of cultural production. Moreover, since the process of "real subsumption" is never even, it is important to acknowledge and account for the co-existence of different social forms within the dominant one, and to clarify their relation. While Raymond Williams's triple conception of "dominant," "residual" and "emergent" social forms retains its useful- ness we need to note that these do not exist side by side, but rather within the "limit" imposed by the dominant social form. The social form that is being colonized and relegated to the "past," for example, may very well preserve significant social practices (becoming hybrid), but its capac- ity to establish its own law over the law of value is denied. So, too, the emergent social form, pointing to future social relations, exists only as an enclave and this limits and shapes its meaning. Thus, the current account takes into consideration so-called "hybridity," or the non-standardized process of "real subsumption," but maintains that such forms receive their meaning only from their inability to impose their own law. The concept of "limit" does this important theoretical work and refines our understanding of global historical processes.

With this historical process in place, we can take up the question of aesthetic form and the category of Literature and propose an outline for a theory that traces the shift from modern world literature to global literature. With the historical shift in eighteenth-century Western Europe from external to immanent determination, three interrelated phenomena take place: First, literary production passes through a process of autonomization, shifting from heteronomous to autonomous aesthetics. Different than in Bourdieu and Casanova, however, the process does not commence with the autonomization of the literary field, but with the broader processes of social abstraction, making possible the emergence of the real fiction of a self-legislating and autonomous subject. Second, at the same time, the category of Literature appears as a discursive category designating a separate and autonomous field of human creativity. Third, the novel becomes a dominant genre of literary production. Ultimately, all three are underlined by the concept of autonomy in its liberal modality, and it is this *specific* social relation and political ideology embedded in aesthetic form that circulates around the world and provides the object of inquiry. Since the rest of the world does not pass through the shift from external to immanent determination just at that time, its literary production is still heteronomous. Through the nineteenth century in Western Europe, given the unevenness of the social world, an autonomous aesthetic based on social abstraction becomes synonymous with Literature as such and turns into the dominant world category. As far as this inquiry is concerned, this is the moment when we may begin to talk about a modern system of world literature as a structure of dominance that distributes aesthetic value, whose main categories are autonomous and heteronomous aesthetics, and whose social forms are based on external and immanent determination.

With the circulation of the novel not simply as genre but as *a specific form of autonomous aesthetic,* and the circulation of the category of Literature from Western Europe to the rest of the world, we notice a divergence in social and aesthetic velocity. As I have argued, in social forms based on external determination in which literature is conditioned by politics (as Casanova argues), social life itself is political, and social abstraction has yet to take place, the literary forms borrowed from Western Europe will be rearticulated within the local heteronomous aesthetic and used to fulfill certain political ideologies that need to be mapped contextually in each reading. In this period, autonomous aesthetic, if and when attempted in the periphery, will be a matter of linguistic abstraction, achieving the status of "Literature" by an aesthetic of concealment that is at odds with local social conditions that have yet to go through the abstraction associated with capitalist social relations. The difference, then, between the social forms in Western Europe and the rest of the world, rather than the difference in the degree of autonomy of the literary field as Casanova would have it, furnishes the reason for the imbalances between literary form and social content discussed in Jameson, Schwarz and Moretti. This mismatch will be true of the discourse of literary autonomy (and its attendant techniques of reading) that might very well arrive in the periphery without its corresponding social form, and thus be at odds with literary production itself, that is, what novelists actually write. For this reason, we cannot simply trace the circulation of the discourse of literary autonomy and its reading techniques without being attentive to the historical conditions that shape the raw materials of the literary artwork. Finally, with neoliberal globalization, once social relations themselves begin to change in the periphery, such qualitative imbalances disappear, and literary abstraction then overlaps with real social abstraction. The telltale sign of this shift is that literariness need not be achieved through linguistic abstraction, for now abstraction, in its neoliberal modality, befalls the very social ground that conditions the literary world. In other words, writers on the periphery no longer need to invent mysterious enigmatic worlds in order to wrest their freedom from heteronomous conditions. Characters can inhabit a "referential" world instead, since plain "locality" has already turned into an abstraction, a reality separated from its constitutive conditions, which procures the conditions of possibility for an autonomous aesthetic. For these reasons, peripheral modernisms, whose forms may very well continue to exist in the neoliberal period, have become obsolete. Since their political imperative—to produce autonomy through abstraction—has been made possible in the real, they exist in form only. This is our current situation, in which literary texts circulate in a global field of equivalence, making possible the shift from World to Global Literature, in which "textuality" and the "investigation" are the dominant ideology and literary type respectively. Here novels differ according to their political ideology, the most typical of which fall into two categories: The first endorses a "ground-less" abstract world based on the experience of private life for which heteronomy enters as an ethical rather than a political problem, usually as an encounter with an "other" who makes a claim on the subject's freedom. The second, on the contrary, seeks the real grounds of this textual world, confronting the subject with the social conditions of their own world. In such global literature the most fascinating object and value, taking many forms, is heteronomy: a desire to re-embed the subject in various forms of obligation, which (consciously or unconsciously) addresses the problem of social abstraction and the futility of a social life rooted in endless accumulation.

Several comments need to be added here to complicate this social and literary narrative. First, as Casanova argues, any account of literary production needs to take into consideration both the national literary field and its relation to the dominant international category of Literature. As far as the national field is concerned, as I have argued about the heterogeneity of the social form itself, any literary field might contain both aesthetic categories discussed here (autonomous and heteronomous) rather than just one or the other. These two, however, will not reside side by side but will be mediated by the dominant social form and the dominant aesthetic category. So, today, the literature of minorities or dominated subjects within a social form characterized by social abstraction, such as Mizrahim and Palestinians in Israel, or Algerians in France, might continue with what I have called here heteronomous literary production. Given the dominance of the category of aesthetic autonomy, these works will be accorded lower aesthetic value, and will sometimes be regarded as nearly non-aesthetic. Since these dominated groups, sometimes existing as a "whole within a whole," are limited by the dominant social form, the literary worlds of such texts will be invested in achieving autonomy, whether individual or collective. When such social forms are broken by capitalist forms of social abstraction (as Haredi life in Israel is today, or second-generation Algerians were in France in the 1980s), we will often see narratives in which the main character transitions from a form of life imbedded in heteronomous relations to one embedded in autonomous relations. As important to acknowledge is the role such dominated social forms play within novels characterized by the dominant autonomous aesthetic: from a conservative or romantic political ideology, the dominated social forms rooted in heteronomy are attributed with a utopian valence, a value that can serve as the alternative to alienation, abstraction and individuality. From a liberal position, these forms of life are relegated to the past; they are to be negated and superseded.

As far as the relation of the national field to the international category of Literature, we can currently identify two poles, commercial and autonomous, with two dominant aesthetic ideologies; both, however, are underlined by a standard of aesthetic abstraction. Both poles are invested in the liberal or humanist universalization of local experience, but whereas the commercial pole favors a referential literary idiom, the autonomous, invested in the autonomy of the literary, favors non-referential forms of representation. The political pole, though it continues to exist within national fields, does not occupy a dominant position in the world republic of letters. I examine, in the next pages, an alternative concept of literature that might resist the dominance of the autonomous category of Literature.

Second, the dynamic I have just described concerns the historical shift between social forms which constitutes the conditions of modern literary production, and it therefore needs to be complemented with the history of literary production that takes place after this shift. We have already noticed the recent disappearance of the political pole as a dominant pole in the international field of literary production, along with the weakening of the state as a project of qualitative collective ends, but we also need to account for changes within the national field. In principle, once the constitutive conditions of social life change and new ones achieve structural dominance, we historicize the shifts between dominant styles and political ideologies that might change in accordance with literary fashions and political and economic upheavals. Thus, any account of literary production involves two types of periodization: one that concerns the shifts in the historical conditions of possibility of literary production, and another that concerns the history within these conditions, in the literary field itself.

Third, although this kind of inquiry affirms the immediate experience of literary producers (writers, editors, publishers, critics, etc.) within the literary field as necessary, it also regards them as insufficient. Thus, if, for literary producers, the main category of literary experience is "style," and its mode of analysis is "criticism," we complement these with "social relation" and "critique." This entails two modes of history, and different epistemological optics: for example, where literary criticism might see a series of changes in style, literary critique, understanding "style" as social relation, might see invariance, that is, the continuation of the same social relation in a different style. This dual optic would change our understanding of the history of the novel: whereas criticism will be interested in tracing a history of national "influence" between, say, Western Europe and the periphery in the nineteenth century, critique will historicize the social relations embedded in the novel and therefore will shift from the category of the "nation" to the category of "social form." Accordingly, it will show that the history of the novel is to be plotted neither along the lines of Western European dominance, nor of hybrid influences, but rather along the lines of the increasing dominance of a particular social and aesthetic relation, namely, autonomous aesthetic and social abstraction.

To complement this general account, I will attempt a series of brief comments on the transformation of three literatures across the globe, moving eastward from the US, to Brazil, and on to China. Different than the readings offered throughout this account, these comments are not based on close readings but rather on synthetic histories of different national literatures and therefore should be treated as no more than preliminary hypotheses.

In the US, the question of the emergence of autonomous aesthetic will revolve around the moment of transition from the colonial form of life to the capitalist one, when social relations based mostly on subsistence are transformed into a value-based economy, and what Tocqueville identified as American individualism becomes possible. While there is still an ongoing debate over whether the transition occurred between 1770 and 1800, during in the 1830s, or after the Civil War,[2] there is some agreement that before the 1830s, the American novel did not resemble its Western European counterparts and exhibited characteristics we associated here with non-Western literature. Nancy Armstrong and Leonard Tennenhouse argue, for example, that literary writing after 1776 and into the period of the American Renaissance, what they call the republican novel, did not exhibit that central feature of the English novel, namely the autonomous liberal subject, but rather a more collective form of subjectivity that becomes marginal or disappears in the 1830s with the importation of romanticism.[3] In such novels, therefore, we might still see the compromise between the imported Western European form and heteronomous forms of life, associated with nationalism, that bifurcate the imaginary world. For Jonathan Arac, who works with the categories of the "national" and the "literary," the latter emerges only later, in the 1850s, with Hawthorne and Melville, together with the commercialization of the literary field. If we agree that in the last third of the nineteenth century, with Henry James, we begin to see the kind of reification typical of Western European modernism, then the question of the onset of

---

2 James Henretta, *The Origins of American Capitalism: Collected Essays* (Boston: Northeastern University Press, 1991); Richard Brown, *Modernization: The Transformation of American Life 1600–1865* (New York: Hill and Wang, 1976); Charles Post, *The American Road to Capitalism: Studies in Class Structure, Economic Development and Political Conflict 1620–1877* (Leden/Boston: Brill, 2011).

3 Nancy Armstrong, Leonard Tennenhouse, "Novels Before Nations: How Early US Novels Imagined Community," *Canadian Review of Comparative Literature* 42.4 (December 2015): 353–69.

autonomous aesthetic will revolve around the period between the 1830s and the 1880s, and the way we read the American romance novel or the sentimental novel of that period. While autonomy as discussed here is not identical with what Arac calls "the literary" in nineteenth-century American fiction, given Arac's claim that the "literary" gave way to the national narrative of, say, Stowe's *Uncle Tom's Cabin*, then we might be able to see in romance an attempt to think autonomy where it did not yet exist as such on the social ground. The history of American literature after the late nineteenth century, moving from modernism to post-modernism, will be in accordance with the narrative suggested here. African-American literature would be considered an aesthetic grounded in heteronomy that continued until the postmodern moment. Using the categories developed here, we may distinguish more accurately between the American and English novel of the early nineteenth century, and rethink the political significance of American romanticism and attempts of what Casanova would call "literarization."

In Brazil, before the second transition to democracy in the 1980s, Brazilian society passed through multiple political forms (empire, republic, democracy, military rule) all based on a strong central state. In this period, it is difficult to talk about any simple separation of private and public spheres where an autonomous, liberal subject may emerge as the basis of literary autonomy.[4] Similarly, the history of Brazilian social form (which included slavery, waves of industrialization, forms of feudalism existing in rural areas at least until the mid-twentieth century, and a small bourgeois class), indicates a hybridity of heteronomous and autonomous social relations which would make literary production very different from Western Europe and the US despite their cultural influences. It is in this kind of historical context, Roberto Schwarz argues, that we should see a "misplaced idea" in the imported Balzacian realism, an idea that does not fit with the social reality of Brazil based as it is on "favor," i.e., forms of direct dependence. Schwarz sees embedded in

---

4   Ernesto Laclau, "Feudalism and Capitalism in Latin America," *New Left Review* 67 (May–June 1971): 19–38; Boris Fauston, *A Concise History of Brazil.* Second Edition (Cambridge: Cambridge University Press, 2014); João M. E. Maia and Matthew M. Taylor, "The Brazilian Liberal Tradition and the Global Liberal Order." In Oliver Stuenkel and Matthew M. Taylor (eds.), *Brazil on the Global Stage: Power, Ideas, and the Liberal International Order* (New York: Palgrave Macmillian, 2015), 35–55; *Cambridge History of Latin American Literature*, Vol 3: Brazilian Literature (Cambridge: Cambridge University Press, 1996); Randal Johnson, "Brazilian Narrative." In John King (ed.), *The Cambridge Companion to Modern Latin American Culture* (Cambridge: Cambridge University Press, 2004), 119–35.

Alencar's novel *Senhora* a split between an imported European autonomous subject and what I would call a heteronomous social subject.[5] Such a split and allegorical mode, where characters stand in for Brazil in complex and multiple ways, could be read then as an attempt to think autonomy in a moment where it is not yet available in terms of social relations. The emergence of *modernismo* in Latin America and its inauguration in Brazil in 1922 is also different than its Western European and American counterparts. Although exhibiting various forms of abstraction similar to those of Western modernism, works such as *Macunaíma* by Mário de Andrade are charged with national meaning that we cannot find, say, in Virginia Woolf's *Mrs Dalloway*, or even William Faulkner's *The Sound and the Fury*.[6] Only after 1945 do we begin to see formalist works based on psychological states, such as those of Clarice Lispector, that might suggest certain autonomy and separation from the social and historical conditions grounding Brazilian society.[7] And yet even here, we can ask whether such abstraction arises as a gesture of aesthetic negation or from the social situation in Brazil. In other words, does Schwarz's claim about Alencar still hold in the case of Lispector? If we understand Lispector's abstraction and others like it as aesthetic negation this would also implicate some of the more formalist works of the Latin American boom—those of Borges, for example, whose autonomy and visibility in the world republic of letters, is bought with the currency of obfuscation. This leaves us to ask whether the transition to democracy in 1985 and later on to neoliberalism brings about abstraction on the social ground itself, and whether the arrival of the postmodern announces autonomy as it did in Israel.[8]

As for China, while its shift to consumer capitalism in the post-Mao era is still very much a state-directed project and its sheer size makes any change uneven, the transformation of mainland China is not too

---

5   Roberto Schwarz, "The Importing of the Novel to Brazil and its Contradictions in the Work of Alencar." In his *Misplaced Ideas: Essays on Brazilian Culture* (London/New York: Verso, 1992), 41–77.

6   Kimberle S. López, "Modernismo and the Ambivalence of the Postcolonial Experience: Cannibalism, Primitivism, and Exoticism in Mário de Andrade's 'Macunaíma,'" *Luso-Brazilian Review* 35.1 (Summer 1998): 25–38; Michael Korfmann and Marcelo Nogueira, "Avant-garde in Brazil," *Dialectical Anthropology* 28.2 (2004): 125–45.

7   Wilson Martins, "Brazilian Literature: The Task of the Next Twenty Years." In Raymond S. Sayers (ed.), *Portugal and Brazil in Transition* (Minneapolis: University of Minnesota Press, 1968), 9–23.

8   Tânia Pellegrini and Laurence Hallewell, "Brazilian Fiction and the Postmodern Horizon: Rejection or Incorporation?," *Latin American Perspectives* 33.4 (July 2006): 106–21.

different from that of many non-Western socialist societies moving from a statist to a market structure. Using the categories of heteronomy and autonomy we may distinguish two periods, the first beginning in 1919 and the second around 1990s respectively. The heteronomous period begins with the launch of the May Fourth nationalist movement, which brought a new concept of literature to the fore. This new concept replaced the older classical writing, imbedded as it was in moral and historical thinking, and ushered in modern Chinese literature.[9] In terms of social form, the transformation in the category of Literature takes place as China shifts from a variant of feudalism to communist form, which means that, different from Western Europe but similar to Israel, Chinese modernity is not so much a matter of bourgeoise and capitalist revolution, but rather a socialist one. Between 1911 and 1978, China went through several political upheavals that punctuated the different periods in the literary field, including the end of dynastic rule and the establishment of a republic, civil war, the Sino-Japanese war and occupation, the formation of the People's Republic of China, and the Cultural Revolution. But in the present periodization, it is possible to see literary production over this entire period as heteronomous, an artform with a pedagogical, political function written in a popular, vernacular idiom. A history of the literary field of this period will then periodize the shifts in dominant political ideologies and styles not only in relation to one another but also in relation to the "limit" of heteronomy. Literary autonomy, the commodification of literary production, and the appearance of postmodern styles, only came about in the 1990s, according to Bourdieusian scholars, with the shift to a market economy and the weakening of state control over the field.[10]

Yet despite this preliminary periodization, many questions remain. First, along with the rise of Chinese nationalism in the early twentieth century that underlined heteronomous literary production, there were also liberal positions such as those of Hu Shih, and individualist positions invested in psychic states and written in romantic registers such as the stories of Yü Ta-fu and Hsü Chih-mo. Borrowed in part from the

---

9   Some argue that the onset of modern Chinese literature is traceable to the writings of Liang Qichao in the early twentieth century, or even to the late Qing period.

10   For an overview of Chinese literature from mid-nineteenth century to the present see David Der-Wei Wang, "Chinese Literature from 1841 to 1937," and Michelle Yeh, "Chinese Literature from 1937 to the Present." In Kang-I Sung Chang and Stephen Owen (eds.), *The Cambridge History of Chinese Literature*, Vol. 2. (Cambridge: Cambridge University Press, 2013), 413–564; 565–705. See also C. T. Hsia, *A History of Modern Chinese Fiction 1917–1957* (New Haven: Yale University Press, 1961).

West, the discourse of autonomy advanced in such texts and others as an antidote to political or propogandist literature at different points in this period might be an example of the different velocities of aesthetic form/discourse and social change that we have discussed. For while the autonomy of the writer and of literature was raised as a concern, it was imbedded within a social reality of national renewal and duty that didn't resemble the kind of autonomy developed in Western Europe in the eighteenth and nineteenth centuries.[11] As for the styles that Jaroslav Prusek calls lyric or subjective, they were always imbedded within the historical and collective reality of China after the revolution and so their meaning is not identical to the Western European forms they import and rearticulate. There are also instances in Prusek, discussing the negativity in these texts, that bring to mind Israeli modernism in the 1960s. If for Prusek one can find in the Chinese sentimental novel a rejection of the older forms of life, one that works through a certain abstraction of character (my term), then it is instructive to compare these attempts to the kind of abstraction we see appearing in Oz, Yehoshua and others as a rejection of Zionist statism.

Today as in the recent past, the subordination of human social relations to abstract forms of domination underlined by endless accumulation have brought about various political responses whose common goal, at least on the surface, is to restore purposive human existence where human needs are prioritized over the production of value. Here arise, at the same time, two seemingly similar but in fact very different social and political patterns: on the one hand, a deep desire for older social forms, embedded in what Postone calls "overt social relations," and on the other, a desire for new, future-looking, post-capitalist social forms. These two patterns need to be distinguished. What is today called a conflict between the concrete and the abstract (whose most spectacular example shows itself in the re-emergence of organic nationalism and xenophobia—what can be called "politics of inequality"—in response to global trade agreements and financial crises) arises from the first social pattern which, however consequential, does not provide an alternative and exists well

---

11 As Michel Hockx argues, "To my mind, the main reason why modern Chinese literary practice does not allow itself to be schematised as easily in terms of only two conflicting principles [political and economic], the way Bourdieu described modern French literary practice, is the presence of a third principle, partly but not fully heteronomous, which motivates modern Chinese writers to consider, *as part of their practice,* the well-being of their country and their people." Michel Hockx (ed.), *The Literary Field of Twentieh Century China* (Honolulu: University of Hawaii Press, 1999), 12.

within the conditions of possibility of abstract domination. So, too, all civil identitarian thinking and struggles, demanding both recognition and redistribution which nonetheless presuppose capitalist social relations, remain within what can be called a "politics of equivalence," for they do not address the fundamental question of human social ends but only the redistribution of means.[12] The second and rarer social and political pattern advances what can be called "politics of equality," a struggle to abolish the law of value and re-establish the priority of human social ends.

Dominant literary production in this moment of global abstraction follows mostly what I call "politics of equivalence." Whether in its commercial or autonomous variants it upholds liberal or humanist values that attend neither to the question of human social ends nor to the question of autonomy as an act of collective making. If a post-capitalist social form is possible it might very well be imagined first not in the available category of Literature but in a new and speculative one whose three preliminary contours—heteronomy, critique, and narrative speculation—I can only briefly suggest in conclusion.

A critical new concept of Literature would begin not with the concept of autonomy in its liberal modality but with heteronomy—the paradoxical trans-historical fact that social freedom and autonomy are not limited by others but made possible by a dependence on others and on nature. And yet, as we know, the illusion of autonomy is not an error pure and simple but one enabled by an abstract social structure which maintains its reality as lived experience. If our thoughts about social autonomy begin in heteronomy, in the fact that the social human is always-already mediated through an historical form of dependence, and yet such dependence is obscured, then our new concept of literature will have to invent narrative forms of this social dependence that will acknowledge the reality of the appearance (of autonomy) but also shatter it through its mediation in social conditions of possibility. Invoking the concept of conditions of possibility brings us back to Kant's first Critique, but in a

---

12   See for example Slavoj Žižek's critique of postmodern politics: "My first observation here is that while this standard postmodern Leftist narrative of the passage from 'essentialist' Marxism . . . to the postmodern irreducible plurality of struggles undoubtedly describes an actual historical process, its proponents, as a rule, leave out the resignation at its heart—the acceptance of capitalism as 'the only game in town,' the renunciation of any real attempt to overcome the existing capitalist liberal regime." Slavoj Žižek "Class Struggle or Postmodernism? Yes, please!" In Judith Butler, Ernesto Laclau, and Slavoj Žižek (eds.), *Contingency, Hegemony, Universality: Contemporary Dialogues on the Left* (London: Verso, 2000), 95.

displaced and historical manner; for his concept of critique (the second contour) now finds its way into the third Critique, as it were, and helps us define not reason but aesthetic form. Rather than separating itself from conceptual knowledge, a critical narrative seeks to make visible the grounds of social experience by inventing an aesthetic of temporal and causal mapping. An aesthetic of critique then rejects the distinction between the nomothetic and the ideographic, science and art, and brings them together in an amphibious aesthetic-conceptual form. But critique alone will not do, and needs to be complemented with speculation. If critique can map the present and past, literary speculation can invent a social world without the production of value, where human social ends would regain primacy over abstract structures of domination, not simply by constructing utopian metaphors for it but by showing us how such a world might come about and what it would feel like. Such speculation, informed by the concepts of heteronomy and critique, dispenses with the ban of graven images and takes the risk of spelling out a future whose imaginary existence would defamiliarize our own and point to a possible way out of the asphyxiating deadlock of the present.

Acknowledgments

In the long course of researching and writing this book I have been guided, aided and advised by many whom I would like to acknowledge here.

I would like to thank first Fredric Jameson, who supported this project since its inception. I owe to Jameson all that I know about Marx, Hegel, symptomatic readings and so much more, and I cannot imagine what course my theoretical and political inquiries might have taken had I not audited his seminar at UCLA in the spring of 2003. I am grateful to the community at UC Berkeley, including Chana Kronfeld for her guidance, and Robert Alter for taking me through the intricacies of medieval Hebrew poetry. I owe profound gratitude to Daniel Boyarin for taking up my project and for providing me with the warmest and most generous advice and guidance. Martin Jay was a caring and patient guide; he kept a close watch on the theoretical elaborations of the argument, presenting me with hard questions and expanding the scope of my reading. I am grateful to Margaret Larkin for opening up the world of Arabic language and literature to me. I would also like to thank Sami Shalom Chetrit whose book on, and commitment to, the Mizrahi question helped me solidify a concept of what a Mizrahi public intellectual might look like.

I had the good fortune to be at Berkeley during a remarkable surge in student organizing, and I thank my friends and colleagues in the student bodies at the time. Much of our political conversation during demonstrations, sit-ins, and planning meetings found its way into this book. Special thanks to the participants of the Interdisciplinary Marxist Working Group: Annie McClanahan, Jasper Bernes, Chris Chen, Shane Boyle, Jill Richards, Neil Larsen and Dan Blanton. Rarely have I seen a more theoretically sharp and politically honest group of people at Berkeley.

Some of my happiest moments at Berkeley were thanks to those who made me feel most at home, including Lena Salaymeh, Yaacov Yadgar, Sarah Levine, Lital Levy, Harsha Ram, Rutie Adler, Noha Rawan, Bluma Goldstein, Candace Lukasik, Callie Maidhof, Deellan Kashani, Aaron Eldridge, Yael Almog, Yael Sigalovich, Eyal Bassan, Hila Avraham, Shira Wilkof, Tara Hottman, Jenny Slattery, Maya Kronfeld, Gilad Sharvit, Satyel Larson, Brandon Schneider, Emily Rabiner, Leslie Elwell, Jenna Ingalls, Natalie Cleaver, Tony Martire, Tamar Lando, Jonathan Combs-Schilling, Jennifer Mackenzie, and Jonathan Rowan. Of this group, Emily Gottreich deserves my deepest gratitude for being there every time I needed a guiding hand and institutional support. I will never forget her kindness.

I would like to acknowledge the Arabic and French language instructors I met along the way; I am especially indebted to my Arabic teachers at Middlebury College, Housni Bennis and Swasan Awad. I will be forever grateful for the patience and kindness that Nevenka Korica—at the time the Executive Director of the Center for Arabic Study Abroad—showed me during my time in Cairo. For helping me with my French and for correcting my pronunciation, I thank Nicole Dufresne of the UCLA French Department. And for being responsible for a magical summer at Bryn Mawr's Avignon French program, I thank Mélanie Giraud, Philippe Osmalin and Martine Dufor.

I am indebted to Samuel Weber for welcoming me as an outside member to Northwestern's Paris Program in Critical Theory. My time in Paris would not have been the same without the conversations at his weekly seminar.

I should also thank *Novel* for their permission to publish an earlier version of my essay on Yeshayahu Koren in Chapter One.

And last, I thank Erica Lee who had my heart during the challenging years of exams and writing, and who was with me in my saddest moments, when no one was around. Like the artwork of Lily Briscoe in Virginia Woolf's *To the Lighthouse*, she possesses that gentleness of a "butterfly's wing" with a resolve "clamped together in bolts of iron," a rarity I was fortunate enough to be around.

Index of Names and Select Concepts